2006   Social Work   Dept

Generalist Social Work Practice

Generalist Social Work Practice:

Context, Story, and Partnerships

Barry Locke
West Virginia University

Rebecca Garrison
Northern Arizona University

James Winship
University of Wisconsin

Brooks/Cole Publishing Company

I(T)P® An International Thomson Publishing Company

Pacific Grove • Albany • Belmont • Bonn • Boston • Cincinnati
Detroit • Johannesburg • London • Madrid • Melbourne • Mexico
City • New York • Paris • Singapore • Tokyo • Toronto • Washington

Sponsoring Editor: *Lisa Gebo*
Marketing Team: *Jean Thompson, Christine Davis,*
    Deanne Brown
Editorial Assistant: *Shelley Bouhaja*
Production Editor: *Karen Ralling*
Manuscript Editor: *Jennifer McClain*
Permissions Editor: *Catherine Gingras*
Interior Design: *Carolyn Deacy*

Interior Illustration: *Lori Heckelman*
Cover Illustration: *Mark Gordon*
Cover Design: *Christine M. Garrigan*
Art Editor: *Jennifer Mackres*
Photo Editor: *Bob Western*
Typesetting: *Graphic World Inc.*
Cover Printing: *Phoenix Color Corporation*
Printing and Binding: *Quebecor*

For more information, contact:

BROOKS/COLE PUBLISHING COMPANY
511 Forest Lodge Road
Pacific Grove, CA 93950
USA

International Thomson Publishing Europe
Berkshire House 168-173
High Holborn
London WC1V 7AA
England

Thomas Nelson Australia
102 Dodds Street
South Melbourne, 3205
Victoria, Australia

Nelson Canada
1120 Birchmount Road
Scarborough, Ontario
Canada M1K 5G4

International Thomson Editores
Seneca 53
Col. Polanco
11560 México, D. F., México

International Thomson Publishing GmbH
Königswinterer Strasse 418
53227 Bonn
Germany

International Thomson Publishing Asia
221 Henderson Road
#05-10 Henderson Building
Singapore 0315

International Thomson Publishing Japan
Hirakawacho Kyowa Building, 3F
2-2-1 Hirakawacho
Chiyoda-ku, Tokyo 102
Japan

Printed in the United States of America

10 9 8 7 6 5 4 3 2 1

Library of Congress Cataloging-in-Publication Data
Locke, Barry
    Generalist social work practice: context, story, and partnerships
/Barry Locke, Rebecca Garrison, James Winship.
        p.   cm.
    Includes bibliographical references and index.
    ISBN 0-534-21876-8
    1. Social service.   2. Social case work.   I. Garrison, Rebecca J.
II. Winship, James.   III. Title.
HV40.L8128 1998
361.3'2—dc21   97-17469
                                           CIP

To all of the people in our lives
who have taught us
and continue to teach us
that
hope,
dreams,
and
change
are ever possible.

Writing this book has been a collaborative process and a true partnership. This photograph represents the beginning of this partnership that led to the dream of which this book is a result. This picture was taken the summer of 1986 at the Eleventh Annual National Conference on Social Work and Human Services in Rural Areas where Jim was elected President; Becky, Vice President; and Barry, Secretary/Treasurer of the National Rural Social Work Caucus. The photograph was taken by Sam Hickman, Charleston, West Virginia.

About the Authors

Barry Locke is Associate Professor and Assistant Dean at the West Virginia University School of Social Work, where he has taught for 23 years. He holds the MSW degree in social group work from Virginia Commonwealth University and the Ed.D. in curriculum and instruction from West Virginia University. He has served as director of both the BSW and MSW programs. He teaches in the areas of social policy, rural community practice, and evaluation research. His practice and research interests include contextually grounded generalist practice, rural social work, poverty, and faculty issues in social work education. He is a certified site team chair of the Council on Social Work Education Commission on Accreditation. He is past president of the National Rural Social Work Caucus, the West Virginia NASW chapter, and the West Virginia Human Resources Association. He was recognized as Social Worker of the Year by the West Virginia chapter of the National Association of Social Workers.

Rebecca "Becky" Garrison is Associate Professor and Coordinator of Field Education with the Social Work Program, Northern Arizona University. She has also taught in social work programs at Colorado State University, Virginia Commonwealth University, and East Carolina University. She holds the MSSW degree from the University of Tennessee at Knoxville and the Ph.D. in social policy and social work, with an emphasis in social work education, from Virginia Commonwealth University. Her areas of teaching are generalist social work practice and field education. Her practice, research, training, and volunteer interests include generalist social work practice, rural social work, enhancing conscious use of self in professional practice, distant learning and teaching via interactive television, crisis intervention and critical incident debriefing, and AIDS education and outreach. She is a past member of the board of directors of the Council on Social Work Education and is currently a certified site team chair for the CSWE Commission on Accreditation. She is a registered representative for and past president of the National Rural Social Work Caucus.

James "Jim" Winship is Associate Professor with the Social Work Program, University of Wisconsin-Whitewater. He holds the MSW degree and the DPA in public administration from the University of Georgia, where he has also taught. He teaches in the areas of social policy, social work practice, and field education. His practice, research, and training interests include rural social work, generalist social work practice, homelessness, family services, international practice, and the uses of storytelling. He is a member of several local planning groups and boards and is active with developing programs that address issues of homelessness in Wisconsin and Georgia. He is past president of the National Rural Social Work Caucus.

Contents

Phase Three: Making Plans and Dreams Real / 186

CHAPTER EIGHT

Phase Four: Evaluating Outcomes and Making Transitions / 232

CHAPTER NINE

The Organization and Social Work Practice / 250

CHAPTER TEN

Living and Working Well in a Changing Community and World / 281

Epilogue / 299

Appendix: Code of Ethics of the National Association of Social Workers (1996) / 301

References / 315

Author Index / 327

Subject Index / 331

Credits / 351

Boxes and Figures

Preface

The world in which social work is practiced is messy and unpredictable. Frequently, when we are learning about and beginning to practice social work, we would like more certainty than exists about how, when, where, who, why, and what to do in the situations we encounter.

For a variety of reasons, there are limits to the certainty a social work practice text can provide and still be faithful to the reality it describes. Humans are complex, diverse, unique organisms, and it is impossible to generalize about what to do when a person, family, or group of people approaches you for service (for example, when a woman flees a violent husband, a group of single mothers wants to form a support group, or the community wants someone to guide its efforts at reducing teenage substance abuse). The background or history of the situation, the previous efforts made to manage the situation, the strength of the support system, and the extent of available resources can all influence the social worker's actions. Sometimes doing social work practice is like trying to solve an algebraic equation with 17 unknowns, and there are no easy answers.

Knowing and understanding the context in which assistance is sought and provided is vital in social work practice, especially generalist social work practice, which is the model of practice presented in this book. Within North America, the context is incredibly varied and constantly changing. Contextual changes are influenced by natural events (the weather, the earth shifting, the seasons, and the amount of sunshine or rain in an area), global and societal shifts in the economy (recessions, depressions, and economic growth), advances in technology (tele-communications and computer processes), shifts in power structures and political processes (locus of power in decision making moving from national to state and local levels), social structures (changes in family and/or community structures), and the ways in which social welfare services are conceptualized, implemented, and delivered (restrictively or holistically).

Differences in geography, values, and resources abound. Because of this diversity, there are clear distinctions as well as similarities in the ways social workers work in different contexts, for example, in South Bronx or on an Indian reservation in the southwest. A "cookbook," therefore, is not appropriate. I (Becky) will never forget my first experience of baking a cake when I moved from 25 feet above sea level to 5500 feet above sea level. I followed the directions in the cookbook very carefully, yet my cake was flat and heavy. I forgot to adjust for the altitude changes; the context affected the baking process. The phrase "stick to reality and a dream" seems to us to be the best approach, in the midst of change, to understanding and practicing social work across localities. An emphasis on the *importance of context* grounds us in the realities of day-to-day living. One of the defining principles of social work is a holistic approach in which the concept of "person-in-environment" is emphasized. One needs to understand the context in order to practice within a holistic framework.

Sticking to a dream is important also, and we do this as we pay close attention to the key concepts and principles that guide social work practice. We discuss in length the way that social work has to be built on social justice, respect for human dignity, and understanding human, ethnic, social, and cultural diversity. Additionally, we explore the importance of appreciating the essential roles of spirituality and religion, hopes and dreams, a strengths and empowerment perspective, and self-determination in the lives of society's members and in the ways in which we practice social work. In our phase model of generalist social work practice, we emphasize exploring people's stories, building on hopes and dreams, taking action to make dreams real, and evaluating learning and making transitions through client system/social worker partnerships.

There is a tendency to load up the reader with almost too much information, to cram the backpack with tools for every eventuality. We have tried to provide the "right amount" of detail to lay out a philosophical and value foundation and to describe our model without overloading the reader. We introduce and reference people internal and external to social work whose work we have found significant, and encourage you to follow up and read the more complete works of those authors whose ideas, beliefs, and approaches to social work practice "speak" to you.

We have chosen to use only real examples in the book from other published work, from colleagues and students, and from our own experiences. As we make frequent use of our own experiences as social work practitioners and educators over the past 25 years, we have chosen to identify the voice present in our personal examples by referencing the illustrations with I (Barry), I (Becky), or I (Jim). Our illustrations and examples come from our practices and life experiences in both urban areas (Nassau County, Long Island, which borders New York City; Richmond, Virginia; Columbus, Ohio; and Atlanta, Georgia) and rural areas (of West Virginia, Ohio, Georgia, Virginia, Tennessee, Wisconsin, North Carolina, Colorado, and Arizona).

This is a book that stresses the power of place. We hope that you can generalize from our experiences and those of others cited in the book as you apply the generalist social work practice principles, key concepts, and phase model of planned change to your own realities and dreams.

Barry Locke
Rebecca Garrison
James Winship

Acknowledgments

It is difficult to know how to express the full measure of appreciation we owe to so many who have supported over the past four years our efforts that are realized with the publishing of this book. Each one of us has many people to thank and we will do so.

Collectively, we wish to thank our families and friends for their love, encouragement, patience, and support as we started, stopped, lost faith, and began again to complete the project. Their steadfast belief and willingness to loan each of us to the project made it possible for us to fulfill our dream.

To Brooks/Cole and our editors Claire Verduin, who brought us into the project, and Lisa Gebo, who has worked closely and supportively with us over the past two years, we owe a debt of gratitude for encouraging us and tapping our motivation to bring this project to fruition. To Karen Ralling, production editor, for her wonderful leadership in producing the final product, we can only say thank you. To our colleagues, especially those who have been faithful participants in the National Rural Social Work Caucus, you have taught us much about social work practice. We hope this book reflects the richness and depth of those teachings. To Grace Lynn Owens-Freeman, we thank you for your creativity and talents in computer graphics and your humility, grace, strength, and courage. To Barbara Locke, Barry's significant other, we cherish your graciousness, nurturance (emotionally and physically), and consistent love. Barbara's wonderful energy and support to the three of us, as over the years we used the Locke home as a base of operations, cannot be repaid. Finally, we owe a great debt to Jim's parents, Pat and Dale Winship, who offered support and their editing skills. Their feedback provided helpful insights to the flow and structure of the book.

For their thoughtful suggestions, we wish to acknowledge the reviewers: Bonnie Bedics, University of West Florida; Sherry Fraser, Concordia College–New York; Susan W. Gray, Barry University; Naurine Lennox, Saint Olaf College; Susan Murty, University of Iowa; Rebecca Turner, Jacksonville State University; Emmadene Winton, Alabama State University; and Charles Young, University of Wisconsin.

I (Jim) wish to credit my wife, Rita Richardson, and my children, Hope and Parker. They give my life meaning and hope and challenge me to make a difference and to be genuine in my writing and my everyday life. I also wish to thank my colleagues, my students, and those who have been in workshops with me. Through our interactions, I am closer to "getting it right."

To Beverly Koerin and Vickie Marks, I (Becky) cherish your everlasting friendship, creativity, humor, insight, encouragement, and wisdom. This has been an incredible journey. Our friendships have sustained me through all the ups and downs, twists and turns, stops and obsessions, and exhaustion and synergy of the journey. It truly has been a path with heart. To John, my son, I am most grateful for the joy you have brought me and the support you have provided through your humor, hugs, and patience. To my colleagues (coauthors; field instructors and other fellow professionals; students; fellow volunteers with Northern Arizona AIDS Outreach; and program, department, and college faculty), I thank you for encouraging and challenging me to broaden my vision and expand my capacities. And to Raoul, who through sharing with me his journey through death continues to teach me about the richness, beauty, and celebration of life, I dedicate my contributions as I join with others in the creation of nurturing social interactions and a more just society.

I (Barry) wish to thank my colleagues who have helped me think about social work philosophy and practice in unique ways. I cannot pass this opportunity to thank my wife Barb for her unwavering love, support, and belief in me and the three of us.

As coauthors, we feel privileged and enriched to have had the opportunity to work together and experience the synergy that emerged and inspired this book. This has been the highlight of our professional careers.

CHAPTER ONE

Principles of Social Work Practice

A thoughtful beginning spared the travelers later difficulty.

ROBERT FULGHUM
(1991, p. 24)

Introduction

Social work practice demands systematic and purposeful professional behaviors that are grounded in knowledge, values, and skills. What separates professionals from others is the ability to understand why they're doing what they're doing when they're doing it—not just flying by the seat of their pants, unquestioningly following agency policies and practice, or merely doing the client's bidding. Our intent is to present the reader with our view of how social workers set about delivering services and carrying out the mission of the social work profession as it functions in the United States.

Within the profession we continue to see important developments that shape how we work and how we see ourselves. Some of these developments include: the changing nature of our ethical code, the changing nature of social work intervention and role expectations, and the changing view of the profession within society.

The 1996 revision of the National Association of Social Workers (NASW) Code of Ethics reflects current social and political processes, issues, and concerns as well as what we have learned about human behavior, interaction and relationships, and practice processes in the 15 years since the last revision. Throughout this book, we will be referencing specific principles, standards, and sections of the Code of Ethics (1996) as they relate to generalist social work practice principles, processes, and skills.

The way social workers practice is an ever-changing process. This reflects both our increased knowledge about what works and what doesn't and our adjustment to the larger issues within the society. To illustrate, brief therapy is becoming more a model of choice in many mental health programs. In part, this reflects what works, but it is also a function of what insurance programs are willing to pay for under managed care. Depending on the setting in which a social worker may choose to practice (assuming that one chooses to work for a service provider), the professional tasks may be quite different from our recent history. In health care, especially in hospitals, the social work function has changed from client support to that of discharge planner/manager, where the emphasis is on helping patients move out of the hospital bed as quickly as possible to control for lost costs under reimbursement plans that limit the length of stay. In many public welfare agencies, social work is moving more into monitoring and evaluation as agencies contract out direct service delivery.

Finally, the view of social work is changing—sometimes for the better and sometimes for the worse. In 1996, a national TV news show (*20/20,* January 27) presented a troubling story about how involuntary commitments to private psychiatric hospitals were being used against older Americans. The story gave major emphasis to the function of the social worker in the process, making those of us in the profession appear to be "senior citizen nappers." At the end of the story, the show's host turned to the reporter and said, "Tell me, just how did those social workers get so much power?" A week later, on another news program, a story about a pregnant teenager presented the social worker in a much more positive light. The point is that our work is very much in the public eye; and, depending upon how society sees right and wrong as well as how skillfully we operate within our theoretical and ethical framework, we are likely to experience differing views of our professional functions.

Professional practice demands that we deliberately draw on what we know with humility and that we remain aware of what we don't know. Social workers need to be more than just employees—we need to be professionals whose behaviors and efforts are guided by professional values and ethics and directed by a commitment to the purposes, functions, and beliefs of the profession.

It is important for social workers to understand the obligations associated with belonging to a profession. One standard reference for understanding what it means to be a professional is the work done by Greenwood (1957). He stated that "all professions seem to possess: (1) systematic theory, (2) authority, (3) community sanction, (4) ethical codes, and (5) a culture" (p. 45). We believe that it is most appropriate to build on Greenwood's criteria and educate ourselves to carry out the professional roles mandated by our professional ethics, by the client (or client system, as we refer to it in this book), and by the community where we are sanctioned to practice. In subsequent chapters, we will explore further what it means to practice as a professional. This chapter is intended to help the reader understand our view of social work practice and the key principles that support that view.

Practice Principles

In writing for a high school newspaper, I (Jim) learned the "five W's and an H" that needed to be present in a story—Why, Who, Where, What, When, and How. We decided that this might be a helpful way to organize our thinking about how to do good social work and to explain our perspective on social work practice.* Our practice perspective stresses:

- the "why" of social work—the foundation of all we do as social workers as well as a guide for the way we do it, with continual attention to achieving social justice, empowering clients and workers, and fostering hope and vision;

- the "who works together in planned change processes"—the people who identify and name the issue of concern, the people who are the focus of the change process, and the people who support and foster the change process;

- the "where social work gets done"—the specific nature, qualities, and characteristics of a locality, which interact to shape the experiences of persons and groups and their sense of what is possible;

- the "what" of social work—the response to immediate concerns using

---

* In our search of the literature, we discovered we were not unique in using this structure. Murphy (1977) uses a variation on this framework for applying problem-solving processes in community practice.

professional knowledge and a strengths perspective, the awareness of the why, and the necessity of working on multiple levels in multiple ways;

- the "when the work gets done"—the importance of responding to the timeliness of and readiness to change;
- the "how" of doing social work—the interconnectedness of attention to outcomes and relationship, the four-phase approach to planned change, and the necessity for the social worker to move between system levels and roles.

We have purposefully organized this chapter so that the five W's, which articulate practice principles, precede the how. This is necessary in our view because social workers need to be grounded in principles for work. Just as parents may think about potential consequences before agreeing to let a child stay away from home overnight or a corporation may consider the potential hazard associated with a new product before bringing it to market, so too the effective social worker takes action based upon a careful thinking about practice principles. For us, several important principles are found in our discussion of the why, who, where, what, when, and how of contextually grounded social work practice.

Why

The foundation of and purpose for social work practice is reflected in the why of social work practice. Boehm (1958) and Hearn (1969) provide us with an understanding of the assumptions on which the whys of the profession are based. These assumptions include: (1) people are important; (2) people have common human needs; (3) steps can be taken to manage people's concerns and enrich human life; and (4) people and systems can change.

The values of the profession, as articulated in the Council on Social Work Education Curriculum Policy Statement (1992), lay out standards for behavior and provide ideals social workers strive to realize in their practice. These values are:

1. Social workers' professional relationships are built on regard for individual worth and dignity and advanced by mutual participation, acceptance, confidentiality, honesty, and responsible handling of conflict.

2. Social workers respect individuals' rights to make independent decisions and to participate actively in the helping process.

3. Social workers are committed to assisting client systems to obtain needed resources.

4. Social workers strive to make social institutions more humane and responsive to human needs.

5. Social workers demonstrate respect for and acceptance of the unique characteristics of diverse populations.

6. Social workers are responsible for their own ethical conduct, the quality of their practice, and for seeking continuous growth in the knowledge and skills of their profession. (pp. 100–101)

These values are discussed in more depth in Chapter 2.

It is significant to say here that the foundation for all that we do in social work practice is based on these values. As social workers, we believe in the worth and dignity of all people; that people have the right and responsibility to determine for themselves their needs and the best way to meet those needs; that society has a responsibility to ensure the well-being of all of its members; and that the members of society have a responsibility to each other (Friedlander, 1976). Human rights and responsibilities are intertwined; we have a responsibility to our fellow citizens to exercise our rights in a way that does not interfere with the rights and responsibilities of others.

We pay only lip service to values when we say we hold them (and maybe put them on a poster on the office wall) but do not act on them. The "big picture"—the values of the social work profession and our own personal values—need to be incorporated into our professional being, so that believing in the values becomes acting on the values. For example, the NASW Code of Ethics (1996) states, "The social worker should not practice, condone, facilitate, or collaborate with any form of discrimination on the basis of race, ethnicity, national origin, color, sex, sexual orientation, age, marital status, political belief, religion, or mental or physical disability" (Standard 4, section 4.02 [Discrimination]; see Appendix). As a result, I (Barry) have asked friends not to share belittling humor (jokes I consider offensive to people) with me, as I believe that to be hurtful and a violation of this value. For us, this is an important part of making a commitment to becoming a professional social worker. Our challenge to the reader is to make the career choice carefully, for you will be called on to live and act in ways that may very well set you apart from friends, family, or others in the community.

The Social Work Professional Code of Ethics provides us with a vision of and framework for what should be with regard to our behaviors as social workers. Throughout the history of the profession, social workers have struggled to maintain a balance between responsibility to the community and responsibility to the self-determination of the person, family, group, organization, and community (Freedberg, 1989). In some cases, applying the principle of maximum self-determination is not difficult. Students beginning to learn social work practice find that starting off an initial interview by giving advice is not a way to facilitate client system self-determination. Students involved in community organizing learn not to use community groups to further their own social action goals if these personal goals do not match the intent of the community group. Yet, applying this principle in other situations is more difficult. Bertha Reynolds (1963), one of the pioneers of social work, wrote that addressing the national issues of exploitation and lack of opportunities was essential if client system self-determination were to be possible. Rothman (1989) argued that, in deciding how directive to be with client systems, we need to take into account other values—the client systems' abilities to make informed and rational choices and the degree of harm that client systems may do to themselves or to others.

Another example of a standard of behavior would be to "respect clients' rights to privacy" and "protect the confidentiality of all information obtained in the course of professional service, except for compelling professional reasons"

(NASW Code of Ethics, 1996, Standard 1, section 1.07 [Privacy and Confidentiality]; see Appendix). At first glance, this sounds like we should never share any information that the client system gives us in confidence. Differentiating between absolute and relative confidentiality is vital when applying this standard of behavior, however.

Absolute confidentiality means that under no circumstances will anything that a person reveals to us be shared with anyone else. There are very few situations and circumstances where this holds true. The primary situations in which people can reveal information that has absolute protection are with their priest, doctor, lawyer, and therapist. In a landmark decision on June 13, 1996, the United States Supreme Court ruled in *Jaffee* v. *Redmond* that therapists have the same right to privilege as do doctors, lawyers, and clergy. This means that social workers who are engaged in a therapeutic relationship with a client system do not have to reveal the contents of the therapeutic sessions in a court of law (Arizona Chapter, NASW, 1996).

However, in other roles as professional social workers, we are not covered under the privileged communication laws in most states. Thus, in most of our practice situations, *relative* confidentiality exists. This means that information may be shared with others on a need-to-know basis. For example, in most practice settings, records are kept for monitoring progress, and clerical and professional staff have access to these client system records; by virtue of this access, the privacy of the information in the records is relative.

Individuals have a right to know whether or not what they share with us may be seen by or communicated with others. I (Becky) have found in my work that most client systems assume absolute confidentiality as the standard when in fact it is most commonly relative confidentiality that exists. Thus, following the behavior code outlined above, I have the responsibility to inform my client systems of what happens with the information and to obtain their permission to share information with other professionals.

There are two primary situations in which not only is it permitted but necessary for the social worker to take action in ways that might mean violating confidentiality. Social workers are required by law to report suspicion of child abuse. Also, violation of confidentiality may occur when a client threatens harm to self or other. In addition, Kirkland and Irey (1978) note that in some rural environments confidentiality needs to be viewed more broadly; for example, in rare situations where confidence might be broken, in the interest of the client system, to stop harmful rumors.

Understanding social work's reason for being and its values and ethical stances is important so that social workers can embody these in their practice. Two organizing principles of all social work practice evolve out of the why:

- Both the outcome of an activity and the process by which it is achieved are governed by the ethics of the profession and by the values recognized in the community. Thus, as social workers, our function is to enable client systems to manage or address issues of concern in ethical ways that enhance competence and foster esteem and empowerment while reaching sanctioned outcomes.

- Opportunities exist for altering or strengthening the context to enhance human capacities and well-being. The goals of social work go beyond working with individuals to include change on the community, state, and national level. The challenge is to utilize our values and ideals in our day-to-day activities. The motto "Think Globally, Act Locally" reflects what we mean. As social workers, our scope and vision of what can be different are broadened beyond the particular needs and concerns of those with whom we are directly working.

The way in which these principles become translated into daily functions and activities depends on who we are as people, the depth and breadth of our knowledge and skill, and our own professional style.

Who

Vital to the change process are the people who identify the issue of concern, who are the focus of the change process, and who foster and support the change activity. We call these people "the ones who work together in the planned change process." Key principles for practice associated with "who" include naming the issue(s) of concern; understanding that those who name issues may not be the focus of change activity; knowing how to identify, at both the formal and informal levels, resources and persons with the ability to address the issue(s) of concern; and valuing the ownership of issues as well as the responsibility for acting on them.

Pincus and Minahan (1973) provide a model for understanding the involvement of people in planned change processes. We think their work is very helpful in naming the elements in the helping process, especially "client system." Adding the word *system* conveys the meaning that the who we work with will be groups of people, families, organizations, and communities as well as one person. This becomes most important when confronted with issues where the efforts of the planned change process are not directed toward the namer of the issue.

To illustrate, think about a single black mother who has just had her house burned down by the Ku Klux Klan because she is living in a white neighborhood. Expecting her to move to a safer neighborhood or to single-handedly make the neighborhood safer to solve "her" problem would not be appropriate. While she might be the person asking for help, the change efforts will be directed toward stopping the harassment and altering prejudices and discrimination within the community. Because effecting these organizational and community changes is a slow process, the mother may *choose* to move or fight back single-handedly.

Using Pincus and Minahan's model, we identify four different whos: (1) who names the issue of concern or initiates the process (client system), (2) who will be joining with the process initiator to facilitate change (change agent/social worker), (3) who or what is the focus of the change effort (focus of change), and (4) who else needs to be involved to enhance the opportunity that the change efforts will be successful (resource system).

The Client System The people who identify the issue of concern and ask for assistance in a planned change effort are the client system. This may be one or more persons who perceive disharmony, discrepancies, discontinuities, and/or opportunities in their own life experience or the life experience of others. They also expect to be beneficiaries in some way of the change effort.

Pincus and Minahan (1973) point out that persons or groups become client systems only when some kind of working agreement has been reached between them and the change agent. People or groups become a client system when they engage with a professional in two separate ways: not only do they engage in the sense of seeking the services of someone for assistance but they also are active in stating how they will be involved in the change process.

For the engagement to be meaningful, the client system and the social worker join together in a mutual process of influencing change. To illustrate this point, many people who seek the services of a professional may see the professional once and never come back. Some of these cases may be attributed to purposeful and effective brief intervention. On the other hand, many of these are instances where the person or people decide against working with that particular professional. In these situations, the "no return" is often the result of a failure of engagement between the two parties that precludes the forming of a client system.

According to Pincus and Minahan, the social worker may attempt to expand the client system by including other persons. They use the example of a worker in a mental health facility, working with the wife of an alcoholic husband, who tries to include the husband and children as part of the client system. The challenge often faced when expanding the client system is an unwillingness of the others to join the process.

Whether the focus of change is internal or external to the client system, ownership of issues is important for change to occur. For example, in the coal mining regions of Appalachia, many of the coal miners (mostly men) have been laid off. They often wait for the mines to call them back rather than seeking other job opportunities, and their wives have begun to enter the workforce through involvement with education or other social services. When these women have asked their spouses to get involved with the helping process as members of the client system, more often than not their husbands have refused. A result has been increased tension between spouses and pressure on the traditional family structure, often with negative consequences.

The Change Agent/Social Worker The change agent is the person who carries the responsibility for working with the client system in a planned change process. In many cases, this is the social worker. For example, parents may come to a social worker in a family service agency seeking help in communicating with their pregnant teenage daughter about the best course of action.

The route by which a person comes into contact with the social worker varies with the setting and with the client system. Medical social workers are known for their ability to assess and link patients with resources or services that facilitate discharge from a hospital in a timely way—a skill that is becoming critical in the efforts to control health care costs. In many instances, the social worker just shows up in the patient's room; the patient often is unaware before the social worker's arrival that there is someone who can be of assistance in this way. Typically, the medical social worker does not supply the needed service or resource after discharge; it may be a home health agency or a Visiting Nurses Program that provides the actual care that makes it possible for the hospitalized person to return home. In these situations, the social worker as change agent has the role (for example, brokering and advocacy) of enabling the client system to obtain the services of other available and competent change agents.

The term *change agent* may not be ideal; the words somehow remind us of fictional secret agents, James Bond and Maxwell Smart. Therefore, we choose to use the "social worker" label throughout the remainder of this book.

The Focus of Change The focus of change is the person(s), organization(s), and community(ies) that need to change. Pincus and Minahan (1973) refer to this as the *target system*. We're choosing *focus of change* as the preferred phrase because target system reminds us too much of Gary Larson's "Far Side" cartoons where characters are walking around with bull's-eyes on their bodies!

Perhaps the most useful part of the work of Pincus and Minahan is in differentiating between the client system and the focus of change. The client system and the focus of change may be the same. People who have a history of episodic outbursts of violence in which they destroy things and hurt others may be placed in a treatment/education group as a condition of their probation. Part of the social worker's role is enabling these involuntary clients to define themselves and their behavior as the focus of change instead of blaming others for their actions. In many instances, however, the focus of change is at least partially external to the client system. If the issue of concern is the high incidence of poverty and unemployment in a community, which may be exacerbating the propensity toward violence in families, the client system may be the locality. A community might identify the focus of change as the city council members responsible for changing zoning laws and tax structures in order to attract new industry to the locality to boost the economy and provide opportunities and resources for its members.

Resources The resources are the supports that can be enlisted or mobilized to do what needs to be done. Pincus and Minahan (1973) refer to this as the action system. Both the social worker and client system face the challenge of thinking creatively about who as well as what (for example, welfare benefits, medical equipment, free meals, or shelter) can be a resource. Webster and Campbell (1978) note that when social workers in rural areas are able to expand their thinking about potential resources beyond traditional tangible services and formal agency staff, rural areas have more potential resources (for example, the postmistress, barber shop owner, implement dealer) than conventional wisdom would suggest.

Human resources may be found within the client system or the external context. The strengths perspective challenges us to see the resources, past successes, and good points in people and communities. What the strengths perspective contributes, as Dennis Saleeby (1992) and others have clarified, is that the social environment is rich in human resources. In describing ways to use a strengths perspective in reintegration of the mentally ill into the community, Pat Sullivan (1992) uses this example:

> *Frank S. was forty-three years old when he was referred to the community support program. He had been recently discharged from the state hospital, his second stay in a twenty-year period. Frank has a diagnosis of schizophrenia. Previously, Frank had lived in rural Kansas, where for most of his life he had worked on the family farm.*
>
> *Frank's recent difficulties followed the death of both of his parents. His increasingly bizarre behavior and inability to care for himself led to his commitment to the hospital. He was subsequently released and was living in a board and care home.*
>
> *At the time of his referral, Frank was basically noncommunicative, had poor personal hygiene, and suffered continuously from auditory hallucinations. These factors, plus his nonverbal threats to leave the board and care home, led to a prediction by the staff that he would soon be hospitalized. Given his current condition, the community support staff did not feel he would be able to benefit from the structured groups offered at the center. Instead, he was placed in a "maintenance group" which was largely devoted to arts and crafts activities.*
>
> *He was subsequently assigned to a case manager, who began the contact by discussing Frank's goals and desires for his life. Like most people, Frank wished to have a job and a place of his own to live. The case manager also completed a strengths assessment, a record of previous and current activities and involvement.*
>
> *The most striking impression of these early meetings was Frank's consistent expression of a continued interest in farmwork. His history of farmwork and clear expertise in this field suggested this as an area of interest worth pursuing. Together Frank and the case manager began an exploration of area farms and ranches that might accept a volunteer. Soon a rancher was found who was agreeable to the idea. The relationship that developed was so strong that the owner of the ranch made it clear that Frank could come as often as he liked. When transportation became a problem, Frank surprised everyone with news that he owned a truck that was stored in his hometown. Even more surprising was the ease with which he passed a driver's examination.*
>
> *At the time contact with the Community Support Program was terminated, Frank was working at the ranch regularly, was providing his own transportation, and was beginning discussions about moving into paid employment. In addition, there were a number of spin-off effects, including improved hygiene and increased interaction with those around him. (pp. 153–154)*

Sullivan (1992) makes the point that

> *[t]he resources used in this example are expandable, reusable, and limitless. By locating sympathetic individuals and programs in the community, we identify and expand the number of natural helpers and propitious opportunities available to our clients. . . . The assets available to our clients may only be foreshortened by failures in our creativity and willingness to work. (p. 154)*

Some of these resources may be present and some may need to be developed. Using a strengths perspective, the client system is encouraged to think of the resources that are present in the context and the way those resources may contribute to the development of capacities for managing the issue(s) of concern. For example, one social worker, in his work with a family on long-term public assistance, discovered that the adults in the family were important resources once the parents were encouraged to entertain the idea of carrying out nontraditional roles. The social worker discovered that the father really wished to stay at home and care for the children and the mother really wished to be employed outside the home. Although this arrangement did not satisfy the agency goal of "getting the father off welfare," it did introduce stability to the family finances and empowered the adults to pursue desired personal goals consistent with other aspects of the agency mission.

Important for contemporary social work practice are the contributions and potential of social networks—another valuable resource. A person's social network includes the individuals, families, and/or groups of people who provide support, encouragement, and energy on an ongoing basis or in situations where assistance is needed. Pipher (1996) noted:

> *Recently I talked with a student therapist. Matt told me about a young mother he worked with who was alcoholic, poor, and alone. I asked about resources, especially those within her family. He said, "I've encouraged her to stay away from them. They're pathological." I thought to myself, if she's estranged from her family, who will help this young woman? Matt's training has left him feeling proud that he identified a "pathological family." Yet he won't be baby-sitting for his client or teaching her child how to ride a bike. Nobody calls out for their therapist on their death bed. (pp. 28–29)*

Germain (1991) summarized the value of social networks

> *as coping resources for dealing with life stressors. They facilitate mastery of the twin tasks of problem solving and management of feelings by providing emotional support, information and advice, and tangible aids, and by under-taking action. They may also serve a primary preventive function in effectively staving off an imminent stressor. In carrying out these functions effectively, informal systems also contribute to the member's self-esteem and relatedness and may enhance the sense of competence and self-direction. (p. 76)*

The idea of people as resources encompasses more than the people them-selves. A person's religious beliefs or spirituality and the intensity of the person's desire for life to be different are vital resources for influencing change. When relevant, social workers respect and facilitate the use of religious and spiritual traditions in the planned change process. Such traditions, where they are real for the client system, may serve as sources of strength for taking action and for providing direction for the chosen action. We are not suggesting that this resource be forced upon the client system, for no meaningful resource can be imposed on another. However, as social workers, we must not fall into the trap of objectivity to the extreme that we are unable to envision other kinds of resources as relevant to the change process.

An example of the inclusion of beliefs and spirituality as resources is the blending of American Indian ceremonies with formal social services. Medicine men are a vital part of the treatment team of a child sexual abuse treatment program in Tuba City, Arizona. If desired by the family, the shamans perform healing ceremonies for child survivors of sexual abuse instead of or in conjunction with the "nontraditional" dominate-society treatment processes.

Another example of religious traditions and spirituality as a vital component of human resources in the process of change was the spiritual courage of Barry's neighbor who died recently from cancer. When I (Barry) visited the family at the funeral home, I was struck by the peaceful presence of my neighbor and the strength his spirit had left for his wife as she faced her future. There was a sense of both loss and joy present within the family.

What can be a resource varies from situation to situation. Sometimes what is most useful for client systems is the knowledge and information (intangible and very renewable resources) that people with whom they interact can provide. In West Virginia, for example, human service professionals created a scanning network to systematically collect information useful for influencing future social policy decisions. The group began to see early signs of "welfare bashing" in other states and acted to publish a fact sheet on public assistance that could be used to educate leaders when public assistance clients came under attack in their state. As another example, the family of an infant child with serious medical problems may need information from a national, state, and/or local support group about caring for a child with that particular disability or from organizations that provide funding for purchasing specialized medical services or equipment.

We consider an expanded view of resources—as more than formal social service agencies or benefits—to be central to effective generalist practice. In Chapter 7, we will discuss how advocacy, brokering, and mobilizing can be used in locating, creating, and employing resources.

Differentiating among Those in the Change Process Differentiating among the client system, the change agent, the focus of change, and the resources is crucial in order to avoid "blaming the victim" (Ryan, 1972). Blaming the victim has been a concern of the social work profession as well as other human services professionals and advocates since the 1960s. The major idea associated with this concept is that issues, needs, concerns, and challenges faced by client systems are often created by or located in their external contexts, yet client systems may be blamed or otherwise made to feel personally responsible for these concerns as an expression of some inadequacy. To illustrate, many of us who work with abused partners are told that, as survivors of the abuse, they feel society holds them responsible for the conditions and events that led up to the abuse and for the abuse itself, when the reality is quite different. Being questioned about why the survivor of the abuse did not leave is one form of this blaming-the-victim perspective. A response that does not blame the victim would reflect an awareness that the abuser is responsible for engaging in violent actions and, thus, responsible for ending the abuse.

Who identifies the issue and the way it is identified and named has a major impact on what happens. During the 1980s and 1990s, federal officials made concerted efforts to name difficulties in social functioning as individual problems and pathologies. They attempted to define the focus of change in purely individualistic terms, excluding any federal responsibility or role that societal change had played in creating and/or exacerbating misery and hardship. Hilman and Ventura (1992) reflected:

Every time we try to deal with our outrage over the freeway, our misery over the office and the lighting and the crappy furniture, the crime on the streets, whatever—every time we try to deal with that by going to therapy with our rage and fear, we're depriving the political world of something.

And therapy, in its crazy way, by emphasizing the inner soul and ignoring the outer soul, supports the decline of the actual world. Yet therapy goes on blindly believing that it's curing the outer world by making better people. We had that for years and years and years. "If everybody went into therapy we'd have better buildings, we'd have better people, we'd have more consciousness." It's not the case. (p. 5)

The categorizations of people in the change process may seem unnecessary in some situations. A neighborhood that comes together to combat the vandalism and crime within its boundaries is both the client system and the focus of change: "We are no longer going to stand by and watch as we destroy ourselves." In this instance, the neighborhood may encompass all four categories—the client system, in identifying the issue of concern or the condition that is unacceptable; the change agents, who encourage neighborhood residents to come together to assist in the change process; the focus of change, in altering the reality of the way in which the neighborhood is valued and perceived by its residents; and the resources, both formal and informal (material, spiritual, environmental), which come from within the neighborhood to support the change efforts.

In other circumstances, these categorizations enable us as practitioners to better conceptualize change processes and their associated activities. A husband comes to see a social worker to change his wife's behavior. In this situation, the husband is the client system; the social worker, the change agent; and the wife, the focus of change. Resource systems have yet to be identified. In this case, however, if the wife does not wish to name the problem as simply her behavior, efforts by the husband to change her behavior in absentia are doomed to failure. What would be more promising is for the husband and wife together to name the issue or concern as a reflection of their interaction and relationship. Stated this way, they are both part of the client system as well as the focus of change.

Identifying the focus of change is important in helping clients understand their responsibility and opportunity to exercise influence over events. Often, client systems assume "blame" for events beyond their control. Clarifying this issue can facilitate action to proceed in healthier ways. On other occasions, client systems may assume little or no responsibility for events and may need assistance in understanding where they do have ownership. Finally, identifying the change agent is important to both the social worker and the client system in clarifying appropriate roles.

Where

The where of social work practice is the context of people's life experiences, influenced by growing up in a particular family in a specific place or places. The context is the specific nature, qualities, and characteristics of a locality that interact to shape the experience of its people. A person, family, or group's life experience influences whether or not a situation is considered to be one that requires action. For example, a locality whose school ranks near the bottom of the state on test scores may not identify education as an issue of concern because the school system is no worse (and may even be better) than it was when the adults of the locality were students in that school. In another instance, a high-status family may not consider vandalism by their teenage son an issue of concern (and may move to keep the incident out of the court system) because the family believes, deep down, that many laws shouldn't apply to them.

Similarly, what is seen as possible and not possible is also shaped by the context. Alex Kotlowicz (1991), in his book *There Are No Children Here,* about a family in a public housing project in Chicago, quoted the older brother: "*If I grow up* [emphasis added], I want to be a bus driver." In an area where gunfire is common and schoolchildren practice hitting the floor when they hear shots fired, the uncertainty about reaching adulthood is understandable.

In some instances, the context defines not only what is seen as possible but also what may be probable. The close proximity of a university, community college, or vocational institute may make it possible for a working single mother to pursue her education while keeping her job and being with her family. If she lives in a community where the nearest college or technical institute is three hours away, however, getting a degree or certification while juggling other responsibilities becomes much more difficult.

Understanding context also aids the social worker in realizing the connection between the place from which the issues of concern arise and the larger environment. This is important not only in understanding resources and constraints but also in not blaming oneself unduly for events over which one has little control. In recent years, the number of manufacturing jobs—jobs with good wages and benefits—has declined drastically. What former workers in manufacturing and the defense industry have had to settle for, in many instances, are jobs in the service sector that pay far less and offer few or no benefits. Inner-city residents were hit especially hard by the drop in manufacturing jobs (Phillips, 1990). An adult who is angry at himself for not being able to find a job comparable to a previously held position is focusing on internal capacities and not on the external realities of the changing world. For example, in Janesville, Wisconsin, in the 1950s and 1960s, a high school graduate could walk into a General Motors plant and be hired for a job with great benefits and enough pay to support a family. Those days no longer exist. An understanding of the changing nature of occupations does not excuse the adult from making every effort to find a good job, or the locality and the larger society of the responsibility to create good jobs, but it does put a person's efforts and concerns in the context of today.

In Chapter 3, we discuss context in depth. Any discussion of the where of practice needs to underline how people's experience of a community may be different due to diversity in race, class, gender, or other characteristics. Clarence Page, a Pulitzer Prize-winning journalist for the *Chicago Tribune,* described situations in which others reacted to him on the basis of his race:

> *What . . . do I think of when I wake up in the morning? Getting to work. I hope the weather's nice, because if it's bad, a taxi will pass me by and pick up a white person halfway down the block. It happens to me all the time. I'm dressed in a*

suit, carry a briefcase. Just like the white guy who got the cab. I'm a member of the Tribune *editorial board, right? I dress the role, right? Just getting to work, I think about that.*

I'm conscious of how I'm dressed because I want this cabdriver to see that I'm not a welfare recipient. The average white guy may go out there in dirty blue jeans and expect the taxi to stop just like that. And it will. It will stop for him more quickly than for me, three-piece suit and all. I learned that if it's dark out and I see a white friend, don't approach him too quickly. Don't startle him because the first thing he's going to see is a black man. (cited in Terkel, 1992, pp. 359–360)

As we review the discussion of the where of practice, several principles emerge.

- It is the context that provides the framework for change, an understanding of the people involved in or influenced by planned change processes, the way in which issues and concerns become identified and defined, the timeliness of initiating change, and the pace of the change. "Starting where the client is" has historically been a primary principle of social work practice. Traditionally, this has meant an assessment of the client system in terms of strengths, concerns or needs, and readiness for change. Adding the dimensions and forces of the context expands the meaning of "starting where the client is" to include forces and factors external as well as those internal to the client system.

- The context defines and shapes the way in which the knowledge, values, and skills of social work practice are applied. Being able to translate what we have learned into the dynamics of the context is the focus of this principle. For example, the skill of empathy, when applied within the context of American Indian populations, appears very different than when applied within white middle-class populations. Empathy with American Indians is conveyed primarily nonverbally—limited eye contact and indirect approaches to the task at hand, with minimal overt discussion of feelings. Knowing and understanding this is vital to the initiation, nurturing, and sustaining of a relationship.

- An expanded view of resources, as we discussed in the "Who" section, depends on understanding the specific nature, qualities, and characteristics of the context. In working with people, we know that as we understand their situation in more depth and develop a stronger relationship with them, we are more likely to be effective. Similarly, as we develop an understanding of a locality and form connections with persons and groups in that locality, we are more likely to be able to identify and use the resources available there.

Examples from a variety of contexts (rural, urban, and inner city) are utilized throughout this book to further illustrate the significance of context in generalist social work practice.

What

What is the social worker trying to accomplish in working with client systems? Obviously, the actions or strategies will vary from situation to situation. Neither practitioners nor students are easily satisfied when experts in an area of practice answer a question such as "How do you treat people who are both schizophrenic and alcoholic?" with the response "It all depends." The rest of the answer, however, is influenced by a range of factors, such as the effects of the schizophrenia, the degree of alcoholism, the strengths and resources of the person, the nature of the context, and so on. When practitioners are able to identify those factors that are important to the change effort, they can help the client system find preferred ways to address these factors. Therefore, "what" principles enable us to discover desirable ways to act.

For the past twenty years or so, the social work profession has adopted the word *generalist* to describe a basic model for carrying out its work, and a number of competing interpretations of what is meant by generalist practice have been given. This book is our attempt to more fully define how we see this form of practice as expressed within our own model. Some of the key ideas of a generalist practice orientation include:

- being able to work with a variety of issues of concern,

- being able to work with diverse client systems,

- being able to influence change at multiple levels (one-to-one and within families, groups, organizations, and communities), and

- being able to apply intervention strategies that address multiple issues of concern within multiple system levels simultaneously.

We will explore each of these more fully as we present our phase model of practice.

The what of social work practice is inextricably related to the why. What we do needs to be within the value stance and ethical standards of the profession. However, it is possible—even easy—to lose sight of social work values and the primacy of social justice when dealing with a number of people whose lives seem to be falling apart. As the sign that's seen tacked up on office walls states, "When you're up to your ass in alligators, it's hard to remember that the objective is to drain the swamp."

In helping client systems identify issues of concern and work on them, social workers try to be mindful both of the alligators nipping at the intruders and of whether or not the swamp needs to be drained. The challenge facing the social worker is not to lose sight of the objective (the why) as we set about facilitating the what. All too often the pressure is on responding to the crisis of the moment. When asked why they don't spend more time on trying to influence "the system," it's not unusual to hear social workers respond with "We don't have enough time!" We certainly can agree with that view, yet achieving desired outcomes demands that we move beyond the personal level of response to the issues of concern. Otherwise, prevention, competency, enhancement, vision, and hope are likely to become things talked about in our classrooms and rarely, if ever, experienced in our careers.

I (Jim) coached a basketball team of fifth- and sixth-grade girls. One of the points we constantly worked on in defense was knowing where the girl you are defending and the ball were at all times. Players on defense need to be aware of both so as not to give up easy baskets. In working with client systems, social workers also need to be constantly aware of more than just the immediate concerns. The skilled generalist social worker

- utilizes the strengths perspective in helping the client system identify or name the issue. As the client system is laying out the conditions and circumstances of concern, the social worker is also listening for capacities and strengths. "There are valuable strengths in our families and communities. These strengths are often hidden from view to those unskilled in noticing them or focused solely on looking for what is wrong" (Graber and Nice, 1991, p. 3).

- applies professional knowledge to reframe capacities and issues. The social worker develops an ability to "see" from a variety of perspectives and thus to overcome *functional fixedness,* the routinized way in which objects (or ideas) are regarded. Cognitive restructuring (discussed in more depth in Chapter 2) is a method for reframing events so that alternative meanings emerge. It is the identification of alternative meanings for circumstances and events that may determine the feelings associated with the event and, ultimately, the actions or behaviors employed to meet the challenge of the event (Burns, 1980). When someone views a situation in terms that are unsolvable (for example, "I've always had this problem with my temper; it's part of who I am"), it is not possible to change. This situation can be restructured as an opportunity (for example, "I have the capacity to respond to difficult situations and frustrations with rage and violence. I can choose whether or not I respond to situations this way or in a different way"). With this restructuring, the situation becomes one where action is possible.

Another way to apply professional knowledge is proposed in the book *Women's Ways of Knowing.* The authors encourage "tuning your ear" to be able to hear the ways that women's paths of learning may be different from men's (Belenky, Clinchy, Goldberger, and Tarule, 1986). Similarly, our knowledge of human behavior in the social environment may tune our ears to enable us to reframe or reconfigure a client system's experience in a way that brings into awareness more options for action than the client system may be perceiving. For example, sharing knowledge of human growth and development might make it possible for a stepfather to understand his eleven-year-old daughter's messy room as normal for that age rather than as an act of disrespect and hostility.

- recognizes when the issues of concern may be connected to and linked with interrelated concerns and a variety of dimensions and systems beyond those identified by the client system. The key here is to be able to identify potentials for change in all relevant system levels—persons, families, groups, organizations, and communities. For example, I (Jim) worked with a client who had schizophrenia and was a member of a group for persons arrested for domestic violence. In group sessions, he would talk about "time hanging heavy" on his hands. He lived independently, received supplemental security income (SSI) for his disability, and had very few expectations for his time. Since I lived in the same town, I knew of a number of other persons in similar situations within our community, so I engaged an active minister and others to attempt to do something that would provide outlets for activity and service for these residents. In this way, I was simultaneously developing a specific resource for the person in the group and influencing a community-level change.

• realizes that no one approach is appropriate all the time. The late Abraham Maslow was reputed to have said of B. F. Skinner and behaviorism, "The person whose only tool is a hammer tends to treat everything as if it were a nail" (Shimkus and Winship, 1977). In the Middle Ages, alchemists searched for the "philosophers' stone," the substance believed to have the power to turn base metals into gold or to cause spiritual or physical regeneration. Especially for beginning practitioners, there's a tendency to believe in a modern philosophers' stone—one practice approach, such as behavior therapy or structural family therapy, that is appropriate in almost all situations. Similarly, practitioners can become fixed on working only on the personal level or, conversely, on believing that only large-scale change is important.

I (Barry) recall a discussion several years ago with a colleague who insisted that most of our emphasis should be on prevention programs rather than remedial services. When I asked what we were to say to the client system who needs and wants change now, my colleague responded that they would have to wait until we made things better (that is, prevented them from occurring), an answer that the client system would surely find unsatisfactory.

When

What is it about "when" that is so significant? It would seem that the time for naming and working on issues is a given. But "when" means more than just the time when a client walks through an agency door or a community group seeks help with an issue. The Greeks had two words for time, *chronos* and *kairos*. *Chronos* refers to chronological time, what time of day or what day of what year it is. *Kairos* refers to time as timeliness and readiness, as in the preferred time to do something. We often tend to think only in "clock time," believing that the time to address concerns or issues is when they appear. As the old saying goes, "Strike when the iron is hot." It's easy to think that people or communities are either ready for change or they're not; however, the reality may be quite different as we come to understand that readiness to change is associated with more than one single system in the planned change process. Client systems may have named external foci that are not ready to change or issues they are not able to face even though they name them as concerns; resources (including staff, programs, and equipment) may not be in place to support the change effort. The concepts of readiness and timeliness, then, become key.

Students beginning to learn social work practice often refer to the level of client system motivation. Especially as it relates to persons, they describe people as "unmotivated" who are not investing much energy in working on what appear to the outsider as obvious concerns. Using the descriptor *unmotivated* not only writes the social worker out of the script ("I can't work with him if he's unmotivated") but also creates a mind-set in which it is difficult to see potential ways of working with the client system or managing the issues of concern. In many cases, one could substitute the words "demoralized" or "utterly overwhelmed" for unmotivated. By this simple act of reframing, the focus shifts from being solely related to whether or not the person wants change to exploring the barriers to change and the energy and resources available for change to occur.

Consider the example of a twenty-one-year-old who squeaked through high school with a C– average, acquiring no tangible job skills. He was unable to find work for more than six months after high school until he found a job in a factory. During a period of economic depression that occurred after the young man had worked for a year, the factory laid him off. For the past year and a half, he has been looking for work; he has applied at a number of places and gotten some interviews but no job offers. He's living at home with parents who are increasingly upset about his not working. It's getting harder and harder for the young man to deal with the rejection of applying for jobs without getting them, and deep down he's not sure anyone will hire him. A social worker who comes into contact with this young adult might consider him unmotivated, but that description does not take into account the effect of repeated disappointments on his self-esteem and hope for the future.

In many instances, involvement with a social worker is most likely to be successful when the client system considers itself ready or believes that the time has arrived for addressing the issue of concern. Investigation into self-initiated and professionally assisted changes in addictive behavior led Prochaska, Di-Clemente, and Norcross (1992) to develop and research a model of the stages through which persons with addictive behaviors progress. The sequential stages they identified are:

- *precontemplation*—people don't see a concern and so do not define a condition (their addictive behavior) as a concern. Consequently, they have no intention to change behavior any time soon.

- *contemplation*—people are defining the condition as a concern and are seriously thinking about taking action but are not yet ready to take action.

- *preparation*—people intend to take action within a short period of time and have already made small behavioral changes (such as smokers smoking five fewer cigarettes per day).

- *action*—people are changing their behavior and environment in order to reach a desired goal.

- *maintenance*—people work so as not to have a relapse and to consolidate and build on gains in the action stage.

According to the results of the survey instruments that were used in almost a decade of research, 0–15% of smokers are prepared for action, 30–40% are in contemplation, and 50–60% are in precontemplation at any given time. People who are coerced into anti-smoking programs while they are in the precontemplative stage are four or five times as likely to resume smoking after the end of an anti-smoking program as are those in the preparation or action stage (Prochaska, DiClemente, and Norcross, 1992).

Using this framework, a person who could be described as unmotivated could also be described as being in the contemplation or preparation stage. The social worker can help client systems identify their degree of readiness and offer to join them at the point that they are ready to engage a change process.

In many locations, timeliness is a crucial consideration for the social worker when planning change activities. For example, in some communities weekends are for families, and all day Sunday and Wednesday evenings are set aside for church activities. Scheduling a community action committee meeting on a weekend is likely to result in skewed and lower attendance. The skillful social worker can work with client systems in identifying the behaviors, feelings, traditions, norms, and other cues to be considered when judging readiness and timeliness for change.

A community's willingness to accept the assistance of "outsiders" may depend on another form of timeliness—the point in time when the outsider is accepted as part of the community. I (Barry) recall living in a small town for almost five years before I joined the local Lions Club. During that period, I often encouraged local leaders to seek the help of the Regional Planning and Development Council on a variety of community needs. They always listened politely, yet nothing ever seemed to come of my recommendations. After I joined the Lions, however, these same leaders started coming to me for more information about how to use regional planning.

I (Becky) was first introduced to the issue of acceptance (or lack of it) during my field placement in the second year of my social work master's degree. One of my responsibilities as a social worker for a preschool for the deaf was to locate children who might benefit from the program, which provided daily transportation to and from the preschool for the child and a parent or guardian.

My territory was the Appalachian Mountain region, approximately 100 miles north of the city in which the preschool was located. Realizing that I was a stranger to the area, I spent over a month just being present in the local store responding to any questions the residents had of me and asking only those questions that would help me better understand and appreciate the locality. Most of the questions asked of me had to do with who I was (who was my family; was my family from the area; did I have any ties to the area) and why I was there (was I there to take any of the children away).

Finally, after much scrutiny, they must have decided that my intentions were okay: I was introduced to the midwife for the region, the person who had the best knowledge of the families in the area. It was the midwife who introduced me to several families with children eligible for the program. Without her assistance and presence, I might still be sitting in that country store.

Another aspect of timeliness has to do with being prepared to work on an issue when the opportunity arises—to seize the day when that day rolls around. For example, a settlement house in a midwestern city, under a very active director, generally had two or three proposals for the neighborhood essentially ready. At the point when notices were issued regarding the availability of funds from the local, state, or federal governments, the settlement house was ready (and was usually first in line).

How

The how of social work concerns the deliberate and selective use of knowledge, values, and skills to achieve the goals of a planned change process. We will present much of the how within our four-phase model for change. The model, which will be fully introduced and developed in later chapters, is built around the concept of the life experiences of client systems as a story.

We have purposely chosen the metaphor of "story" because it fits how we think about reality. The life process tends to be one that is full of uniqueness, unexpected twists and turns, surprise, joy, sadness, drama, and triumph. Just like a well-developed story, life is exciting, unpredictable, and riveting. Additionally, viewing life in this way normalizes the functions of social work so that social workers may be viewed as useful, potentially desirable, resources.

In the box below, we present the four phases of our model to be presented in later chapters.

Phase One	→	**Telling and Exploring the Story**
Phase Two	→	**Describing a Preferred Reality**
Phase Three	→	**Making Plans and Dreams Real**
Phase Four	→	**Evaluating Outcomes and Making Transitions**

Summary

We began this chapter with the assertion that social work is a profession and, as such, it has systematic practice theory, authority, community sanction, ethical codes, and a culture. Through our discussion of the five W's and the how of social work practice, the roles of ethical codes, community sanction, and authority have been clarified. Furthermore, we have identified the importance of the application and development of systematic theory and proven approaches in striving to work effectively with client systems. In addition, we have communicated that social work's history, traditions, and ways of viewing the world and what is important provides social work with a culture and a mission that is valuable to client systems, localities, and the nation.

As you prepare to move on from this chapter, we suggest that you give some thought to the following questions:

1. How do the five W's and the how fit with the way you have personally experienced life?

2. Can you think of examples of issues where the client system and the focus of change involve different persons or groups of people?

3. How may human diversity issues shape the life stories of some of our client systems?

4. Think about times you have wanted to achieve a particular change. How have the principles of timeliness and readiness for change been part of your process?

CHAPTER TWO

Key Values and Concepts That Ground Social Work Practice

The challenge is in the moment. . . .

JAMES BALDWIN

(1995)

Introduction

Where do we start? The question seems odd, as does the answer: The client system is paramount; start where the client system is. We adhere to this belief and use these as well as other words we string together, which we call *key values and concepts.*

As we noted in the Preface, books often tend to contain admonitions about what to do in every contingency. The world is moving swiftly, and knowledge is outmoded quickly—the half-life of information in many areas is five years, often less. Skills, however, can last much longer; for example, much of what we teach about listening and advocacy has remained accurate for a long time.

Values, concepts, and principles withstand the test of time. When we try to figure out how to practice in a way that respects the dignity of individuals and groups, how to affirm the capacities of others, and how to foster social justice, we are naming issues that people have been thinking about and struggling with since the birth of the profession and will still be struggling with as you are retiring. Yet, to struggle with them, you not only have to understand something about the abstract values and concepts but you must also formulate your own view of what they are and what they mean for you.

Just as no two practitioners will practice exactly the same way, neither will any two practitioners believe exactly the same thing, even though they share much in common. In this chapter, we present the values and philosophical and theoretical ideas and conceptualizations that shape the social work profession. What you believe and understand can then be companions, guides to action. In situations with client systems that are incredibly complex—where no "cookbook" will suffice—these values and concepts will serve you well. Listed below are the major themes that serve as our organizing framework for discussing the values and concepts we identify as vital for contextually grounded, generalist social work practice.

- The Societal Goal: social justice
- The Human Condition: (1) construction of meaning, (2) respect for human dignity, (3) human and cultural diversity, and (4) spirituality and religion
- Ways of Connecting with People: (1) belief in hopes and dreams, (2) self-determination, (3) strengths perspective, and (4) empowerment

We are indebted to Siporin (1975) for his work on and definition of ideology as a "system of beliefs and attitudes, expressing moral values and ideals about society and human relationships, which motivates people to act so as to realize these values and transform society" (p. 355). As reflected in Siporin's definition, an ideology is inclusive of more than professional values; it enables a profession and its members to work toward a preferred reality. The values and concepts can be used as signposts. We understand that on some days and at some places you may not get too far toward that reality, both at work or at home, and the best you can do will be just to get through the day. However, a professional ideology provides us with a foundation, the basis for our work with client systems. When we don't have an ideology that guides our actions, we become technicians instead of professionals.

We are committed to the position that, even though the ideology of the social work profession currently may not be in vogue, we have a responsibility to ensure that our practice, in all ways, reflects fundamental values and concepts. The point to this is that, as you think about entering the social work profession, it is important to understand that the profession has an ideology that we as social workers are expected to embrace as we set about our professional practice and take action to make the world a healthier and more sustainable place to live. However, we do note that this view may not be politically popular, and we see the social work profession as facing challenges and attacks because we have not abandoned our sacred positions. Nor should we.

The Societal Goal: Social Justice

When we think about social justice, we are considering the bases on which we make decisions about allocation or redistribution of scarce resources. There are three major philosophical approaches used to consider society's choices and obligations regarding resource use.

The *egalitarian theory* is a redistributive theory. According to John Rawls (1971), its foremost proponent, the needs of all persons must be considered when decisions regarding the distribution of resources are made. The disadvantaged have a right to at least the basic resources for living; the most vulnerable in society should not be left out or disregarded by the rest. Redistribution of scarce resources then becomes a moral imperative.

According to the *utilitarian theory,* redistribution of scarce resources is appropriate when it meets the interest of the common good (Conrad, 1988). The needs of individuals as well as of those of minority groups are subservient to the good of the majority. An example of the application of utilitarian theory is in the use of DRGs (Diagnostic Regulatory Groups) in hospitals and other health care settings. Insurance companies and Medicare authorities generally permit patients to receive a treatment or stay in a hospital only for a certain number of days when that treatment or that length of stay has been indicated as generally applicable. The needs of the "statistical majority" are given the primary consideration, not the personal needs of a patient.

Adherents to the *libertarian theory* reject any obligatory redistribution of resources, holding that each person is entitled to any and all material resources he or she has legally acquired. This approach is grounded in the autonomy of the individual, emphasizing the importance of freedom from coercion to share with those who are less fortunate. Any charity or service to others is considered supererogatory, beyond obligation, and is based on the voluntary contribution of the benefactor rather than rooted in the right of the recipient to basic resources (Nozick, 1974).

In *Social Welfare and Social Justice,* Beverly and McSweeney (1987) define social justice in distributive or redistributive terms: "Justice then as we define it means fairness in the relationships between people as these relate to the possession and acquisition of resources based on some kind of valid claim to a share of those resources" (p. 4). If fairness is the prime concept on which decisions are made, then all persons must be treated in essentially the same way. It follows from this that "the allocation of resources by government must give priority to meeting basic human needs in the areas of food, clothing, and shelter for all people within the jurisdiction of that government" (Beverly and McSweeney, 1987, p. 8).

Organizer and songwriter Si Kahn (1991) expressed the same idea in clearer words:

We need to abandon the concept
of fixed incomes
and insist instead
that people have fixed needs
and that these needs
have to be met
no matter what. (p. 315)

Social justice can be thought of in terms other than distributive or redistributive justice. According to the *American Heritage Dictionary,* justice is "fair treatment and due reward in accordance with honor, standards, or law" (Morris, 1982). Fair treatment is the province of the courts as well as legislative bodies; Supreme Court cases such as *Brown* v. *Board of Education* and recent legislation such as the American Disabilities Act and the Civil Rights Act of 1991 have been instances when branches of the United States government moved toward fairer treatment for some of its citizens.

Social justice, however, is more complicated than just giving priority to meeting basic human needs. The philosopher Michael Walzer (1983, 1986) states four requirements for distributive justice in a society: a shared economic, social, and cultural infrastructure; a system of communal provision; an equality of opportunity; and a strong democracy.

Decisions that we as citizens make about the *economic, social, and cultural infrastructure* influence the range of options and capacities of the members of the society. To the degree that we support public education and mass transportation, people who don't have cars and cannot afford to send their children to private schools will likely have more options than if we neglect these institutions. As Walzer (1986) stated, "In an egalitarian society, the decay of the infrastructure has differential effects, constraining the activities, limiting the scope of some people and not others. These constraints have never been ratified democratically, and they are, in any case, inconsistent with a democratic social life" (p. 139).

Even with a strong infrastructure, a *system of communal provision* is necessary in any society to assist people who are unable to care for themselves. Every nation makes provisions for people in need, depending on the values and economic realities of that nation. In the United States, we have provided governmental assistance not only for those who are most at risk (the poor, those with physical and cognitive disabilities) but also for many middle-class people (for example, tax deductions for mortgage payments).

Walzer (1986) notes that "the idea of a safety net is a more powerful idea than is commonly thought. It means that the first commitment of the welfare state is to its weakest members; nothing else can be done until their position is secured" (p. 142). Even if there were agreement on the safety net as the first commitment of society, there would still be a range of opinions on what the safety net should be like—how strong? how wide? how long can persons be supported? For example, the 1996 Federal Welfare Reform Bill signed into law limits the notion of a federal safety net for poor parents to five years in a lifetime and cuts over $50 billion from public assistance programs in a six-year period (Pear, 1996).

Walzer (1986) believes that "the safety net be constructed so as to secure for everyone whatever it is we collectively believe to be the central values of our culture, the needs that must be met if we are to stand with one another as *fellow* citizens" (p. 142). The safety net, weakened with the 1996 Federal Welfare Reform Bill, is even less secure than it has been.

The major arenas in which *equality of opportunity* is important to achieving distributive justice are in the workplace and professions, in gaining money or market power, in freedom of religious expression, and in attaining political power. Walzer (1986) cites the lessons of history, noting that those who have unlimited access to the world of work, money, religious expression, and political power tend to close off opportunities to others, especially to those most unlike them (women and members of disenfranchised groups). Professions and craft unions have been well known for acting this way.

License requirements, apprenticeships, and other entry mechanisms have traditionally been used to control access. While we have seen recent changes in the professions, especially law and medicine, such changes would not have been as assertively pursued, in our judgment, without public policy interventions that extended the idea of equal opportunity.

A shared definition of equal opportunity is even more elusive than coming to agreement about the substance of a safety net. The philosopher William Galston (1986) proposes that equality of opportunity has to take into account the profound range of abilities and talents of the members of any society. Equality of opportunity can lead to the full development of each person. The results of this will vary widely. Full development for a person with cognitive disabilities will not be the same as for a person with strong mechanical or communication skills, for example. Galston (1986) states that, in a good society, "the range of social possibilities will equal the range of human possibilities. Each worthy capacity, that is, will find a place within the society. Further, each worthy capacity will be treated fairly in the allocation of resources available for individual development within that society" (pp. 193–94).

Finally, a *strong democracy* is essential to the concept of distributive justice because decisions that affect the shape and vitality of the infrastructure, the system of communal provision, and the nature and range of equality of opportunity are all decisions that are made within the democratic process (Walzer, 1986). A concern for justice, then, carries over to a concern with the role of big money in politics and the ways in which large campaign contributions can have much more power over the decisions made by politicians and political bodies than do a much larger number of private citizens without deep pockets to contribute to legislative campaigns.

On this issue, Walzer (1986) cautions:

> *Political justice, or democracy, is the immediate form of justice. But democracy, though it rests ultimately upon a substantive distribution of power—one citizen, one vote—takes in practice the form of a procedural allocation of power—chiefly through free elections. And elections have unpredictable outcomes; the resulting distributive decisions are, sometimes, unjust.* So justice requires that justice itself be democratically at risk. This means that your favored conception, or mine, of infrastructure priorities, or the necessary forms of welfare, or the nature of available opportunities, or the division of this or that factory's profits, may be rejected *[emphasis added]. (pp. 148–149)*

Walzer's requirements for distributive justice are useful, but they are only a starting point. The involvement of social workers in shaping the definition of social justice (and its requirements), in making efforts to change the nature of our relationships with each other, and in changing the rules and the playing field itself are vital in supporting the voices of the oppressed and disenfranchised.

The rapid pace of social change means that definitions can become outmoded as fast as computer operating systems. Defining what is needed in a safety net, how to provide equality of opportunity without too many unanticipated negative effects, and what is essential in developing and maintaining the infrastructure is an ongoing process.

Perhaps even more crucial than the actual ongoing work of defining justice is the work of redefining our relationships with each other in the society. On a utilitarian level, this may be necessary in order to prevent civil unrest and maintain the unity of the United States. As philosopher Judith Sklar (1986) states, the perception of justice (and injustice) is the main cause of revolution. Walzer (1986) added in the question, "How are we to live together if we are not to oppress and injure each other?" (p. 137).

Feminist philosophers, especially Carol Gilligan (1982) and Nel Noddings (1984), have noted that the writings on social justice from Immanuel Kant (1964) to John Rawls (1971) rely on an ethic of morality to support the idea of justice, without taking into account the ways that caring and concern for others contribute to our sense of what is right and fair. We need to reframe our understanding of interdependencies in ways that make it possible for people to view the connections between themselves and others who are not members of their family, who don't live in their neighborhoods, and who may not look or act like them. South African writer Nadine Gordimer called us to acts of "rational empathy," to recognize the situation of others as if it were our own (cited in Sklar, 1986).

The African proverb "It takes a whole village to raise a child" is not universally accepted, and part of our work as social workers may be to engage others in the dialogue about what constitutes a caring community. "Caring involves stepping out of our own personal frame of reference into the other's. When we care, we consider the other's point of view" (Noddings, 1984, p. 24). The general society in the United States is not at this point in its development.

Equality of opportunity and a stronger safety net are not enough to achieve a "good society." Walzer (1986) stated that when the only change in society is to open old opportunities to new groups of competitors, the immediate effect is to intensify the competition, to generate the classical rat race. Some of the divisions in society today, which include a backlash against women and minorities, come from increased competition for higher paying jobs with generous benefit packages at a time when the number of such jobs is shrinking. In their book *Global Dreams,* Richard Barnet and John Cavanagh (1994) write, "[a]n astonishingly large and increasing number of human beings are not needed or wanted to make the goods or to provide the services that the paying customers of the world can afford" (p. 1).

Social justice may best be thought of using the metaphor of an organized game, such as baseball. One application of social justice is to ask questions about fairness, such as "Who is allowed to play?" Using the baseball analogy, it wasn't until 1947 that African Americans were allowed to play major league baseball and only in the 1970s that girls were allowed to play Little League. Another question, and a larger one, asks whether the current societal game that leads to a few winners and many losers is the game we want to play, or whether we need to work at changing the rules or inventing a new game. For instance, I (Barry) know some parents who have organized community games events where the issue is not competition but, rather, cooperation among participants—without naming winners and losers.

The Human Condition

A Construction of Meaning

Before we introduce the guides to social work practice, it is essential to look at how we know what we know. And we believe that much of what we call reality is not objective; rather, the meaning of events is constructed or generated by the people experiencing them. In other words, we know what we know because of who we are and where we've been.

Certainly, this does not mean to say that we literally construct the world without reference to the laws of physics and motion. If an instructor is standing in front of a class and drops a textbook from a desk to illustrate the reality of physical events, all the students in the class will see and hear that event. But the meaning to them will undoubtedly vary. Some will likely see it as a good illustration. Others may see it as silly.

We can clarify this concept with several more examples. If the indoor coed soccer team of which I (Jim) am a member loses a game 9-8, some team members will walk away angry at the refs and dejected at having lost. Others will feel good about how well the team played or how well they played individually. Others will consider it a good experience because they got a good workout. All of us were at the same facility at the same time, but the meanings (and therefore the experiences) are different.

Ronald Takaki (1993), historian at the University of California-Berkeley, wrote:

> *I had flown from San Francisco to Norfolk and was riding in a taxi to my hotel to attend a conference on Multiculturalism. Hundreds of educators from across the country were meeting to discuss the need for greater cultural diversity in the curriculum. My driver and I chatted about the weather and the tourists. The sky was cloudy, and Virginia Beach was twenty minutes away. The rearview mirror reflected a white man in his forties. "How long have you been in this country?" he asked. "All my life," I replied, wincing, "I was born in the United States." With a strong southern drawl, he remarked, "I was wondering because your English is excellent!" Then, as I had many times before, I explained: "My grandfather came over here from Japan in the 1880s. My family has been here, in America, for over a hundred years." He glanced at me in the mirror. Somehow I did not look "American" to him; my eyes and my complexion looked foreign. (p. 4)*

According to Gergen (1985), knowledge is not something people have somewhere in their heads but, rather, the process of a shared activity by people. As people act and interact as both observers and participants, we figure out what makes sense both for us and for the larger social context. It is the social context that enables us to understand more clearly the definition and meaning of behaviors and feelings.

This social constructionist viewpoint about knowledge differs from that of the positivists, who held that there was a reality that could be known if only we tried hard enough. The English poet John Keats, in the poem "Ode on a Grecian Urn," concluded with the lines:

> *"Beauty is truth, truth beauty"—that is all*
> *Ye know on earth, and all ye need to know.*

Truth is dependent upon what we know at any particular point in time, given the state of our knowledge acquisition tools. During the 13th century, the world was thought to be flat. It was only as efforts to sail off the end of the world failed that we began to discover another truth about our planet. We operate on the best knowledge we have about objects, people, places, and/or events until that "best" knowledge is expanded.

Our experiences and the stories we tell about those experiences influence how we see the world and how we make meaning of what we experience. All of us tend to view upcoming events either with anticipation or dread, depending on our past experiences with similar situations. A technical explanation for this comes from the work of the cognitive scientist Roger Schank. According to Schank (1990), people know how to act in common situations because they've "been there, done that" before, and they have a generalizable idea about how people are going to behave. These scripts, to use Schank's phrase, enable us to act without thinking much about what is appropriate and without even being aware that we are using the scripts. We also use scripts when we are in conversation. Given that it is markedly more difficult to create new thoughts on the spot, most of us most of the time are repeating scripts that we have heard before or told in another time or place.

When we encounter a new situation, we tend to understand it in terms of the other stories we know, including the ones we tell ourselves about our own lives and experiences. According to Schank (1990), "[g]eneralizations about narrative tend to be limited by the kind of cultural commonplaces and generalizations already in circulation in a community" (p. 30).

When you hear a story, it has an impact greater than other kinds of knowing. Schank proposed that stories can make a point without stating it directly, and that the more work that the hearers do, the more they get out of the story. He used a story to illustrate the point:

> *A friend and I were discussing stories and then moved on to a discussion about Jewish attitudes toward intermarriage. He said that two Jewish friends of his mother had gone out when they were young women, and when they'd returned home, their mother had asked them what they had done that day. They'd responded that they had played tennis. Their mother had asked whom they had played with, and they had said, "Two guys." The mother had then asked what kind of guys, and they had responded "Italian," to which the mother had said: "Another day wasted." (Schank, 1990, p. 11)*

Listeners are more likely to remember the point of this story than if they were told, "Some mothers don't want their daughters spending time with men they believe to be unsuitable prospects for marriage."

Modernism and Postmodernism We live in a time in history that can be characterized as the end of the modern era, the beginnings of postmodernism. Modernism was born in the 17th century, with Galileo seeing the solar system clearly through a telescope (Parry and Doan, 1994). The philosopher Descartes proclaimed, "I think. Therefore I am." Nature could be understood and controlled by science, and rationality would replace superstition, mysticism, and religion (Gorman, 1993).

In Europe, people had seen their lives up to that time in terms of their place within the "dominant story" of their society, shaped by the role of the church and the rulers of the country. Societies were generally steady-state ones, in which children followed in the footsteps of their parents. Both geographical and social mobility was extremely limited for the vast majority of the people (Parry and Doan, 1994).

With the Enlightenment and the Industrial Revolution in the 18th century came a loosening of the power of large landowners and the church over the lives of people. What the modern age promised was progress, propelled by scientific inventions and the power of rationality. Modernism was seen as a way of understanding the world and its progression, another dominant story that replaced the earlier one (Parry and Doan, 1994).

Postmodernism arose in the last half of the 20th century, partly because the stunningly rapid pace of change outstripped the ability of any one story or "grand narrative" to explain the world. In the fifty years since the explosion of the atomic bomb, science is no longer seen as a blessing. Similarly, at least in the Western world, scandals and revelations about politicians and politics have left many people skeptical about the possibility of rational solutions to societal problems (Parry and Doan, 1994).

Moving from One Dominant Story to Many Stories   Another force moving us away from a single dominant story, either about how the world works or about American history, is its exclusionary nature. Women and members of ethnic minority groups are rejecting the grand narratives in which they do not see themselves. According to Parry and Doan (1994), without grand narratives,

> *we now live in a world in which personal narratives essentially stand alone as the means by which we pull together the text of our own lives. . . . Our own stories stand alone as the codes by which we interpret the significance and meaning of the text of our own lives and of those who concern us. (p. 25)*

While the dominant story may be less important to many, social workers might find it worthwhile to build links between personal narratives and the grand narrative. In fact, building such links may be vital to strengthening communities and assisting them in caring for and being a resource to others.

Respect for Human Dignity

Social workers believe that all people have worth and the right to be treated with dignity. However, it is rare in social work professional literature that social workers define dignity and specify ways in which it is affirmed and denied or assailed in actual practice.

Defining Dignity   At its root, *dignity* means worth or value. It has three basic components: the intrinsic worth of all people, the person's view of the intrinsic worth of self, and the person's intrinsic worth as affirmed by others.

Human dignity was first proclaimed as a right in 1948, with the United Nations' adoption of "The Universal Doctrine of Human Rights," thus codifying the concept of the intrinsic worth of all people. Article I of that document reads: "All human beings are born free and equal in dignity and rights" (United Nations, 1987, p. 166). The declaration that all people are "equal in dignity and rights" means not only that laws apply equally to all but that people have a right to be *treated equally* regardless of their actions or place in life. According to Seltser and Miller (1993), "[t]here is a surprising consensus in our religious and philosophical traditions concerning a dignity in human life that is independent of any of the vagaries or accidents of social standing or personal action. There is an inner worth that is to be acknowledged, respected, and acted upon" (p. 95).

In this country, the strongest voice speaking out for human dignity was that of Martin Luther King, whose fight for civil rights began in a revolt against the indignities of segregation inflicted on the Negroes riding the public buses in Montgomery, Alabama. The resistance was sparked by Mrs. Rosa Parks, whose "personal sense of dignity and self-respect" was affronted by the order of the white bus driver to vacate her seat and move to the back of the bus. Her refusal to do so moved the country one step closer to desegregation. This event also started King's struggle for human dignity. In Dr. King's speeches and writings, the "achievement of human dignity" is presented as the major aspiration of the

American Negro. Thus, in his "Letter from a Birmingham Jail," he proclaimed the "dream of a positive peace where all men will respect the dignity and worth of human personality" (Spiegelberg, 1970, p. 41).

As King well understood, to be treated equally before the law does not by itself ensure that one is treated with dignity. To be seen as a person of worth is first and foremost to be seen as *a person,* not just a member of a racial or ethnic group, not defined by a label or a stereotype. We are reminded by Robert Coles (1992) that all efforts to put people into categories should be looked at skeptically. In 1968, Maslow wrote: "To place a person in a . . . [category] takes less energy than to know him in his own right, since in the former instance, all that has to be perceived is that one abstracted characteristic which indicates his belongingness in a class, e.g., babies, waiters, Swedes, schizophrenics, females, generals, nurses, etc." (p. 126). We do not want to be thought of just as social workers or students, and we do not like it when others use a single fact such as our gender, race, or occupation to define us. When we see people in their complexity, and acknowledge the forces and experiences that are most important in shaping them, we are treating them with the dignity they deserve.

Intrinsic worth is an abstraction; it becomes internalized when people carry themselves with dignity and act in ways that proclaim that they consider themselves to be of value and are worthy of recognition and acknowledgment. Dignity in this sense can be equated with the more commonly used term *self-esteem.* If my self-esteem is high, then I will behave in a way that non-verbally communicates to the world my image of myself. Many civil rights movements have understood this important point, including Operation PUSH, which had as its rallying cry the phrase "I am SOMEBODY!"—an affirmation that was chanted at rallies and meetings to voice (and reinforce) a sense of self-worth.

One's self-esteem, however, is based on more than just self-image. According to Coopersmith (1967), the messages one receives from others about one's worth are important in shaping a sense of competence and self-esteem. It is possible to claim that we have dignity even if no one else treats us with dignity; but the term is social and psychological as well as philosophical. In reality, it would be hard to act with dignity if no one else affirmed it. Both conditions are required: we carry ourselves with dignity, and other people respond to us as people with dignity (Seltser and Miller, 1993).

Being treated with dignity and maintaining a sense of dignity can also be equated with the current use of the term *respect.* In 1993, many of the nation's most powerful and violent urban gangs held a Gang Summit. According to one observer, "No word was heard more often than respect. 'Don't disrespect your brother or sister' was a continual refrain. Respect is what those young men and women have felt the least of from their society; it is what they most seek for themselves and their communities" (Wallis, 1994, p. 245).

The sociologist Elijah Anderson (1994) wrote about a code of the streets—informal rules governing interpersonal public behavior in urban neighborhoods:

At the heart of the code is the issue of respect—loosely defined as being treated "right" or granted the deference one deserves. However, in the troublesome public environment of the inner city, as people increasingly feel buffeted by forces beyond their control, what one deserves in the way of respect becomes more and more problematic and uncertain. This in turn further opens the issue of respect in sometimes intense interpersonal negotiation. In the street culture, especially among young people, respect is viewed as almost an external entity that is hard-won but easily lost, and so must constantly be guarded. . . . The person whose very appearance—including his clothing, demeanor, and way of moving—deters transgressions feels that he possesses, and may be considered by others to possess, a measure of respect. . . . Many inner-city young men in particular crave respect to such a degree that they will risk their lives to attain and maintain it. (p. 85)

According to Gewrith (1982), "[t]o treat someone with dignity is to accord her certain kinds of consideration: to treat her as an end, not only as a means or as an object to be exploited, to treat her with respect for her basic needs, and for herself as worthy of having these needs fulfilled" (p. 15). Seltser and Miller (1993) added that people deserve to be related to

in a manner that allows them to have an inner attitude, a world of dreams and hopes and intentions toward the future. To attack the dignity of others is to treat them as if they merely mirror their circumstances, as if they accept others' interpretations of their lives and are subject to other peoples' agendas. (p. 93)

There are some actions and ideas that are incompatible with respect for the inherent dignity of a person or of people. Schacter (1984) notes two categories of these affronts to dignity: (1) behaviors and ideas that directly offend, put down, or denigrate the worth and dignity of people and (2) ideas that are incompatible with the basic philosophy of the inherent worth and dignity of people. Among the affronts to dignity that he cites are:

- statements that demean and humiliate people or groups because of their origins, status, or beliefs;
- vilification or derision of beliefs that people hold in reverence, teaching that particular races, ethnic groups, or religions hold "ridiculous" or dangerous views, or otherwise belittling cherished beliefs;
- dissemination of negative stereotypes of groups (ethnic, religious, social) and implications that members of such groups are inferior;
- denial of the capacity of a person to assert claims to basic rights;
- degrading living conditions and deprivation of basic needs; and
- abuse and insolence by (government) officials, especially to people suffering from infirmities or social opprobrium (oppression).

Dignity Affronted and Affirmed in Human Services   Peoples' dignity and sense of identity are both reinforced and attacked as they have contact with human service agencies and workers. The number and variety of situations in which a person's sense of identity may be vulnerable are many. Here are some examples:

- Social workers who work with single mothers experiencing homelessness report that few of them volunteer for parenting classes. Why is this? It may be difficult for them to acknowledge that their parenting could use some improvement when their primary identity is in being a parent. If they are not in the job market, and not in a more or less permanent relationship, their identity may be largely in their relationship with their children. They may also feel they are doing a better job of parenting than their parent or parents did with them. And, because of their circumstances, their self-esteem may be low. For many parents, not being able to provide a roof over their heads and those of their children assaults their own sense of identity. Initiatives or assumptions by agencies that imply that parents are not taking good care of their children just because the family is homeless can erode their image as parents.

- Staff who work with men who are single and homeless report that it is common for these men to lose their driver's licenses or other forms of identification. There are few places in shelters to safely leave their possessions, and in the moving around from place to place, things get lost, left behind, or stolen. The longer that people have been on the streets, disenfranchised, the less important the ID (literally, their identity) becomes to them (Truax, 1995).

- In rural areas, families that are well known to agencies can acquire a negative identity. Workers may know that the family or some family members may not have willingly worked with the agency on some issues in the past. What too often happens is that workers and the agency assume that the family is not motivated to work on other issues, so the agency responds half-heartedly to current concerns.

When people need assistance from human service agencies or when they are in contact with governmental agencies, feelings of powerlessness are often high and their sense of dignity can be especially at risk. Three areas where dignity becomes an important issue are: being treated as persons, being treated as people who are important, and being aware of issues of power, autonomy, competence, social participation, and inclusion.

Being Treated as Persons Social welfare programs in this country are generally designed to meet specific needs, and eligibility criteria are usually strict. If a person's income level is low enough and he or she has facilities and resources for cooking, that person might qualify for Food Stamps in some states. If a parent or couple's income is still lower, they have children under 18, and meet other requirements, they might qualify for public assistance. If a child's learning disabilities are severe enough, that child can get special assistance from the schools. In all these cases, however, the personal situation, in all its complexity, is not considered. What often happens is that a person or family may have needs or circumstances that don't fit the array of services or programs available—square pegs and only round holes. The frustration and anguish that people feel on hearing that their needs cannot be responded to is related to their sense of identity and esteem. They don't want to be categorized as "welfare recipients" or "disabled"—they just want help that mirrors their situation.

In interviews with social workers, several reported instances in which their client systems came back to them upset that other service providers had not appeared to listen to their concerns. "They didn't hear a thing I said!" exclaimed a client. Social workers who are sensitive to the issue of dignity reported using reflections and other techniques to communicate that the client system is being heard. One social worker gave a testimony to what can happen when clients are treated as people. She works in a combined human service agency in a rural county.

> *One day, a man who applied at the Income Maintenance side was referred over, because the Income Maintenance worker thought he was depressed. I was lucky in that I had an hour open, and tried to intently listen. What emerged, piece by piece, was that this biker, a member of the Diablos Locos motorcycle gang, was a Vietnam vet and was a late-night cross-dresser who wanted a sex-change operation. The sources of his depression came clearer. Without the time, and without the attention, none of this would have come out. (Danielson, 1995)*

Being Treated as People Who Are Important "Human dignity is the worth of a person who is worth being for his own sake, regardless of his usefulness for another. It is because of this worth that he is worthy of personal respect" (Spiegelberg, 1970, p. 59). The way in which people are treated by agencies and by workers clearly communicates a sense of how important they are in the eyes of that worker or agency. One aspect of this is the agency's appearance. There is an incredible variance in the decor and furnishings of public welfare agencies: some are well kept with plenty of light and appear like doctors' waiting rooms; others are dim, with furniture in need of repair and seven-year-old *Readers Digests.* This communicates a message to the applicants (and to the staff, we would add) about how valuable they are.

As another example, the staff of an organization that serves the homeless reported receiving from a manufacturer boxes of clothes, for older children, that had been sitting in a warehouse for at least a decade. The staff debated about whether or not to distribute the clothes because wearing the clothes would set the children apart from others.

In another instance, a worker in an agency that provides in-home services to families spoke of another worker whose middle-class orientation alienated her from the families with whom she worked. She would not sit down when she was in the home and refused offers of food or something to drink. These actions clearly communicated to the family her sense of their value.

As a further example, a case manager for persons who are HIV-positive and have AIDS talked about how her clients are very aware of situations in which service providers demean them, how they are often spoken to in a manner that communicates that they are less of a person than others, not deserving of services. For example, a worker in a county agency told a family member of one man with AIDS that she "wouldn't blame a nursing home for not accepting a person with AIDS, because AIDS is an awful thing."

There are also reported instances of people with AIDS being treated with dignity, of workers talking to persons with HIV and AIDS as if they were talking to other professionals, of workers who shook their hands on greeting and put an arm on their shoulder in walking out of an office. In some situations, to treat people "normally"—as others are generally treated—is to treat them with dignity.

Many agencies and organizations make special efforts to safeguard and reinforce the dignity of recipients. In some settings, adults are always called "Mr.," "Mrs.," or "Ms." instead of their first name. A unique organization in Winston-Salem, North Carolina, provides hospice care for people in the last six months of life, respite care for families of children with cognitive disabilities, mediation services, and wellness planning free of charge. Staffed entirely with volunteers and funded by contributions only, they put a strong emphasis on working with all those who come for services. Referring to their work with people who are dying, one volunteer talked about the agency's commitment to their wishes: "If they want to waltz, we'll waltz. If they want to shag, we'll shag" (Human Service Alliance, 1995).

Being Aware of Issues of Power, Autonomy, Competence, Social Participation, and Inclusion Human beings need to have a sphere of action, an arena in which they make choices and have some control and discretion. Many people who are homeless find themselves in shelters or other facilities that are heavily regimented, with rules that seem to cover all situations.

In one shelter, dinner is served at 5:00 p.m. and families are not allowed to have food in the main living area after dinner. For parents whose children get hungry again before breakfast, the only choices they have are to stay on the street and not in the shelter, ignore their children's requests for food, or sneak food in and hope they don't get caught. "When our lives are severely restrained, we are less able to see ourselves as moving through our own world, as influencing what happens to ourselves and to others" (Seltser and Miller, 1993, p. 99).

It is hard for people to hold onto their dignity when they are in contact with a professional helper who has control over resources or some other kind of power. A white nurse wrote about seeing an elderly black man in an emergency room:

> *When I had completed my specific tasks, I really listened to Mr. B. Besides offering his symptoms, he had entered into a master/servant relationship with me. His answers were often 'Yes, ma'am,' 'No, ma'am,' or 'Thank you, ma'am.' He was, of course, concerned about his physical condition, but more than that, he appeared to be saying that he knew I had the power to help him and he did not want to upset that relationship. (Gosline, 1993)*

In rural America, the path to homelessness for many families starts with an old car breaking down, missing work or not being able to get to a job at all, and ultimately not being able to pay the rent, resulting in eviction. People in this situation are not only without a stable roof over their heads but they are also lacking an arena to demonstrate their competence and abilities. At this point in time, they are dependent on the kindness of strangers or the availability of a room or beds at facilities for the homeless. "When luck becomes the major explanation for feeding one's children, any sense of accomplishment or self-respect is likely to disappear" (Seltser and Miller, 1993, p. 105).

When people are homeless, they are often outside the contexts of a neighborhood or community or of a web of family and friends within which they can participate, and so find meaning. A woman who prided herself on the way she kept up her small apartment (and was complimented on the apartment's appearance by guests) lost the opportunity for competence and inclusion when she became homeless (Seltser and Miller, 1993). From small actions like asking residents in a transitional housing facility to paint trim to helping people experiencing homelessness organize around political issues, creating opportunities for competence and inclusion in the larger world can lead to a sense of belonging and mastery.

A social worker in rural New Hampshire told me (Jim) about a woman in her town who was losing her apartment and had nowhere to go. When all other options had been exhausted, the social worker decided to call one of her clients, another woman who received disability benefits and lived alone in a house. The social worker asked her if she could put up the woman at risk of homelessness until other arrangements could be made. The woman readily agreed, and added, "No one ever asked me to help anyone before." When we offer people the opportunity to help others, we are affirming their worth.

It may be as important to the social worker as to the client system that we do our job in a way that respects and affirms the dignity of those we are privileged to serve. In the hectic pace of our work, it is easy to think only of what is effective and efficient in the provision of services. People become cases, and what is uppermost in our mind is not sinking under the workload and paperwork. To affirm *our own* personhood, it is essential to remind ourselves of the importance of treating people with dignity.

It is also important to realize that, at times, it is impossible to absolutely honor dignity in assisting client systems with meeting their needs. For example, a person may be faced with the options of homelessness or acquiring shelter in a dangerous high-rise public housing complex where parents worry about their own safety and that of their children (Hopps, Pinderhughes, and Shankar, 1995). Social workers who are mindful of the importance of dignity recognize that their role is to support the person in making a choice, even though the range of options may not be healthy or desirable.

Treating client systems with dignity becomes more difficult when the client system is angry or aggressive. Not taking the anger personally is essential. Workers can remind themselves that in some situations people feel they have very little power and few choices; getting angry at someone in a position of authority may be their only way to assert themselves.

Human, Ethnic, Social, and Cultural Diversity

In the years around the close of the century and the dawn of a new millennium, few challenges are as important (and as daunting) for social workers as understanding diversity and working in ways that are culturally competent. In this section, we will explore the complexities of this issue and present an expanded view of diversity.

Demographic Changes We live in changing times, and demographic changes are among the most noticeable in our society. In 1980, one out of five United States residents was a member of an ethnic minority group (African, Latino, Asian, or

BOX 2.1

Demographic Changes: 1980–1990

The demographic makeup of the United States is changing.

- 30 million African Americans, a 13% increase since 1980

- 22.4 million Latinos, a 53% increase since 1980

- 7.3 million Asian Americans, a 107% since 1980

- 2 million American Indians, a 38% increase since 1980

Regional and urban/rural changes are significant.

- 82% of the population in the Northeast and Midwest, 72% in the South, and 67% in the West are white American; one in five persons living in the West is Latino.

- The states with large ethnic minority populations will continue to be coastal and border states, especially those states on the southern U.S. border from Florida to California.

- Half of the population growth in the 1980s was in California, Texas, and Florida.

- It is predicted that California will have a nonwhite American majority by the year 2000, or at the latest, by 2005.

- 73% of Asian Americans, 69% of Latinos, 58% of African Americans and 46% of white Americans live in large metropolitan areas.

American Indian); in 1990, the figures were one in four (U.S. Bureau of the Census, 1992). One-third of the current United States population does not trace its ancestry to Europe (Takaki, 1993).

Demographic changes usually happen slowly—iceberg slow. This is an iceberg on roller blades! Box 2.1 illustrates the specifics of these changes.

Parallel to the demographic changes have been other social changes. One of the legacies of the Civil Rights movement of the 1960s has been an increased level of awareness and activism among traditionally oppressed groups. No longer are African Americans content to sit at the back of the bus, gays and lesbians to stay in the closet, or persons with disabilities to stay locked up in institutions or as adults in their parents' homes. Active efforts have emerged in which groups are telling their own stories and demanding to be accepted as full partners in society.

An example of this, regarding the experience of many American Indians, comes from the work of anthropologist Edward Bruner:

According to a 1992 Census Bureau projection:

- during the next four decades (until 2030), the white American population will increase by 25%; the African American population by 68%; the Asian American, Pacific Island, and American Indian populations by 79%; and the Latino population by 187%.
- by the year 2080, the U.S. might be 24% Latino, 15% African American, and 12% Asian American.

As a nation with a population of 260-plus million, our population is growing at a slower rate than in the past, largely due to lower fertility rates (the average number of children each woman has in her lifetime).

- The fertility rate needs to be at 2.1 for population replacement.
- Currently in the U.S., the fertility rate is 1.7 for white Americans, 1.3 for Cuban Americans, 2.4 for African Americans, and 2.9 for Mexican Americans. The fertility rate differences by class are stronger than the differences by race.

- The average white American is 31 years old, the average African American 25 years old, and the average Latino is 23 years old. The lower the average age, the more potential children.

These demographic changes will be reflected in work environments.

- In 1990, 42% of the workforce were white American males.
- Only 15% of all new entrants into the workforce in the next 10 to 15 years will be white native-born males; the remainder will be people of color, women, and immigrants.
- The rate of growth of minority populations in the workforce will continue from approximately 17% in the late 1980s to over 25% by the year 2000. In 1990, one-fourth of the companies surveyed already had a minority workforce of more than 25%.

Source: Statistics from the U.S. Bureau of the Census (1992).

Bruner demonstrated how the interpretation of [American Indian] current living circumstances shifted radically with the generation of a new story that proposed an alternate history and future. In the 1930s and 1940s, the dominate story about the Native Americans constructed the past as glorious and the future as assimilation. In attributing meaning to current circumstances within the context of this story, anthropologists and Native Americans alike interpreted the "facts" of the daily lives of the Native Americans as reflective of breakdown and disorganization, as a transitional state along the route from glory to assimilation. This interpretation had real effects. For example, it justified certain interventions [by] the dominate culture, including those related to the appropriation of territories.

In the 1950s there emerged a new story, one that constructed the past as exploitation and the future as resurgence. Although it could be assumed the "facts" of the daily existence of Native Americans did not significantly change through this period, with this new story providing the context, a new interpretation of the facts arose. They were now considered to reflect not disorganization, but resistance. This new interpretation also had its real effects, including the development of a movement that confronted the dominant culture with the issue of land rights. (cited in White and Epston, 1990, pp. 10–11)

Diversity as Inclusive As Lum (1996) points out, there is a tendency to view differences from the "American norm" as deviant. White American students on university campuses at times complain about Asian Americans being too quiet and African Americans being too loud. Both of these judgments, of course, are made in reference to their own communication style.

As we move away from the deficit-based view of diversity, there has been a tendency to equate diversity or cultural difference only with race, or with those groups clearly defined and identified as minorities and protected under antidiscrimination law: African Americans, Latinos, Asian Americans, American Indians, persons with disabilities, and women. The Youth Service Bureau (1994), which serves youth who run away and are homeless, expanded the definition of cultural diversity to encompass more of the nation's range of differences as follows:

- ethnic/racial background
- socioeconomic/educational status
- sexual orientation
- gender culturalization
- physical capacity
- age/generation
- personality type
- spirituality/religious beliefs
- regional perspectives
- new immigrant socialization

To this particular list, we would add geographic location, mental capacity, and immigrant status as well!

An inclusive view of diversity is also reflected in much of the training currently being conducted in large corporations. Their efforts at diversity training for the past decade or more have been motivated toward increasing personal productivity, decreasing interpersonal conflict, improving work relationships through greater employee knowledge of diversity-related issues, and increasing their ability to recruit and retain the most qualified employees (Sundstrand Corporation, 1993).

Among the characteristics identified as part of one corporation's diversity program were race, ethnic background, gender, sexual orientation, marital status, religion, education, nationality, age, weight, blue-collar or white-collar employee, educational degree, recent hire or long-term employee, long-term resident or from outside the community, and smoking preference. The purpose was to illustrate that all employees (and all of us) belong to in-groups and out-groups, and employees need to look at the variety of ways in which they can exclude, or be excluded by, others (Sundstrand Corporation, 1993).

Similar to categorization, dichotomous definitions such as male/female or black/white can have the unintentional consequence of reducing people to only one aspect of their lives. Various experiences and memberships in groups, cultures, and subcultures have shaped our journey through life. All of us, in some sense and in some contexts, are insiders as well as outsiders, and the nature of our interactions with various groups and cultures as well as the larger society contribute to our sense of identity.

As we discuss concepts of diversity, it is crucial to define what we mean by terms such as culture, ethnicity, and race. *Culture* can be defined as a set of meanings or understandings shared by a group of people, a framework, a world view, or a cognitive map that is used to make sense of the world. Culture also can be understood as a way of life of a people or society, consisting of norms of behavior, beliefs, values, and traditions. An expanded definition would include language, religious ideals, habits of thinking, artistic impressions and expressions, and patterns of social, interpersonal relationships.

Culture provides us with our fundamental sense of belonging and our fit within society as a whole. Our group identities—the "we's" that shape us—influence our experience by determining whether we are relaxed and can speak in the shorthand of others who share the same basic world view and experience or whether we have to translate ourselves to others who would not understand the way we interpret the world (Markowitz, 1994).

Culture can serve to hold people together and provide them with a personal and collective sense of purpose and continuity. As part of this, culture also aids in defining in-groups and out-groups. Unfortunately, sets of shared meanings and ways of life are seldom seen as cultural assets; they are more often labeled as liabilities.

Abraham Verghese (1994), a physician whose ethnicity is East Indian and who grew up in Ethiopia, wrote of his experience in east Tennessee during the mid-1980s while working with young adults with AIDS:

> *As I got to know more gay men, I became curious about their life stories, keen to compare their stories with mine. There was an obvious parallel: Society considered them alien and much of their life was spent faking conformity; in my case my green card labeled me a "resident alien." New immigrants expend a great deal of effort trying to fit in: learning the language, losing the accent, picking up the rituals of Monday Night Football and Happy Hour. Gay men, in order to blend in, had also become experts at blending in, camouflaging themselves, but at a great cost to their spirit. By contrast, my adaptation had been voluntary, even joyful: from the time I was born I had lacked a country I could speak of as home. My survival had depended on a chameleon-like adaptability, taking on the rituals of the place I found myself to be in: Africa, India, Boston, Johnson City (Tennessee). I felt as if I was always reinventing myself, discovering who I was. My latest reincarnation, here in Johnson City, was my happiest so far. (p. 58)*

Dr. Verghese is a master at recognizing cultural nuances and adapting to different cultures. For people immersed in a culture, these meanings are generally more unconscious than conscious—like fish who don't know they are swimming in water. Persons whose roots are in the white American middle-class helping professions might not realize the cultural values reflected in such phrases as "enmeshed family" and "co-dependent" to describe family structures and inter-actional processes (which generally reflect behaviors defined by the white middle class as dysfunctional).

Traditionally, culture is passed from one generation to the next by way of stories, rituals, ceremonies, and traditions. Cultures remain distinct to the degree that the values, beliefs, behaviors, and habits of thinking are embraced by the next generation.

An *ethnic group* is a group of people who hold a subjective belief in their common descent because of similarities of physical type, or customs, or both—or because of common memories of immigration and oppression. The term "hyphenated Americans" refers to groups that include ethnic heritage as part of their identity (for example, African Americans, Asian Americans, or Irish Americans).

A person's sense of ethnic identity may be self-defined or defined by others. A teenager, whose parents had moved from Korea to the Chicago area before he was born, was vacationing on the West Coast when he was asked where he was from. He replied "Chicago." The questioner asked the question again. "Chicago, Illinois," the teenager replied, thinking his answer wasn't clear the first time he replied. Again the question was repeated. Confused, the teenager replied the name of the Chicago suburb where he lived, before his mother interjected to tell the curious person that his parents (she and her husband) had originally lived in Korea (Governors State University, 1993).

Consciousness about ethnicity and its value varies widely from person to person and even within ethnic groups. For some people, their ethnic heritage can be a pivotal factor in shaping their identity; for others, it may be seen as incidental, to be brought out in cooking or festivals a couple of times a year. Similarly, one's ethnicity may be experienced as a source of pride or as a source of shame (Devore and Schlesinger, 1991).

Race is a notoriously slippery concept that eludes serious attempts at definition. The term is used so frequently that we can forget how imprecise it is.

Historically, in this country, race was used to signify immutable differences. About the 1896 Supreme Court decision, *Plessy* v. *Ferguson,* that affirmed the legality of separate but equal, Justice Bradley stated:

> *A statute which implies merely a legal distinction between the white and colored races—a distinction which is founded in the color of the two races and which must always exist so long as white men are distinguished from the other race by color—has no tendency to destroy the legal equality of the two races. (cited in Kromkowski, 1995, p. 21)*

In addition, there are legal distinctions based on racial differences; for example, one is legally black, white, or American Indian. In 1983, a woman in Louisiana sued to change her racial classification from black to white, challenging a state law that declared anyone who was 1/32 or more black be classified as black. The court upheld the state law, in spite of the testimony of a retired geneticist from Louisiana State University that the average white person in Louisiana owed 10 percent of his or her genetic structure to African heritage. Up to 30 percent of the genetic composition of African Americans is from European or American Indian ancestors (Shreeve, 1994).

The concept of race has a shaky scientific base, especially when it is used to explain physical or intellectual differences. Professor Richard Lewontin of Harvard, one of the country's leading geneticists, stated that more genetic diversity exists within a race than between races; only six percent of genetic difference can be explained by race (Begley, 1996).

The label of a group of people as white has no meaning outside of race-based systems. Immigrants originally identified themselves in terms of their country of origin (for example, Italian, Swedish, Scottish, Irish, or Japanese), not their skin color. In much of the world where racial classifications exist, they use gradations to describe differences in color or ethnicity without the dichotomy of white and black found in the United States (Takaki, 1993).

Additionally, many groups and many people do not fit neatly into a racial category. The term *Asian* is used to refer to people from such places as China, Japan, India, Pakistan, Korea, the Philippines, and other Pacific Islands. Latinos or Hispanics are neither a race nor an ethnic group. The terms are used to refer to immigrants from places such as Argentina or Chile as well as descendants of people who lived in northern New Mexico in the 1600s, when the area was still a part of Mexico and before the United States seized half of the land mass of Mexico in the 1840s. On census forms, Hispanics can list themselves as black or Caucasian. Labels such as Asian or Hispanic deny the richness of cultural and historical difference (Wood, 1995).

In 1990, Americans claimed membership in nearly 300 races or ethnic groups and 600 American Indian tribes. Latinos had 70 categories of their own. The fastest growing collective in the United States is multiracial, and there is strong sentiment as well as strong opposition to a category that enables people to identify themselves as multiracial or multiethnic on the census for the year 2000 (Fost, 1995).

While race as a social construct is a mixture of prejudice, superstition, and myth, racial identity has real implications in day-to-day life for many people. The following is excerpted from an interview with Clarence Page and appears in Studs Terkel's book *Race: How Blacks and Whites Think and Feel about the American Obsession* (1993):

> *When I wake up in the morning and see my pregnant wife beside me, I know from ultrasound that we'll probably have a boy. A young black male. How different I think as a father of a young black male than if I were a father of a white male. There's a certain level of expectations society has of my kid different than the other one. If he's a teenaged boy walking down the street wearing Adidas basketball shoes, jeans, and a troop jacket, he's regarded differently than a white teenager wearing Adidas basketball shoes, jeans, and a troop jacket. They wear the same outfit, yet are looked upon so differently.*

I think of moving to the suburbs because of the schools. But I think: "Where will I be welcome? Where will I possibly be burned out?" In 1990, I think about that. If I were to move into a predominantly white suburb, the first thing that crosses their mind is not the Pulitzer Prize, it's "it's a black family in our neighborhood." Even among the most liberal white families, the question is: "Is it bad for my property values?" (p. 76)

African American author Paula Giddings (1984) explains: "When and where I enter, then and there, race enters with me" (p. i). For those of us who are white, we can go days or weeks in many environments without our whiteness being an issue; it stays in the background.

Part of the tragedy in contemporary America is that many people are accepted or not accepted on the basis of only one characteristic. As illustrated in the quote by Clarence Page in Chapter 1, the cab driver who did not stop for him did not notice that the black man hailing the cab was a middle-class, well-dressed, middle-aged professional. He saw only a black man. A college student who uses a wheelchair complained that others "do not see the person in the chair, only the chair."

Leticia, a graduate of the social work program in which I (Jim) teach, wrote this vignette in a paper for one of the classes I taught.

I moved to Dallas (from a town on the Texas-Mexico border) when I was eighteen. As I was walking into a mall, a group of teenagers (all white) called out "Hey, taco!" I just kept walking but I knew they had been yelling at me because I was the only one walking in and I know this is a word people use to refer to a Mexican. That day I realized that I did not fit into the American world. I was not like them. I did not have blond hair and light eyes. If I had been, then I would not have been called names. . . . I had an image of who I was. I was a Mexican who did not want to be Mexican. (Monroe, 1994, p. 2)

When Leticia recounted this incident in class, the reaction among her white classmates was profound: shock that someone would treat her so badly. One aspect of her life that was different from theirs had become clear to her colleagues. What was less visible but more significant for Leticia were her identities as a parent, a feminist, and her growing identification with the social work profession. Proudly, she has now included Latino as a significant part of her identity.

Power, Privilege, and Diversity   Because of the different ways people are treated in our society, power and privilege are concepts that warrant being addressed again. Elaine Pinderhughes (1983) notes that, generally, social workers—especially white middle-class social workers—are uncomfortable with examining their own power and privilege in United States society. White middle-class people know they seldom have as much power in our society as do the upper-class, well-connected members, yet they seldom acknowledge the power and privilege they have in relation to other members of our society.

To illustrate, Peggy McIntosh (1993) writes: "As a white person, I realized that I had been taught about racism as something which puts others at a disadvantage, but I had been taught not to see one of its corollary aspects, white privilege, which put me at an advantage" (p. 209). She describes white privilege as "an invisible weightless knapsack of special provisions, passports, code books, visas, clothes, tools, and blank checks" (p. 210).

As we reflect on the idea that special privileges artificially accrue to the dominant members of a society, it is important to think about how these benefits may have shaped many of our experiences in ways we may not ever have considered. To illustrate, I (Barry) have benefited from being of the dominant group in a variety of ways. As white-skinned, I have not had to worry much about how others perceive me as I go about my day-to-day activities. As a middle-aged, tall male, when I enter a place of business, I don't have to fear being watched to see if I am going to steal something. When I attend a meeting of professionals, I can expect to have a voice more easily than others. It has been a common experience to attend a public hearing with some of my female colleagues and have the sponsors address me first as the expert. As I have learned more about privilege and artificially attributed benefits of dominant membership, I am conscious about trying to reframe that experience by appropriately stepping to the background when I feel my views should not be solicited preferentially just because of my height, gender, or race.

I (Becky) experienced the profound effects of white privilege during the early 1970s. As an employee of the Department of Public Welfare located near the eastern border of a southern state, I was driving several of my professional colleagues to a conference near the western border of the state. With confidence and comfort, I had turned off the highway to seek gas in a small community on the way to the conference. Unexpectedly, I heard one of my colleagues gasp and anxiously suggest that I return to the highway and keep driving. As my gas gauge indicated that the tank was empty, I replied that I had no choice. The alarmed companion was an African American female; she informed me that not only could she not enter this particular community safely, anyone accompanying her was also in danger. Ultimately, to ensure our safety, she lay flat on the floor of the back seat covered with an old blanket from the trunk of my car until I was able to fill my gas tank and return to the highway. As a white-skinned person, I had never before had to be cautious about which towns or cities I entered.

I (Jim) don't have to worry about my children's schoolteachers treating them differently because of their skin color (white). My family and I can choose to eat in restaurants in any part of Wisconsin without wondering if we will be the center of attention or even if we will be seated. I can run (or jog) in any residential area I choose without having to fear being stopped by a police officer for an ID check. African American colleagues and friends share tales indicating that their experiences are quite different from mine in schools and restaurants, and in other aspects of their lives.

It is important that we are mindful of the existence and effects of White-Skinned Privilege. At the same time, we do not assume that this privilege generalizes equally to all white people. I (Jim) had a student in class who was starting college in her mid-thirties after experiencing a disability from working in a factory. She was white, and her family background would be considered by sociologists as lower class. She described it as "white trash." Because of the family's poverty, she generally grew up in the only neighborhoods the family could afford—places where she and her family were outsiders, occasionally mistreated, and not accorded any special benefits because of the color of their skin. Her experience has been that, sometimes, when she dresses just right, she can become invisible. Far more often, however, mainstream white culture recognizes the difference in class and socioeconomic status, and thus she is not privileged in the same way middle-class whites are.

Creating hierarchies of privilege and oppression is not what we are suggesting here nor is it a useful exercise (Lorde, 1993). It is vital that social workers listen to and understand the perspective of the variety of persons and groups of people with whom we live and work. As Michael Novak (1993) reminds us: "Why do the educated classes find it so difficult to want to understand the man who drives a beer truck, or the fellow with a helmet working on a site across the street with plumbers and electricians, while their sensitivities race easily to Mississippi or even Bedford-Stuyvesant?" (p. 33).

Understanding Diversity, Understanding Self For social workers, self-awareness includes cognizance of our ethnicity, privilege, and the ways past experience and context have shaped our perceptions of others as well as our feelings, values, spirituality, attitudes, behaviors, and such. Social work must be recognized as cultural phenomena—ways a culture has devised to address certain social and personal issues.

Those of us who are white and those of us from middle-class upbringings seldom experience the ways other people are treated differently (and in many ways, oppressively) in this society. This means that the responsibility is ours to listen to and read about the experiences of diverse cultures and populations.

The book *Ethnicity and Family Therapy* (1982) was instrumental in alerting family therapists to recognize, often for the first time, that what might appear to be idiosyncratic behavior in a family could be a reflection of cultural patterns and ethnic diversity (Markowitz, 1994). In relation to this point, McGoldrick (1994) writes:

> I have myself only recently become aware of the constraints of class, culture, gender, and race on the structure of who I am. I have been coming to realize that most of us have never been safe, since home in our society has not been a safe place for women, children, or people of color, in light of the persuasiveness of abuse in the form of corporeal punishment of children, child sexual abuse, mistreatment/devaluing of women, and the appalling institutionalized racism in our society. I had no awareness of these issues until a very few years ago. They were, to borrow the phrase from Betty Friedan, issues with "no name"—invisible issues that I only now realize defined the entire construction of relationships in my family, my schooling, and the communities in which I have lived. None of these issues was ever mentioned in my childhood, my adolescence, my college or graduate experience, or in my study of family therapy. (p. xiii)

In the challenges and opportunities to becoming *culturally competent,* understanding self is the first step. Attention, commitment, and action are crucial to mastery of the knowledge and skills, as well as the internalization of social work values and ethical standards, necessary for developing competency in working with people who are different from us.

Human and cultural diversity contribute to the richness of our lives, experiences, locality, and society. The benefits and challenges associated with understanding diversity and practicing in ways that reflect a sensitivity to the differences of others are addressed throughout this book. In particular, in Chapter 9, we will address issues relevant to the ways the agencies in which we practice are responsive to human, social, cultural, and ethnic diversity.

Spirituality and Religion

A graduate student in social work wrote the following in a paper on spirituality and social work:

> *While working on my undergraduate social work degree, I was given an assignment to do a psychosocial assessment and report to the class. The person who agreed to let me interview her told me the tragic tale of her bittersweet life. She had started out a very devoted wife and mother who was a very devoted Christian. A series of adverse events led to her husband leaving, a drug dependency, the loss of custody of her children, etc. At the time we spoke, she had been clean for almost a year and was anxiously awaiting the return of her children from foster care. She said she knew it would be difficult, but wanted to create a happy family for her children. In the summary section of my assessment, I indicated that I would like to help her reconnect to her lost spirituality for strength. My professor went crazy, and proceeded to give an hour-long lecture on separating out any spiritual or religious aspect from the social work profession. (Brunner, 1996, p. 1)*

Certainly, not all in the profession make that clear a separation between social work and spirituality and religion. However, neither the concept of a higher being nor the distinctions between spirituality and religion are discussed much in social work education.

Definitions and Distinctions Although the terms spirituality and religion are often used interchangeably, important distinctions between the two need to be made. *Spirituality*—from the Latin *spiritus,* breath of life—is best understood in the context of searching for meaning to life and existence. Spirituality can be a search for meaning that involves both transcendence (the experience of existence beyond the physical/psychological) and immanence (the discovery of the transcendent in the physical and psychological world) (Decker, 1995). *Religion*—from the Latin words *re,* together or again, and *ligio,* to bind—can be considered the organized attempt to facilitate and interpret that search. Religion "binds together" followers of a certain set of beliefs in group worship and other group activities. In addition to belief in a deity that exists outside of the temporal and human world, religions have traditions that make demands of some kind on those who are members of the group (Carter, 1993). Canda (1989) believes that religion exists and persists because it helps people understand why humans make mistakes, why we suffer, why the world is an unjust place.

Spirituality should be understood as broader than the term religion, which is most often used to denote a specific and formal institutional context. In this sense, the link between spirituality and human behavior is direct and straightforward, while affiliation with a formal religious institution (for example, a church, temple, or synagogue) is one means of expressing spirituality. There can be an institutional context for spiritual beliefs and practices, and spirituality can be experienced and expressed outside of religious contexts.

Other interpretations about spirituality and religion come from these papers of graduate students:

> *After several years of searching and questioning, I realized that I already practiced a sense of spirituality within myself. To me, spirituality is standing on the edge of a mountain peak and looking over a great lake or forest, breathing in fresh ocean air on a warm, cloudy day, or simply staring up into a starry sky. I also truly love and have faith in living things. I feel as if any child could be mine, and that they are incredibly precious, yet vulnerable little beings. The same feelings occur as I think about all of the animals and wildlife on this earth. I have an intense passion and a deep connection with both life and nature . . . a truly wonderful gift and to share with others. (Paul, 1996, p. 1)*

> *Religion to me is the gathering place, the coming together of people in search of a common community belongingness. This connection to things/people outside ourselves is part of what I would call spirituality. Spirituality is also about inspiration and that which touches us in profound and deep ways. (Lichtenstein, 1996, p. 1)*

> *"Religion is for people who are afraid to go to hell; spirituality is for people who have already been there." As a recovering alcoholic, who has lived a type of hell on earth, I can relate to this. (Martin, 1996, p. 1)*

National Attitudes toward Religion and Spirituality Stephen Carter (1993) notes that a widespread cultural belief exists that downplays the importance of religion in our lives and in our social, economic, political, and educational structures. Additionally, tension exists in our society about the degree to which it is acceptable to be public about our beliefs. We propose that part of this downplay of religion and the tension about public pronouncement of beliefs may grow out of western society's trust in the classic science paradigm. Beliefs that come from religion and spirituality are mistrusted precisely because they are not based on rationality. The reliance on empirical evidence in our society tends to promote a belief in absolute truth and in the potential for factual knowledge about all things. The ultimate proof of the existence of God, except as a part of faith and belief systems, has eluded us.

According to Carter (1993), the public views religious participation as an activity akin to building model airplanes, a hobby that is permissible but not really the kind of thing intelligent people do. For example, if beliefs are strong, believers can engage in actions and practices unpopular or not sanctioned by prevailing views. These occurrences are most dramatically illustrated by the mass suicides of

Jonestown and Heaven's Gate members. While these acts often puzzle us and challenge our understanding, they also may serve as opportunities to re-examine and explore in more depth our own belief systems, resulting in enhanced clarity and understanding.

While religious freedom is protected by the United States Constitution, there is much public dialogue and debate about the role of religious activity and spiritual beliefs in the public arena. We view this questioning as desirable and encourage social workers to be active participants in this process.

Social Work and Religion and Spirituality   The social work profession has had an uneasy relationship with religion. As in other developments in the practice ideology of social work, Sigmund Freud was influential. Freud, in *The Future of an Illusion* (1957), connected religious ideas to man's obvious helplessness in the face of life's mysteries. He then connected this helplessness to the child's predicament and referred to the condition as an infant prototype (Freud, 1957). He also likened the effect of religious thinking to that of a narcotic (Coles, 1990). Religion, according to Freud (1957), was a mere illusion, or neurosis, composed of fairy tales and derived from human wishes.

There are other reasons, more rooted in modern life and thought, for the social worker's discomfort in this area. Cornett (1992) believes that many clinical practitioners

> *have an almost instinctive negative reaction to the introduction of the word "spirituality" into clinical discussions. In some cases this reaction seems to represent a distaste for something that is not quantifiable or totally observable. In other cases, it appears to spring from a fear of imposing a specific perspective (for instance, conservative Protestant theology) on clients through the therapeutic dialogue. In yet other cases, this reaction appears to [be a] spiritual perspective in itself: that of the organization of the universe around the rational, problem-solving ego of the individual.* (p. 101)

It is likely that this graduate student speaks for many when she writes:

> *At my placement I don't know if clients bring their view of god into discussions with me because this will make them seem like "good clients," that this is what they are supposed to do to successfully complete the program, or if god is really that primary in their lives. It makes me a little bit uncomfortable, like I'm supposed to say something in agreement or nod and smile, but god forbid(!) should I say I don't agree. My mother always told me, it's best to avoid discussing religion and politics.* (Jackson, 1996, p. 2)

Yet, when we avoid discussing religion, we may be missing something very important. Recently, I (Barry) had a profound experience with spiritual belief. On the first day of a fall term at my university, I learned that my mother had experienced an aneurysm and had survived the surgery but was in critical condition. This had taken place on a Monday, and by the following Friday, it was clear that many of her organs were not functioning and that additional surgery to remove one leg was immediately necessary.

The future did not look good. By this time, she had been transferred from the community hospital where the surgery had been done to the teaching hospital at my university because of her need for advanced care. Our first message from the new physician was that she had agreed to having one leg removed. While I found that unusual, knowing how my mother had always expressed a fear of losing her mobility, if she wanted to go ahead I was not going to challenge that wish.

As the family (including my brother, sisters, and father) waited, we were asked to meet with the head of surgery. He explained that my mother's condition had worsened to the point that he was not sure she could survive another operation, nor was he convinced that it would leave her with any quality of life. His visit with her had left him convinced that she was not alert enough to choose the next steps, and he needed to know the family's wishes.

My mother's pastor had joined us by this time; as he listened to the doctor, he started to poll the family on our wishes by asking me what I thought. (I am the eldest child and no doubt that influenced the pastor to start with me.) I indicated that I would not speak for anyone else, but I would rather not put her through any more. As each family member spoke, they talked of our mother's faith and how she would be with her Lord in the afterlife.

After the decision to discontinue treatment and remove her from life support, the doctor—a gentleman in his sixties who had taught the young doctor that had performed the original surgery and literally saved Mom's life that day—thanked the family and asked if we would join him in prayer . He then proceeded to lead us in a powerful and healing prayer of thanksgiving for my mother, her life, and the courage of the family in arriving at this hard decision. My family and I were struck in a positive way by his behavior. Later, we joined my mother in a room at the hospital and remained with her as she quietly passed on. Our family members all remember with great respect the caring of the doctor and his healing prayer.

A social worker reflecting on her own experiences struck a similar note:

> *I became a case manager for elders in the community. At that time, I did not consider spiritual leaders to be an important referral source for my clients. I find it interesting that it was terribly easy to overlook an important source of support and guidance for my clients. Sometimes I thought about it, and sometimes I did not.*
>
> *When my mother was involved with hospice care, she was offered a social worker in addition to a clergy person. She rejected social work, but depended upon the help of the church to meet her needs as she "passed on." I learned a great deal about the need for spirituality during this period of my life. I tend not to "just" forget the religious needs of others after this experience. (Cates, 1996, p. 2)*

Robert Coles, a child psychiatrist whose psychoanalytic training reflected Freud's teachings on religion, became convinced, little by little, that the spirituality and religious beliefs of the children with whom he worked were important. In 1962, he was talking with an 8-year-old, one of the first children to integrate the schools in her community. The child talked about how her faith was important to her in this struggle. When asked to elaborate on this, she said:

"I was all alone, and those segregationist people were screaming, and suddenly I saw God smiling, and I smiled." Then she continued, with these astonishing words: *"A woman was standing there (near the school door), and she shouted at me, 'Hey, you little nigger, what you smiling at?' I looked right at her face, and I said, 'At God.' Then she looked up at the sky, and then she looked at me, and she didn't call me any more names."* *(Coles, 1990, p. 19)*

What these three stories have in common is the realization that the spiritual dimension of life is important to many people—to us at times, to a family member, to a person or the people with whom we are working. This can alert us or remind us that it is a dimension to which we may not pay enough attention. As Canda (1989), a social work educator who also has a doctorate in comparative religions, documents: religion and spirituality are universal aspects of human experience. If your world view does not contain convictions about or beliefs in religion or spirituality, it is wise to remember Hamlet's words to Horatio in Shakespeare's *Hamlet,* "There are more things in heaven and earth, Horatio, than are dreamt of in your philosophy" (Act I, sc. v). One can understand that spiritual and/or religious beliefs are important to people without sharing or understanding them ourselves.

The Role of Religion and Spirituality in a Flawed World Religion and spirituality often come into play in times of loss or during life-shattering or life-shaking experiences that contradict our assumptions about the safety of the world, about a Creator, and about ourselves. Herman (1992) suggests that trauma challenges one to be a theologian, to ask "big picture" questions when experiences change our perception of the world. Alice Seabold testified to this loss of security: "When I was raped I lost my virginity and almost lost my life. I also discarded certain assumptions I had held about how the world worked and about how safe I was" (cited in Herman, 1992, p. 50).

Combat veterans, who saw and did things on the battlefield that most of us only experience watching movies or in nightmares, often have trouble reconciling their experience with the faith with which they grew up. Believing that, in wars, "God is on our side," that we fight for "one nation under God," assures soldiers that they are engaged in a just cause. "The truth about combat is quite different, however. God seems malignantly absent in the caldron of madness, savagery, and malice that is war. Grace, redemption, mercy, kindness, love of nature—the stuff of New Testament faith—are incompatible with the killing rage of combat" (Mahedy, 1995, p. 6). For many young soldiers, their battlefield experiences shattered their conceptions of right and wrong, and the exposure to evil resulted in strong feelings of shame and guilt. Thirty years later, many combat veterans are engaging in spiritual practices to promote their healing (Salois, 1995).

In hospice care and other settings where death and dying are more present than they are for most of us, religion and spirituality can be important in enabling people to understand (or make meaning of) their lives and life itself. One social worker employed as an alcohol and drug counselor stated, "I frequently work with my clients on these issues, and currently am co-facilitating a grief group where we address religious and spiritual beliefs and convictions of the group members since they very much affect how people view death and dying" (Rogalla, 1996, p. 3).

Religion and Spirituality as Culture and World View In the previous section on diversity, we defined culture as a set of meanings or understanding shared by a group of people, a world view or cognitive map that is used to make sense of the world. For many people, their world view is influenced and shaped by their sense of spirituality and/or religious beliefs.

Social workers who are uncomfortable with religion but attuned to the importance of culture-sensitive practice may want to think about their work with people who have strong religious beliefs as cross-cultural communication. One social worker who realized this reported, "Once I start listening to the language of the client and using their terminology while advocating that a client start listening to their wisdom, I am amazed how many people begin to describe a greater sense of comfort regarding their decisions" (Cates, 1996, p. 3).

Ways of Connecting With People

Belief in Hopes and Dreams

Social workers operate in a problem-saturated environment. There is a crisis at home that propels someone to seek assistance, or a circumstance or action (poverty, abuse, difficulties in daily functioning) that prompts a community or governmental agency to intervene. Yet, when we focus only on "the problem," we may not be paying enough attention to the role of hopes and dreams in people's lives; to the future they want for themselves, their family, and their community; and to the ways in which hoping and dreaming can be driving forces for action.

Hope is the belief that the dreams will become real—a trust in the possibility that, with work, things can be better. When people *dream,* they are affirming their capacity to imagine or envision a reality that is in some way different and better than the present.

Without dreams, there may be little motivation for change. Many people find themselves stuck in the eternal present and don't really believe that things can or will be better. They see their lives as continuing in the same way, and they see their community and the nation not much differently. A single mother, homeless at the time, with whom I (Jim) was working, voiced a common refrain when she said, "There's really no place in the country for people like us."

When children grow up in situations where the future does not look promising, if the dreams don't die, they get downsized. This occurs far too often for children growing up in distressed neighborhoods. In *Amazing Grace* (1995), author Jonathan Kozol's story of his encounters with families in the worst neighborhood of the South Bronx, he writes of being introduced to Damian, the top student in the fourth grade at a neighborhood school. When Kozol asked Damian what he wanted to be when he grew up, Damian replied, without conviction, "an X-ray technician" (1995, p. 123). Jim Wallis (1994), a minister who has worked in inner-city Washington, D.C., lamented that children talk with each other about their favorite kind of caskets, not their favorite style of bikes or cars.

The social philosopher Cornel West (1993) writes that conservatives tend to blame the plight of poor African Americans on the lack of proper values—hard work, frugality, or delayed gratification—while liberals highlight structural factors—discrimination in housing and employment, the changing nature of jobs, and underfunded schools. He notes that neither perspective attends to the nihilism that pervades many poor black communities. Nihilism, he clarified, is "the lived experience of coping with a life of horrifying meaningless, hopelessness, and (most important) lovelessness" (p. 14). With the eclipse of hope in nihilism comes a disregard for property and for one's own life and the lives of others.

Perception and Possibilities   People tend to dream of what they see as possible. It's no accident that a dramatic growth of state-run lotteries and tribal casinos has occurred in the 1980s and 1990s, a time when wages and possibilities have been shrinking for many people. I (Jim) used to refer to hooking your future with winning the lottery as *castillos en el aire,* a Spanish phrase for dreams that have no foundation in reality. However, for many working people who see their wages stagnating or dropping, the slim chances of winning the lottery seem the most likely avenue for improving their economic well-being.

Nathan McCall is a reporter for the *Washington Post* who grew up in segregated Norfolk, Virginia. After graduating from high school, he was arrested for armed robbery and spent three years in prison, where he learned printing as a trade. In *Makes Me Wanna Holler: A Young Black Man in America,* he remarks on the print shop instructor's final words before he was released:

> *"Make sure that whatever you do, you find a job in an atmosphere that is psychologically comfortable for you."*
>
> *I appreciated the intent, but I needed that piece of advice like I needed a .25 automatic with extra clips. It was clear to me that, as a white man, my instructor came from a reality that gave him enough choices to be able to look for a comfortable work environment. But that was a foreign concept to me, a contradiction in terms. I know that if I worked, I'd likely work for white folks. So how could that be comfortable? I figure that if I followed my instructor's advice and looked for a comfortable work environment, I'd be unemployed all my life, unless I worked for a black-owned business or started one myself.*
>
> *I politely thanked my instructor for the advice and moved on, thinking "He meant well. He didn't know any better." (McCall, 1994, p. 214)*

Later in the book, McCall reflects on why he and his friends, growing up in the neighborhood that they did—most of them in two-parent, hard-working families—made the violent choices that they made. Thinking about one close friend, Shane, who breezed through school but had spent most of his adult life in prison, McCall writes:

> *Shane and I and the others in our loosely knit gang started out like most other kids. Yet somewhere between adolescence and adulthood, something inside us changed. Our hearts hardened, and many of us went on to share the same fates as the so-called disadvantaged.*
>
> *I'm not exactly sure why, but I've got a good idea. A psychologist friend of mine explained that* our fates are linked partly to how we perceive our choices in life [*emphasis added*].
>
> *Looking back, I see that the reality may well have been that possibilities for us were abundant. But in Cavalier Manor, we perceived our choices as being somewhat limited.* (p. 402)

There are several implications for social workers and social work in these passages. In a previous section, we introduced the concept of White-Skinned Privilege and also wrote about how our own backgrounds influenced our sense of the possible. We need to be constantly aware that the same opportunities are not available for everyone, that the road of life is rougher for some than for others. And we may also need to assist some people in realizing that there are more options and opportunities than they currently can envision.

A Sense of Hope as a Source of Energy   When people believe that their actions will lead to a better reality or that something important awaits them, it can be energizing. In *Anatomy of an Illness,* Norman Cousins wrote about his own successful efforts (using Groucho Marx movies, among other things, to prove that laughter *is* the best medicine) to combat a life-threatening disease. He stated that part of his motivation came from early experiences; he had tuberculosis at age 10, and remembered that those patients who were confident that they would improve did better than other patients (Cousins, 1981).

In contemporary times, perhaps the strongest advocate for the power of hope in human functioning has been Viktor Frankl, the founder of logotherapy, an approach that stresses the importance of people finding what gives meaning to their lives and acting on this discovery. Frankl survived a Nazi concentration camp during World War II, and he uses those experiences to explain: "The prisoner who had lost faith in the future—his future—was doomed. With his loss of faith in the future, he had lost his spiritual hold; he let himself decline and became subject to mental and physical decay" (Frankl, 1963, p. 117). He quotes Nietzsche, "'He who has a *why* to live for can bear almost any *how.*' In the Nazi concentration camps, one could have witnessed (and this was later confirmed by American psychiatrists both in Japan and Korea) that those who knew that there was a task waiting for them to fulfill were most apt to survive" (pp. 164–165).

Dreaming of a preferred reality can be a starting place for action. In the work I (Jim) do with parents, I ask them to think about how they would like things to be six months down the road (no winning lottery ticket, no miraculous personality change in their children). With some time and a safe, comfortable space for this kind of active dreaming, they can often think of situations that would be healthier and less stressful—that would involve some work but are not impossible. In this way, they are able to approach the next steps with much more energy than when they are focusing on "problems."

Some professionals have difficulty with the element of hope, fearing that some client systems may put too much emphasis on hope when it is unwarranted. For example, people living in violent situations frequently express the hope that, if they can just survive the abuse, everything will get better; or they attribute the cause of the violence as somehow related to their own failures and deficiencies and express the hope that, when they change, the violence will stop. As social workers, our developing knowledge about the cycle of violence provides us with an awareness that, without some form of intervention for change, the violence not only continues but generally intensifies over time. The cycle becomes a rut. And the deeper the rut (as the cycle is repeated), the harder it becomes to get out. Knowing this, some professionals are reluctant to acknowledge—let alone build on—the hope expressed during the romance stage of the cycle, that the violence will stop and the situation will improve.

It is not the hope that things can be different that is to be feared, however. Without hope, there is despair; and despair leads to entropy, a state of less differentiation (all parts begin to be alike), less organization and effectiveness, and less capability of using energy and carrying out the system's function (Munch, 1995). What is required is a context for the hope. This can be accomplished by sharing our knowledge and understanding about the dynamics of the situation and exploring with the client system ways in which the situation can be different. One way to support and build on the expressed hope is to affirm the hope that is present and to examine the elements of the situation over which the people who are being abused have potential control. The people being abused do not cause the abuse, and therefore, do not have control over the abusive behavior. But they can exert control through their response to the abuse by pressing charges, leaving, staying and enduring, or (which often happens) identifying with the abusers and behaving in ways similar to them. Providing this context puts into perspective the hope that exists and creates opportunities for imagining the options available for working toward a preferred reality.

Connecting Family/Personal Hope with the Community/National Perspective
As valuable as the work of imagining a preferred reality and building on the dream is, it is incomplete if one's preferred reality or that of one's family is seen apart from that of the context. We tend to separate the two.

It is common for parents in our communities to speak with concern about the general challenges facing teenagers, including drugs, teen pregnancy, violence, and an uncertain economic future. Yet, when asked how they see their children's future, these same parents speak confidentially that their own children will not be impacted by the challenges. It is almost as if the headlines in the news do not apply to them.

This phenomenon of what appears to be denial may occur because many of us have tacitly given up on the idea of things changing for the better for many people, so the dreams become smaller and more individualized. Jim Wallis (1994) writes that we live in a time when people are asked to accept the current political and economic situation as the way things always will be. To believe otherwise is considered nonsense; but it is that kind of "nonsense" that can lead to changes in thinking and, ultimately, to changes in society. He notes: "The nonsense of slave songs in Egypt and Mississippi became the hope that the oppressed would go free. The nonsense of a bus boycott in Montgomery, Alabama, became the hope that transformed a nation" (p. 238). Hope, then, becomes the door from one reality to another—believing in spite of the evidence, acting on the beliefs, and watching the evidence change. In Chapter 6, "Describing a Preferred Reality," we explore further the way hope can be a resource in working with client systems.

Self-Determination

Self-determination has been one of the capstones of the values that social workers hold dear; it is linked with acts of personal power, autonomy, opportunities for competence, social participation, and inclusion. When asked what values are important, confidentiality and client self-determination are the ones that most social workers would first identify. To understand the significance of client system self-determination in social work today, we examine the evolution of the principle of self-determination within the context of the nation and the profession.

A Historical Perspective In *Habits of the Heart: Individualism and Commitment in American Life,* Robert Bellah and his colleagues (1985) write about the continuing importance of individualism in American life. For the early settlers, self-reliance was seen not only as a necessity for survival but also as a value. This was expressed most clearly by Benjamin Franklin (1924) in *Poor Richard's Almanac,* which contains sayings about right living and how to become wealthy (such as, "God helps those who help themselves"). For many Americans influenced by Franklin's work in the 1700s and 1800s, individual self-improvement was so important that the larger social context was not seen as significant (Bellah et al., 1985).

The emphasis on individualism—with the continuing loss of community—continues to this day. Recently, I (Barry) was talking with a young couple about life and society. I asked them what they wanted from the government. They responded just to be left alone. They were doing just fine in their view. What they failed to understand was just how dependent, in the reciprocal sense of that word, they, in fact, are. They have good roads on which to drive, a nice house, free baby-sitting when they need some time away; yet, they fail to consider how mutually dependent they are on others for these things.

It may be uniquely "American" (limiting the word to those of us in the United States) to think this way, and we need to understand both the limits and opportunities associated with this perspective. Certainly, many prosper in a highly individualistic society, and just as many, if not more, do not. We need to think carefully about just how self-reliant we really are. Robert Bellah, interviewed by Bill Moyers, noted that "to me the most critical question is how can we give interdependence—which is so obvious in connection with everything we do—a moral meaning?" (Flowers, 1989, p. 279). Finding the moral meaning within our individualism may be the key to how we and others can exercise our self-determination more responsibly.

With the birth and growth of social work as a profession in the 20th century, self-determination was held to be very important. In the 1930s, within the larger context of worrying about the rise of fascism in Italy and Germany and the crisis confronting democracy, self-determination was seen as an extension of democratic values. Bertha Reynolds and other progressive social workers stressed the importance of self-determination so that social workers not become unwitting agents of wealthy and privileged classes that oppressed and exploited individuals and groups (Freedberg, 1989).

After World War II,

> *[a]s the social service delivery system served more middle-class clients during the relatively affluent 1940s and 1950s—clients who felt more in control of their behavior and had more invested in the social system than clients of an earlier time—self-determination took on greater significance as a professional concept. (Freedberg, 1989, p. 37)*

Client System Rights versus Social Worker Obligations Self-determination as a value provides the basis for client systems to choose alternatives from what is possible rather than solely from the perspective of what is morally or legally correct (Bellah et al., 1985). In the most recent revision of the NASW Code of Ethics (1996), self-determination is recognized as an inherent human right: "Social workers respect and promote the right of clients to self-determination and assist clients in their efforts to identify and clarify their goals. Social workers may limit clients' right to self-determination when, in the social workers' professional judgment, clients' actions or potential actions pose a serious, foreseeable, and imminent risk to themselves or others" (Standard 1, section 1.02 [Self-Determination]; see Appendix).

Note the exception that is made in the event that the client system's actions indicate potential or actual harm to self and other. In a number of fields of practice, there is a constant dilemma for social workers in trying to strike the balance between a client system's right to act in ways that can be destructive and a social worker's obligation to prevent harm to the client system and to others (Reamer, 1993b). One way to hold to the value of self-determination while not endorsing actions that are destructive, outside legal limits, or against other social work ethics is to redefine the term. In his review of the concept of self-determination in social work literature, McDermott (1982) notes that self-determination is often equated not with making choices but with making choices that are prudent, rational, and socially acceptable. According to Bernstein and others, self-determination should be supported only:

- when the rights of others are protected;
- when client system choices are realistic, rational, reasoned, and constructive (rather than unexamined impulses);
- when those choices fit the law, the agency, and society; and

- when those choices are within the client's capacity to self-determine (cited in Rooney, 1992).

We share the concern expressed by Rooney (1992) and McDermott (1982) about viewing self-determination from the perspective proposed by Bernstein and others. We believe that this limits self-determination to what the worker may perceive as appropriate, socially acceptable, externally defined goals. If humans didn't act in ways that got them into trouble, then respecting self-determination would not be difficult. As McDermott (1982) states, "[e]xcept in the most arbitrary of tyrannies, it is only when one begins to deviate from the accepted social norms that any real need for the protection afforded by a right of self-determination arises" (p. 82).

Closely related to the belief in the right to self-determination is the right to privacy and confidentiality. In many states, social workers have the "duty to warn" third parties from harm if they learn of a possible threat of harm from a client system with whom they are working. (The precedent-setting decision that resulted in the duty-to-warn requirement was the 1974 Supreme Court of California ruling for *Tarasoff* v. *Regents of the University of California* [Gibbs, 1991].) In other states, the professional has "an obligation to use reasonable care to protect the intended victim against such danger" (Gibbs, 1991, p. 19).

Ultimately, the client system has the right to determine goals and the actions to take to reach those goals. And inherent in this right are the consequences and responsibilities associated with the actions. For example, social workers have a duty to report any suspicion of child abuse and neglect to the appropriate authorities. In some states (Arizona for one), there are legal requirements regarding the reporting of adult abuse and exploitation as well. A client system's choice of behaviors may "put into motion," or have as a consequence, therefore, actions that must be taken by the professional. As social workers, we have the responsibility to explore with and inform our client systems of the potential consequences of their choices.

The Importance of Self-Determination Self-determination can be viewed as a foundation for affirmation and participation in one's family, community, and world. Further, self-determination as a value that informs practice reinforces the principles of mutuality and partnership of client system and worker in the change process.

Professional expertise and knowledge are essential to effective social work practice. However, mutuality of the process requires that social workers use their professional knowledge and skills to address the issues, needs, opportunities, and desired outcomes as they are named by the client system, in a partnership framed within the context of the community and social justice. This point is important because it places self-determination in the larger context of social principles and values and acknowledges the consequences and responsibilities associated with rights and choices.

While the client system must carry a primary responsibility for naming the issues and goals of the work, this does not mean that the social worker has no voice. Our obligation in the partnership is to clarify, bring in new information, encourage, challenge, and otherwise support the client system in having the information necessary to make informed decisions. One challenge in this process is being able to offer support for choices when we would personally choose a different action. Our ethics bind us to an awareness of our very human capacity to sometimes coach people to make the same choices we would. As a result of this awareness and attention, we can better avoid this imposition on the client system.

There are also other reasons to practice within the constraints of client system self-determination:

it is utilitarian—participation is enhanced and learning fostered when people are self-initiated and self-determined;

it is existential reality—the reality is that people have choices. Our function as social workers is to affirm this reality. Some decisions, such as to get help or not, or to get well or remain ill, require the commitment of the person(s) involved or nothing will happen (Rothman, 1989);

it contributes to competency development—in making decisions and following a path, a client system is building capacities.

A client system demonstrates self-determination as it acts to reach its goals, desires, or wishes. We can further divide this into *positive* self-determination—having the knowledge, skills, and resources needed to pursue one's goals—and *negative* self-determination or autonomy—engaging in actions that are forced, coerced, or made under undue pressure or influence (Rooney, 1992). In order to promote client system self-determination, then, social workers guard against manipulation and undue coercion and provide client systems with the information necessary to make informed choices. There are consequences associated with all our choices and actions.

The difficulties with self-determination are lessened if we think about it as one important principle, not the *only* one. Just as "There is nothing as dangerous as the man who has read only one book," it is folly to hold to only one precept. When we realize that self-determination is one value and principle among many, we can better appreciate the wisdom of philosophers like John Stuart Mill who clarified the boundaries of self-determination this way: the point where one person's begins, the other's stops. When a person's acts endanger others, the security and basic needs of those in peril take precedence over the person's right to act as she or he wishes (Reamer, 1993b).

As with social work practice, self-determination is best understood within the context of personal and social realities. Our client systems may have dreams that do not fit well with their talents or likely opportunities; and while we always respect the dream, we may need to offer supportive challenges reflecting the reality constraints that impact its realization.

I (Becky) worked with a 14-year-old client who was born with no forearms or hands and one leg. Her IQ was estimated at 60. She had outgrown the prostheses she had for her arms and leg, and she had adapted quite well without them. She could groom herself and perform multiple household chores, including the intricate task of sewing with her "nubs" (as she referred to her arms and leg).

I met "Jane" when I responded to a report of child abuse. I found her to be a remarkable young woman. Her dream was to become a secretary. My initial gut reaction was one of "impossible, unreal," and "there is no way she can pursue that as a career." Not wanting to squelch her dreams, I responded in a way that together we could explore, clarify, and honor her desires within the context of her potentials as well as her capacities. What did being a secretary mean to her? What was it about being a secretary that appealed to her? What was her understanding of what a secretary would be expected to do?

In our discussions around these questions, we discovered that her dreams were to interact with lots of people in a polite and kind way, to provide information about whether or not a person was available to be seen, to schedule appointments, and to answer phones. With the exception of scheduling appointments (as her reading and writing skills were limited), the identified tasks were all within the realm of her current capacities! As social workers, we have a responsibility to help clients frame their hopes and dreams within the context of their capacities and environments so that they may work more fully from a position of informed choice—even when that choice goes against best professional judgments.

I (Barry) recall the story about a young man in my hometown who was advised by his high school teachers and counselors not to attempt college because of his intellectual limitations. In spite of their best judgments, he went ahead with his plans to enroll in college. He started slowly with a few courses; five years later, he was the feature subject of a front-page story, as he was graduating number one in his class. The point is obvious but worth making over and over: We can be wrong, and client systems should be self-determining. Even if the teachers had been right in their assessment, I feel the young man had the right to try, even if he might have failed.

We interfere with client self-determination when:

- we interfere with the actions or intentions of client systems;
- we fail to disseminate all available information or deliberately withhold information from client systems that could open up other options; and
- we deliberately disseminate misinformation.

As social workers, we are reminded by the principle of self-determination to keep our persuasion above ground; there must be very good reasons to maneuver or compel people into acting against their own wishes. We need to be aware of "the opportunity for manipulation available to the social worker in exercise of his or her authority, both legitimate authority and the pseudoauthority with which she or he is often credited" (McDermott, 1982, p. 85).

Self-determination is a guiding principle; it fits well with the other principles outlined in this section and with a democratic, pluralistic society. Our challenge is to seek ways to partner and work with client systems and to remain open to other visions and options that may not be within their view.

The following example, from a hospital social worker in West Virginia, is an illustration of how a social worker can "keep on keeping on" in order to assist client systems in fulfilling their self-determination and reaching their goals.

I worked with a critically ill man who had become bedfast from a rural county in West Virginia, approximately 100 miles from the hospital where he was being treated. He required continuous oxygen therapy; his lungs would also fill up with fluid, bringing him back into the hospital in a week or less after his discharge home. An assessment of needs was conducted at the patient's bedside; his wife was on the phone because it was difficult for her to find transportation to come in to see her husband.

One of the needs identified was for equipment necessary for turning the patient in order to heal the decubiti on his back. A hospital bed with an overhead bar was requested and an air-pressure mattress.

The next problem was to train the patient's wife to give the patient chest physical therapy to keep the excess fluid out of his lungs. A training session was scheduled with the pulmonary therapist nurse assigned to the patient to teach decub care and the equipment provider to teach use of the inhalation therapy unit.

The day after the teaching/learning session, the patient was discharged with the assistance of home health nursing care. But the patient returned in two weeks with the same diagnosis. The doctor could see no other alternative but nursing home placement. Neither the patient nor his family wanted nursing home placement. I began to go over the patient's schedule of care at home with the wife to identify a possible breakdown in teaching and implementation of care at home. We discovered that the wife was not performing the chest physical therapy properly because she was afraid of hurting her husband and would not turn him when he was asleep thus leaving him in one position too long. A respiratory therapist volunteered to make a home visit to observe the wife during the therapy, and found she did not have the strength to continue the therapy more than five minutes and then completely forgot to turn the patient on his side for proper drainage. I contacted the insurance case manager for permission to purchase a chest percussion machine to assist the wife and also to provide more visits from [the] home health nurse, who was also present for the teaching session. Everyone felt more comfortable with the procedure, and the patient was able to stay at home and out of the hospital for four months before returning with another need. (Barbara A. Locke, 1995)

Strengths Perspective

The Spanish philosopher José Ortega y Gasset (1957) proposed that who we are can be understood by where we focus our attention. Social work, along with psychology and other helping professions, has paid a great deal of attention to what's wrong with the people with whom we work.

In the previous section entitled "A Construction of Meaning," we discussed the processes by which people explain and define themselves and the world. If we can accept as a given that the words we use have an effect on what we see as important and what we do, it is a cause for concern that social work and other helping professions tend to focus on problems, deficiencies, deficits, and pathologies.

Neither the concept of pathology nor that of strength are objective facts, but are instead social constructions that reflect public and professional attitudes and beliefs. Goldstein (1992) states that, "within the culture that we call social work, the ritual terms that shape theory and practice are not concise concepts, purified by the scientific method, but rather socially constructed abstractions" (p. 32).

Strength—a value-laden, subjective term—is an expansive rather than a reductionist concept. On the other hand, naming mental illness, the sole purpose for the language of psychopathology, results in reducing people to a label and placing negatively sanctioned terms on them. While this may have not been the intent behind the development of this language, it is, in our judgment, difficult to deny that this has been the outcome.

Many of the metaphors and ways of thinking used in social work and other helping professions have been borrowed from psychology:

> *The historical accident that made Freud a physician who thought in medical metaphors has cast a long shadow. He tried to fit the discoveries that he was making about people's emotional makeup into the mechanistic medical model in which he had been trained. Since physical pathology always had substrata of dysfunctional organs or cells, he made the same assumption about psychopathology. Each layer of emotional sickness was thought to rest on a deeper layer, and the investigation of these deeper layers was thought to be appropriate treatment. The deeper one went, the better; the more attention one paid to the psychopathology, the closer one was to the deepest layer of disease, and the greater the chance for a cure. (Waters and Lawrence, 1993, p. 57)*

Social work as a new profession in the early years of the 20th century, unsure of itself, embraced Freudian thought as a source of potential prestige.

It may also be, as Waters and Lawrence (1993) note, that most ways of thinking or talking about resources and strengths seemed superficial and simplistic, whereas psychological events seemed more intriguing and dramatic. They observed that "[t]herapy has always been good at focusing on what to move *away from,* but weak on what to move *towards*" (p. 3).

When we focus our practice on the pathology, on what is wrong, a person can be easily equated with a diagnosis or label. "Purely psychopathological orientation focuses exclusively on the distorted process and ignores the healthy impulse behind it. It takes the distortion as the important or 'real' process, and sees the person as his psychopathology: He is an obsessive compulsive, we say, as though that captured the whole person" (Waters and Lawrence, 1993, p. 8).

Reflecting on working with persons suffering from severe mental illness, Rapp (1992) writes:

> *The central belief of our program is that these people are not schizophrenic or chronically mentally ill but that they are people with schizophrenia. It is only one part of their being. They, like us, have a history of pain as well as accomplishment, of talents and foibles, of dreams and aspirations. Interestingly, a recent study of effective programs in Kansas found that the most prevalent common denominator was the managerial and direct service staffs' holistic view of clients. (p. 56)*

When we look for what is wrong, not what is right, we may become oblivious to patterns of health and striving for health. "Ascriptions such as defense mechanisms, denial, resistance and dysfunction equally convey a quality of morbidity and defect on the part of the client" (Goldstein, 1992, p. 28). It is a common experience for undergraduate students to take an Abnormal Psychology class and notice during the course of the semester how everyone on the floor of their residence hall is severely troubled with at least one major psychological condition. If enhancing competency and empowerment goals are to be real, it is important for social workers to move beyond deficit thinking in our practice.

Standard theories support the idea that the human state is relatively uniform, consistent, and predictable. Social workers often see people when they are in a state of crisis and are not functioning well. It very well may be that in other contexts and in other times the person functions much better. When we ask about these other times, we may get another perspective on the person's situation. Symptoms may be adaptive attempts gone awry, and people may have adopted protective behaviors for past situations that are no longer necessary or functional. A suit of armor may serve one well in a battle fought with broadswords, but may not be very helpful in a foot race. Client systems, our experiences tend to tell us, are doing the best they know how to do. As their actions become less effective and their circumstances more difficult, social workers can be most helpful by enabling them to examine old responses and choices and to explore more effective ones.

It is not only social workers who accentuate the negative. People in general tend to look at what's wrong in a situation. In parenting groups, a parent might exclaim that her child has been awful all week; upon questioning, she has trouble recalling any time that the child's behavior was not horrible. When prompted with "What about Thursday? Any good times on Thursday?" the parent can then recall times that were not difficult.

The problem or pathology focus blinds us to concentrating on what is good. As college teachers, when we read student comments after the end of a course, we are more likely to focus on the one or two negative comments—"This course was a waste of time"—than on the far larger number of positive comments. There may be something about human nature that focuses our attention on the negatives; or, in a society that is so success oriented, anything less than the best is defined as failure!

In sensitizing ourselves to the strengths in those with whom we are working, we are choosing to notice more than what is wrong. "If one searches for pathology, one finds it. If one searches for competence, one finds that as well" (Waters and Lawrence, 1993, p. 5). What we need to do is to look at people and situations in ways that foster seeing more than failings and deficiencies. An example of this kind of ability comes from Henry Louis Gates's memoir (1994) of growing up in a black neighborhood in a segregated, small West Virginia town:

> *Mama and I would go to a funeral and she'd stand up to read the dead person's eulogy. She made the ignorant and ugly sound like scholars and movie stars, turned the mean and evil into saints and angels. She knew what people meant to be in their hearts, not what the world had forced them to become. She knew the ways in which working too hard for paltry wages could turn you mean and*

cold, could kill that thing that had made you laugh. She remembered the way you had hoped to be, not the way you actually were. And she always got it right, even if after the funeral Daddy would wonder aloud which sonofabitch had been put in the casket instead of that simple-assed nigger So-and-so. Mama'd always laugh at that; it meant that she had been real good. (p. 31)

While most social work practice books, including this one, discuss the need to focus on the client system's strengths, we are distressed that far too often we see social workers still operating out of a deficit model. Yet, we are persuaded that any other view leaves our practice doomed to be less effective. Seeing the potentials and strengths within client systems enhances the resources available for change efforts. A social work education leader, Ann Weick (1992), captures this notion clearly:

a simple truth: that each person already carries the seed for his or her own transformation. A steadfast belief in that potential is one of the most powerful gifts a social worker can offer. By understanding in a deep, reflective way what it means to say that people have strengths, it is possible to recast what has been, for much of social work, a glibly stated maxim. Rather than viewing it as an ancillary and easily expendable belief, it becomes the measure against which all practice is judged. (p. 25)

Empowerment

Empowerment is a concept that has been so widely used in the 1990s that any clear meaning is almost lost. Politicians use the phrase to obscure, so we hear comments like "we empower people on general assistance by cutting off benefits that make them dependent on government" (which leads to homelessness in the guise of empowerment). Yet, even at the risk of using a word that has limits in communicating our intent, we feel that the concepts behind the empowerment principle are too important not to include in defining the ideology of social work.

By empowerment, we mean persons, families, groups, organizations, or communities who know the competence and voice they possess and who are capable, or become capable, of using this competence and voice in working to realize their hopes and dreams. The following are three tenets of empowerment:

1. People are empowered when they experience a level of competence or mastery in living and meeting needs within the natural, social, and physical environment.

2. People are empowered when they develop an active self-concept and a sense of self-competence. Generally, people do not try to influence the world unless they have some sense that their efforts have a reasonable probability of success.

3. People are empowered when they are more aware of the actual role of external forces on their lives and are able to develop a sense of "critical realism," which enhances their understanding of the natural, social, and physical environment.

Understanding Power and Powerlessness To understand empowerment, we start with the concept of power. Power can be defined as the capacity to produce a change or movement in one's life (including thoughts, emotions, or actions in economic, political, or social realms) and to influence one's own life and the lives of those one cares about. When we have power, we have a measure of mastery over our lives, some ability to make a difference.

Solomon (1976) identifies three potential sources of powerlessness:

- *negative self-evaluation*—the attitudes of oppressed people about themselves;

- *negative experiences*—the interactions between the victims of oppression and the outside systems that impinge upon them; and

- *larger environmental systems*—which consistently block and deny effective action taken by powerless groups.

Surplus powerlessness occurs in situations where people have been buffeted by societal forces and consequently develop a mind-set (emotional, intellectual, and spiritual) that prevents them from taking advantage of possibilities that in reality do exist. For example, many southern Appalachian coal miners who lost their jobs are still waiting to be recalled to the mines—a very unlikely event—and are not seeking other employment or educational opportunities. The longer this path is followed, one might predict, the more likely they are to feel powerless about securing employment.

The Importance of Empowerment If we accept that people have power, and one of our principal roles is to enable persons and groups to increase the influence they have in their own lives and the lives of those close to them, then we need to review all that we do in practice to foster this. One of the questions worth asking is, "Will the client system have more competence and options after our work together?" Practicing from a perspective of competency and empowerment provides a foundation for working with client systems as partners in the growth and achievement of desired outcomes.

I (Barry) have a colleague who is truly gifted as a social work educator. She teaches social welfare policy courses and uses a policy journal assignment. This requirement has come to be viewed by the majority of her students as an empowerment tool for them. By the end of the semester many have grown in their understanding of public issues and the need for informed citizens to have a voice in the policy process to the point that they are in active communication with the elected officials that represent them. Such behavior is critical to the success of a democracy and students come to believe in it, thereby increasing the power they have as citizens.

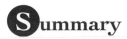ummary

In this chapter, we have introduced several key ideas and concepts that ground social work practice. These ideas have included the centrality of social justice as a goal for all social work practice; a more complete understanding of the human condition and how it is shaped by shared meanings, human dignity, human and cultural diversity, and spirituality and religion; and views that enable us to better connect with people, including understanding the benefits of hopes and dreams, valuing and operationalizing self-determination, building from a strengths orientation, and facilitating an empowering process.

As the reader leaves this chapter, we hope that our sense of optimism about the important privilege social work enjoys as a helping profession has become clearer. We value a planned change process that affirms, values, and facilitates a true partnership with our client systems. Such a process, we believe, moves us closer to social justice in that it places client systems' voices and stories at the heart of our work and recognizes their strengths and capacities for realizing their hopes and dreams. Understanding the relationship of self-determination (and its limits) to naming hopes and dreams is important in supporting the work of creating a more just society and in supporting client systems in claiming their legitimate roles, rights, and responsibilities as citizens and collectives.

Before continuing with the next chapter, we ask that you take some time to reflect on the following questions:

1. As you think about the human condition and working with diverse populations, what beliefs and values might you encounter that will be uncomfortable or difficult for you?

2. Think about how you have experienced the labeling process thus far in your life and how that process has shaped your response.

3. We suggest that social work and its traditional belief in fighting for social justice and working to eliminate oppression might not be popular in society during the final years of the 20th century. How does this affect your feelings about being a social worker?

4. How have you experienced issues of dignity and respect? How well does our society practice this view in the ways in which we manage our interactions with each other?

5. Think about the ways you have experienced human diversity in your life. What have those experiences taught you about this concept?

6. Think about your hopes and dreams. How have your life circumstances shaped them? In what ways have you been challenged to grow beyond your ideas about your capacities and potentials? What lessons have you learned from these experiences?

CHAPTER THREE

The Context and Social Work Practice

*The world is a beautiful book, but of
little use to him who cannot read it.*

CARLO GOLDANI
(1993)

Introduction

There's a story about a man stumbling around on a city sidewalk late at night, obviously intoxicated. A police officer walking his beat comes by and asks what he's doing. "Looking for my door key," the man responds. After a couple of minutes of helping the man search for his key, the police officer asks, "Where exactly did you drop the key?" "Over there," replies the man, pointing some 20 feet away. "Then why are you looking here?" asks the exasperated officer. Leaning against the lamppost for support, the man responds, "Because there's more light here." In their search for illumination in understanding people in crisis and trying situations, and in searching for ways to be of assistance, social workers have too often, we think, looked only where the light is.

Aaron Rosen and his colleagues have conducted a number of studies that ask social workers to analyze case records and ascribe the client systems' difficulties to personal, interpersonal, or environmental causes of their concerns (Proctor and Rosen, 1983; Rosen and Livne, 1992). They have found that many social workers tend to de-emphasize both the impact of the surroundings or social environment and the significance of interactions and relations with others. Instead, they overemphasize the role of personal difficulties—the ways the client system's behavior, cognitions, or emotions contribute to difficult situations.

The more the social workers held to a psychodynamic interpretation of human behavior, the more likely they were to see the situation in principally intrapersonal terms, as a personal deficit. As Rosen and Livne (1992) concluded,

> *a psychodynamic orientation . . . may conflict with the professional value of 'starting where the client is.' A biased attribution of the locus of clients' problems could endanger the extent to which social workers can address the reality of a client's needs and formulate ultimate treatment outcomes that are consistent with such needs. (p. 95)*

To avoid looking only where the light is, social workers need to understand the context of practice; specifically, the locality in which they are practicing. Central to this chapter is the concept of context as the major locus within which we come to understand the issues and concerns presented by client systems. Our intent is to define context and to provide key questions and themes that social workers may use to better understand client systems within their contexts.

> *A community may or may not provide the social system through which its members' needs are met. It may or may not provide a sense of identity for its members. What a community does provide is what some sociologists now call locality, a geographically defined place where people interact. How people interact shapes the structures and institutions of the locality. Those structures and institutions in turn shape the activities of the people who interact. (Labao, 1990, cited in Flora et al., 1992, p. 15)*

We will be using the word *locality* to help us define the physical nature of context. We make this choice out of our concern that the word *community* has come to lose its association with place. While we think community is a powerful concept, it is often used to describe network and non-place associations. For example, we (Barry, Becky, and Jim) are members of a community of scholars known as social work educators, members of a community of social workers interested in rural social work practice, and members of communities known as Flagstaff, Arizona; Shinnston, West Virginia; and Whitewater, Wisconsin.

To minimize confusion, defining the physical location as a locality allows us to better understand the complexities of place. To the maximum extent possible, we will refer to locality when discussing the physical space where human interactions most frequently occur.

By *context,* we mean the specific nature, qualities, and characteristics of a locality that interact dynamically to shape the experience the social worker is seeing and participating in. Locke (1988), in a survey of NASW members of a mid-Atlantic state, found that, while the skills utilized across the survey sample were the same, the way in which the skills were exercised differed by virtue of the locality or region in which the social worker practiced.

This dynamic interplay between people and environments—be they actively embraced or imposed environments—is a reality experienced by all human beings; environment does shape human behavior. Germain (1991) presents a useful description of this process in her work *Human Behavior in the Social Environment: An Ecological View.* Her work is helpful in thinking about the various definitions associated with community. She discusses the value of "network communities that provide a safe communal haven to members. Two examples are the gay community and the lesbian community, in which the members may not live in proximity to one another. Yet they share the functions, structures, activities, solidarity, sentiments, and reciprocal support that other communities do" (p. 39). While we prefer the word *locality* to describe places, we agree that context even for non-place communities is important to its members' sense of well-being.

Context, as it influences and shapes human behavior, especially in western societies like the United States, is best viewed as the present shaped by the past and holding a vision of the future or preferred reality. Therefore, context shapes people's beliefs and expectations and is a definer and shaper of potentiality. Understanding the context—for both social worker and client system—explains the past, frames the present, and illuminates the future.

Systems theory enables us to better understand the nature and relationship of interactions between persons, families, groups, organizations, communities, and society by linking these systems in relevant ways. The experience of any locality is embedded in larger realities, namely, the state, region, nation, and world. Here too is an interaction effect: the localities have an impact on the larger contexts, and the larger contexts at the same time influence the localities. The challenge, for both the social worker and the client system, is to understand these linkages and their role in shaping choices, barriers, and opportunities.

Contexts are modifiable and changeable. This truism is at the heart of social work practice. In fact, the belief that change is both possible and necessary has been part of our professional history from the very beginning, regardless of the prevailing ideology of the time. This is not to suggest that social work has held a consistent ideology over the years, for the social work profession has tended to reflect the tensions between conservative, liberal, and radical forces. However, the emphasis on working toward change has always been a part of social work practice.

The Role of Context in the Evolution of Social Work Practice

The role and function of context in social work practice is reflected in the works of:

Mary Richmond (1917), who originated the idea of social (as opposed to medical) diagnosis of human problems; Gordon Hamilton (1940), who developed the psychosocial orientation of casework that predicated the broad knowledge base and the dual focus of interventions with the person and environment; Virginia Robinson (1930) and Jessie Taft (1937), who developed the idea of problems defined by agency function, and elaborated on the processes involved in casework practice; and Bertha Reynolds (1942), who emphasized the impact of the social/political environment upon people's lives. (Meyer, 1983, p. 14)

Perlman (1957) introduced the paradigm of person, problem, *place,* and process as the primary components of casework in practice; however, she limited the notion of place to the function and structure of the social agency within which the practice takes place. Gordon Hearn (1958, 1969) linked social work practice with systems theory, which broadened the association of place to include other units, both internal and external, with which the person interacts. With this linkage, the role of social units as influencing human behavior is still emphasized.

Bartlett (1970) notes the significance of the "person-in-situation" as the central focus and orientation of social work practice. She defines social functioning as "people coping with life situations," which requires a balance between the demands of the *social* environment and coping skills (p. 130). The social environment includes "problems (conditions) of central concern," "responses and behavior of people involved in the problem," and the "demands and supports from the environment" (Bartlett, 1970, p. 148). The models of Meyer (1976), Germain (1981 and 1985), Northen (1982), and, most recently, Gutheil (1992) are examples of social work practice paradigms that include units beyond the social environment (such as physical and institutional variables) as part of the practice approach.

As Gutheil (1992) summarizes, there are two levels of environment that operate simultaneously: concrete and symbolic. "Concrete aspects of settings affect people in similar ways. Symbolic aspects, or the meaning objects take on, vary with the perceiver (Pennartz & Elsinga, 1990); people perceive and react to the same environment differently" (p. 391).

With an understanding of key contextual elements, we are able to identify that which is "given" and that which can be altered or changed. For example, the

Opportunity Riding on a Dangerous Wind

Figure 3.1 Chinese symbol for crisis

actual distance between points A and B doesn't change, but technology provides alternative ways in which people can get together, which represents a modification of the environment. As we begin to understand the patterns of a locality, we can visualize the capabilities and potentials for a preferred reality.

These contextual realities define and shape the way in which social workers put into practice what they know, believe, and do. How one views the context is also very important: understanding what kinds of change are consistent with the customs and rhythms of the locality and viewing a situation through a strengths perspective so that resources for, and constraints to, supporting change are identified. One of the many challenges for the social worker is being able to see the potential in contextual adversity. For us, the Chinese symbol for crisis is appropriate here—"crisis is opportunity riding on a dangerous wind" (see Figure 3.1).

For example, in 1985, the state of West Virginia experienced extensive flooding that destroyed many small communities around the state. Although the loss of life and property destruction were traumatic, as the small communities set about the task of rebuilding, they used the crisis to re-create their localities in a way that made many of them better (for example, sounder housing, recreational facility improvements, infrastructure improvements) than before the flood. They were able to seek the opportunity within the crisis.

A Framework for Understanding Context

The importance of assessment is well documented in social work literature. We will briefly discuss some of the common frameworks for assessing the context before detailing the key elements we would identify for assessing a locality and the client system.

Netting, Kettner, and McMurtry (1993) present a framework for conceptualizing community, which includes the following factors: a) identifying target variables; b) determining community characteristics such as boundaries, social problems, and dominant values; c) recognizing differences, including identifying formal and covert mechanisms of oppression and evidence of discrimination; and d) identifying structure, which includes recognizing locations of power, determining resource availability, and identifying patterns of resource control and service delivery. They also list McNeil and King's guidelines for community assessment, which include: target population groups, health resources, welfare resources, educational resources, housing resources, recreational facilities, and additional resources, such as criminal justice and consumer rights.

Other frameworks that have been used include Lamb's "Suggestions for a Study of Your Hometown" (1977a); Murphy's guide for analyzing a community (1977); Hasenfeld's guide for analyzing a social service agency (1984); Sheafor, Horejsi, and Horejsi's 15 areas for exploration to understand a community (1994); and Martinez-Brawley's guide for understanding the small community (1990). These frameworks are valuable to explore, as each of these guides leads to the discovery of information about important social institutions, services, population characteristics, values, and history.

We now turn to those contextual elements that we think are important for social workers to understand as they partner with client systems in planned change processes. The specific elements include:

- geography and environment
- history, traditions, and culture
- economic, political, and social structures

Geography and Environment

Environment and geography include such factors as population density and area demographics, weather, place, location, and the natural environment that impacts how one lives, plays, and experiences life.

Location, Opportunities, and Isolation Geography is not destiny. However, where a person or family lives does have a bearing on what kinds of opportunities and services are available and on how isolated the person and community perceive themselves to be.

Knowing that a person lives in an urban or rural area is not enough to assume whether or not opportunities exist in the locality. A 1989 study on changes in rural America revealed that some small towns were surviving and prospering. The most prosperous rural communities were those:

- within 100 miles of a metropolitan area
- near a major highway (usually an interstate highway)
- with a country courthouse or a major medical center
- with a major merchandising center containing an anchor store such as Wal-Mart (Brown, 1989).

In other small towns, many of the young adults have left, and the retired elderly prop up the town. In nearly half of the Kansas counties in 1985, 44% of income came from transfer payments (social security, retirement, public assistance) and property income (Brown, 1989).

When we think of isolation, we typically think of rural areas. For example, the high plains of Arizona are relatively dry, lava land characterized by either dense evergreen forest or sparse vegetation such as sage and piñon trees. The Arizona plains are characterized by vast open spaces, low population density, and drastic weather changes such as high winds and sudden storms. The terrain is most suited for the grazing of sheep, cattle, and horses. However, because of the scarcity of vegetation, vast acreage is necessary to support a single herd. Dwellings are near the grazing land, not in a small town. Visiting the nearest market town may take all day; households must plan to complete all their errands before returning home. Blizzards, winds, and thunderstorms can mean hazardous travel.

A negative stereotype of people in areas like these is that poor families have misguided priorities when they own a new, expensive-looking pickup truck and live in rundown, substandard housing. But put yourself in the place of someone who lives, as many in Northern Arizona do, in a vast open area where the closest neighbor is three to ten miles away, by dirt road, and the closest community is anywhere from 15 to 60 miles away. Reliable transportation that can take the beating of travel over dirt roads, drive through snow drifts, wade through high water from storm runoff, or manage the mire of mud resulting from seasonal flooding becomes vital to survival—economically, culturally, socially, and emotionally.

Geography and environment are connected with the cultures and traditions of the locality. Vast distances between populations and service centers define the nature of social, political, and economic structures as well as the nature of social interactions and service utilization.

Urban dwellers have their own difficulties with isolation. According to demographer Harold Hodgkinson (1989), more than half of all daily commutes in urban areas are between suburbs—in other words, residents of one suburb commute to work in another. Public transportation, when it exists, operates between the suburbs and the commercial downtown at hours serving the needs of the middle class. Poor workers who live in inner cities or outlying areas and who do not own cars are cut off from jobs in other suburbs or from evening or night jobs. I (Jim) worked in a settlement house, a private social service agency, in Columbus, Ohio. The agency served the Near North neighborhood, an area marked by the Olentangy River on the south, an interstate highway on the north, Ohio State University on the west, and downtown to the east. There were 10- and 11-year-old boys I worked with who had rarely been out of their neighborhood. Their lack of contact with the "outside world" contributed to their discomfort outside the neighborhood, and, in my opinion, served to limit their aspirations.

Landscape and geography can create barriers; as in southwestern West Virginia, where how many mountains you are away from somewhere else is more important than how many miles. You may be only 35 miles away, but if it's over three mountains, it can take an hour or more of travel time to reach your destination.

In urban areas, the barriers may come from the perceived ownership of territory, rather than from landscape or geography. In many areas, the issue of gang turf may mean that youth are not able to play outside or are forced to take a certain route to school so as not to trespass on hostile turf and risk injury or harm to themselves. Territory or turf issues are important in other ways. In one study, older adults were found not to take part in meal programs or other programs for senior citizens if they considered the site to be one that belonged to another race—whites were less likely to go to a site in a black neighborhood and vice versa (U.S. Commission on Civil Rights, 1982).

Geography shapes life experience, defines reality, and influences vision. A social worker from Kansas relocated to West Virginia and wondered why so few locals seemed concerned about events beyond their immediate communities. The towns are surrounded by mountains and poorly bridged streams, and the residents could not readily "see" outside events as important for their lives. The social worker came to realize that her own view of the world as open and accessible had been shaped by her growing up in Kansas with its wide open spaces, not to mention global wheat deals. When asked to think about how a geography of "closed-in-ness" (surrounded by mountains) versus a geography of openness (a world of wide horizons) could shape one's view of the world, she immediately saw a connection.

Effects of Weather and Natural Resources Another significant aspect of the geography and environment of an area are the available natural resources and the way in which these resources are managed and utilized to influence daily activities and lifestyles. Examples include the effects of weather, climate, and terrain, and the availability of water. There are regions of the country—Alaska, for example—where, because of the seasons or other natural phenomena, the sun may not shine for extended periods of time. Scientists have discovered that there is a relationship between exposure to the light from the sun and mental and physical health.

A locality that is traditionally sunny and relies on sunny skies for maintaining a solid economic base centered around tourism may be currently experiencing a major change in weather patterns and climate, creating unusually lengthy periods of cloudy and overcast days. With the climate change, the locality may lose most of its business. If we are not aware of these factors, we may miss vital information in understanding and assessing present concerns.

Meaning of Place Another very important part of geography, one often closely tied with culture, is the meaning of place. Two examples from the southern mountains and one from the Southwest illustrate this.

Peter Carlson (1992) wrote an article for the *Washington Post Magazine* titled "West Virginia Mountain Paradox," in which he discusses his experiences as he traveled around the state over a three-week period. He concludes with this observation:

Along the way, I'd met dozens of West Virginians who basked in the beauty and suffered the scars and the heartbreak with quiet toughness and feisty humor. They also exhibited a love of place stronger than any I'd ever seen. Between West Virginians and their land is a bond so intense that it transcends poverty and pollution and the pitiless whims of nature. (p. 26)

Later in the same article, Carlson reported the words of a very bright high school student regarding her desire to return to West Virginia following her college experience. Her answer is an elegant statement about the importance of the meaning of place as it relates to locality. "There's something in the mountains," she said. "You breathe it. You feel it. It's part of you. I think it's the hills and the way they feel and the way you feel when you walk through them barefoot. There's some kind of magic in these mountains" (Carlson, 1992, p. 27). As a fellow native of West Virginia I (Barry) can identify immediately with this young woman.

Land is important to other cultures as well. To illustrate this, we share statements told to anthropologist Keith Basso (1986) by residents of a dispersed settlement of 1000 Cibecue Apaches living on the Fort Apache Indian Reservation in east central Arizona.

Mrs. Annie Peaches, age 77: "The land is always stalking people. The land makes people live right. The land looks after us. The land looks after people."

Ronnie Lupe, age 42: "Our children are losing the land. It doesn't work on them anymore. They don't know the stories about what happened at these places. That's why some get into trouble."

Nick Thompson, age 64: "We used to survive off the land. Now it's no longer that way. Now we live only with money, so we need jobs. But the land still looks after us. We know the names of the places where everything happened. So we stay away from badness."

Lewis Benson, age 64: "I think of that mountain called 'white rocks lie above in a cluster' as if it were my maternal grandmother. I recall stories of how it once was at that mountain. The stories told to me were like arrows. Elsewhere, hearing that mountain's name, I see it. Its name is like a picture. Stories go to work on you like arrows. Stories make you replace yourself." (pp. 40–41)

Basso continues with this historical tale:

Long ago, a man became sexually attracted to his stepdaughter. He was living below this rock formation with his stepdaughter and her mother. Waiting until no one else was present, and sitting alone with her, he started to molest her. The girl's maternal uncle happened to come by and he killed the man with a rock. The man's skull was cracked open. The girl's maternal uncle dragged the man's body up above to a place called "coarse-textured rocks lie above in a compact cluster" and placed it there in a storage pit. The girl's mother came home and was told

by her daughter of all that had happened. The people who owned the storage pit
removed the man's body and put it somewhere else. The people never had a wake
for the dead man's body. It happened at "coarse-textured rocks lie above in a
compact cluster." (Basso, 1986, pp. 41–42).

In all of the preceding examples, the places have names, the names have meaning, and there is power, warning, and healing in referring to the places. In addition to everything else—places, events, moral standards, conceptions of cultural identity—historical tales are about the person toward whom the story is directed when it is told. This is because the telling of a historical tale is often prompted by a person having committed one or more social offenses to which the act of narration, together with the tale itself, is intended as a critical and remedial response.

When an Apache storyteller tells a story to a social offender, the narrative is understood to be accompanied by an unstated message from the storyteller that may be phrased something like the following: "I know that you have acted in a way similar or analogous to the way in which someone acted in the story. If you continue to act in this way, something similar or analogous to what happened to the character in the story might also happen to you." Apaches contend that if the message is taken to heart by the social offender at whom the tale is aimed—and if, in conjunction with lessons drawn from the tale itself, he or she resolves to improve his or her behavior—a lasting bond will have been created between that person and the site or sites at which events in the tale took place (Basso, 1986).

One commonality in all of these examples is that they are situations in which the place where the person lives has meaning to the person. The meaning of place is related to the two levels of environment as identified by Gutheil (1992): concrete and symbolic. The symbolic aspects are the meaning and significance of the geography and environment for the people of the locality. To understand this symbolic significance of land is to understand the basis for various land disputes.

For instance, American Indian traditions include a spiritual connectedness to the land, especially lands significant to sacred legends, such as the creation of the tribe. The United States government's arbitrary delineation of reservation lands did not take this into consideration. An example of this is the current dispute between the Hopi and Navajo tribes over land that was redistributed by the United States legislature (Law PL 93-531) in 1974. Until that date, there were what was regarded as "joint use lands" shared by the Hopi and Navajo tribes. The 1974 law eliminated joint use designation and redistributed these lands as either Hopi or Navajo. This has resulted in the relocation of numbers of Navajos from newly designated Hopi lands and Hopis from newly designated Navajo lands. One area affected by this redistricting of reservation boundaries is Red Mountain, sacred land for the Navajo that was identified as being within the new boundaries of the Hopi lands. The Navajos living on Red Mountain are refusing to be relocated off their sacred lands.

Many readers, especially those who have lived in a particular area for a significant length of time, may identify with one or more of these examples. A number of Americans, however, have little sense of place. People grow up in one or more places, go to school elsewhere, and move to a large urban area to find a job after school. For them, the following statement is accurate: "If the job is good, and the recreational opportunities and restaurants are fine, then one place is as good as another." Persons for whom place is relatively unimportant need to be sensitive to client systems for whom place is very significant. Likewise, people for whom place is important also need to treat the experience of those for whom place is not meaningful with respect and understanding.

In working with children who are homeless, it is essential to realize that a major impact on the child may be the loss of living in a familiar place. The impact of the loss of a sense of place is different and often greater on children than it is on adults.

Children's surroundings begin to shape their lives, their personalities, and their cognitive, social, and emotional development from their earliest moments. The experiences of being loved and cared for, or being abused, happen within a context grounded with people, objects, sights, smells, and sounds. The loss of a home is a traumatic experience for anyone; for children, however, "this loss comes at a point in their lives when the absence of stable, nurturing settings is most injurious, when they are developing a sense of themselves, of their own identity, a sense of what they are capable of doing and their own self-worth. It is a time when some degree of consistency is important to these personal identity processes" (Rivlin, 1990, p. 24).

In the *Power of Place,* Galagher (1993) describes how children learn state-appropriate behavior during childhood. They learn how to match emotional states and behavior (for example, sleep, excitement, and concentration) to specific places: home, playground, and/or school. This is a part of establishing their identity and, in familiar settings, can be a more powerful determinant of children's behavior than their personalities. Being homeless disrupts this sense of identity with the loss of predictable places where the child has learned what she or he can and cannot do.

No less important to our understanding of client systems is the way their life choices are, in part, defined by the meaning of place. Equally important for our practice is our notion of the ways in which our shared meaning of place and space can affect our sense of vision and potentiality. One vital skill for social workers is the capacity for self-understanding and the ability to stand apart from the potential limits of experience—to see the range of choices present in any issue around which they are working, so these choices can be made available to client systems. A tall challenge indeed!

Esteem and Identity of the Locality Understanding the esteem and identity of a locality helps us better understand the locality's meaning for both residents and non-residents. Identity and esteem are influenced by culture and history (the focus of the next section) as well as place and geography. They often involve the process of labeling or using complimentary or derogatory descriptors for the locality; for example, the "sticks" or "boonies" for living in the country a notable distance from the nearest town, or "uptown" for the wealthier residential areas of a city.

Labeling of locality appears to be a very ancient tradition. Recall the question, in the Christian tradition, asked about Jesus: "Can there any good thing come out of Nazareth?" (John 1:46). The social worker must strive to understand how external perception, most often as presented within modern media, influences the world view and behaviors of residents within the locality.

Responses of a locality's residents to negative labeling can take many forms; however, common ones include denial ("we don't have that concern here"), isolationism ("those outsiders don't understand us and are not welcome"), and superiority ("we are better than those others"). The response of superiority is frequently made in reference to perceived "undesirables," including those victimized by institutionalized prejudice; it is often revealed by the barriers to and the ways in which members of the victimized group gain access to resources (for example, jobs, housing, and education).

As we have already stated, proximity does not always produce community. However, one of the qualities to look for is whether or not there exists a *sense of community* within the locality. By sense of community, we mean the collaborative identification of commonalities, a sense of joining, unity, and belonging, and an identifiable connectedness. Part of the process of identifying the existence and nature of a sense of community includes an assessment of the degree to which the esteem for and identification with a locality are universal and shared.

When assessing a locality's identity and esteem, the role of stereotypes in shaping perceptions of both outsiders and residents is a significant factor to consider. The perceptions others have about a locality may be either idolized or derogatory. The difficulties this creates for the residents of a locality are similar to the difficulties people experience when the perceptions of others don't fit the realities. This notion is often referred to as self-fulfilling prophecy.

The residents of a locality may take on an idealized identity and be faced with having to deny issues and concerns that exist but that, if faced, might be perceived as a threat to the locality's sustenance or existence. In some localities, the residents may take on a deprecatory identity. But in others, an ownership of issues of concern emerges, and residents are then in a stronger position to address them.

Often, a positive sense of place can facilitate the ownership of concerns necessary for taking action and can be an important resource for its members. In the words of poet and environmental activist Gary Snyder (1992):

> [a] commitment to place is not just good environmentalism, not just a move toward resolving social and economic problems, but also a means for us to become citizens in both the natural and social worlds. If the ground can become our common ground, we can begin to talk with one another again. (p. 92)

Indeed, we believe a positive sense of place, esteem, and identity are crucial to taking action in developing and working to create communities more responsive to the needs of all residents.

Another factor to explore regarding identity with and esteem for locality is the history of this perception and esteem. Many rural communities are experiencing tremendous shifts in identity. Historically, there has been pride in being characterized as a farming, mining, or logging town. The town centers were service centers vital to the survival of the community. Now, in many areas, these same communities are experiencing tremendous decline. The town center may resemble a modified ghost town, with stores closed and buildings boarded up. The community pride may have vanished, possibly even replaced with a sense of dread and shame. Along with examining the history, it is important to consider forces or events that have influenced the evolution of resident identity with and esteem for the locality.

In summary, we see questions such as the following as key to understanding the importance of geography and environment in defining locality:

- What are the physical characteristics of the locality?
- Who lives within the locality (for example, population demographics, distribution, and seasonality of residence)?
- What is the relationship between physical resources and economic opportunity?
- What role, if any, do weather patterns play in shaping life?
- What special meanings for its residents and members, if any, are associated with the locality?
- To what degree is there a sense of community? How is it experienced and expressed?
- How is the locality perceived by outsiders?
- How do the insiders of the locality perceive themselves?
- Are there differences between outsider and insider perceptions?
- What is the history of insider and outsider perceptions of the locality?
- Has the locality always been perceived this way, or has it been different? If it has been different, how was it different and what happened to alter the perception?
- Is language empowering of members or a barrier to connectedness and sense of community?
- What is the role of myth in shaping perceptions of both outsiders and residents?
- How universally held is the shared identity?

History, Traditions, and Culture

The Spanish philosopher José Ortega y Gasset (1962) wrote that we are shaped by our experiences, as children and throughout our lifetimes. What is true for a person is also true for a locality. The collective experience of people in a locality is local history that can influence how people see what is and what can be.

History provides vital insight into a locality. It is through history that we access a perspective on the roots, patterns, growth, decline, rebirth, and development of a locality. History provides us with a window that connects us to the past, a mirror reflecting the strengths, weaknesses, resources, and coping mechanisms for the present, and a crystal ball providing clues to hopes, dreams, and visions of a preferred reality.

Learning the history and traditions of an area can help a newcomer or outsider understand some of the reasons people see the world or act the way they do. A study of the patterns of voluntary contributions to general relief programs by county in the state of Georgia revealed that the residents of Chatham County, where Savannah is located, contributed far more per capita than other urban counties. When questioned about this, the county public welfare director replied that recent efforts by a prominent local businessman had been responsible for increasing the amount provided for general assistance but that the county's allocations had always been relatively generous. He pointed to the county's involvement in child welfare, dating back to a county-run orphanage in the 1830s, as an example of the county's history of involvement in social welfare (Winship, 1984).

The willingness of the residents of a locality to become involved in change efforts may also be influenced by local and family history. A community organizer working in the Appalachian mountains recounted how it was much easier to organize in areas where the United Mine Workers had been active in the 1930s and 1940s. In those communities, there were memories of parents and grandparents going to meetings and working together, and adults whose childhood experiences contained those memories seemed to be more receptive to participating in change activities (Winship, 1984).

How one views current events is also influenced by previous events, by local history. I (Barry) recall the 1968 mining disaster near my homeplace in West Virginia. I had relatives working in that mine who, fortunately, were not on shift at the time of the explosion. However, because of the history of the mine in question and the locality it drew its miners from, there was great tension about sealing the mine without getting the victims of the explosion out. To understand the depth of emotion around that decision, one needed to know that local stories suggested that a decision to seal this mine after an explosion some 14 years earlier had been made too quickly, and that legend had it that men had been sealed in the mine alive. So beyond the normal grief one would expect with such a major tragedy, prior history added to the depth of tension and the anger of those impacted by the current event.

How residents of a locality view outsiders may be revealed in small ways. Whitewater, Wisconsin (with 3,500 permanent residents), sponsors an annual Fourth of July parade. The local weekly newspaper, in announcing the event, once stated that "The parade will follow the normal route," assuming that readers knew where to go to get a good view. Newcomers would not necessarily know the route, and also would not know that the celebration, which included food and rides in a park, was one of two annual occasions where residents gathered for a shared experience.

As we discussed in Chapter 2, culture is the organized pattern of "the totality of meanings, norms and values possessed by interacting persons and carried by material vehicles, such as ritual objects or works of art, which objectify and convey these meanings" (Coser, 1977, pp. 177, 465). This includes the identification of significant norms and values that determine what is important to the community and its members, and the rituals and traditions used to express them. Examples of various cultures and traditions include the interconnectedness of humankind and the natural world and the ceremonies that celebrate this significance for American Indian nations and tribes; the revered place of Jesus Christ and the religious traditions associated with his birth, life, and death in Christianity; and the central place of the weather and seasons for some localities and the festivals and celebrations associated with each.

In their book *Community Organizing in a Diverse Society,* Rivera and Erlich (1992) write about how important it is for organizers to be thoroughly grounded in the customs and traditions of the locality in which they are working. Their words are applicable for any social worker:

> *For example, how have the dynamics between organized religion and the community changed throughout the years? Ignored, its effect may imperil a whole organizing effort. Both the definition of the problems and the setting of goals to address them are involved. A number of Latino mental health and advocacy programs regularly consult with priests, ministers, and folk healers about the roles they all play (or might play) in advocating for mental health needs. These mental health activities are very clear about the importance of these other systems—formal and informal—in the community's spiritual life. The superstitions and religious activities are addressed by a variety of representatives, thereby making the advocacy work that much more relevant and effective. The American Indian nations give deference to their medicine man, with no actions being taken until he has given approval. Similarly, the Vietnamese, Cambodian, and Laotian communities have strong religious leaders who help to define community commitments and directions. (p. 14)*

Understanding a locality's history, culture, and traditions provides the social worker with important knowledge about the pace and process of life within the locality, including how services and help are provided. For example, rural areas are traditionally tied to the land and the rhythms of nature. Time takes on a different meaning and the pace of living is different from the urban and inner-city environment.

Social workers must take the time necessary to learn about the norms and traditions of the area where they practice. Social service agencies, often established under federal guidelines and laws, operate within the context of the history and cultural traditions of the locality and region. To illustrate, the hunting traditions in many rural West Virginia counties have resulted in the closure of some county school systems on the first day of deer season. Some may view this as a lack of respect for education, but it is better viewed as honoring a tradition growing out of the history of the state while not penalizing those who would choose to participate in the tradition and miss school.

Sensitivity to the culture and lifestyle of one's clientele has been a universal social work practice principle. This principle is especially important to the social worker in small towns and rural areas, given the traditions of human relationships based on trustworthiness of the person rather than on professional role or credentials (Ginsberg, 1976; Neale, 1982).

Additionally, rural areas have been characterized by greater visibility for the social worker (Fenby, 1978; Ginsberg, 1976; Whittington, 1985). It has not been unusual for one's business to be common knowledge in small towns and rural areas. This has meant that social workers must be sensitive to confidentiality issues for their client systems, as well as prepared to encounter client and resource systems in contexts other than a professional one.

The NASW Code of Ethics (1996) addresses this issue of dual relationships as follows:

> *Social workers should not engage in dual or multiple relationships with clients or former clients in which there is a risk of exploitation or potential harm to the client. In instances when dual or multiple relationships are unavoidable, social workers should take steps to protect clients and are responsible for setting clear, appropriate boundaries. (Dual or multiple relationships occur when social workers relate to clients in more than one relationship—whether professional, social, or business. Dual or multiple relationships can occur simultaneously or consecutively.) (Standard 1, section 1.06[c])*

Social workers have related the experience of having a sensitive discussion in the morning with client systems only to run into the person, family, or committee members that evening at the local market while shopping for the evening meal (Fenby, 1978). Such realities mean that the worker must be prepared to relate to client systems as professionals, as citizens, and as neighbors—a task that requires sensitivity to the local communication network and the meaning of being helped in the small town or rural area where one practices.

I (Becky) have discussed with client systems during our initial meeting the ways in which they would feel most comfortable handling dual relationship issues, such as meeting on the street, at church, during recreational activities, or in other public places ("When we meet, how would you like me to respond?") or my continuing to be a patron of the client system's business or service. With neighbors or family members of colleagues, the discussion also includes clarifying issues of confidentiality and boundaries.

To illustrate, during the time when I served a small community as an auxiliary police officer and crisis intervention team member (the other member was a local minister), an incident occurred that shook the community and the local police department with which I was associated. A relative of a police department staff member was under the influence of drugs and, while on a rampage, wounded several patrons of a local market and killed a relative of another department staff member.

To handle the crisis with sensitivity and clarity, the other crisis team member and I decided (with the client system input and permission) that we would work individually with each of the staff members and his or her family, relatives, and friends. Together, we provided critical incident debriefing for officers and staff of the police department.

Mental health center staff worked with the manager, victims, patrons, and community members impacted by the shootings in the market. This division made it possible for my crisis intervention team colleague and me to relate to each client system with dignity, respect, genuineness, and empathy. Immediately, we clarified our accessibility and roles—that I did not have privileged communication status and that my colleague and I would be consulting with each other for support and assistance to ensure that we were able to continue providing effective and competent services.

In the rural community, the family has been and remains the central institution. To work well in small towns and rural areas, social workers need an appreciation for the value of family (Collier, 1978; Jacobsen, 1980; Whittington, 1985). The concern for the family in rural areas has been a long-standing one. The Country Life Commission, established in 1908, called for action on behalf of the family farmer and for strengthening the rural family; this commission continues to this day. Josephine Brown (1933) regarded the family as a central focus in her classic text on social work within rural areas.

The plight of farm families, as economic conditions force more families off family farms, is well known. Of concern as well, if not so widely publicized, is the condition of the non-farm family (Johnson, 1980). This has been the fastest growing group in rural areas, subject to the same stresses and issues as its urban/inner-city counterparts. What is necessary for social workers in small towns and rural areas to understand is how these families cope with the problems encountered in the rural context.

Related to this understanding of the importance of family and social institutions for small towns and rural areas has been an expectation that social workers who practice in small towns and rural areas be committed to preserving the lifestyle of the community and locality. Irey (1980) suggests that a commitment to the rural area is important if the social worker is to be seen as part of the community. Unless this status is achieved, it is likely the social worker will be less effective.

Jacobsen (1980) affirms that a commitment to the small town or rural area is important, and indicates that the social worker's willingness to become involved in the community development process could facilitate this acceptance. An additional benefit is the reduction of isolation that can be felt by those who practice in the rural environment. Also, the social workers' effectiveness is thought to be positively impacted by a continuous involvement with the rural community, as this involvement enables the professional to acquire the knowledge of when and where best to focus in interventions (Hanton, 1978). While we are less clear about how important this involvement is seen for our colleagues in urban areas, we think the view that social workers in rural areas must "be of, as well as live in" the locality is one worth serious reflection.

The ways in which resources are utilized and services are delivered are also influenced by the dimensions of history, culture, and tradition. Resources may be physically and geographically accessible but not culturally accessible to the population. I (Becky) worked in a mental health center located in the center of a poor, densely populated, primarily African American community. The director and staff of the center worked very hard to be responsive to the cultures and traditions of the population by providing walk-in (no appointment necessary), outreach, community, and off-site services as well as the traditional in-office scheduled therapy sessions. A unique program of this center was our Welcome Wagon service for newcomers into the community. Staff made a home visit carrying a basket of food, household supplies, and a community resource manual for the new resident.

Studies of services to older adults in urban areas reveal that cultural appropriateness as well as geographic closeness are important in elders' decisions about whether or not to use services. In Tulsa, Oklahoma, a senior citizen community meal program attracted a smaller percentage of American Indian elders than expected. When interviewed about why they didn't take advantage of this free program, one of the most common reasons was that the food was an Anglo menu that did not have fried bread or other foods that the American Indians valued (U.S. Commission on Civil Rights, 1982).

Learning all about a locality's history, culture, and traditions can seem overwhelming to the social worker new to the area. One effective way to acquire this understanding is to ask questions and listen to the stories people tell about their locality. Social workers can encourage community members and client systems to tell their own story in their own words; they can also listen to the stories told in waiting lines in banks and other places where people gather. We will return to the importance of story for social work practice in Chapter 5.

One potential dilemma facing social workers who practice in rural areas is when the role of citizen, someone who preserves community values and lifestyles, comes in conflict with the role of social worker, someone who is concerned about the quality of life for *all* citizens and, therefore, bound by professional ethics to identify and raise controversial issues. This dilemma occurs when the integration of personal and professional is challenged—when personal priorities tug against professional standards and practice principles or vice versa. The balance of the two is not always equal.

To illustrate, I (Becky) was one of three professionals to initiate the development of a family violence prevention program in the small town in which I lived and worked. We were six months into the developmental process when a 14-year-old boy shot and killed his father.

During the crime investigation, it was discovered that both the boy and his mother had been victims of the father's violence for most of the boy's life. The boy had marks on his neck from the time his father had tried to hang him and had been frequently seen at school with switch marks, multiple bruises, and burns. The incident that sparked the killing was when the boy came home from school with his report card showing one C and the rest of the grades A's and B's. He and his father were in the kitchen where his father kept a rifle propped up against the wall by the entryway. His father went to the knife drawer to select a knife for the boy's punishment. While the father had his back turned, the boy picked up the rifle and fired, shooting his father in the back and killing him. One of my longtime friends, an assistant district attorney, was selected to prosecute the case.

The board of directors of the violence prevention program, whose members were community leaders, survivors of violence, and helping professionals, saw this tragedy as presenting an opportunity for enhancing community awareness about the prevalence and trauma of family violence. One of the cofounders of the program, a social worker and another longtime friend of mine, was selected as program spokesperson. However, she was identified as a possible expert witness for the defense and could not speak publicly. So I was to take her place in meeting with the media and being a guest of a local radio station for a community interest program. Out of respect, I called my attorney friend to let her know what I would be doing as a representative of the program. Unfortunately, my friend appeared not to understand my role and my ethical responsibility to bring to the attention of the community the amount and seriousness of the family violence. As a result, our friendship was altered.*

The history, traditions, and culture of this small town, which served as a service center for the area, reflected the belief that "a man's home is his castle. What goes on at home is nobody else's business." Raising the issue of family violence and its prevalence in the area was not very popular in the community. The change of my friendship is one example of the challenges faced when confronted with the dilemma of being committed to the community while at the same time being ethically bound to raise tough issues and concerns.

In summary, we see questions such as the following as key to understanding the role of history, traditions, and culture in defining locality:

- What are the significant historical events of the locality?
- What cultural heritage is reflected in the diversity of the locality?
- Is there a dominant cultural group?
- What role has geography and environment played in creating cultural traditions and norms?
- What traditions are elevated to a position of sacredness in the locality?
- What aspects of the culture and traditions are important to keep in mind in working with the residents?

Economic, Political, and Social Structures

In this section, we will be looking at the organized patterns of behavior that sociologists call social institutions and how they may affect life processes and experiences of the residents of a locality. The benefit of this understanding is directly tied to the ethical obligation to improve society (NASW Code of Ethics, 1996). Goldberg and Middleman (1974) state:

> *Examining the structures of a locality presupposes that social problems are caused by inadequate social arrangements that systematically victimize large segments of the population . . . that large segments of the population—the poor, the aged, and minority groups—are neither the cause of their problems nor the appropriate target for change efforts aimed at alleviating their plight. . . . Implicit in this assumption is the directive to focus change efforts on environmental structures—not as a means to modify a client's behavior, as in the case of intervention methods based on operant psychology, but as the ultimate*

---

* The young man was found innocent by reason of self-defense. The county was assessed with the responsibility of paying (no matter where the family lived) for unlimited counseling or psychotherapy for both the young man and his mother because school and social service personnel had not intervened in a timely or effective manner.

objective of intervention in each instance. Although it is recognized that change in the social environment may lead to change in a client's behavior, behavioral change is not the goal. To the contrary, clients are viewed as adequate people confounded by inadequate resources, limited choices and lack of access to means for changing their plight. (pp. 151, 154)

If social workers are to act upon the view taken by Goldberg and Middleman, economic, political, and social structures need to be well understood.

Economic Structures The economic structure of a locality provides residents with the means to earn a living and to provide for themselves and their families. The social worker needs to understand how most residents support themselves financially. Answering this question leads to an understanding of the role of paid employment, as well as income transfers, for the locality. If a locality has a robust economy with many jobs and low unemployment, wages and earnings may be stable and the residents living there relatively well-off and able to support a wide range of social programs. If, on the other hand, the area is characterized by high unemployment and large numbers of persons living on fixed incomes, it may not have sufficient resources to address important social needs. When meeting a newly unemployed person for the first time, the social worker's awareness of this type of information is important for seeing the range of available options.

Equally important to economic health and the existence of quality social services is the diversity found in the local economy. By diversity, we are referring to the breadth of economic activity as well as the range of employment opportunities. The greater the range of economic activity, the greater the stability. If the locality is not economically diverse, an important consideration becomes the stability of the dominant employer.

Barlett and Steele (1992) present an excellent analysis of how economic instability and lack of responsible corporate citizenship in the United States over the decade of the 1980s has changed—often for the worse—the life choices and experiences of many citizens across the land. Much of their work focuses on areas dominated by a major employer who, for various reasons (including narrow self-interest) closed a factory or destroyed pension plans and left thousands of persons without decent jobs or economic stability. In such instances, residents of the locality are often left with feelings of betrayal and despair.

Understanding how the locality's residents are experiencing, perceiving, and explaining these economic shifts provides the social worker with insight into alternative choices and opportunities the residents may be defining for them-selves, as well as the emotional impacts such events have on how they see their choices and future opportunities. It is not unusual for persons who have invested much of their lives with a single employer to find it difficult to see other choices, even when they may be present, because of the emotional impacts of unemploy-ment (for example, grieving over the loss of one's economic identity).

Additionally, social workers, using the generalist orientation as presented in this book, seek ways and create mechanisms to address the necessity of main-taining economic vitality in a locality. We are persuaded that it is no longer appropriate, if indeed it ever was, for citizens to leave economic activity to the so-called experts. Therefore, we would encourage social workers to understand how the economy of a region or locality is defined and influenced and, as responsible citizens, to seek ways to influence change. For example, working to pass levies that would be used to create a stronger infrastructure (schools, roads, housing, zoning) could be a most important activity for social workers, in our citizen roles, to carry out in the service of our local areas.

Such activity must take into account the economic history of the locality: how the number and types of jobs have changed, how job requirements have changed over the years, and so on. Even though attendance and graduation rates associated with higher education have not grown as rapidly as desired, it is becoming an economic reality that more employers are demanding educational credentials that a few decades ago would not have been necessary for the same job. When assessing the economic arena, it is important to be aware that this insistence on credentialing means that many low-income persons face an additional barrier to economic sufficiency.

Finally, in understanding the economic structures of a locality, the social worker needs to understand the ownership patterns in the local economy. Who owns the firms and businesses of a region can have a direct impact on the way the life opportunities are experienced. Over the years, partly due to the powerful book *Night Comes to the Cumberlands* (Caudill, 1963), we have heard many advocates and other professionals living in central Appalachia (a section of the United States that includes parts of Kentucky, Tennessee, Virginia, and West Virginia) speak of this area as an American colony. In part, this view grew out of an assessment of economic ownership.

The central Appalachian region has historically been dominated by the coal industry. As this industry came to be controlled by absentee corporate ownership, local influence became harder to maintain.

When decisions that determine job opportunities are made in the boardrooms of New York City, Pittsburgh, Los Angeles, and, increasingly, overseas in Europe and Asia, there is a sense of emotional loss of control over these decisions, so that locals no longer have much, if any, say in events that shape their daily lives. The result has been a mistrust of corporate leaders, outsiders, and "company men" that continues to shape local relationships to this day.

In summary, we see questions such as the following as key to understanding the role of the economic structure in defining locality:

- How is the money necessary for living maintained (for example, through wages or transfer payments)?
- How many residents are employed in the locality?
- How diverse is the local economy?
- How stable is the local economy?
- What economic changes have affected the locality?
- What has been the recent history of economic activity within the locality?
- What are the ownership patterns in the local economy?
- What are the dominant commuting patterns associated with economic activity in the locality?

Political/Power Structures Every locality has some form of political structure and associated power holders. An understanding of these institutions is important for social work practice in that many of the programs and services in a locality are tied directly to some level of government or power-holder decision making. To illustrate, the siting of a senior citizen center may reflect the view of a powerful local leader about where such a center should be located, rather than other factors such as ease of access. Knowing who has power and how it is exercised is important to understanding how resources are distributed locally.

In recent years, much of the public debate about the federal government has focused on how to downsize and return power to the states. This movement to return control to the states appears likely to continue for the immediate future. If it does, social workers will need to shift more of their attention to the state level and, we would imagine, to the local level as arguments for the devolution of power from state to local governments are made, especially in the arenas of public education, environmental regulation, and social service delivery.

All of this means that social workers may be in key roles to use our human relationship skills to build networks with local and state decision makers. We are not suggesting that we abandon a role for the federal government in social welfare; only that, as the political context changes, we need to be able to interact with the new reality as we work for professionally sanctioned ends.

While identification of power holders is a complex process, I (Barry) have heard many social workers who practice in small towns and rural areas across the country discuss how one can enter a new locality and begin to know who some of the key decision makers and power brokers are. While there are a variety of ways to do this, many use a strategy of asking people with whom they come into contact, "Who within your locality would you turn to if you wanted to get something changed in the community?" Once this question has been asked several times (there is no magic number for how often), the same names begin to surface over and over. It is the people who are repeatedly named that may be the key stakeholders, power brokers, or decision makers within the locality.

An important point to note is that often the names one may learn about are not those of elected officials. This is not to suggest that elected officials are not important to know, because they are. However, oftentimes power brokers operate behind the scenes; when seeking to change or influence the resource structure of a local area, it may be necessary to seek access to these behind-the-scenes persons as well as to publicly identified leaders.

The naming of natural helping and support networks can be an important resource for social workers as they address issues of concern presented by client systems (Martinez-Brawley, 1990; Netting, Kettner, and McMurtry, 1993). Asking a different question (To whom within your locality would you turn in a time of need?) may provide information about natural helping and support networks. These processes are applicable in urban and inner-city communities as well.

Si Kahn (1991), a community and union organizer, writes of the complexity in identifying leaders in poor communities:

> *Often an easy way of identifying them (the leaders) is to ask key members of the power structure who the "responsible leaders and spokesmen" of the poor*

community are. Those who are identified as such by the power structure will usually be persons who are influenced or controlled by the power structure, and who represent its interests. On the other hand, those identified by the power structure as "troublemakers," "agitators," "irresponsible," "sorry," "out for themselves," or "a discredit to their race" will often turn out to be real leaders of the poor, a part of and in touch with the poor community. (p. 42)

Understanding the power structure of a locality and the linkages to larger systems becomes important in helping social workers meet their ethical obligation to pursue societal improvement and promote social justice. We believe that a central focus for the social work profession—enhancing societal responsiveness to human needs and social issues—needs attention. If social workers are to work well within their localities, they must be able to provide effective direct service and must be skilled in influencing change within the political arena. It is in this arena where much of the opportunity for social policy change is encountered. How social workers can accomplish this, given the very real limitations they may encounter in the workplace, will be discussed in Chapters 9 and 10.

Haynes and Mickelson (1991) present solid justification for the significant role of social workers in influencing change within the political arena and provide helpful guides for such important influential activities as lobbying and coalition development. Effective lobbying involves knowing the issue as completely as possible, creating or joining a campaign group to write and call as needed on the issue, getting a supportive lawmaker with clout to sponsor relevant legislation, knowing the steps in passing a bill in the legislative process, and being visible at the capitol to answer legislators' questions and to intervene with the opposition (Haynes and Mickelson, 1991, p. 72).

In developing coalitions, social workers are urged to follow a carefully thought out planning process that begins with clearly identifying a need or issue of concern, recruiting others who share an interest in the need or issue, identifying people who will serve as leaders in the change process, generating data and information relevant to planning the change strategies and activities, and implementing a plan with ongoing monitoring of the effect of the change efforts (Haynes and Mickelson, 1991, pp. 83–85). Working to influence the decisions of powerful stakeholders is by definition a significant and necessary component of contextually grounded generalist social work practice.

In summary, we see questions such as the following as key to understanding the political/power structures in defining and understanding locality:

- Who are the power brokers?
- Do they hold powerful positions or are they "behind the scenes"?
- How are decisions that shape the locality made?
- What groups are generally involved in decision-making processes at the local level and what groups are frequently left out of these processes?
- Who are the political representatives and elected officials of the locality?
- How much of the power rests with absentee owners?
- What form does local government take?

- What linkages exist in the locality with state, regional, and national public and private decision-making bodies?

Social Structures Closely aligned with understanding the economic and po-litical/power structures is knowledge of such social institutions as the church, the educational system, the family, and voluntary organizations and of the nature of social relationships within the locality. People, as social creatures, are dependent upon opportunities to interact and belong in order to maintain a functional state of health. Traditionally, the institutions identified above have carried this primary responsibility. While many of the relationship opportunities within these structures are formal in nature, the social worker needs to be equally aware of the informal, interactional patterns, processes, and opportunities within the locality.

I (Barry) in my social work practice classes always ask students to discuss where they go for help when confronted with a difficult issue or concern. Almost universally, they identify friends, specific family members, maybe a member of the clergy, and, rarely, a professional helping person (social worker, psychologist, or planner). I use this exercise for two purposes: (1) to raise awareness of the difficulty associated with seeking formal help and (2) to demonstrate the role, utility, and limits of natural helping systems in planned change processes.

The Role of Churches Earlier in this chapter, we discussed the importance of understanding the way religious values can affect a locality. The church, as a formal institution, can also be an important resource in the life story of a locality. Social workers need to understand the role of specific churches in the locality to be effective in working with client systems for whom the institution holds meaning and in working within the locality.

In some localities, the role of the church is extremely significant to the life and survival of the locality, meeting more than just spiritual needs. The role of the African American church in this country has traditionally been one that has encompassed strengthening the family and working toward social justice. A recent survey of over 1000 African American churches in the Northeast dem-onstrated that the African American church today plays a vital role in mental health, family support, and promoting the well-being of youth (Billingsley and Caldwell, 1991).

The church continues to be a central organization for most rural communities as well. It has served not only to help people with their spiritual needs but also to define what is acceptable in the daily life of the community (Ginsberg, 1976). It is not uncommon for social workers to report that the success or failure of their intervention efforts was influenced by the views held by a powerful lay leader or minister about the service in question.

Several years ago, when employed by a public welfare agency, I (Barry) was involved with doing Food Stamp outreach. The idea of outreach, a sound and important generalist social work role, is to assertively reach out to the com-munity to educate its members about programs and services for which they might qualify and use to their benefit. In this instance, we were making sure that all folks who might meet the eligibility standards for the Food Stamp program, which was being expanded throughout the state, knew about the program and were invited to apply.

On one visit, I introduced myself and the reason for my visit and was kindly invited in by a woman who was living on a small disability grant. The lady was very kind and patiently listened as I explained the Food Stamp program and its potential benefits to her. I noticed after a bit that she seemed perplexed, and as I was nearing the end of my review, she started to tremble throughout her body and speak in a language that was not familiar to me. At first I feared she was experiencing a seizure, but I quickly realized by the movement of her arms and body that she was speaking in tongues.

I sat quietly at the kitchen table and waited for her to rejoin me. She looked at me with some embarrassment and quickly explained that she had been warned by her pastor not to use Food Stamps as they represented the mark of the beast or Satan. I was not prepared for this explanation and replied that I was not there to force her to use the stamps and would not wish to have her go against her religious beliefs. I asked her if she minded sharing her pastor's name as I would like to learn about his views. She was uncomfortable doing that, so I asked her to have him call me if he would and left my name and number with her.

As I left, I thanked her for sharing her concerns with me and invited her to call me if she wanted to discuss using the stamps or other services. I never heard from the minister and, as far as I know, the lady never followed up to apply for the Food Stamps.

The church in small towns and rural areas has been a powerful influence for many of the client systems social workers are likely to encounter. This point has not been lost on some authors. Turner (1985) suggests that collaboration between the rural church and the social worker is an area in need of development. She identifies the common ground between the church and the social work profession and notes that the problems of rural America are complex enough to require the efforts of both groups. Duncombe (1982) also notes that the rural church is seen as an important and central place in the provision of social services; she is making efforts at collecting data that defines how that role is viewed by residents of rural areas.

In other localities, while spirituality may be important, the structures for the gathering and expression of this spirituality are less organized or more integrated within the community and are expressed through community rituals and ceremonies. In some localities, both can occur, with inherent conflict between memberships. For example, in some American Indian communities, the traditionalists are those members of the tribe who have held onto the spirituality and beliefs of the tribal ancestors, whereas the nontraditionalists are the tribal members who have assimilated the organized religion and beliefs of the dominant culture.

The situation is further complicated by the political stands that national denominations and local churches take and the effects that these stands have within states and localities. Churches interpret religious truths in various ways and take differing positions on issues such as abortion and protection for gays and lesbians. This diversity of interpretation can produce local tension. Yet, as Robert Bellah and his colleagues (1992) state in *The Good Society:*

Many powerful institutions that influence our lives and consume much of our energies—economic, governmental, educational—pull us apart; they seem to pressure us to compete for individual advantage rather than to combine for the common welfare, and they empty out meaning from our lives when they structure our existence as a competitive race for money, power, prestige, or the consumer goods that symbolize them. Religious communities do not simply give us membership and recognition—qualities in short supply in America ([as illustrated by the] example of the storefront church whose members can say to the single parent "We know who you are; you're important.") They also help us grapple with the ultimate problem of meaning, of trying to find a way to live that is based on something more than cost-benefit calculation or desire; of whether we have a place in the universe at all and any abiding purpose to pursue here. (p. 218)

One dilemma that has challenged the social work profession, and continues to be relevant, is the tension between religion (as expressed through the church as a social institution) and a fear that the social worker should not be about the business of converting client systems to a particular form of faith. We share that important concern; however, as we discussed in Chapter 2, we think religion and spirituality are resources too valuable to be held at bay by the profession.

The Role of Education The United States has a long tradition of valuing education—at least in public pronouncements. Education has long been seen as the way to success for the majority of the population. What has changed is that education used to be only one of the avenues that led to economic well-being. In the 1940s, half of the students who started school did not complete high school, and that was not seen as a social problem. There were jobs, often well-paying manufacturing jobs, for persons without a high school diploma. With the shrinking of the manufacturing sector, and the increasing need for workers in manufacturing to be literate and numerate, education is becoming a necessity.

Many groups see educational opportunity as the means to address many of their concerns, be it education in the formal sense of schooling or educating the locality to be sensitive to the legitimate needs of diverse members. Social workers are increasingly being employed within school systems, and if not employed directly, they are often invited to work with children and their families. That this is an important area for social work practice has been made obvious by the successful use of social workers in Head Start programs. Key issues that need to be assessed about the role of education within a locality include:

- how responsive educational leaders and personnel are in developing policies and programs that address the special needs of children and adults;

- which members of the locality are included in or excluded from decision-making processes about the structure and function of the educational institution (for example, populations identified by geographic location of residence ["right or wrong side of the tracks"], by whether they receive or provide services, by race, by gender, by marital status, and/or by family status);

- what views are held about education within the locality (for example, is education seen as supportive or destructive of local traditions and norms);

- what roles are assigned to the educational institution within the locality (for example, to provide a day care service versus educational opportunity); and

- how integrated the schools are within the life of the locality, especially as related to lifelong learning issues.

It is important to identify how the opportunity for learning and instruction is structured within the locality. Many communities provide formalized instruction in public or private school settings, others through ritual and ceremony. Residents' perceptions of the educational system are often related to its structure: the locality may be supportive of education but not of its forms over time.

For example, education serves a vital role for most American Indian nations and tribes. It is through ceremony, ritual, and lore—a significant educational avenue—that the traditions and the knowledge, values, and skills necessary for survival have been passed on to tribal members. However, the decision was made by some members of the dominant culture that American Indian children needed to be more assimilated into the dominant culture and its educational structures. As a result, boarding schools were developed for American Indian students, which frequently required that the children be sent away to school for extended periods of time. Many American Indians see this program of education as having destroyed or undermined American Indian cultures and traditions. Thus, education as defined by the dominant culture may be perceived as a destructive rather than a constructive force by many cultures.

Education's role in the locality may take a variety of forms, and educational structures may serve as a primary socialization mechanism. In Indiana, there are communities of 800 with high school gymnasiums seating 2000. High school basketball, as shown in the film *Hoosiers,* is a primary way for community members to share and express their identity. It is often through schools that values and beliefs of the culture are transmitted. Schools may provide the only means for acknowledging and attending to the special needs of children and their families or the lifelong learning needs of adults of the locality. Educational structures may also be the primary economic support of a locality or an avenue for political expression. The social worker's challenge is to explore and identify these aspects of the educational structures and processes in the locality.

The Role of the Family   There is much discussion and debate about the family and our society today. Such debate is important, and the tensions, needs, and roles of the modern family merit our serious attention. As social workers, we will often encounter client systems, including families, that need our best efforts to support them in carrying out their responsibilities. Central to our ability to do this is an understanding of how families are viewed by the residents of the locality, including those residents that make up our client systems. The key questions that a social worker needs to understand include: (1) What meaning does the word *family* hold both for client systems and for other residents of the locality? (2) How are alternative lifestyles perceived by the members of the locality? (3) How are families defined in terms of roles they are to perform? and (4) How does the locality support its families? Many families in our society are burdened by a lack of resources to fulfill their roles (for example, no day care or access to health services). However, our traditions hold them accountable for providing these things without vesting a sense of the responsibility in the citizens of the locality.

Mary Pipher (1996) addresses the significance of family in this way:

Family need not be traditional or biological. But what family offers is not easily replicated. Let me share a Sioux word tiospaye, *which means the people with whom one lives. The* tiospaye *is probably closer to a kibbutz than to any other Western institution. Until the 1930s, when* tiospaye *began to fall apart with the sale of land, migration, and alcoholism, there was very little mental illness. When all adults are responsible for all children, people grow up healthy.*

What tiospaye *offers and what biological families offer is a place that all members can belong to regardless of merit. Everyone is included regardless of health, likability or prestige. What's most valuable about such institutions is that people are in by virtue of being born into a group. People are in even if they've committed a crime, been a difficult person, become physically or mentally disabled or are unemployed and broke. That ascribed status was what Robert Frost valued when he wrote that home "was something you somehow hadn't to deserve." (p.23)*

Voluntary Organizations It is through voluntary organizations and associations that the residents of a locality organize themselves according to common interests and needs. Such organizations include the Kiwanis, Masons, Rotary Club, Veterans of Foreign Wars (VFW), Mothers Against Drunk Driving (MADD), and self-help groups (Alcoholics Anonymous, Al-Anon, Adult Children of Alcoholics, Overeaters Anonymous).

It is important to identify not only which voluntary organizations are present but also their role in the locality's functioning. These organizations serve multiple purposes—as important resources for networking and as support mechanisms for taking on community projects and providing information about how potential changes are likely to be received within the locality.

As previously mentioned, natural helping networks are an important area of study within social work and related helping professions. Central to assessing the strengths and capacity present within a locality is identifying naturally occurring resources; that is, those that operate independent of formal resource networks.

Webster and Campbell (1978) argue that the historical view of rural areas as resource-poor may not be at all accurate if one expands the definition of resource. This would appear to be equally true for isolated urban or inner-city neighborhoods. Therefore, social workers would be well served to identify the naturally occurring helping networks and the voluntary organizations and associations that provide additional resources within the locality.

The Nature of Social Relationships In our opinion, one of the advantages of using the term *locality* rather than *community* is that it is to easy to assume that residents of a community have many things in common. In urban areas, segregation along racial and class lines can leave neighborhoods isolated from each other in multiple ways, with mutual fear and distrust prevalent among residents of diverse neighborhoods.

In his book *There Are No Children Here,* Alex Kotlowicz (1991) writes about a family living in the Henry Horner public housing projects, located near Chicago Stadium and downtown office buildings. Children playing near the commuter train tracks were alert to oncoming trains.

> *They had heard that the suburb-bound commuters, from behind the tinted train window, would shoot at them for trespassing on the tracks. One of the boys, certain that the commuters were crack shots, burst into tears as the train whisked by. Some of the commuters had heard similar rumors about the neighborhood children and worried that, like the cardboard lions in a carnival shooting gallery, they might be the targets of talented snipers. Indeed, some sat away from the windows as the train passed through Chicago's blighted core. For both the boys and the commuters, the unknown was the enemy. (p.7)*

Residents of a locality can also have different goals. Fisher (1987) states that community "organizers assume a unity of interest between the power structure and the neighborhood and assume a willingness of at least some in power to meet community needs" (p. 389). Important here is not only the willingness to meet community needs but the degree to which community needs are seen as the province of anyone other than those affected. We have previously mentioned the African proverb "It takes a whole village to raise a child." Whether people on the other side of town (or county) view as important the raising of other people's children influences the locality's response to such a need.

In social work practice, understanding how the residents of the locality relate to one another is vital for contextually grounded social work practice. How do residents regard and relate to diversity like age, gender, race, sexual orientation, ethnicity, class, or lifestyle? What are the social norms and controls of the locality or of its different groups? What is the role of language in relationships? Does language enhance or impede social participation by members? How mobile and/or stable are social relationships over time? What are the quality and character of social networks? How are outsiders received and perceived? How stratified is the locality by income and other power attributes? How permeable are these stratifications? These questions provide a framework for exploring and assessing the nature of the social interaction within a locality.

In rural areas and small towns, how a family or person is perceived affects the kinds of informal helping or resources that are available in times of need or crisis. Sharon Hanton (1980) identifies five types of families that may need services and support. They are: (1) the family involved in abuse or neglect, on the run from authorities; (2) the mobile family, who stays in a locality while one of the adults has a temporary job and then moves on; (3) the permanent, low-status, marginal family, where the adults are not involved in voluntary associations or in the life of the community; (4) the newcomer family, often urban dwellers who have come to the country for an alternative lifestyle; and (5) the permanent, high-status family.

According to Hanton (1980), families on the run, mobile families, and newcomers seldom receive informal helping. Permanent, low-status families receive support from natural helpers, churches, and voluntary associations in times of crisis or emergency and then retreat to the margins of the locality. Permanent, high-status families not only receive informal support in times of crisis and emergency, but the locality may also support behaviors of high-status members that are unlawful or self-destructive because of their place in the community.

Hanton (1978) recounts the example of a social worker in Montana who went to an isolated community because a rancher had been reported for child abuse. The social worker, unfamiliar with that part of the county, called the sheriff's department and arranged for a deputy to accompany her. The deputy stated that he wasn't too familiar with that part of the county either, and they drove around for hours looking for the ranch in vain. The social worker learned the next day that the rancher and the deputy were hunting buddies, and they probably would have driven around indefinitely without finding that ranch.

In summary, we see questions such as the following as key to understanding the importance of social structures in the locality:

- What are the views associated with religion and churches?
- Do churches see a social role for their service to the locality?
- What is the relationship between the school system and the locality?
- How inclusive are the schools within the area?
- What resources exist to support special education for children and adults?
- How is the family viewed in the locality, especially as related to alternative family styles?
- What types of families are present in the locality?
- What types of voluntary organizations are present?
- What special missions and/or functions do the voluntary organizations fulfill (for example, services for the disabled or community beautification)?
- Do any of these missions and/or functions include developing services and resources within the locality or activities directed toward enhancing responsiveness of the locality's members to the varied needs and concerns of diverse populations of the locality?
- What are the social norms and controls?
- What is the role of language in social relationships?
- How mobile and/or stable are social relationships over time?
- How are outsiders received and perceived?
- How stratified is the locality by income and other power attributes and how permeable are these stratifications?

Contextual Elements and Social Work Practice

We have reviewed three primary contextual elements that impact social work practice: environment and geography; history, traditions, and culture; and economic, political, and social structures. We have done so out of the conviction that good professional social work practices depend on an understanding of the context of the client system and the potential impacts that context has for the choices available to address any issue of concern.

In applying this material on the context of practice to working in localities, it is important to remember that:

- the interconnections between the contextual elements (geography and environment; traditions, history, and culture; and economic, political, and social structures) of the where of social work practice are as important as the elements themselves;

- looking for patterns in the interconnections of the contextual elements can be helpful not only in enabling the client system to gain a fresh perspective on what is but also in identifying what can be; and

- contexts are continuously changing.

Interconnectedness of Contextual Elements

Each of the contextual elements portrays a specific, significant component that aids in knowing and understanding a locality and enhances our use of social work values, knowledge, and skills in practice in the locality. However, it is the synergy (combined force) that evolves from the interaction of the elements that characterizes each locality as truly unique. It is the interaction of the elements that determines the direction change takes. When, as social workers, we can understand the ways that these elements interact with each other, we are able to fully capture the depth and breadth of that particular locality. In that respect, no locality is like any other. There may be commonalties, yet each has its own nature and soul. The direct practice corollary is the concept of individualization of client systems: we see every client system as unique, while recognizing the commonalities they may share with others.

In his book *The Skilled Helper,* Gerard Egan (1990) writes of the importance of identifying themes and building bridges between the islands of client systems' feelings, experiences, and behaviors. The same kind of pattern-recognizing behavior is important in understanding context.

Contexts in Transition and Change

One of the assumptions we are making is that change is a given. Realities are fluid, some more rapid than others. In teaching, I (Jim) tell my students that a decade ago, when I was teaching about issues in localities, the problems of homelessness, AIDS, and crack cocaine were not nearly as important to the life and health of the localities as they are now. A decade from now, there will be other emerging concerns that localities will have to face.

National and international events and trends affect the largest of cities and the smallest of towns. In the late 1970s, I (Jim) went with a group of university professors to Rabun County, Georgia, to see how we could help with economic development. Rabun County is in the mountainous area of north Georgia, where the movie *Deliverance* had been filmed a few years before. One local resident at that meeting was talking about the difficulties they were having with kids smoking pot, and she blamed the drug use on the film crews that invaded their county. I recall thinking that practically every other small town in the United States was experiencing increased drug use among adolescents during that time.

Change in one of the contextual elements can cause other changes that ripple through a locality. The proposal of an interstate highway that connects historically isolated, distant communities may in and of itself be sufficient to create a boom situation for pivotal communities. Once the highway is built, what were once communities with a stable population may become very mobile localities whose members are transient. This may have a dramatic impact on the environment and geography (mountains literally have been moved to make way for highways); the cultures and traditions; and the economic, political, and social structures (occupations, voting patterns, and the nature of social relationships).

Summary

This chapter has presented our view of a vital component of social work practice; namely, the ways to better understand the context of the client system. At any moment in time, we are taking a snapshot of a locality—things will change. The three key elements for understanding context are: geography and environment; history, traditions, and culture; and economic, political, and social structures and institutions.

We have suggested illustrative questions that we think social workers can use to better know their locality on an ongoing basis. Such knowledge is essential to effective social work practice within a locality.

The examples we have chosen for each of the elements of the context were selected to illustrate aspects of that context. What should be clear to the reader is that, in most situations, understanding these elements in combination is crucial. The geography and environment shape a locality's history, traditions, and culture, for example, and the interaction of all of the elements shapes the locality's unique identity.

In addition, there is interaction between the residents of a locality and the contextual elements. While the issues and concerns presented by client systems may be centered in one or two of the contextual arenas, we believe it necessary to extend our services by exploring and using resources found in all contextual elements.

As you prepare to move on to learning about our model for generalist social work practice, we ask that you reflect on these questions.

1. Think about the locality or localities in which you grew up. How would you describe them in terms of each of the contextual elements?

2. How have the geographical and environmental contexts of your life experience influenced how you see your world?

3. Think about your values and identify the ways in which the contextual elements of the locality or localities in which you have resided shaped them.

4. What influence have the contextual elements of the localities in which you have resided had in shaping your views and beliefs about other cultures and people who are different from you?

CHAPTER FOUR

Introducing the Phase Model

*The recipes in the cookbooks and the
meals we really eat are not the same
thing.*

ROBERT FULGHUM
(1991, PP. 13–14)

Introduction

Our model incorporates our collective experience as generalist social work practitioners and educators over the past 25 years; it also draws upon a variety of knowledge systems that we think are particularly useful in preparing for professional generalist social work practice. These knowledge areas include content selected from the social, political, economic, and behavioral sciences, as well as wisdom gained from the experiences of a number of our social work colleagues and students who have been kind enough to share with us over the years.

As we developed our phase model, we were influenced by and remain indebted to the work of Gerard Egan (1990), especially his discussion of developing preferred scenario possibilities (pp. 39–41, 274–283). While we have chosen slightly different language for Phase Two (that is, exploring and thinking about preferred realities and futures), Egan's work helped us become more clear about the importance of being able to name and embrace a desired reality as a necessary condition for change and movement.

We were also influenced by others who have worked to bring the concepts of story and narrative to the forefront of the helping professions: White and Epston (1990), Parry and Doan (1994), and Howard (1991). Our familiarity with Donald Schon's work (1987) influenced us to think about the last phase as one that focuses on learning and making transitions rather than termination.

Effective social work practice involves integrating values, knowledge, and skills for work in specific situations. Figure 4.1 graphically portrays the way in which we see the relationship of these three elements in generalist social work practice. Our knowledge, values, and skills are always present and, hopefully, available to us in our work. The uniqueness of client systems and their contexts shape the ways in which our knowledge, values, and skills are applied.

Being grounded in the professional values supportive of our practice is crucial, but values are hard to implement without an idea of the goals of practice.

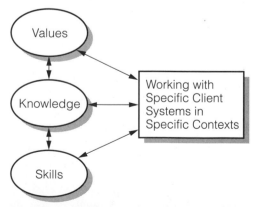

Figure 4.1 Professional Practice in Context

The National Association of Social Workers (NASW, 1981) identifies four objectives of social work practice: (1) to enhance people's issue management, coping, and developmental capacities; (2) to link people with systems that provide them with resources, services, and opportunities; (3) to promote the effective and humane operation of systems that provide people with resources and services; and (4) to develop and improve social policy.

In its most recent curriculum policy statement, the Council on Social Work Education (CSWE), the national accrediting body for social work education in the United States, conceptualized the purpose and goals of social work practice as

> *the enhancement of human well-being and the alleviation of poverty and oppression. The social work profession receives its sanction from public and private auspices and is the primary profession in the provision of social services. Within its general scope of concern, professional social work is practiced in a wide variety of settings and has four related purposes:*
>
> *1.   the promotion, restoration, maintenance, and enhancement of the functioning of individuals, families, groups, organizations, and communities by helping them to accomplish tasks, prevent and alleviate distress, and use resources;*
>
> *2.   the planning, formulation, and implementation of social policies, services, resources, and programs needed to meet basic human needs and support the development of human capacities;*
>
> *3.   the pursuit of policies, services, resources, and programs through organizational or administrative advocacy and social or political action, so as to empower groups at risk and promote social and economic justice; and*
>
> *4.   the development and testing of professional knowledge and skills related to these purposes. (1992, pp. 97, 135)*

A comparison of the NASW's goals with the purposes reflected in the CSWE Curriculum Policy Statement reveals a number of similarities and a few important differences. There is an emphasis in the CSWE (1992) statement on "the alleviation of poverty and oppression" and the need to "empower groups at risk and promote social and economic justice" (pp. 97, 135). These additions reflect the profession's increased emphasis on social justice and empowerment as a result of limited opportunity for many members of our society.

As we work to achieve the goals of social work through practice, we do so through the process of selecting knowledge, skills, and techniques consistent with professional values and standards for ethical practice as reflected within the NASW Code of Ethics (1996). Similarly, we need to filter the planned use of knowledge and skills through these values and purposes to support their achievement.

In this book we argue for an empowerment and competency orientation to practice that recognizes and builds on strengths. The social work profession regularly supports such practice; however, many of our practice theories have been developed within the framework of the medical or deficit model of practice. We think this reflects an inconsistent selection of knowledge. One continuing challenge to professional social workers is to evaluate the goodness of fit between their interventions and the value base and professional purposes set forth above. We believe that social workers fulfill their professional responsibilities by working toward the achievement of the following aims:

- facilitating the effective functioning of client systems and working toward preferred realities in their context;
- linking client systems with needed resources from the social context through providing information, brokering, and advocacy;
- supporting client systems by working with them to strengthen their social supports and social network;
- working with client systems and with others to alter the social, economic, and political structures of the context so they are more responsive to the needs of persons, families, groups, and communities and more conducive to social justice; and
- carrying out these aims in ways that strengthen competencies of and increase options for client systems.

Distinctions exist between this conceptualization and the purposes outlined by both NASW and CSWE. First, we put an additional emphasis on strengthening supports and social networks. Since, in many cases, people need to manage issues over a long period of time, the need to strengthen available support or create access to new forms of social support is all the more important. Second, the concept of *competency* is woven through everything we do in social work. Regardless of whether we are working with a person, facilitating a group, linking a family with needed resources, or working with others to strengthen a community's responsiveness to a common concern, one of the aims of practice must be to increase client system competence and mastery.

We also recognize that there are important similarities between this conceptualization of the aims of the profession and the goals and purposes identified by NASW and CSWE. Social work has traditionally, in its generalist foundation, understood that issues are expressed and experienced at multiple levels. Additionally, the profession has been concerned with responding to both private concerns and the public causes linked to them. Finally, the profession has supported the primacy of client system interests to the maximum extent possible, realizing that such interests are best understood within the context of a democratic society with both rights and responsibilities.

System Size and Points of Intervention

Central to the generalist orientation to practice is the idea of multiple client systems and points of intervention. System size is distinguished by the number and association of the people with whom one is working. Social workers can influence change one-on-one, with couples and families, in small groups, and within organizations and communities, and they may be called upon to work with these different-sized systems simultaneously. The idea of multiple points and levels of intervention is associated with how we come to select the "best intervention" for the issue or concern. Often, especially if we practice within social service agencies or in private clinical practice, the intervention focus is on achieving changes that are desired by the person or family with whom we are working. However, the issues and concerns we encounter in these situations are frequently linked with contextual realities that need to be influenced and changed. Our efforts at effecting contextual change, including public or private policy, exemplify this concept of selecting the best intervention point to influence the client system's issue or concern. In many instances, the social work practitioner is moving between intervention levels, as illustrated by the following example:

> *Trying to raise children in an inner-city, low-income neighborhood plagued by inadequate housing, racism, drug abuse, and crime can be a brutal experience for single mothers of color. Workers in a child-development center devised a several-step plan to address the individual child-rearing concerns of a group of low-income single mothers mainly Hispanic and African-American, and then to help the women to move toward a societal explanation for their children's school problem, leading to social action to change school conditions.*
>
> *Initially, support groups helped the women identify the source of their problems as family stress, dangerous neighborhood, and an inadequate school system. In subsequent skill-building groups, the women learned more effective parenting behaviors. The women also learned skills in group facilitation and in the final stage of intervention, the social action phase, the group was client-led. When concerns about the educational system arose repeatedly, the group, with the workers' support, initiated a class-action suit against the board of education. The case was subsequently won, and had a positive impact on children throughout the city. According to one of the workers, "This example indicates how in less than one year, these women moved from feeling overwhelmed by their young children to feeling capable of confronting the city board of education. Although these women set out to learn how to become more effective parents, they quickly became interested in having an impact on those external conditions that made their role so difficult." (Gutierrez, 1990, p. 151)*

How would you place the level of intervention in this case illustration? We recognize that the initial choice by each mother to seek a day care service was important. At the same time, acknowledging common needs among the mothers contributed to the creation of support groups and the discovery of a concern that could be addressed only through legal action. Figure 4.2 illustrates the levels of intervention used in the case above.

This case also illustrates another important dimension of the context of practice. Reamer (1993a) writes of "the persistent tension between case and cause, between amelioration of individual suffering and social change that addresses the structural flaws in the culture that foster the varied ills that individuals experience" (p. 4). In carrying out the functions and fulfilling the aims of social work, the practitioner will not only move between levels but will also

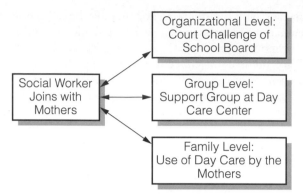

Figure 4.2 Intervention Levels

move from issues that are nonpolitical and generally noncontroversial (case) to ones that are more political and more controversial (cause). As issues are encountered, the need to deal with the causes underlying them often presents the social worker with a challenge of taking collective action or otherwise seeking the involvement of influentials who can be advocates.

Understanding the use of power is important here. Social change, by its very objective, involves power: its use and abuse, and its imbalance as it is held within society and our communities. It is vital to the process of influencing change that social workers understand the power they and their client systems possess and that they support the client system in the effective use of this power.

Linking individuals with services in most cases focuses on smaller system interventions. An example would be working with the family of a 9-year-old with a severe speech impediment to obtain a computer with speech capability for use in school. However, when the client is a person with AIDS seeking admission to a nursing home, linking with resources can become advocacy and the issue of protecting the right to service.

Not all larger system interventions are related to alleviating oppression and achieving social justice. Adding the dimension of case and cause enhances our understanding that the levels of practice are connected and what we learn in working with persons, families, and groups may spur us to work on changing policies and programs. Reamer (1993a) states:

> *It is essential for modern day social workers—even the majority who are aiming for careers in some form of direct practice—to understand their special mission. We cannot afford to equip students with clinical skills alone, although such skills are imperative. To do so would relegate this noble profession to the variety of "helping professions" that are hard to distinguish from one another. Our mission is unique. No one can link and explain as well as a well-trained social worker the sprint to address the immediate pains of suffering in people's lives and the marathon involved in the thoughtful design of long-term, policy-based solutions. (p. 4)*

Attention to cause as well as case brings us back to the purposes and aims of social work practice. Abromovitz (1993) reminds us that "any social work method can be used to preserve or transform the personal or societal status quo" (p. 8). We understand this important observation and would challenge the reader to be mindful of our professional responsibility to be *transformers,* especially at the societal level. Preserving the status quo is rarely the question as client systems name their issues and preferred realities.

Our Model for Influencing Change

Rationale for the Model

Much of social work practice, especially those models designed to support generalist practice, are presented as versions of the problem-solving paradigm. For example, Bloom (1990) identified his task model as proceeding through seven ordered steps. Johnson (1992) also presented her model for problem solving as involving seven stages, moving from problem statement to evaluation of the plan. Kirst-Ashman and Hull (1993) described a six-step model, from assessment to follow-up, and O'Neil (1984) identified a six-sequential-stage model for her general method of social work practice.

We have a concern about the notion of social work practice as problem solving. In part this has to do with the negative connotations that may be associated with the word itself. The idea of having a problem is in part dependent upon who names the issue. Goldstein (1984) expresses this quite well:

> *The notion of a problem is relatively meaningless until we gain some apprecia-
> tion of where it fits within the pattern of the client's living, how it is understood
> and what it means to him or her, what is at stake either in perpetuating or
> changing the problem, and whether a solution is possible. As a "problem," the
> abuse that the battered woman has suffered so long takes on radically different
> meanings when she finally concludes that all hope for the future of the
> relationship is lost and that an alternative way of life is either necessary or
> possible. The alcoholic's "problem" doesn't really exist as far as they are
> concerned until their illusions no longer serve them and another solution is
> called for. (p. 284)*

In Box 4.1 are several other points we think help in understanding the power of language and the difficulties associated with only seeing and working with problems. We do not wish to overstate the concern here, although we do not believe that would be possible in the current state of affairs. The degree to which helpers (including social workers, counselors, planners, psychologists, and teachers) see themselves as working with problems raises the possibility of seeing people as problems. Once this leap is made, the issues noted in Box 4.1 become more likely to define the change process; when this occurs, we are less likely to experience the process of seeking and giving help as building competencies.

Believing in the power of words, we are concerned that this historical language, especially in a success-oriented society like the United States, forces people who feel a need (or desire) to seek or consume social services to perceive

BOX 4.1

Critique of "Problem" Terminology

In Oregon, an agency working on a program to focus on family unity and family strengths developed this critique of "problem" terminology:

1. *Problems do not resolve anything.* Strengths are what resolve issues of concern.

2. Use of the word *problem* in our society often carries heavy overtones of *shame, blame, or guilt.* The overlay of those emotions makes it difficult to discover the real issues of concern.

3. Asking someone to share their "problems" with you puts the listener in a *"one-up" position* on people. The unspoken word is often, "You have problems and I don't." I do not believe a person can be an effective helper from a "one-up" position.

4. People's reaction to having their "problems" aired is often resistance, anxiety, fear, anger, embarrassment, or reluctance, which can cause the listener to make *negative assumptions* about them. Looking for problems, one not only misses what is "right" about someone, but often misjudges what the real concerns are as well.

5. Looking for "problems" increases the tendency to *label people.* Labeling happens most often when you don't understand or know how to explain a person's behavior. *Labeling is basically unhelpful. It speaks to a person's limitations, not their strengths.* No one gets well because of a label attached to them. On the contrary, they may get worse, mired in the fear of what the label may mean to you. Labeling not only limits your options, it increases the burden on the person you are trying to help.

6. "Problems" have a way of paralyzing both the people sharing as well as those listening. *The frustration with the paralysis leads to hopelessness on the part of the person sharing, and advice giving on the part of the helper.* Common words from counselors at this stage of the process are, "Well, what you need to do is. . . ." (which is basically a disrespectful response). People do not get stronger by pointing out what is wrong with them.

7. Pointing out "problems" invites *defensiveness, hostility, and excuse making* (it is basically a stuck position). Families accept "issues of concern" terminology much better than "problem" terminology. Issues of concern often are not the same as problems. Concerns take issues to a different and oftentimes more workable level and open avenues to pursue strengths and good will behind the difficulties many families experience.

Source: L. Graber (1992).

themselves as having failed in some important way. We do not at all believe this to be an accurate or useful constructed reality for social service consumers and social workers to bring to the planned change context.

Weick (1992) presents a powerful argument for reframing our views on this matter and for adopting a strengths perspective of social work practice. We find her views compelling:

> *The strengths perspective consciously creates a new agenda for practice. It draws attention away from increasingly technique-laden approaches to human situations and reminds us of a simple truth: that each person already carries the seed for his or her own transformation. A steadfast belief in that potential is one of the most powerful gifts a social worker can offer. . . .*
>
> *It may be tempting to diminish the force of this claim by asserting that social work has always practiced from a strengths perspective. But it is a precarious position to maintain in the face of the themes of pathology, problems, and human deficiency that lace social work texts, journals, and professional workshops. The commitment to working with people's strengths has an admirable tradition in social work. But putting it at the center of practice will require an effort that consciously challenges both cultural and professional shibboleths. Until we can come to a point where it is strengths rather than problems that most significantly identify who an individual is, we will know that we have not overcome the seduction of pathology. (p. 25)*

An emphasis on problem solving reinforces the idea—for the client system, the social worker, and the community—that the client system is somehow deficient. The idea that the situations in which client systems find themselves are problems is interpreted by many people as "there's something wrong with us." It is a familiar experience for social workers to get a negative response when we mention the availability of mental health services that might be of use to a person. A common response to such a suggestion is, "I don't need to see a therapist (or shrink or social worker). I'm not crazy! I don't have a problem."

A related issue with the problem-solving or deficit model is the idea that many of our social programs appear designed to reinforce the stigma felt by client systems as they participate in them. We believe that public and private policies, historically and currently, are constructed in a way to maintain a sense of stigma as client systems seek help. Trattner (1994) discussed the role of the Charity Organization Society, in the late 19th century, in shaping the social casework model of practice and its belief that helping was at best a necessary evil and should be done only as a last resort and in a way that would encourage most people to avoid seeking assistance. The use of stigmas therefore became (and still remains) an important and, in our opinion, inappropriate way to deliver service and help. This is not at all empowering and, in fact, is one of the major barriers to practicing in an empowering way. As Chapin (1995) notes, "despite the time-honored emphasis on strengths in the social work literature, as Cowger pointed out, 'there is very little empirical evidence indicating the extent to which practitioners make use of strengths in their practice' (p. 140)" (p. 507). We believe the social work profession has a responsibility to take this charge seriously and to provide such evidence by embracing a strengths and competency-building orientation to our practice.

A baseball coach tells the players, "Keep your eye on the ball," knowing that it is impossible (or very difficult) to concentrate on a lot of things at the same time. If we concentrate on problems, we're not focusing on strengths, and we're not focused on working toward a time when things are better than they are now. The situation may be the same, but the people involved may approach the situation differently if what is identified as the focus of the change effort is, for example, "strengthening the marriage" rather than "fixing the problems."

At all levels of our practice, we believe that this view serves the interests of our client systems and the profession well. The classic social work maxim of building on strengths fits here. We do not know how to build on weakness and suggest that models of practice that encourage and support social workers to do that prevent us from achieving our purpose.

Related to the concept of "problem" is the idea of solution. In a positivist-rational society, we pride ourselves on being able to find a final solution to our problems; however, people tend not to fit this paradigm so easily. "People" issues rarely have final solutions—rather, we may be better served to think about issue management and developing strengths and resources so that the client system has a broader range of desirable choices. A person with a long-term history of abusing alcohol can be helped by treatment for his alcohol abuse or alcoholism. However, with effective treatment comes the message that one doesn't solve addiction but works to manage it over the course of a lifetime. Persons who have struggled to lose or maintain a desired body weight also realize the fallacy of considering weight gain as a problem to be solved; they know that it is an issue that needs to be managed.

While employed by a public welfare agency, I (Barry) recall a man with whom I worked who was diagnosed as mentally retarded. This gentleman had family members with major illnesses that required frequent trips to a major hospital some distance from his home. He managed to keep an old clunker of a car in running order by trading for parts and doing the repairs himself so that he could get his daughter to the doctor; however, neither he nor I ever thought of his transportation issue as solved. He managed it well, but he was always actively concerned about it, and much of our work together focused on his thinking through how best to keep his car on the road.

A focus on problem solving also tends to devalue the importance of the relationship between social worker and client system. An examination of the problem-solving models cited earlier in the chapter reveals the following:

- they often place the social worker in the position of being the expert with solutions;
- they appear to suggest that there are ideal solutions for all issues identified;
- they are presented, admittedly with cautionary caveats, as linear models that oversimplify the ebb and flow of the change process.

Social workers who see their client systems as possessing capabilities and competencies will seek to partner with them in working toward desired ends and preferred realities. The planned change process, understood in this light, assumes that there are always issues and concerns with which people may wish to seek, or be forced to seek, help. In this sense, we think social work best realizes its potential by enabling a society and its members to see such help seeking as a normal process of living.

Models and Language

We share the profession's commitment to knowledge-guided practice. A hallmark for social work professionals is that they know what they know, why they know what they know, and how to articulate that knowing to others. One useful way to organize what we know is to create models. In this sense a model can be defined as a guide or a standard of excellence to be imitated.

For these reasons, we have arrived at language we believe fits better with a view of generalist social work practice as strengths oriented and competency based. We would rather discuss issues of concern when thinking about needs or desires presented by client systems than to call them problems that are most often seen as system failures. For similar reasons, we talk with human service consumers about issue management rather than solutions. While this discussion may strike the reader as strange or much ado about little, we would only ask you to consider the many meanings associated with or implied by the term *problem.*

You might react differently to a friend depending on which of these statements he or she made: "I've got to get all A's and B's this semester or else!" or, "Though I'm concerned about getting good grades, this semester is a great opportunity for me to learn a lot!" The situation hasn't changed, but the person has stated it as an opportunity rather than a problem, an issue to be dealt with because there are desirable outcomes.

Explanation of the Model

We have discussed our concerns about the use of the phrase *problem solving* as the operating paradigm for social work practice. This concern is also shared by Saleebey (1992), who has written about the strengths perspective in social work practice. The strengths orientation incorporates the concept of constructed reality, which suggests that what we come to see as real is in fact real for us, independent of others' constructed realities. We think this is a powerful idea to be aware of if the client system's world view is to be understood.

Therefore, we have created a four-phase model that is designed to place the client system at the center in determining how the aims and processes of social work practice unfold and flow. We devote much of Chapter 7—Phase Three of our model—to a discussion of how the aims of the profession are part of the phase of making plans and dreams real. For now, it is important to understand that each of the aims we outlined earlier in this chapter—designing strategy, linking with resources, providing social support, influencing the social, economic, and political context, and increasing client system competence and capacity—are to some degree present in each of the phases of our practice model. Like the model itself, the primacy of the aim may be more (or less) important depending in part on how the client system and the social worker come to agree upon preferred realities associated with their work together.

As we look at the practice models cited earlier, it appears to us that they are worker-centered models—the social worker assesses, plans, and intervenes with client systems. While the worker's activities are important, we are persuaded that the activities of the client system are equally important, and the intent of our model is to shift the power relations in the planned change process from one dominated by the worker to one where power is respectfully shared by the client system and the social worker in partnership. This is a subtle but important shift in emphasis.

In formulating this model, we are not implying that structure is not important. In reviewing metastudies of the effectiveness of social work practice and case management, Corcoran and Videka-Sherman (1992) concluded that "effective interventions had structure; they were clear and specific about what problems to resolve, the goals of treatment, and the procedures followed to reach those goals" (p. 18). What we are suggesting is that how the social worker and the client system understand and view structure influences the way in which the process is experienced.

Expert models, in the traditional sense that professionals have used them, place consumers in a secondary position. We think these practices need to be reframed so that the people with the issues and concerns fully participate in their naming and action efforts. In the following chapters, we will present the details of our model for how such practice may best be accomplished.

The metaphor that we imagine for our model of influencing change is one that uses the image of the phases of the moon. One of the reasons for choosing this image is that, as with the moon, the movement from one phase to another is gradual and fluid, not abrupt. The difference between the first and third phase is clear, but the dividing lines between contiguous phases are much less obvious.

Another consideration for using the progression of the moon as a metaphor for our model is that the moon is constantly in the process of change through its phases; and depending on where you stand on the planet Earth, that change process will look slightly different. So too are our client systems, as well as ourselves, in a constant process of change, with phases and transitions not exactly clear all the time and perceived differently by the participants in the process.

The dividing line from one phase to another may be especially blurry between the second and third phases of the planned change process. For purposes of explaining the model and organizing material, we make a distinction between these two phases. In many situations, linear planned change models—where phase one leads to phase two, which leads to phase three—is not an accurate reflection of the process that human beings at all levels of their interaction are likely to follow.

Taking action with client systems is rarely a lockstep process. For instance, in an emergency situation we might be forced to act initially without complete information of how the emergency came to be. Other times, we might move from exploration to understanding to action and back again. We will be discussing our model in sequential chapters with the hope that you understand that, in our experience, influencing change does not always follow such a structured path.

Process and Relationship

Social work has historically been a profession concerned with both process and outcomes. This concern recognizes that the means utilized are never fully justified by the ends achieved and that desired ends or outcomes are not sufficient in and of themselves. To illustrate, a social worker may decide that the most efficient way to help a family in need of income is to go with the family as they make an application for public assistance and to answer the eligibility worker's questions while guiding the family through the bureaucratic process. The worker is able to get the family financial assistance, and the family begins to receive a monthly check. The income goal is realized by getting the family public assistance. However, the worker notices over the next few months that every time the family identifies a need, they seek her out to go with them to secure it. One day, she was approached by the family when she was quite involved with another crisis. She asked them why they always sought her out. They replied: "You always take care of our needs."

The worker realized that her behavior—that is, the process of conducting her work with the family—had helped them become quite dependent upon her. Most of us in this society would say that overdependence is not desirable for people. In this illustration, we can see that desired outcomes were realized; however, a less than desirable outcome (increased dependence on the worker) was also created.

We call this concern for both *process* (the way we work) and *outcomes* (the results realized in our work) *attending to the dual processes of social work practice.* Process is defined as "a continuing development involving many changes; a particular method of doing something, generally involving a number of steps or operations" (Guralick, 1978). Outcome is defined as "result, consequence, aftermath" (Guralick, 1978). Several authors have provided useful insights into the contributions each of these make to practice.

Bloom's generic problem-solving approach (1990) requires that the social worker attend both to task functions and to relationships. Pincus and Minahan (1973) discuss process in terms of the worker needing a purpose for each activity, as well as for the whole change effort. They further suggest that this process needs to be actively connected with the preferred end state or outcome. Johnson added to our understanding of the importance of process in social work practice by linking it with the work of John Dewey (1933). She appropriately noted the Deweyian contribution of reflective thinking and scientific process to social work practice (Johnson, 1992). What all of these authors appear to have in common on this issue is that they perceive social work practice as a cyclical and directional process over time.

Our four-phase model highlights the process aspects as well as the task accomplishments of social work practice. We value process equally with task or product and don't want to give the impression that the only thing that is important is what gets accomplished.

The relationship between process and task or outcome may be seen like the relationship between the drawing of either a cup or a face that is used in psychology texts: what you see depends on whether you're concentrating on the foreground or the background. Within the discussion of process, we want to consider the attention to what is going on both in the interactions and in the nature of the relationship between the worker and the client system.

The Helping Relationship Historically, relationship has been seen as very important in social work practice. In *The Casework Relationship,* Felix Biestek (1957) defines relationship as "[t]he dynamic interaction of attitudes and emotions between the caseworker and client, with the purpose of helping the client achieve a better adjustment between himself and the environment" (p. 12). The seven principles of a helping relationship, according to Biestek (1957), are individualization, purposeful expression of feelings, controlled emotional environment, acceptance, nonjudgmental attitude, client system self-determination, and confidentiality. Biestek's focus is on client system adaptation rather than challenging the reasons for things being as they are; however, his work was influential in highlighting the importance of relationship.

In her books *Social Casework: A Problem-Solving Approach* and *Relationship: The Heart of Helping People,* Helen Harris Perlman (1957, 1979) puts forward a problem-solving process for social work, with the relationship between the caseworker and the client system essential to the process. She writes that "in professional helping relationships, caring is concern for the welfare of those one seeks to help. It does not imply that one needs to 'love;' it implies, rather, that one cares about the person's hurt and/or about the hurtful consequences of his behavior, whether for himself or others" (1979, p. 59). The concern, according to Perlman, is for social as well as personal well-being. We are concerned about the effects of the client system's actions on others. In medical terms, we also worry about the contagion potential—about the client system's behaviors affecting others.

More recently, feminist philosopher Nel Noddings (1984) has highlighted the importance of caring in professional as well as personal relationships. In an interaction with a client system, we make the effort to understand the client system. According to Noddings, understanding is the basis for caring; otherwise, we are attending to an image that we have of the person's world or concerns without real knowledge of the person. Noddings (1984) states: "I shall reject the notion of universal caring—that is, caring for everyone—on the grounds that it is impossible to actualize and leads us to substitute abstract problem-solving and mere talk for genuine caring" (p. 18).

In a related vein, Berg and Miller (1992) note:

> *The traditional emphasis on obtaining the cooperation of the client, is, however, hopelessly one-sided and therefore, does not constitute cooperation at all. In fact, cooperation, as routinely described by treatment professionals, is analogous to a therapeutic* Animal Farm, *in which the rule is that all participants in therapy must cooperate equally, but some participants must cooperate more equally than others—the latter referring chiefly to the client. In the "intervention" process described above no attempt is made to see the problem from the client's perspective, to speak his or her own language, to work within his or her unique frame of reference, to negotiate a mutually agreeable treatment goal, or to utilize*

existing strengths and resources in an effort to solve the problem. The entire process is based on the idea that the client is "delusional" and "out of touch with reality" and must be forced to "cooperate" with the treatment as recommended. Cooperation, as Sesame Street's Big Bird is so fond of pointing out, means working together with *one another. Therefore, in a truly cooperative therapeutic relationship, not only must the client cooperate by working* with *the worker, but the worker must cooperate by working with the client.* (p.15)

The stronger the relationship between worker and client system, in general, the more open the communication will be and the more the worker will be trusted. We can help strengthen the relationship by being as present as possible in our interactions, by demonstrating that we have some things to offer, by following up on what we promise to do, and by communicating that we care about the person.

Components of a Helping Relationship   Four basic components can help define the nature of the relationship between the social worker and the client system: engagement, nurturance, sustenance, and transformation. Engagement is the way in and the degree to which we connect and join with the client system in the process of change; nurturance, the way in which we attend to the basic human needs of the client system (belonging, safety, physiological well-being, esteem, and actualization); sustenance, the degree to which we address and work on the relationship; and transformation, the way in which the relationship changes throughout the process of our work together.

In crisis intervention, we may be engaging, nurturing, sustaining, and transforming within a very limited and intense time frame. Or in case management or program development, we may have a longer period of time in which we are working with a client system and thus be able to spend more concentrated time on each or any one of the relationship components. All four of these components are essential in any relationship we develop with a client system, regardless of the duration or nature of the change effort.

The Process   In being an effective helper, it is necessary to attend to the ebbs and flows of the process. As mentioned earlier, by process we refer to the way the work unfolds and how it is being done. Consistent with a generalist orientation, our comments have application to all sizes and levels of client systems.

Social work is a profession that attempts to work within a value base of self-determination, respect for the dignity of others, and a continuing belief in the hopes and dreams of our client systems. The process of influencing change is very much connected with these values.

Before a social worker can be allied with a change process, a relationship must be established. The social worker who communicates genuineness, respect, empathy, and concern for the primacy of the client system's interests is likely to earn the privilege of experiencing with the client system a positive and productive change process.

Stages of Group Development

forming	beginning stages of groups; characterized by emergence of group feeling; attention focused on organizing and getting acquainted; stage of testing and dependence.
storming	stage of intragroup conflict and emotional expression; characterized by resistance of group members to group pressure; attention focused on desire to be a member of the group without losing sense of self and identity; exploration of fit and role with group; approach-avoidance type reaction.
norming	stage of developing group cohesion; characterized by beginning differentiation of roles and clarification of rules; attention focused on development of interactive and feedback processes.
performing	stage of functioning in efforts to meet agreed-upon goals; characterized by completion of group efforts, group decision making; attention focused on finishing business and producing results.
transforming and mourning	stage of ending characterized by review and evaluation of group efforts; attention focused on parting and the feelings associated with endings.

Source: Brown (1979, pp. 65–73); Tuckman (1965, as cited in Brown, 1979).

Being focused only on outcomes or achieving a tangible goal to the neglect of the learning opportunities associated with how that goal was realized is incomplete at best. At worst, it leaves client systems more dependent upon the worker for their future well-being. As we review the phases of our model later, it is important to consider the elements of achievement associated with each phase—both process and outcome.

In working with groups, it is equally important to be aware of the process of the group as well as how it is achieving its tasks. In conceptualizing the stages of group development, we have utilized the work of Brown (1979) and Tuckman (as cited in Brown). We propose five stages of group development, as illustrated in Box 4.2. As with all processes, the sequential nature of the stages may vary depending on the circumstances and context of the group.

If group members are not communicating with each other or if some members are being excluded, the group will not function as effectively as it could. Hepworth and Larsen (1993) remind us that attending to process issues within the group involves at least two foci—one on how the group and the social worker are establishing trust in their relationship, and another on how the group members are managing this task with each other as well.

Attending to group process is like maintenance of an automobile. Forgetting to change the oil until the dashboard oil light comes on will not lead to longevity of the car's engine. Similarly, when a group, community, or family does not attend to the process in an ongoing fashion, serious difficulties can develop.

Relationships in Cross-Cultural Context Proctor and Davis (1994) note the challenges the social worker may face in cross-cultural helping; namely, the development of a relationship qualitatively different than either party may have previously experienced with a racially or ethnically dissimilar other. We think the key to working well with those who are different from ourselves is found in our capacity for sensitivity and openness to learning how the difference is seen by each party in the helping relationship. Differences of gender, race, sexual orientation, class, and lifestyle are important considerations. As social workers, we need to be clear about how we feel about these differences and about how the client system may experience them.

While there has been much discussion about the capacity of social workers to work well with persons different from themselves, we are not of the view that such work is impossible or ineffective. However, we do agree that working with difference requires us to be clear about our language and the impact of words and behaviors as forms of cultural expression.

For example, we have worked with some concerns about improving race relations in the communities where we live, especially between university students and community merchants. One issue that African American students regularly identify as a concern is the feeling that, when they enter a store, they come under different scrutiny than do white students who may enter the same store. This feeling is well understood in the African American community, and efforts by merchants to overcome this kind of behavior have been difficult at best. Should we fall prey to similar behavior in helping situations, the trust necessary for work to go forward is not likely to develop.

Some research suggests that effective work is possible where the race of the worker and the client system is different. Taylor, Neighbors, and Broman (1989) investigated how African Americans assessed their experiences with seeking help. Almost four out of ten respondents indicated that the person they saw in the social agency was also African American. For those respondents who were not assisted by an African American, 58.5% reported that the race of the social service worker made no difference, 26.4% indicated that they would have preferred being helped by an African American, and 15.1% said that they preferred not to be helped by an African American. When asked whether they would return to the social service agency for assistance, 85.2% of the respondents answered affirmatively.

One of the more consistent findings of this analysis was that the respondents gave positive appraisals of the assistance they received from social service providers. Most of the respondents indicated that they were satisfied with the services they received, would return to the agency if they had similar problems, and would recommend the agency to their relatives and friends.

Facilitating Work

While it is not possible (or desirable) to provide a cookbook for practicing effectively, there are useful skills and tools we will identify as we progress through the phase model in the chapters that follow. In thinking about things that help facilitate effective practice, we would lump them into two major categories: worker traits and facilitating skills.

Worker Traits Worker traits, as presented in the list below, are those values in action, personality traits, and world views that reinforce our ability to practice effectively. They include:

- *being authentic*—communicating a natural sense of oneself in an open, real, and sincere way;
- *being respectful*—communicating an attitude toward others that is warm and accepting and that views them with unconditional positive regard;
- *being self-aware*—having enough self-understanding to not act in ways that harm client systems' abilities to work on their issues and concerns;
- *being assertive*—knowing one's personal and professional power and being able to use it in appropriate ways to serve client systems;
- *believing in change*—actively believing in the possibility of growth and change, both for people and for the contexts in which they live.

Facilitating Skills Facilitating skills are the actions of social workers that support the effectiveness of the process and outcomes of their work with client systems and others. Our list, not intended to be exhaustive, includes:

- *listening*—hearing, observing, and remembering the message of another;
- *speaking*—the conscious use of one's voice and word choices in ways that help others hear and understand the message;
- *asking questions*—inviting the message of another through encouraging, probing, and clarifying to aid understanding;
- *reflective responding*—the process of reflecting the messages, feelings, and experiences of another through paraphrasing and empathy.

The Danger of Paternalism We will return to these traits and skills as we move through the four phases of the practice model that follows. There is a final point, however, that we need to make as we reflect on how to practice in an encouraging and strengths-centered way.

We are concerned with how the helping process can sometimes slip into paternalism. When this occurs, client systems are harmed and left unempowered.

Simon (1994) offers some guides that social workers can use to assess the degree to which their practice may be perceived as paternalistic.

> 1. *With what degree of concentration do I listen to and consider the explicit and implicit communications of the clients or constituents to whom I am responsible?*
>
> 2. *Do I silently discount the opinions of any client, client group, or constituent? If so, why so? And what can I do to exchange my silence for dialogue with that person or group?*
>
> 3. *When I recommend a particular course of action to a client, do I take ample care and time to elicit from him or her alternative proposals before seeking agreement of the nature and sequence of steps to be taken?*
>
> 4. *Has any client given me feedback that I have been remote, intimidating, or inaccessible? If so, what more can I learn from that person about the basis for her or his impression of my unavailability?*
>
> 5. *Do I use acronyms, abbreviations, proper names, or specialized language that are foreign to clients in their presence without defining those terms?*
>
> 6. *When circumstances force me to rush a client or constituent or to keep him or her waiting, in what ways do I make amends?*
>
> 7. *When my professional duty requires me to violate a client's preferences, do I explain my actions and reasoning to that client in as open, direct, and respectful a manner as possible?*
>
> 8. *When I feel protective of a client, do I inspect the situation with special care to make sure that I am not underestimating the client or exaggerating my own importance or capability?*
>
> 9. *When I find myself thinking primarily about the problems that a client faces, do I make a conscious effort in my contemplation to pay closer attention to his or her strengths and imagination? (pp. 188–189)*

Phases of the Model

In the chapters that follow, we will present specific details associated with each phase of our generalist practice model. For now, we wish to introduce the phases and briefly share with the reader how we arrived at each.

We have chosen to call them phases to express our belief that social work practice, as we have experienced it, is not rigid or linear. The word *phase* is often used to mean the way something develops or unfolds, and we think this appropriately describes the social worker and client system experiences of the planned change process.

As the moon travels through an orderly process each month following its course around the earth, we know the whole moon is in the night sky, yet we see only certain parts of it as it continues its journey. The moon is different each night we look at it, even though the differences are often subtle and difficult to detect. So too are the stories associated with the issues and concerns and the hopes and dreams of those with whom social workers work. It is a rare event to learn the whole story at a first meeting, yet by careful work, especially with effective process, we can hear it. The box below names the phases of work in our practice model.

Phase One	→	**Telling and Exploring the Story**
Phase Two	→	**Describing a Preferred Reality**
Phase Three	→	**Making Plans and Dreams Real**
Phase Four	→	**Evaluating Outcomes and Making Transitions**

In naming the phases of our model, we have attempted to capture the work, both as process and outcome, that is of primary importance in each. So we begin with careful exploration and storytelling and move toward examining what we have learned and transitioning to other opportunities and challenges.

As we move through the experience, the beginning and ending of each phase is deliberately fuzzy and not always clear. This is because we think most of us live our lives this way, with few clear-cut and distinct beginnings and endings. In this sense, we hope to present generalist social work practice as a dynamic and ever-changing experience designed to work with people in naming issues and hopes and in taking action toward realizing their goals, all the while understanding that the work of living well is always incomplete and unfolding.

Summary

In this chapter, we have shared our views about social work practice as both a process and an outcome. We have identified a competency orientation and a strengths perspective as central to more fully realizing the aims and purposes of the social work profession.

Equally important, we hope the reader has an increasing appreciation for the importance of language and meanings in our interactions with others. The discussion of our concern with viewing social work practice from a problem-solving perspective is one illustration of the influence of language on the effect of practice.

We have also reminded the reader that life is rarely ever experienced as a linear process, of moving from point A to point B in the most efficient manner. People and their contexts are more complex than that, and our phase model reflects this understanding as central in any planned change process.

Finally, we have raised the need for social workers to be mindful of and attentive to both the process of work that facilitates movement toward desired outcomes and the outcomes realized. In our outcome-oriented society, process may often be discounted; yet, effective processes build the competencies and capacities of both client systems and social workers for managing future concerns and issues.

As you move on to learning in greater detail about Phase One, Telling and Exploring the Story, please consider the following questions:

1. What feelings and reactions did you have to the discussion of our concern with the concept of problem solving and the idea that, as professionals, we need not be the expert?

2. Think about how you choose a course of action. Do you see a decision as a final solution or the best choice for that point in time? How do your thoughts about influencing change and the nature of outcomes fit with our views?

3. Think about your growth and development. In what ways have others around you acted that were beneficial to your learning? In what ways have others around you acted that were detrimental to your learning? How might this understanding be applied in your practice?

4. Based on your own experiences of seeking and receiving help, how have the ways in which you have been helped influenced your perception of the results of these experiences?

5. Can you think of examples of realizing desired outcomes that were not very satisfying because of the ways in which the outcomes were achieved? Or can you think of examples of when you might not have reached the outcomes identified but the process was beneficial and inspired learning, growth, and competency?

CHAPTER FIVE

Phase One: Telling and Exploring the Story

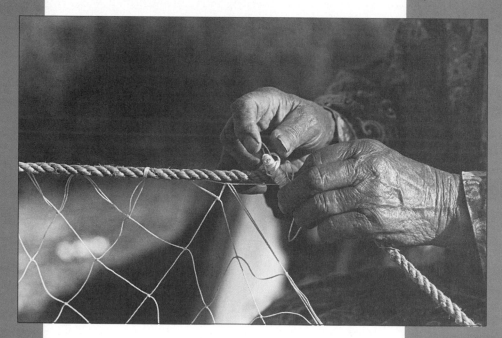

Let us tighten our bond with each other, as a knot would, and unite in love's great power to redirect the present conditions we are facing in our lives.

LENA SOURS
(1883–1993)

Introduction

Central to our model of generalist social work practice is the metaphor of life as a story. This metaphor is useful in thinking about the lives of the members of client systems, inasmuch as persons, families, organizations, and communities have histories, present situations, and future possibilities that can be thought of as a story unfolding. Our model is built around the idea of discovering the story that is important to the concerns and issues of the client system with whom we are working.

The metaphor of story is also valuable in thinking about the work of the social worker with a client system. This story, from the viewpoint of the social worker, begins where the client system and the worker first meet or when the worker is asked to work with a client system or the individual or institution that is the focus of change by a referral source.

The first phase of our model of social work practice is Telling and Exploring the Story, which provides the foundation for the other phases of the model. In this chapter, we will be describing the knowledge, values, and skills that help the social worker explore the story with the client system.

Given the variety of client systems, settings, and roles of social workers, it is difficult to generalize to the initial contact between workers and client systems. Here are some examples of first contacts from practicing social workers.

- A family preservation worker makes a home visit in a situation where the mother has called the police department to complain that she cannot handle her 9-year-old son.

- A 32-year-old man, convicted of battery for beating his wife, comes in for an assessment with a social worker to see if he qualifies for a group for men who batter, as the judge has stated that completing a group is a condition of getting off probation.

- A 15-year-old girl stops in without an appointment to see the high school social worker; there are problems at home, and the word around school is that the social worker can be trusted.

- A case manager for an agency that serves persons with HIV and AIDS in three rural counties sets up an appointment to see a new client, a man who just moved back home from the city where he had been living.

- A social worker who is a member of a group, the Family Resources Coalition, convenes the first meeting of an action team comprised of agency and community representatives interested in expanding and coordinating a range of services that support positive family, parenting, and life skills.

- A social worker is approached by members of his church to assist them in developing a food pantry.

What has led the client system to seek assistance or be in contact with that agency or social worker is usually not simple, and social workers need to be aware that they cannot presuppose an understanding of the situation immediately.

The process begins with a respectful invitation to the client system to tell the story and then with active listening on the part of the social worker to hear and understand the story. The process is a joint one, and through the process of telling and exploring the story, both the client system and the worker may understand the situation better. This is the goal for Phase One of our model.

Rethinking Diagnosis and Assessment

The choice of the words used for key ideas in any practice model is important. As we discussed in regard to the construction of meaning in Chapter 2, we believe that language matters—especially as it may have negative impacts for the client system. We think the language we use to name our models of practice, or the components of those models, is important in influencing and shaping how we do our work.

It is not uncommon for many practice models to start with the idea of conducting a problem assessment or arriving at a diagnosis. Historically, words like *assessment* and *diagnosis* have been commonly understood as things the social worker does to help set and define the goals and interventions associated with social work practice. Hepworth and Larsen (1986) present their views on assessment and diagnosis by noting that "Assessment has been referred to elsewhere (Hollis, 1972) as 'psychosocial diagnosis,' but we have chosen to eschew the term *diagnosis* because of its negative association with symptoms, disease, and dysfunction" (pp. 165–166). They proceed to define assessment as

> *the process of gathering, analyzing, and synthesizing salient data into a formulation that encompasses the following vital dimensions: (1) the nature of the clients' problems, . . . (2) the functioning . . . of clients and significant others, (3) motivation of clients to work on the problems, (4) relevant environmental factors that contribute to the problems, and (5) resources that are available or are needed to ameliorate the clients' difficulties. (p. 166)*

Pincus and Minahan (1973) refer to the worker doing a "problem assessment" to guide the planned change effort. They go on to note that "[t]he purpose of the worker's problem assessment is to help him understand and individualize the situation he is dealing with and to identify and analyze the relevant factors" (p.102).

Meyer (1976) describes social work assessment as

> *a generic function of social work practice. The assessment process is based upon a triumvirate of assumptions. It assumes that all human phenomena are best understood in a multi-causal interacting framework; that the concept of needs and resources reflects the intentions, purposes, and values of the social work profession; and that person-in-situation can effectively become the vehicle for selection of the unit of attention. (cited in Vigilante and Mialick, 1985, p. 35)*

In the work of influencing, modifying, and creating resources in the social context, social workers *proceed through a series of steps designed to gather as much useful information about the problem as can be made available. The steps involved in compiling this information include: (1) identifying an organizational or community condition; (2) collecting supporting data; (3) identifying barriers to condition resolution; and (4) determining whether the condition is seen as (or can be made to be seen as) a problem. (Netting, Kettner, and McMurtry, 1993, p. 204)*

While most social work authors seem to prefer the word *assessment,* often for reasons similar to those of Hepworth and Larsen (1986) outlined above, the issue of diagnosis as a first step remains with us. The state of West Virginia recently established the "Clinical Social Worker" level within its licensing law. Like other states, such as Florida and Maine, social workers must present a minimum of three graduate credits in psychopathology to qualify for this level.

A primary tool for understanding issues associated with psychopathology (at least in the traditional mental health sense) and, increasingly, a requirement for receiving third-party payments from insurance companies or other programs like Medicaid or Medicare is the *Diagnostic and Statistical Manual of Mental Disorders* (DSM-IV), published by the American Psychiatric Association (1994). The increasing dependence upon this tool to secure funding is an area of concern for some social workers, and an important issue for the social work profession to address. (We discuss the DSM-IV in more depth later in this chapter.)

If social workers use the DSM-IV, or more traditional methods of analysis, they will be looking at different variables than if they are also considering the context and the person-in-situation. In the traditional approach, it is the worker who is doing the diagnosis or assessment, with the role of the client system generally seen as merely providing the raw materials (information) for the expert to make the diagnosis.

Assessment from an empowerment perspective is different. Miley, O'Melia, and DuBois (1995) discussed assessment as a process of discovery, especially the discovery of resources. Assessment also includes the social systems of which the client system is a part. As identified at length in Chapter 3, we propose a framework for assessment of the client system's locality, which encompasses the characteristics of geography and natural resources; history, traditions, and culture; and social, economic, and political structures. With knowledge of these aspects of locality—in the context of the client system's experience—the social worker is able to join more clearly and comprehensively with the client system in exploration of the story.

Exploring the Story

In the process of exploring the story, both the client system and the social worker are jointly engaged in discovering meaning and uncovering places to start work. In this sense, assessment is the appropriate term, as long as assessment is a joint process.

Both the client system and the worker bring knowledge to this process. The client system is the expert on his or her situation, knowing it far better than anyone else. The social worker brings professional expertise: the ability to generalize from other situations, the ability to relate knowledge about social systems, human behavior, and system interactions, and the ability to provide an outside perspective from which to view the situation.

We think telling and exploring the story is essential, for the following reasons:

• *Exploring the story lessens the tendency for workers, especially new workers, to "jump to solution."* One of the virtues of process and planned change models is that they force the worker to refrain from leaping immediately to remedies or solutions to concerns. Our experience is that the most common mistake that social work students doing role-play simulations make is that they want to start suggesting alternative solutions within 45 seconds or a couple of minutes of the time the client system in a role-play starts to describe the situation.

In a "Calvin" cartoon, Calvin, a 6- or 7-year-old, is sitting behind a cardboard box on which is crudely lettered "CANDID OPINIONS." When a female classmate comes by, Calvin tells her, "You're a bat-faced, bug-eyed, booger-nosed, baloney-brained, beetle-butt." In the last frame, Calvin and the box are demolished. He mutters, "This volunteer social work just isn't for me." The kind of advice and suggestions that beginners can give are not as bad as Calvin's (so much for volunteer social work), but it can be inappropriately premature, nonetheless. Emphasizing the need to hear and explore the story lessens the likelihood that students will be leapfrogging to solution of the concern.

• *Exploring the story enables the worker and client system to understand the present situation as a continuation of the client system's life experience.* Gerald Caplan (1974) writes about how, in doing crisis intervention or in working with people who have been hospitalized for mental distress, we see only the person in crisis who is not functioning well. Our tendency is to not see the person as someone who has functioned well in other times of his or her life.

A family seeking help in despair over a teen who's running away and a parent's alcohol abuse may have been a family that "worked" at other times. It is important for both the worker and the client system to understand there have been times when functioning was different as well as to recognize the events, actions, and/or forces that have contributed to the difficulties the family is currently experiencing.

Beloit, Wisconsin, a city of about 35,000, has a number of pressing concerns. The unmarried pregnancy rate for African Americans is among the highest in the nation, and there are concerns about drug abuse, gangs, and persistent poverty in central-city neighborhoods. In working with this community, it is important to know that the central city was made up of thriving, working-class neighborhoods 30 years ago. The industries in Beloit paid good wages, and one wage earner could support a family. But the loss of many manufacturing jobs over the years has been a major factor in the decline of these neighborhoods. Knowing the history, or story, of these areas is essential in understanding that things were not always as they are today.

• *Exploring the story enables the worker to understand (or begin to understand) the world view of the client system as a foundation for building a helping relationship.* Individuals and groups experience wellness and disease, happiness and mental distress, within the framework of their world view. Assisting the client system to reveal the story with much detail enhances the worker's understanding of the client system's world view.

As social workers, we try to act in ways so our own biases and world views do not get in the way of our work with client systems. As professional social workers, we are ethically bound not to let our personal world view inappropriately dominate how we come to understand the world view of the client system. Yet, as humans we know that it is impossible to be truly objective—that who we are and what we have experienced shapes our view of the world. The following are examples of the difficulty of understanding the world view of others.

1. A study by Davidson and Jenkins (1989) of policies and practices in battered women's shelters illustrates the ways in which our past experiences and upbringing affect how we see the life and life options of others.

    Staff members can begin to develop an understanding of the world as women from the working class see it—for example, a battered woman's reluctance to embrace independence, single parenthood, or feminism as personal goals. Although shelter staff members may see these goals as synonymous with violence-free living, working class residents may aspire to nonviolence without any enthusiasm for the other goals mentioned. Staff members must be realistic about future prospects for women entering society as single heads of households, walking the thin line between "cheerleading" to encourage women toward success and fatalism about their chances to be successful in an economically hostile society. (p. 494)

2. According to Denton (1990), many social workers have trouble working with families who are religious fundamentalists. This may be in part due to the values of many social workers that are not consistent with fundamentalist churches and to the concerns with ideologies that stress dominance of the church over the family and men over women. Yet, members of fundamentalist churches derive things of value from their church attendance and membership.

    Fundamentalist churches, like other social organizations, can be an important source of social support. They often provide members with a sense of belongingness and spiritual direction that helps them become clearer about the values and norms by which they wish to live. A study of marriage and family therapists in North Carolina found that, in effective therapy with members of fundamentalist churches, it was important to "first gain an understanding of the fundamentalist family's belief system and then frame interventions which use these beliefs to reinforce treatment" (Denton, 1990, p. 9).

3. Another way in which world view differences may exist between social worker and client system is found in this reflection of a social worker on her experiences in the first year of working in a residential setting for juvenile offenders—13- to 16-year-olds whose behavior had been judged dangerous enough for them to be incarcerated outside of their own communities.

What seems obvious to us is not always obvious to them. Because of their backgrounds, which can include neglect and abuse, being moved around a lot, being in foster homes, many don't know what feelings are. In an Anger Management group, it's clear that many of the boys are only in touch with being angry or happy—not any other emotions. When we ask "How are you feeling today?", they don't know how to respond. They also have high level reactions to a low level criticism; what we see as "constructive criticism" is interpreted as being "punked" or put down, as a personal attack on who they are. (Wolf, 1994)

One indication that we are making the transition from viewing situations from our own personal perspective to viewing them as professional is when we start to understand that others may interpret a situation differently than we do. We still may not understand how they happen to experience the world, how a world view different from our own functions. But when we don't understand another's world view, we can seek clarification.

Our knowledge of human behavior in the social environment provides us with a framework from which to ask questions to foster understanding. For example, we may ask parents about the nature of their social support system, based upon on our understanding of the role of a strong social support system in preventing child abuse. Or, our understanding of social systems theory may lead us to ask a local minister about the probable reaction of the local community to having a new domestic violence shelter established there. Failure to explore this carefully may result in the expenditure of scarce resources to acquire property, only to have the community mount a campaign against the placement of the shelter. Knowing enough to know what more we need to know is an important first step.

• *Exploring the story enables both the worker and the client system to listen for and identify strengths, resources, and opportunities that can be of use in working on the issue.* Careful listening to the story can yield more than a better understanding of the world view of another. In their book *Women's Ways of Knowing,* Belenky et al. (1986) challenge teachers to "tune their ears" to listen for the stages of intellectual development of their students, so that the teachers can respond to their students appropriately.

Similarly, we ask social workers to tune their ears to listen for the resources and strengths in the current situation and behaviors as well as in past accomplishments and successes; and to be aware of areas of life in which the client system is functioning well, of people in the support system who are potential resources, and of other actual and potential strengths. By clearly hearing the client system's strengths, resources, and accomplishments, the social worker can help the client system reclaim ownership of them for use in the work phase.

• *Exploring the story enables the worker and client system to listen for ways in which the client system processes information and experiences.* Humans have amazing abilities to hear what we want to hear and only accept information that fits within our perception of reality. As we listen closely to client system stories, we may hear the instances in which distortions could occur in the way messages are given and/or received.

David Burns (1980) provides us with a framework for identifying distortions in the messages we give to ourselves about the events and situations in our lives, and then for creating messages that challenge these distortions in order to respond in a more effective way. This framework of cognitive restructuring is based on the premise that the messages we give ourselves about a situation or event influence how we feel about that situation or event and ultimately determine how we behave in relation to it. He clarifies this with regard to

> [t]he relationship between the world and the way you feel. It is not the actual events but our perceptions that result in changes in mood. . . . [The world is] a series of positive, neutral and negative events. . . . You interpret the events with a series of thoughts that continually flow through your mind. This is called your internal dialogue. . . . Your feelings are created by your thoughts and not the actual events. All experiences must be processed through your brain and given a conscious meaning before you experience any emotional response. (p. 30)

Burns (1980) identifies ten basic ways in which thoughts might be distorted, illustrated in Box 5.1. The challenge for the social worker and the client system is to identify the distortions that may exist in thought patterns and develop a reframing or challenge for the distortion. For example, a challenge for all-or-nothing thinking ("I can't do anything right" in response to flubbing an oral presentation) might be, "Nobody's so perfect as to be all bad." A way of reframing the feeling of total imperfection might be, "I may have flubbed this presentation; however, I had the courage to try. I am proud of myself for putting the work into it that I did."

• *Exploring the story enables the worker and client system to understand the present situation as contextually relevant and as shaped by the changing context.* In Chapters 1 and 3, we proposed that personal or systemic conditions need to be understood within the context of the locality, the nation, and the world. As client systems tell their stories, we hear information that can help them and us put their concerns in perspective.

Perspective is shaped by the contexts most relevant to the client system. A family is shaped by its experience as a family within a larger family network, within the neighborhood, the position of that neighborhood within the larger community, and so on. Similarly, community, as the client system, is influenced by its context, which includes its relations with the economic sector, the county government, the state, and beyond.

To fully understand the issues and concerns of the client system, both the social worker and the client system need to place these concerns within the changing contexts. For example, a small county that has just lost 1000 decent-paying jobs over the past year is faced with the challenges of understanding and responding to the fears and sadness of workers who have built houses, raised families, and otherwise connected themselves in the community. Faced with an uncertain future, it is not surprising to keep hearing stories of anxiety and stress in local families. This story is also best understood within the national

BOX 5.1

Ten Basic Thought Distortions

1. ALL-OR-NOTHING THINKING: You see things in black-and-white categories. If your performance falls short of perfect, you see yourself as a total failure.

2. OVER-GENERALIZATION: You see a single negative event as a never-ending pattern of defeat.

3. MENTAL FILTER: You pick out a single negative detail and dwell on it exclusively so that your vision of all reality become[s] darkened, like a drop of ink that discolors the entire beaker of water.

4. DISQUALIFYING THE POSITIVE: You reject positive experiences by insisting they "don't count" for some reason or other.

In this way you can maintain a negative belief that is contradicted by your everyday experiences.

5. JUMPING TO CONCLUSIONS: You make a negative interpretation even though there are no definite facts that convincingly support your conclusion.

   a. *Mind reading.* You arbitrarily conclude that someone is reacting negatively to you, and you don't bother to check this out.

   b. *The fortune-teller error.* You anticipate that things will turn out badly, and you feel convinced that your prediction is an already-established fact.

story of redefining work away from having a full-time career with the same employer.

• *Exploring the story enables the worker and client system to understand the connections between their story and the national superstory.* One useful way to assist client systems in discovering opportunities to exercise influence or control within their issues of concern is to make efforts at linking their story with the stories of others and the national superstory. The superstory is the story of the society in which client systems find themselves and includes the myths and beliefs about the nation-state's place in the world, including the rights and obligations it carries.

The superstory may be experienced as positive or negative, depending upon the ways client systems perceive their place within the society. For example, many current multicultural historians express concern about the United States' superstory as only a reflection of a Eurocentric world view and rightfully note that important contributions by minority subgroups such as American Indian, African American, and Mexican American peoples are largely ignored in defining who we are. An obvious consequence of this practice is to lose the rich

6. MAGNIFICATION (CATASTRO-PHIZING) OR MINIMIZATION: You exaggerate the importance of things (such as your goof-up or someone else's achievement), or you inappropriately shrink things until they appear tiny (your own desirable qualities or the other fellow's imperfections). This is called the "binocular trick."

7. EMOTIONAL REASONING: You assume that your negative emotions necessarily reflect the way things really are: "I feel it, therefore it must be true."

8. SHOULD STATEMENTS: You try to motivate yourself [and others] with shoulds and shouldn'ts, as if you [or the other] had to be whipped and punished before you [or they] could be expected to do anything. "Musts" and "oughts" are also offenders. The emotional consequence is guilt. When you direct *should* statements toward others, you feel anger, frustration, and resentment.

9. LABELING AND MISLABELING: This is an extreme form of overgeneralization. Instead of describing your error, you attach a negative label to yourself: "I'm a *loser.*" When someone else's behavior rubs you the wrong way, you attach a negative label to him: "He's a . . . *louse.*" Mislabeling involves describing an event with language that is highly colored and emotionally loaded.

10. PERSONALIZATION: You see yourself as the cause of some negative external event, which in fact you were not primarily responsible for.

Source: Burns (1980, pp. 42–43).

contributions of these groups to our present and to deny members of the subgroups access to valuable historical information as well as place them in second-class and oppressed citizenship roles. As stated by Adrienne Rich (1986), "When someone with the authority of a teacher, say, describes the world and you are not in it, there is a moment of psychic disequilibrium, as if you looked into a mirror and saw nothing" (p. 199). A challenge that remains for the United States is to take more seriously the need to embrace and affirm the contributions of our diverse membership to our story. In this sense, when we leave out the history and traditions of some of our members, we are all the poorer for this omission.

People in need or in crisis tend to think that not only are they the only ones in the situation but also that they are entirely the cause of their predicament. In my work with families experiencing homelessness, I (Jim) use the handout illustrated in Box 5.2. It has proved useful in enabling the adults to understand their situation as connected to larger realities.

Access to perspectives that illustrate the way in which personal situations are connected to the big picture can become a source for feeling empowered and valued within the society. Similarly, being able to link the client system's story with

BOX 5.2

National Changes That Contribute to Homelessness

INCOME

- One-quarter of women and a tenth of all men are in low-paying jobs.

- Wages for manufacturing jobs have gone down almost 10% in real dollars since 1975; family income for all but the well-off has stayed the same or gone down.

- AFDC benefits nationally in real dollars are 40% less than they were 20 years ago.

DOMESTIC VIOLENCE

- Over 5000 women are battered by their husbands/male partners each day; the rates of child abuse are higher.

- Approximately 40% of all homeless women are fleeing abuse.

HOUSING

- Rental costs for housing have gone up 13% in real dollars in the last 20 years.

- In most large cities, there are twice as many low-income renters as there are affordable apartments.

- A modest two-bedroom apartment rents for more than a monthly AFDC benefit for a family of three.

GOVERNMENTAL SUPPORT FOR HOUSING

- Federal funds for housing programs have been cut over 80% in real dollars since 1978—funds continue to be cut.

- Only 36% of all poor households receive any form of housing assistance.

- Tax subsidies to the upper and middle class are more than four times as much as what the federal government spends on low-income housing.

Being homeless is more common than most people think. At least 7% of all adults in the United States have been homeless at some point in their lives; 13% have either been homeless or "doubled up" with a relative or friend.

others, especially in contextually relevant ways, can be a powerful mechanism for taking action on issues of concern. Client systems who know they are not alone in their struggles and challenges find support to act. As identified by Germain (1991), a significant association exists between social ties and personal well-being.

One role of the social worker is to assist the client system in connecting with others to reduce the sense of isolation that often can accompany issues that have escalated to the point of crisis. Many years ago while a graduate student in field placement, I (Barry) recall leading a public assistance mothers' group in a large southern city. As the group formed and became a support system, I was struck by how important it was in helping members share their stories and struggles. It became a source of comfort to the members as well as a part of their coping network. Information was exchanged about what worked and what didn't, and the members were constantly reminded that they were not alone with their concerns. By the end of the time-limited group, these women had established relationships that went with them as they lived in their neighborhoods and continued to operate independently of the service agency that had sponsored the group.

We think helping client systems claim their legitimate roles as citizens is an important one that social workers can support. Examples of how this can be done include providing information about benefits, opportunities, and responsibilities associated with the client system's issues of concern. In Phase Three, when we talk more about taking action, we will return to this issue in discussing the social worker as advocate.

- *Exploring the story enables the worker and client system to identify the focus of the change efforts.* The client system with whom you are working may or may not be the focus of change. We have defined competence as the ability to influence one's life and the lives of significant others. Competence-oriented social work practice would seek to extend that range of influence, which can include targeting systems that are limiting to people, and that are important to a person, family, or organization. In the example in the previous chapter where a group of mothers started out with their own parenting issues and moved to successfully sue the school board, we see how the focus shifted from personal concerns to include more systemic issues.

- *Exploring the story can facilitate an understanding of the story for the worker and the client system.* In talking in detail both about tough times and about the times when things were going well, the client system's life situation in all its complexity can emerge. This is invaluable not only for the social worker but also often for the client system, who might not have considered the situation in quite this way.

A new awareness or understanding often places the concern in a new light that makes it possible for the concern to be seen as more manageable within the client system's resources. When this occurs, the client system often experiences a sense of competence that leads to action.

- *Exploring the story provides a foundation for describing a preferred reality and taking action.* "Strategies are both plans for the future and patterns from the past" (Mintzberg, 1989). The unfolding story can be a means for identifying and examining the patterns from the past and their use in the present, as well as their potential in helping to shape the future. To use another metaphor, in exploring the story the social worker and client system can become aware of what roads still need to be traveled. The point to all of this is that, as we come to greater understanding of the issues and concerns, we are in a better position to state the preferred reality. This reality becomes more possible where we are able to build linkages with past patterns that have worked and that support the desired outcomes. As we stated in Chapter 2, we can learn to identify strengths and possibilities as we listen to client systems speak.

Benefits of a Well-Explored Story

Story exploration is the basis for the work that is to follow in other phases of our model. If we do not obtain a well-grounded understanding of the story, we may be confronted with a shifting-sands quandary where, just when we think we know something to be true, the sand settles in a new area and we realize that we are not in touch with the issue or issues of concern for the client system.

We do not mean to suggest that the client system's story is perfectly knowable; the reality is that it is probably not. Our challenge is to explore with client systems their story as much as is possible within the constraints of the situation. It is possible through our careful listening and reflective talking that we can come to a level of understanding that makes work possible.

We do believe that we can know another to the point that trust is established, a critical relationship stage that must be achieved for the story and work to unfold. As the story emerges, the trust that develops as we communicate our interest in understanding results in a mutual respect that facilitates our working together with the client system.

While this phase of the model is likely to be the focus of the social worker and client system at varying times throughout the relationship-building and change process, there are tangible outcomes of a well-explored story early in the process that facilitate movement to imagining a preferred reality.

1. There will be increased understanding of how the past has moved into the present in influencing and shaping the story. Often client systems present themselves to the social worker in a state of crisis. The social worker should not lose sight of the whole story. Thus, when the time is appropriate, the social worker can assist client systems (who may have lost sight of their past capacities and experiences), through revealing, identifying, and reclaiming these resources and strengths, in choosing how to act and in managing the issue of concern.

2. This phase of work provides the social worker with the opportunity to facilitate the creation of a relationship that communicates a concern and respect for the client system's dignity, humanness, and well-being. Such demonstration should result in the client system's perception of the social worker as someone worthy of some measure of trust.

3. Finally, this phase should provide both the social worker and the client system with some agreement on the locus of change. As noted above, the focus of change can be internal (within the client system) or external to the client system (within other systems with whom the client system interacts), or both. Once this is known, there can be an awareness of what can be influenced, of what is more resistant to change at a particular point in time, and of the readiness to change and to exercise the influence that is available to the client system in the situation.

Starting Where the Client Is

Most books on social work remind the reader, "Start where the client is." Others would add, "but don't leave them there!" We would agree with this and add, "Start where the client is *and act with them!*"

We concur with de Shazer (1991) that full understanding is rarely possible, yet "good action" is possible. We can find an explanation for concerns or situations if we try hard enough to do so, but that may not move us closer to managing the situation.

For the change process to be effective, it must come from the client system. This is a profound idea on which it is often very difficult to act. Part of the difficulty comes from how we view the expert in our society (more about this later) and the idea that client systems who seek help are not able or do not know how to address their concerns. Story exploration, done with genuine respect and a desire to better understand, makes it possible for the client system and the social worker to envision the next steps and to have the courage to take action.

Focusing on changes that are desired by the participants, the heart of Phase Two of our process, is applicable to working with systems of all sizes and is best done as a collaborative process with client systems, community members, and workers. Both the process and the outcome components of change are enhanced when we listen to and involve client systems and community members in planning. Consider these examples from Melaville and Blank (1993) of programs that were shaped without listening to and participating with client systems in program development.

> *A Central Harlem adult literacy program has far fewer students than expected. Residents confided to a home visitor that they were too embarrassed to participate. They wanted to learn to read, but tutoring was done in the main room of the branch library where everyone, including their children's friends, would see them and know that they were illiterate.*
>
> *A mentoring program could not involve young Latina girls because service providers underestimated parental concerns about their daughters' safety. Although very interested in joining, the girls could not convince their parents that they would be safe going to a community center after school and spending*

time with strangers. The parents had not been invited to meet the potential mentors, and the only communication between the school and parents was a formal permission slip written in English.

Health care providers in some communities experience lower-than-expected treatment success rates because they fail to work with key family members. Family involvement is often necessary to ensure the best home care and follow-up. At the same time, health care providers need to realize that parents or children are not always the primary caregiver. In many Southeast Asian cultures, for example, a senior member of the extended family, rather than a parent or child, may be in charge of family health matters. In many African American families, grandmothers, aunts, or other family members may be the key persons.

Substance abuse programs that are not sensitive to gender issues overlook the special conflicts women face in getting help. Many women who abuse drugs also have been physically and sexually abused by men and are often unwilling to enter a program staffed largely by males.

The parent who may approach the child protection social worker about giving up his or her child is met with stony silence because our national story precludes our hearing this as anything other than dysfunction or pathology. (p. 11)

In all of these situations, if the persons who were to receive the service had been involved with the planning, it is unlikely that the services would have been planned in the same fashion.

These stories also point up a common dilemma faced by social workers. We will often have programs designed or policy decisions made that do not have client systems' voices as part of the process. If we know that this will present difficulties, we have an ethical obligation to act.

The NASW Code of Ethics (1996) reminds us that we hold the rights of client systems to be primary. If we take this responsibility seriously, then we are obligated to act in order to encourage and support the inclusion of client systems' experiences and views in agency decision making.

In some agencies, administrators and key decision makers such as board members may not be social workers. Therefore, it is vital that we act in ways that educate these decision makers about the need to facilitate the inclusion of client system perspectives in decision-making processes.

Values, Knowledge, and Skills for Story Exploration

Stating why it is important to explore the story and knowing how to explore the story with client systems are not identical. There is a Spanish proverb, "It is not the same to talk of bulls as to be in the bullring." The values, knowledge, and skills presented below aid the social work practitioner in working with the client system to effectively explore the story.

It seems obvious to us that there are differences between values, knowledge, and skills, and yet the distinctions between these are not clear-cut. The way in which one values and honors the client system's right to seek help depends on skill level, and there is a knowledge base implicit in the value and skill components. However, at least for purposes of organization, we have divided a number of important attributes of social work practice into these categories.

Values

Values that are especially important in this phase of practice include: respecting the dignity of the client system, valuing the unique views and beliefs of the client system, and affirming the rights of and exploring opportunities for the client system. Professional values inform the NASW Code of Ethics (1996), which is an important guide to professional practice.

In the Code of Ethics, Standard 1, "The Social Worker's Ethical Responsibility to Clients," section 1.01, places the interests of the client system as the primary concern for the social worker. Without the careful exploration of the client system's story, we do not know how to do this.

Below we discuss other values that we feel support and guide effective practice in Phase One.

- *Honoring the client system's right to seek help.* The intersection of personal and societal values makes it difficult for many people to seek help. To have to ask for help from a stranger or from a social welfare or social service agency is incredibly difficult. A person has to admit, at that point in time, that he or she is having trouble making it—an admission that is difficult to make, especially in a society in which individualism is revered and many believe that "God helps those who help themselves." In many respects, this is one area where the social work profession has set itself apart from the general society.

Our values prize help seeking. While it may be easy for some to say that is because our jobs are dependent on having client systems, we doubt that is the real reason! Social work honors help seeking because we believe it is a client system right. Indeed, knowing that one desires to work with a social worker on an issue or concern is a strength.

Finally, we also know that none of us are truly self-sufficient. This latter point may be a difficult one to believe in a society that prizes individualism. However, we would ask you to reflect for a moment on the issue of true self-sufficiency and name how you are fully capable of independently meeting your needs for belonging, safety, food, clothing, shelter, and esteem. To belong requires others. We depend on others to produce the materials and goods we desire. Esteem is shaped by the interaction of self with other. In short, we depend on others for our existence and well-being.

People who need aid with shelter or money are not generally valued. There used to "just" be a stigma about applying for welfare, Food Stamps, or public housing. The vilification of welfare has increased in the mid-1990s. In the Personal Responsibility Act of the "Contract with America," it is stated that "government programs designed to give a helping hand have instead bred illegitimacy, crime, illiteracy, and more poverty" (Gillespie and Schallas, 1994, p. 65). Describing benefits for people needing assistance in these terms makes it even more difficult for people to consider applying for aid when they need it.

When I (Jim) work with parents who are experiencing homelessness, they often say, "I'm not like those people on welfare. I really need the help!" In many cases, it is difficult for them to see themselves as being in need of assistance, as they have bought into the stereotypes of welfare recipients and their situation does not mirror that image.

• *Valuing the fact that it is very difficult to ask for help and to consider changing.* In his book *Giving and Taking Help,* Alan Keith-Lucas (1972) states that it is important to realize that many people who ask for help in actuality do not want to be helped. What explains this apparent contradiction? Keith-Lucas believes that a fear exists about getting help.

> *We can understand this fear better, perhaps, if we consider what asking for help demands. The person who asks for the kind of help that will really make a difference to him must, in fact, do four things. He must recognize that something is wrong with or lacking in the situation which he can do nothing about by himself. He must be willing to tell someone else about his . . . [difficulties]. He must accord to this other person at least a limited right to tell him what to do or to do things for him. And finally he must be willing to change in some way himself. This means giving up whatever adjustments he has been able to make to his present situation—adjustments that may have and probably have cost him a great deal to make and have become part of himself and wholly necessary to him—in favor of a new kind of life, which he may have some reason to believe will be more satisfactory but which, at the same time, is an unknown quantity, full of possible dangers. (p. 20)*

We do not wish to suggest that all people come to the helping experience with this view. However, it is important that the social worker appreciate the probable existence of this fear and be prepared to work with the client system in exploring and managing it.

Client systems seeking help reluctantly, or involuntarily, who are invited to be there and are received with dignity and respect, may be able to reframe their views about help seeking and move more quickly into a positive exploration of their story. Social workers who understand the challenges in seeking help, as well as the privilege they have in being sought out to help, will be in a better position to serve the client system who experiences these concerns.

• *Respecting client systems' right to self-determination as they construct their own meaning of their own experiences.* In Chapter 2, we wrote about the centrality of self-determination. This can be *positive* self-determination—having the knowledge, skills, and resources needed to pursue one's own goals—or *negative* self-determination—being forced, coerced, or made under undue pressure or influence to take action.

We believe self-determination starts before action in affirming the right of persons and groups to construct their own meanings, hopes, and dreams. For the social worker to fully support this cardinal value, it is necessary to understand the story of the client system's issues and concerns, including how these issues and concerns came into being.

- *Respecting the significance to the client system of the experiences reflected in the story.* A 15-year-old girl in tears because her boyfriend "dumped" her comes into the office of a school social worker. The social worker, from her perspective as an adult as well as a professional, is very certain that this is one of those wounds that time will heal—maybe even pretty quickly. But she honors the pain that is expressed, and responds to it, for the pain at that moment may be as intense for that 15-year-old as it would be if a family member had died.

The social worker's ability to hear the story respectfully is key to enabling a relationship that can lead to productive work. As in the example above, we may often have a story presented to us as a crisis and we know from our experience that it is not. If we are not careful in how we respond to these times and fail to connect with the feelings presented, we may leave the client system feeling discounted.

I (Barry) was recently teaching a graduate research class, which was on the same night after an important meeting the students had about their field placements. As class began, it was apparent that several students were upset. I came to learn that they were confused about a field policy and felt that they might not be able to meet the school's expectations.

I could have ignored their distress because my twenty-plus years at the school have taught me that we do a good job of dealing with the special circumstances that arise from time to time for students. Instead, I chose to explore their concerns and attempted to "clear the air" so that their distress might be acknowledged. This proved to be a wise choice in that several students indicated that they came away with a clearer understanding of policy around their issues, as well as a sense that their concerns were heard and addressed.

The newly adopted Council on Social Work Education Accreditation Standards (1994) pays particular attention to the importance of social workers understanding issues associated with human diversity. Traditionally, this has meant giving attention to issues of oppression and discrimination. From a social justice view, this makes great sense. Oppression and discrimination remain entrenched within our society, and social work has the responsibility to keep itself at the forefront of the challenge to these practices.

The important addition in the accreditation standards is the expectation that social work education will also include content about the positive contributions diverse populations make in our society. Diverse cultures bring strengths that require recognition in the helping process, as well as talents important to the quality of life of the community. Social workers need to be comfortable with and respectful of difference in seeking to understand the client system's story.

- *Hearing the strengths, competencies, and possibilities in the story.* One of the most powerful applications of the strengths perspective to social work practice is the reframing and reorientation of our way of looking at client systems' lives so that we are not focusing on pathologies. A mutual help organization that focuses on persons with mental illness, GROW, helps its members view difficulties not as hurdles but as opportunities, as reflected in the following verse:

Mostly, when things go wrong,
They're meant to go wrong—
So we can outgrow
What we have to outgrow
You've got a problem? That's good!
(Rapaport, Reischl, and Zimmerman, 1992, p. 89)

Communicating this value to client systems whose degree of self-oppression is high can be difficult. Without denying their reality that things are really bad at the present, it is vital that we treat people with dignity—as people of value and worth—and address the possibilities as well as the pain in the present situation.

• *Controlling one's own biases.* All of us are influenced by our own biases and beliefs. As Nurius and Gibson (1990) state:

[beliefs, values, and theories] generate certain expectations that are used to filter relevant from irrelevant information, and to read or assign meaning held in events and behavior. . . . These cognitive building blocks thereby play an enormously influential role. They not only produce selective attention to cues and events consistent with expectations, but also fuel active searches for expected input from the social environment and discount or overlook informa-tion or possibilities inconsistent with expectations and proclivities. (p. 20)

While holding biases may be unavoidable, one can control them by careful attention. One way to do this is to think about one's thinking, to carefully reflect on one's actions and words and the biases that may lurk therein. If we start with the assumption that we all have biases and prejudices we have acquired in our lives (from family, friends, and a society that in subtle and not-so-subtle ways is permeated by prejudice), then we have the necessary precondition of awareness that leads to action for preventing our biases from burdening the client system. In writing this book, the authors have learned from each other to look at our words and actions that may have been racist or sexist in ways we were not aware.

When we increase our knowledge about the group (or condition) with whom we are working, we are less subject to "old husbands' tales" or media images for our base of reference. Later in this chapter, we will introduce several tools that client systems (with the worker's assistance) can use to gain an additional perspective on a particular situation. As we gain more information about client systems and their contexts, we are able to attend more to who the client system is and less to our preconceived notions about who the client system is or should be.

Knowledge

The etymology, or root meaning, of the word *knowledge* comes from the Old English words for "know" and "lock." When we speak of knowledge, we're not referring just to facts and information learned at some point in time, but to information that has been integrated and internalized into a view of the world or an understanding of a particular situation. For example, I (Jim) clearly remember the first time I came across Kübler-Ross's stages of grieving (1969). As I learned about the grieving process, I became aware that it was okay to "get mad with God" when someone important to you had died. I understood grieving as a natural human process. This knowledge has affected the way I approach situations of loss ever since.

While it is appropriate to use knowledge to understand and work with situations more effectively, it is equally important to make sure it fits the context in which you wish to use it. Sometimes, as illustrated by the following story, the theory that explained similar events in other contexts may not apply.

Leola Furman (1994) has been actively studying social work and spirituality for the past few years and shared the following story of her experience. After her husband died, her faith was a source of comfort and support. Many social workers she met who knew of her recent loss operated from an assumption that she had to be angry with God for taking her husband, when in actuality she was not. We need to check out our assumptions before jumping to conclusions with them. Knowing differing interpretations helps us ask encouraging and clarifying questions so we do not drive client systems away as a result of our misunderstanding.

Forms of Knowledge   The specific knowledge that will be needed in Phase One clearly varies from situation to situation.

> *Without loss of commitment to the client's unique perspective on his or her personality, relationships, and social situation, and so as to have a frame of reference for understanding the client, practitioners of a profession must draw upon general knowledge about the class of clients of which the particular client may be a representative, and about the general nature of the problems indicated in the case. The reliance upon general knowledge to help explain a unique case situation is one of the distinguishing features of a professionally educated vs. a volunteer or agency-trained worker. (Meyer, 1993, p.10)*

Remembering the uniqueness of each client system with whom we work is important; yet, in each phase of our work, there are some forms of common knowledge that can be helpful. In thinking about understanding the story, such knowledge might include: knowledge about how to communicate effectively, knowledge of the context of the client system, knowledge of initial contacts and forming relationships, knowledge of social systems, and knowledge of various helping roles. Examples of the kind of knowledge that is useful to the social worker include the following:

• *Learning from people and communities who have experienced similar situations.* In many respects, the real experts on how to survive and even triumph in stressful or dangerous situations are the people who have experienced those situations. How we do this with client systems is important. When we share others' stories so the client system may benefit from them, we need to be careful not to violate confidentiality or minimize the experiences of the client system with whom we are working. This is an important way to communicate empathy and demonstrate trustworthiness.

Asking the client system to talk about others they may know who have had similar experiences can aid in identifying possible resources in their networks. Thinking about the struggles of others with our issues and concerns can be a source of hope as we think about how we wish to manage our troubles.

A child welfare agency in Alaska identified a lack of attention to native cultures in its service provision. To remedy this, the agency integrated a Cultural Awareness Program, staffed by an Alaskan native, into its program planning and staff development and instituted culturally specific activities and counseling for native children. The native children responded positively to these efforts, and staff could see that they were having an impact.

Unexpectedly, some children of non-native origin began to develop an interest in these cultural activities. The stories of native Alaskans' ways of coping, surviving, and triumphing had something to teach the youth. Carroll (1986) stated that they (and we) could learn much from the Eskimo's knowledge of human development and survival in an environment of climatic harshness, the Aleut's willingness to survive irrespective of the savagery of more powerful forces, and the Eskimo's belief that children belong to everyone.

Secondary information, that which has already been compiled by another organization, can assist us in learning about the experiences of people and communities, albeit in a statistically based fashion. An examination of data from the United States census and from local agencies can yield information on indicators for measuring the status of a number of different populations within a community or region. It provides greater clarity when these indicators are differentiated by relevant categories such as age, gender, income, household composition, and ethnic and minority group membership. As an example, the indicators that might be useful for measuring the status of children and families are listed in Box 5.3.

• *Understanding the effects of help seeking on some persons.* In the previous section on values, we discussed how it was difficult and stressful for people to seek help because of the stigma and/or the pain involved in change. When I (Jim) was working at a settlement house in Ohio some years ago, we had a small amount of emergency aid that could be granted. Invariably, on Friday afternoons after 4:00 p.m., one or two persons would show up, needing money or facing immediate eviction or some other crisis.

At the time, I was young and unmarried, and originally was angry with people showing up with complicated situations at a time when I did not want to delay my Friday night plans. When I realized that, in some cases, people had known for a couple of days that they were going to need assistance and were putting off seeking help because it was so difficult to admit the need, then I was able to stop blaming and understand the behavior.

Some client systems learn that the way to get help is to scream. A social worker at a hospital was asked to meet with a mother who was new to the community and had a daughter with mental retardation and a serious health problem. When the mother did not like the fact that the social worker did not have an immediate answer for one of her questions, she complained to the administration. Even though the social worker had followed up by providing the mother with the

BOX 5.3

Indicators for Measuring the Status of Children and Families

- poverty rate
- literacy or basic skills level
- student mobility rate
- primary grade retention
- number of people on day care waiting lists
- number of new and reopened public assistance cases
- percentage of 9th graders who finish the 12th grade on time
- percentage of higher education–bound high school graduates
- immunization rates for young children

- housing mobility rates
- reported and substantiated cases of abuse and neglect
- number of foster care placements
- chronic absenteeism rate and numbers of suspensions from school
- youth unemployment figures
- voter participation rates
- percentage of substandard housing
- requests of families experiencing homelessness for aid
- percentage of babies with a low birth weight

Source: Melaville and Blank (1993, p. 39).

desired information, the mother's prior experiences elsewhere had taught her that the way to get action was to complain. The social worker's ability to understand this made it possible for her to see the strengths and capacities in this mother and to see her as someone who cared about her daughter rather than as "a problem parent."

- *Having enough knowledge to put the situation in context.* In Chapter 3, we discussed the significance of understanding the context of the client system and the ways in which geography and environment, history, traditions, and culture, and political, economic, and social structures of a locality can influence how people see the world and what they see as possible. In specific fields of practice, there is important general information that can be very useful in understanding and helping a client system gain a fresh perspective on the situation.

Parents of young children, especially of a first child, often have difficulty realizing whether a child's behavior is normal or a cause for concern. According to the noted child development expert Burton White (1975), if a child does not speak at 18 months, that's not troubling; this is within a normal developmental range. However, if a child doesn't seem to understand what parents are saying at 18 months, the child's hearing needs to be examined immediately. A worker who understands this about child development can provide the information necessary to parents who may have a concern about their child's speech development.

Similarly, parents who come out of abusive families are often concerned (having seen the "cycle of abuse" public service announcements on television) that they will abuse their own children. It is often reassuring for parents to hear the data that, while parents who were abused as children are more than twice as likely as other parents to abuse their own children, less than half of those abused in their childhood years abuse as parents.

Common sense can't help social workers in these situations. They need to acquire the specific knowledge that promotes understanding and to share this understanding with the client system.

This is applicable when working with organizational and community systems as well. Knowledge of the social forces that contribute to social issues and the intervention strategies that have been documented as being effective can be useful when developing programs or engaging in social change and action.

For example, the organizers of the Family Violence Prevention program (with which I [Becky] had the privilege of being associated as a founding mother and board member) soon discovered that there was a pressing need for providing a safe place for recipients of abuse. Our first challenge was to examine the literature to find out what worked and what did not work. One particular question we had was whether or not the location of the safe place was to be made public or kept hidden. Though the findings in the literature were inconclusive (documentation revealed that there were as many benefits to publicizing the location as there were to keeping it hidden), based on our knowledge of the context and the dynamics of abuse, we concluded that the benefits of the public knowing the location of the facility outweighed the difficulties associated with the location being known.

• *Having enough knowledge to ask relevant questions.* There's an old saying, "There's nothing as dangerous as the person who has read only one book." When we know a little about something (one book's worth), there is a tendency to think that we understand more than we do, that we can generalize our information farther than the information warrants.

As we have said, understanding the story requires careful listening by the worker. Equally necessary is the ability to ask "good" questions. Good questions are questions that result in increased understanding by both the client system and the social worker. For example, asking "how you feel about" a specific event, person, or experience may be a good question when the desire is to explore the affective meanings of issues. Unfortunately, this question, used indiscriminately, is the seed corn for numerous social work jokes!

Knowing that a community is a border town, that a family is Latino, or that a person has lost through death several family members close to him or her in the past 14 months does not enable us to completely understand what is going on within the community, the family, or the person. There are too many variations in border towns, within Latino families, and in the ways people react to and experience grief. Through research and investigation, however, we can know of theories, frameworks, and approaches that *may* apply to a given situation. On the basis of this knowledge, we are able to identify areas for exploration and clarification in order to understand and appreciate the uniqueness of client systems. To illustrate, we can ask about the interaction between the residents of the border town and their nonresident neighbors. We can explore with the Latino family the meaning of "family" to them and the influence of extended families and godparents in their family, because often "family" means much more than one's parents and siblings. And we can observe and explore with the grieving person his or her reactions to the losses.

The information that follows may appear out of place. However, our intent in placing it here is to raise a cautionary word about a powerful tool that is widely used within the social work profession and elsewhere, and to remind us to ask relevant questions about the tools we use. The DSM-IV is one of those tools that is best seen as a double-edged sword, in that it facilitates access to funds that support the delivery of certain services like mental health supports and counseling while placing client systems at risk of having to wear a more-or-less permanent label. Given the stigmas and growing use of divisive and derisive labels in our society, we feel a need to present our concerns about this tool.

The DSM-IV   *The Diagnostic and Statistical Manual of Mental Disorders* (fourth edition), or DSM-IV (American Psychiatric Association, 1994), is different from other tools the social worker might use in that the DSM is used exclusively by professionals to diagnose clients' conditions. Other tools such as the ecomap and the genogram (discussed in more detail later in this chapter) are used jointly by the social worker and the client system to discover patterns and information.

In the introduction to the latest version of the DSM, this caveat is provided:

> *Although this volume is titled the* Diagnostic and Statistical Manual of Mental Disorders, *the term* mental disorder *unfortunately implies a distinction between "mental" disorders and "physical" disorders that is a reductionistic anachronism of mind/body dualism. A compelling literature documents that there is much "physical" in "mental" disorders and much "mental" in "physical" disorders. The problem raised by the term "mental" disorders has been much clearer than its solution, and, unfortunately, the term persists in the title of DSM-IV because we have not found an appropriate substitute. (American Psychiatric Association, 1994, p. xxi)*

Recognizing these limitations, advocates for the use of the DSM point to its common use. It is routinely used by mental health professionals, and it is the common language—the *lingua franca*—in writing diagnoses and justifications for treatment for third-party payers.

According to Anello (1992), one-quarter of all social workers use the DSM daily. If social workers in mental health were not familiar with the DSM, they would be out of step, and it would effectively sever their partnership with other professionals. Anello (1992) points out another reason for being conversant with the DSM: "As advocates, social workers should be able to critique and challenge inaccurate evaluations where sufficient evidence is lacking for diagnostic conclusions offered—when expert in the tools of diagnosis" (p. 141).

Critics, on the other hand, identify shortcomings and difficulties in using the DSM:

> *It has five axes—1) a list of "clinical conditions" (a concept that is not defined or explained anywhere in the manual); 2) a list of developmental and personality disorders; 3) physical disorders; 4) a one-digit numerical rating of social stressors; and 5) another numerical scale that represents a global assessment of functioning. Only the first three axes are part of the "official system." Surveys of practitioners have found that most do not use axis four or five, the only two axes that might give the DSM some dimensionality, because the first three axes are merely lists of disorders.*
>
> *But even if most practitioners faithfully used axes four and five, they have serious shortcomings. For instance, single numerical ratings of stressors or single numerical ratings of social or psychological functioning hardly qualify DSM for an assessment of coping capacities, of social networks, of family strengths, of intergenerational ties, of community resources, and so forth. Proponents of DSM quickly and correctly point out that DSM was never intended to include those factors. This is precisely why DSM is inadequate for use by social workers! It does not concern itself with those domains of human functioning that are the* sine qua non *of social work. Social work has a viewpoint that is different than psychiatry's regarding mental health problems, a perspective that is much more focused on interpersonal relationships and social conditions. (Kirk and Hutchins, 1992, pp. 150–151)*

Turecki (1994), a noted child psychiatrist, confides:

> *I'm deeply concerned that diagnostic labels are increasingly applied to normal individual variations in behavior and development. Over the past couple of decades, in sequential editions of the* Diagnostic and Statistical Manual, *the number of mental disorders has expanded considerably. Indeed, the present edition defines pathology so broadly that many of us could find ourselves within its pages. (p. 20)*

The latest edition, for example, includes "developed arithmetic disorder" as one of the new categories.

I (Barry) know of friends or colleagues who have sought therapy or other counseling and have had to have a DSM diagnosis established in order to have their insurance company cover some of the costs associated with seeking help. They have come to me expressing concern and questioning if they were crazy because they now have a diagnosis. I share my doubts about the helpfulness of labels and remind them that the agency professional from whom they had sought help was required to come up with the diagnosis as a way to get paid.

The pervasiveness of the DSM compels social workers to be familiar with its form and use, as well as its limits.

Skills

Skill may be thought of as the ability to act effectively, based on one's knowledge. To increase our knowledge base and thereby our understanding of the story, the following skills are particularly useful: exploring and clarifying, generalizing and individualizing, respecting the client systems' beliefs, enabling the telling of the story, externalizing the concern, using visual aids to tell and understand the story, assessing the community context, and using focus groups to gain information. These skills, used in effective combination, can help us better understand the story. We outline some of them below.

- *Exploring and clarifying the story.* Listening and asking questions are important skills in story exploration and clarification. The social worker invites the client system to share issues and concerns and seeks to facilitate an increased level of clarity and understanding by both parties in the process. Specific techniques like observing verbal and nonverbal behaviors, using appropriate eye contact, actively listening for meanings, communicating accurate emotional tones and responses, and asking relevant questions are useful in this phase.

Reframing issues and concerns is one particularly useful technique in this phase. Reframing helps the social worker and the client system think about issues and concerns in a new light. This communication technique asks that social workers and client systems look at issues and concerns in a different way than that currently being presented. I (Jim) was working with five fifth graders on a creative project. The group was moving slowly, and the students were frustrated with their progresss. I reframed the situation as a function of the group's containing five highly intelligent, strong-willed leaders, and no followers. Group members accepted the reframing, and it helped them accept the pace of their work.

- *Being able to generalize and individualize.* Social work practice cannot be reduced to a set of formulas. This is due not only to the complexity of human behavior and the wide variety of contexts in which people live; it also is related to the way in which rapid social change is transforming the landscape. As Meyer (1993) states:

> *In this last decade of the twentieth century, it is very difficult to find stability in social structures: people, events, lifestyles, ideas, and so on, simply do not stand still long enough for them to be viewed as reliable or permanent. Mobility and change in gender, age, family, work, ethnic, and class roles have so strongly affected American society that they often outdistance one's ability to analyze their impact. This phenomenon may well contribute to the notion that assessment is not possible because it must straddle the two conceptions of uniqueness and generality. How can we determine "what is the matter?" if we don't know what the norm is? (p. 8)*

The challenge, then, for the social work practitioner is to continually work on finding a balance between individualizing client systems and relating this grounded understanding to what is increasingly being learned about people in general and client systems in similar situations.

In discussing individualization, Hepworth and Larsen (1993) note that the social worker "must also enter the other person's world, endeavoring to know how that person experiences life, including thoughts, feelings, world view, daily stresses, joys, hopes, longings, disappointments, hurts, and all of the myriad facts of human experience" (pp. 65–66). A tall order indeed!

• *Respecting client systems' belief systems and inviting them to talk about what is important and life-giving to them.* In most circumstances, people generally only talk about issues they feel are not taboo. Kreutziger (1995) writes, "I . . . discovered that families were often reluctant to talk with professionals about religious matters because of their astuteness regarding the invisible barriers signaled by professionals uncomfortable with this area" (p. 30).

Social workers can use open questions that invite client systems to talk about spiritual or religious issues if they wish. Some examples of the types of questions that might elicit this understanding are:

• What is your source of strength?

• On what is your hope based?

• What gives meaning to your life?

• What do you value most?

When people are willing to talk about these aspects of their lives, it behooves us as social workers to respect alternative ways of looking at sources of strength, healing, and criteria of concerns. While practitioners do not need to hold the same beliefs as the client system, we can enhance our effectiveness by respecting client system beliefs and practices.

• *Enabling client systems to tell their story in ways that are more useful to them.* As Meyer (1993) notes, client systems are not schooled in presenting themselves in an organized or coherent fashion. They may present the situation in a problem-saturated fashion, one in which perhaps there is no possible escape or in which they bear no responsibility for the turn of events. When clients describe their life in incoherent terms, the description fits their perception. As one character says in the movie *Untamed Heart,* "My life makes as much sense as watching 'The Three Stooges' in Spanish."

Howard Goldstein (1984) writes about the way in which clarity can help client systems to redefine their reality:

> *The extent to which clients begin to perceive their circumstances more keenly, find that there are some gaps in their conclusions about how things are, discover the need for more information, or otherwise increase their awareness by a few degrees, would create the need or the prompting to risk taking another view of their version of reality. It needs to be said again that this heightening of consciousness is effected not by a "doing to" but by a doing with. (p. 294)*

Goldstein (1984) asserts that, by our respecting the client system's right to tell the story, the client system feels freer to tell the story. When the social worker explores with the client system areas the client system has not explored before, this process can lead to greater clarity and understanding—and to other avenues to pursue. The worker can also help the client system reframe experiences in ways that are more useful. Living through a painful childhood, for example, can be seen as evidence of survival capacities and skills rather than being marked for life.

In working with involuntary clients, I (Jim) have found that, in the process of the work, the story changes. As people feel more comfortable with a group or worker—the result of effective relationship building—they are able to talk about themselves in ways that admit mistakes and imperfections. It also happens that they may have learned some ways of looking at the world that change their interpretation of their life. One person with whom I was working realized that the sentence he had repeated for years, "I drink a lot because all the males in my family do," didn't have to be true for him for the rest of his life.

• *Externalizing the concern.* One recent approach that has proved useful in helping people think about and tell their story in a useful way is to objectify and externalize the concern. Michael White (White and Epston, 1990), an Australian family therapist, has developed such an approach.

White worked with a number of families with young children who had a concern that was resistant to resolution. The family's description of their situation would become increasingly problem-saturated, and the family's story would revolve around their unsuccessful attempts to manage the concern.

One family that came to White were a couple, Ron and Sue, with a 6-year-old son, Nick. Every day Nick had accidents that soiled his underwear. Over time, the "poo" became Nick's playmate or toy, and he smeared it on walls, flicked it behind cupboards, and hid soiled clothes. The poo had affected the family by isolating Nick from other children. He didn't feel comfortable inviting other children to his house or going to other children's homes for sleepovers.

It affected the parents as well. Sue was questioning her capacity as a parent to the point that she felt like giving up. Ron felt deeply embarrassed and didn't feel that he could talk about the issue with family, friends, and workmates. Ron and Sue focused so much of their attention on the difficulty with poo that they had little energy for each other.

White externalized the concern for the family, asking the family members to map the influence that "Sneaky Poo" was having on them. They discovered that:

1. Although Sneaky Poo always tried to trick Nick into being his playmate, Nick could recall a number of occasions during which he had not allowed Sneaky Poo to outsmart him. These were occasions where Nick could have cooperated by smearing, streaking, or plastering, but declined to do so. He had not allowed himself to be tricked into this.

2. There was a recent occasion during which Sneaky Poo could have driven Sue into a heightened sense of misery, but she resisted and turned on the stereo instead. Also, on these occasions she refused to question her competence as a parent and a person.

3. Ron could not recall an occasion during which he had not allowed the embarrassment caused by Sneaky Poo to isolate him from others. However, after

Sneaky Poo's requirements of him were identified, he did seem interested in the idea of defying these requirements.

4. Some difficulty was experienced in the identification of the influence of family relationships in the life of Sneaky Poo. However, after some discussion, it was established that there was an aspect of Sue's relationship with Nick that she thought she could still enjoy, that Ron was still making some attempts to persevere in his relationship with Nick, and that Nick had an idea that Sneaky Poo had not destroyed all of the love in his relationship with his parents. (White and Epston, 1990, pp. 46–47)

By externalizing the concern, the focus of change became not Nick but Sneaky Poo. White asked the family what they wanted to do to diminish the influence of Sneaky Poo. Nick thought he was ready not to be outsmarted by Sneaky Poo, Sue declared that she wouldn't let Sneaky Poo push her buttons, and Ron said that he would confide in someone about the concern.

Two weeks later, there had only been one minor incident, and Nick said that he had not given in when Sneaky Poo tried to win him back. Ron had talked to a couple of people at work about the situation, and later one of them confided that his child had similar issues. Over time, the family increased their social contacts and Nick was doing better at school and with friends (White and Epston, 1990).

Externalization of the concern is different from projection (the coping mechanism in which there is a denial of ownership of feelings and behaviors and these feelings and behaviors are identified as belonging to another) and more than just reframing a situation. It is a way for client systems to gain control over a situation they have acknowledged as troubling by distancing themselves from the concern (not the person), challenging it, and defeating it (Kilpatrick and Holland, 1995).

• *Using visual images in telling and understanding the story.* People live in social contexts, and to understand reciprocal relationships requires an ecosystems approach. Meyer (1993) explains the value of using graphical representations of situations:

The [ecosystems] perspective requires a dense description of relationships and interconnectedness. This is where the values of words alone can be questioned. Just as when people want to describe a complex event, they "talk with their hands" because they cannot present the event in a linear way, so images do better in describing the interactive, person-in-environment events of a case viewed in an ecosystems perspective. (p. 266)

Two common tools useful for better visualizing and understanding the context of the client system are the genogram and the ecomap.

A genogram is a tool that is somewhat like a drawing of a family tree. The family is asked to draw the history of the family going back at least two generations and to present the history of family patterns using a set of defined symbols (see Figure 5.1). This enables the family and the social worker to visualize how relationships have evolved as well as to identify important events that have occurred; for example, deaths, marriages, divorces, or extended absences. See Figure 5.2 for a sample genogram.

An ecomap is a tool that is drawn jointly by the client system and social worker to understand the relationships within the social context. Boundaries, relationships, and the nature of those relationships are represented graphically.

The relationships within the family are depicted as in the genogram, and then placed within the context of connections to one's extended family, friends, social network, work (or school), and formal helpers. Identifying the nature of the social interactions, both in terms of sources of stress as well as sources of support, enables client systems to understand their situation better and to see what the next steps might be (Sheafor, Horejsi, and Horejsi, 1994). Figure 5.3 presents a sample ecomap.

- *Assessing the community.* Community groups can profit from looking at a situation and telling their stories. This fosters an understanding of the ways in which the members of the community group perceive the situation and can lead to possibilities of action. Residents who want to work toward more responsive or efficiently coordinated services in their community need clarity as to what exists

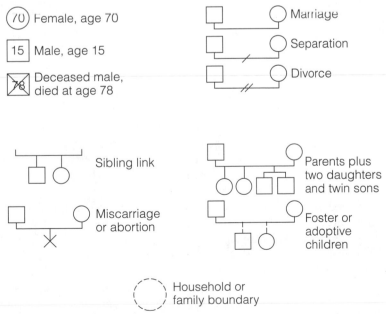

Figure 5.1 Genogram Symbols [*Source:* Sheafor, Horejsi, and Horejsi (1994, p. 268).]

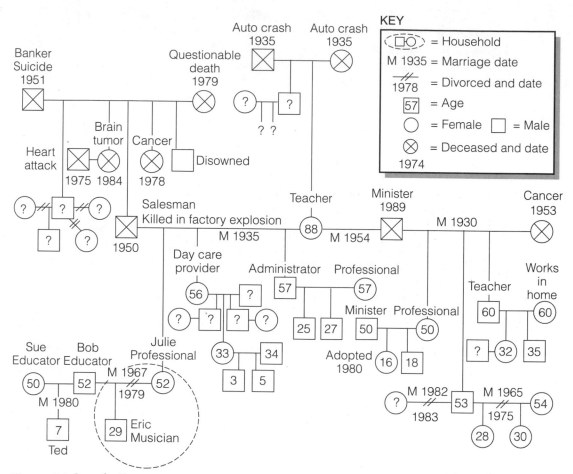

Figure 5.2 Sample Genogram

as well as what is desired in the community. The specific purpose of the community assessment will shape the form, process, and content of the change effort. As with other aspects of practice, influencing organizational or community change must be tailored to the situation and the context. The following example illustrates this point.

A social worker was asked by the Family Resource Network (FRN) to do a community needs assessment for a rural county. The FRN is charged with planning more contextually appropriate services for children and families of the area. The social worker's response was that she would do this if she could first do a resource assessment. By responding in this way, she recognized the value of knowing community capacity as well as meeting unaddressed concerns. The differences between assets and needs approaches to community assessment are illustrated in Figure 5.4.

- *Using focus groups to obtain needed information.* Focus groups have become an increasingly popular tool for enabling social workers and other human service providers to assess client systems' voices and stories. Focus groups are used to explore and clarify concerns by bringing together a group of persons who share experiences central to the concern. For instance, bringing together a group of public assistance single moms could be a desirable way to learn about what being recipients of public assistance might mean and the ways it influences their life choices. The value of this approach rests in the creativity and ideas that emerge from shared discussions. The following examples identify a series of questions one might use with focus groups.

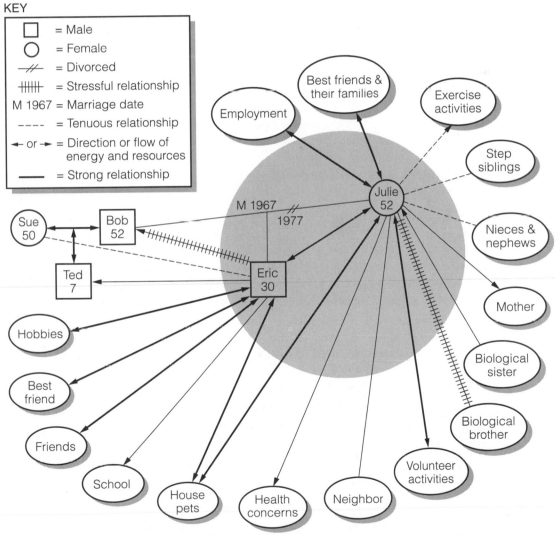

Figure 5.3 Sample Ecomap [*Source:* Key adapted from Germain (1991, p. 80). Ecomap created by authors.]

Community Assets Map

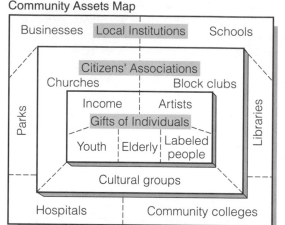

Neighborhood Needs Map

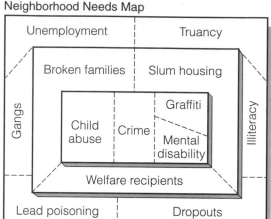

Figure 5.4 Differences Between Assets and Needs Approaches to Community Assessment [*Source:* Kretzmann and McKnight (1993, pp. 3,7).]

Discussion questions for a Service Provider focus group whose purpose is to discuss the needs of children and families and what agency barriers make it difficult to meet those needs:

• *What do families gain from or how do families benefit from the services you provide?*

• *Describe the barriers that families may encounter when they attempt to obtain services from an agency. For example, language difficulties may prevent clients from communicating their needs.*

• *What barriers does your agency experience that keep it from effectively providing services to these families? For example, some agencies might have strict rules on the documentation required before providing services.*

• *What has been your experience in working with other agencies which provide services for these families? Have you experienced any barriers to working collaboratively? Please be as specific as possible in identifying bureaucratic problems.*

• *If you could change one specific policy or procedure in your agency to improve services for these families, what would it be?*

• *What activities, policies, and procedures are working well at your agency? (Melaville and Blank, 1993, p. 41)*

Discussion questions for Community Residents/Consumers of Services focus group whose purpose is to discuss their experiences in getting help they need:

• *What services do you and your children need most?*

• *What problems or barriers do you experience when you attempt to obtain services?*

• *Describe your most positive encounter with a service delivery agency.*

- *Describe your most negative encounter.*
- *If you could change one aspect of the present delivery system, what would it be? (Melaville and Blank, 1993, p. 42)*

The Goals of Phase One

In telling and exploring the story, several things happen. First is understanding. One hopes that the social worker understands the client system's story better than when the process began and that the client system understands it better as well. Also, through the use of questions, tools, and perspectives for examining the situation, the client system is looking at the situation with fresh eyes, which is preparation for movement into the next phase: Describing a Preferred Reality.

In Chapter 4, we wrote about the need for mutuality, for a working alliance between the social worker and the client system. In respectful listening, clarifying, and mutually exploring the situation, the social worker is communicating more clearly than with mere words that he or she is engaging with the client system in an equal partnership in the change process. This attitude, effectively communicated, sets up the second phase of work, in that it says to the client system, "You are important to me, and together we will understand your story as it shapes your vision of a preferred reality."

As we facilitate the client system's exploration and telling of the story, we are sharing tools that can be used in future situations—new ways to look at troubling situations. This is an important condition for being able to hope and dream in describing a preferred reality.

Summary

The goal of Phase One is to realize a more complete understanding of client systems' stories associated with their issues and concerns. In the course of this chapter, we acknowledge several key points: (1) the story can never be completely known, (2) client systems are the experts when it comes to their story, (3) client systems possess unique stories that may not always reflect the grand or superstory of the society because of the selective memory associated with national stories, and (4) the goal of social workers is to maximize our understanding of client systems' stories so our professional knowledge, skills, and values might be used appropriately in the work of planned change processes.

Successful attention to both the process (how we join with the client system in the discovery of the story) and the outcome (our understanding of the story) are important for the work that is to follow. The benefits of a well-carried-out telling and exploring of the story include the emergence of a helping relationship characterized by increased empathy and trust, and an increased knowledge that enables the social worker and the client system to identify goals and hopes that address the issues and concerns that brought them together.

As you prepare to move on to Phase Two of our model, please consider the following questions:

1. Think about the national story for the United States. How does the story include certain groups and leave other groups marginalized?

2. Think about your own family story. How does it reflect the national story? How is it different?

3. Think about times when you have needed some form of help. What behaviors attitudes, and actions of the persons you approached for assistance with your concerns were beneficial in building a relationship and addressing your concerns?

4. Think again about your help-seeking experiences. What behaviors, attitudes, and actions of the persons you approached for assistance with your concerns were not helpful?

5. Think about times when you were confused or ambivalent about a situation or course of action. What responses from the people you approached for assistance (listening, speaking, asking questions, reflective responding) were beneficial to you in telling and exploring your story? What responses were less helpful?

6. Think about people you have met in professional relationships that you came to trust. What behaviors and attitudes did they exhibit that helped you know they were trustworthy? What lessons do you see for your own practice as a social worker?

CHAPTER SIX

Phase Two: Describing a Preferred Reality

Where there is hope there is life,
where there is life there is possibility,
where there is possibility, change
can occur.

JESSE JACKSON
(1995)

Introduction

Phase Two combines the activity of thinking about the desired outcomes of the change process—even dreaming about how it could be better—and identifying ways those images of preference might become reality. Goal setting and contracting are a part of this process.

Describing or imagining a preferred reality enables the client system to base whatever action is to be taken not just on issues of concern or difficulties being experienced but also on an idea of how things could be different. This builds a vision of the story toward which it is worth working and focuses on the capacities and other resources available to the client system. Envisioning desired outcomes emphasizes the significance of hope in the process.

Thinking about one's preferred reality, about how life could be better, is incomplete by itself. Therefore, the second part of Phase Two is to translate the image of a preferred reality into plans that can be realized. Setting a contract is a crucial part of this component.

Imagining a Preferred Reality

Having a vision of the future to work toward or imagining a reality worth fighting for can be a powerful stimulus to action and a motivator toward continued resolve and effort. A poem by Alice Walker (1968) illustrates this.

> *Women*
>
> *They were women then*
> *My mamma's generation*
> *Husky of voice—Stout of*
> *Step*
> *With fists as well as*
> *Hands*
> *How they battered down*
> *Doors*
> *And ironed*
> *Starched white*
> *Shirts*
> *How they led*
> *Armies*
> *Headragged Generals*
> *Across mined*
> *Fields*
> *Booby-trapped*
> *Ditches*

To discover books
Desks
A place for us
How they knew what we
Must *Know*
Without knowing a page
Of it
Themselves. (p. 68)

When people permit themselves to speculate about a preferred reality and to dream, they talk about themselves in ways they and the social worker may not otherwise experience. As we mentioned in our discussion of Phase One, people often use problem-saturated descriptions to describe their experience and can devote all of their energy to dealing with today's crises.

When people believe that the future will not be measurably different than the troubled present, they do not spend time thinking of a "better place" and how to get there. When opportunities are not available for some people or for people in some neighborhoods, the range of choices that they perceive to be open is constricted. The issue of perception in relation to available opportunities is an important one. In many situations, people who are oppressed have more options than they are able to see because they are immersed in daily challenges and crises. To prevent oppression from becoming internalized, the opportunity to dream is necessary.

In writing about hope in Chapter Two, we used a number of examples of youths growing up in distressed neighborhoods whose sense of hope in the future had been blighted. For these youth, hopelessness as a perception increased their sense of their own powerlessness and further limited their vision of the possible. This diminution of hope is a social justice issue. As the philosopher John Rawls (1971) states, "If we would not choose to live and work as overwhelmed people do, then we must commit ourselves to whatever it takes to improve their lives" (p. 24). In Chapter 10, we address this challenge.

The Role of Oppression in Inhibiting Dreaming

For persons and groups, not thinking about the preferred reality can result in a blind acceptance of the present situation and the tacit agreement that other people's ideas of who you are and where you are going are correct. As Judy Merritt (1994) states, "If you don't tell people who you are, they will tell you who you are. If you have people telling you who you are, you will be powerless" (p. 52). Reinforcing the feeling of powerlessness is a key variable in maintaining oppression.

While it may be difficult for many of us to think of oppression as an issue in the United States, we need only remember that oppression manifests itself in many ways. For example, practices that keep people from jobs, education, and/or housing because of how they are viewed are all oppressive.

The social justice interest of the social work profession requires social workers to be concerned about practices that oppress others and to actively work toward their elimination. For instance, the continuing debate over affirmative action as a national policy challenges the profession and the society to think about how opportunities and benefits are distributed. Within the values and policy positions of the social work profession, it is not okay for racial minorities and women to earn, on average, much less than white men. The challenge for us and our profession is to work within society to embrace our vision for greater equality.

In considering these issues of oppression and our response to them, the thoughts of Freire (1989) may be helpful. He notes that those who would work to fight oppression must make a firm commitment and keep it.

> *Those who authentically commit themselves to the people must re-examine themselves constantly. This conversion is so radical as not to allow . . . ambiguous behavior. To affirm this commitment but to consider oneself the proprietor of revolutionary wisdom—which must then be given to (or imposed on) the people—is to retain the old ways. The man who proclaims devotion to the cause of liberation yet is unable to enter into communion with the people, whom he continues to regard as totally ignorant, is grievously self-deceived. (p. 47)*

Only when their voice names the issues and directs the goals can people move out of oppressive situations. This phase of our model is designed to enable the social worker and the client system to dream, hope, and plan actions consistent with the voice of the client system. We will discuss later in this chapter ways of doing this.

Trusting the Process

However, one important point needs to be made now. This process is not a passive one for the social worker, nor for the client system. Sometimes it will be most difficult for the client system to name the dreams and the goals associated with these dreams. Nonetheless, we have faith based upon our experience that, ultimately, it is possible for client systems to eventually name their dreams. Trust the process! Trusting the process requires patience and tenacity to avoid providing the answers and to help unlock the dreams. We do this by the way we listen, clarify, and encourage the client system to dream.

Trusting the process can be difficult, especially when we are on the receiving end of someone who is confused and frustrated, and we are not suggesting that trusting the process is magical. Rather, it is the result of the hard work of listening, reflective responding, and respectful questioning to understand the dreams as they emerge.

One November, I (Jim) asked the participants in a parenting group I was leading to think about how they would like things to be different by July Fourth. The participants were all receiving public assistance and were referred to the parenting group by child protective service workers.

I was surprised by some of the answers. One woman talked about wanting to enroll in vocational school by that time so that she could get off public assistance. Another mother, whose family consisted of herself and her sons, ages 2 and 4, spoke of a family situation where she shouted less and managed sibling mayhem better. Often, both of the women had seemed stuck in the eternal present, where the day-to-day troubles were so overwhelming that coping and making it through that day were all that they were thinking about. Asking the question created the opportunity first to think about a preferred reality and then to begin to plan toward the desired outcomes. Frequently, since that day, I have used this question with client systems and have found that, more often than not, the process of looking ahead not only yields direction but also creates energy for what needs to be done now.

The technique of asking reflective "miracle questions" is another way we might encourage dreaming about desired realities. Such questions may be phrased along the lines of, "If the fairy godmother visited your neighborhood and waved her magic wand one night while all of you were sleeping and brought the desired change to your neighborhood, how would you know she had been there the next day?" These reflective questions are designed to enable the client system to dream, to name the direction of desired change, and to identify goals for working toward a different reality. In Chapter 8, we will expand on the use of reflective questions to evaluate outcomes of the work together.

Lending a Vision

Social workers not only encourage people to explore the options associated with hopefulness; sometimes they also need to "lend a vision" where client systems are too dispirited to dream. Sharing the experiences of other persons or groups who have successfully confronted similar issues of concern is one way to lend vision. One of the reasons Alcoholics Anonymous works is that persons who do not feel ready to quit drinking, or who are having trouble making it through another day without a visit from Jack Daniels, hear the stories told during meetings from persons who have been sober for a year, or three years, or thirteen years. This lends a vision, providing an example of someone who has accomplished what the struggling individual would like to attain.

Another way social workers can lend a vision is to communicate their belief in and respect for the ability and capacity of the client system. Nonverbal behaviors and a voice that communicates, "I care about you and believe in you and your ability to move toward a preferred reality" can be a powerful, encouraging message.

Dreaming, or imagining a preferred reality, however, will not lead to change if its connections to reality are too tenuous. I (Jim) had a client, a man in his fifties, who talked of a former girlfriend whose chief interest was playing the lottery. Such a preoccupation is not unique—the phenomenal growth of state-run lotteries since the early 1980s occurred at the same time that the "American Dream" of owning a home and having a life better than the preceding generation seemed to slip away from many people.

There are more than a few individuals who pin their hopes on winning the lottery, or on a knight in shining armor coming to rescue (or marry) them, or on the factory that moved to Mexico last year coming back and doing wholesale hiring. This point applies to larger systems as well. It is not uncommon to drive around economically blighted areas and see undeveloped industrial parks with signs inviting new tenants. These industrial parks are not likely to attract many new tenants because the resources are not available to the locality to make the dream real.

These kinds of dreams generally do not have the substance to move toward reality. They are what we referred to earlier in the book as *castillos en el aire*—castles in the sky.

Phase Two of our model, Describing a Preferred Reality, departs from conventional models in that ours is based more on what the client system wishes to pursue than on solving problems. From the point of imagining a preferred reality, the similarities between our model and more traditional models increase, with both putting an emphasis on goal setting and contracting. After the client system begins to think of ways that the situation could be different, alternate ways of looking at what needs to be done emerge.

Actions and Their Effects

Management consultant Tom Peters (1995) writes of the value of plunging ahead even when everything is not planned out. "People act in order to think," he quotes researcher Karl Weick as saying (p. 2). Peters believes that, in business, those who begin to act while things are still unclear will learn faster from taking action—any action. Smart people, according to Peters (1995), will act their way into clear-headed thinking. He quotes British prime minister Benjamin Disraeli, who remarked more than a century ago, "Thought is the child of action" (p. 2).

When an effective process is mapped out, we can proceed before all the details are in place. As noted earlier in this book, I (Jim) am currently involved in my small town with a transitional housing project for families who are homeless. In one meeting, we were talking about future directions after the housing units were established. We realized that, as the program began to function, we would become aware of unmet needs and other concerns of the families we serve. As the program develops, we are establishing policies and priorities.

David Burns (1980) proposes that action "primes the pump"; action activates and stimulates motivation. At times, a small step is all that is needed because it can lead to or snowball into more action and provide the additional motivation necessary to address more challenging concerns.

In addition to simply taking action, being successful in an initial effort can also have powerful effects on a person's or group's self-efficacy, the sense that success is possible. According to O'Hanlon and Weiner-Davis (1989):

> *Once a small positive change is made, people feel optimistic and a bit more confident about tackling further changes. Couples seeking treatment often provide clear examples of this phenomenon. Blaming and withholding typically characterize these relationships. However, when person A undertakes one small gesture which pleases person B, person B reciprocates, which in turn stimulates person A to respond in kind, and so on. (p. 42)*

For example, I (Barry) have a sister who lost her job to downsizing after twenty years of loyal service. She decided to go back to school (to study computer technology), but with a certain amount of anxiety because she had been out of the classroom since high school.

I called her toward the middle of her first term and asked how school was going. She had just gotten back her first exam results and had earned a high A in all classes but one, and that grade was a B. I told her how great that was and she said, "Well, I'm proud of myself." This was quite a statement for her, as she had grown up thinking she could not do well in school because of a childhood illness and a doctor's interpretation of its likely impacts. This early success continued in future classwork and her future looks brighter as she prepares for a new career.

While I (Barry) share in the pride my sister feels, the important point to this story is that it serves as an example of the ways in which the story changes as it unfolds: going back to school and being successful changes the self-image and thereby alters the story. The input coming from external systems (such as a teacher, a parent, or a public assistance agency worker) that "you're not good at this!" often becomes the reality that is accepted. Similarly, statements like "I'm too old to change" can become the reality if left unchallenged.

In Phase One, we wrote of the danger of premature advising or suggesting a plan and alternatives within a short period of time after engaging with the client system. What we are presenting here is different. After the client system has determined at least a general direction for a change effort, then the best next step may be a small one. A single mother, age 28, who is contemplating going to college may decide to take one class to "put a toe in the water." In taking that one class, she will learn something about her abilities, both in the classroom and in the juggling of work, school, and family responsibilities. This learning will be invaluable in a later decision about whether or not to return to college to pursue a degree. Through action, what needs to be done in goal setting and contracting becomes more clear and thus more possible.

Goal Setting and Contracting

As stated by Egan (1994), "All clients need focus and direction in managing problems and developing opportunities; what that focus and direction will look like will differ from client to client" (pp. 224–225). Frequently, in imagining the preferred reality, client systems come up with dreams and images that are too vague to be implemented. "As a family, we need to communicate better," "We want a neighborhood that is safer," and "I want to get a better job so that we're not struggling so much with bills" are all vague preferred realities. One of the major tasks of Phase Two is to enable client systems to set goals that are attainable.

Setting goals can make the planned change process comprehensible and can be empowering for client systems. Goals focus client systems' attention and action and mobilize their energy and efforts. In addition, goals stated in specific terms increase client system persistence and motivation to seek ways and means to realize them (Locke and Latham, 1984).

As client systems set goals, they are moving beyond just talking about a situation or concern to taking action and developing a process to do something about the concern. This step is not an easy one in many cases. There can be a certain level of comfort both in telling the story and in speculating about the preferred reality. Taking action by deciding to make the desired outcomes real is a scarier step; it involves moving from intention to commitment, which can be difficult.

Egan (1994) observes that helpers sometimes can be coconspirators in enabling client systems to avoid goal setting. He identifies several reasons why this happens.

> 1. *It can be uncomfortable for the worker as well as the client to "move into the uncharted waters of the future."*
>
> 2. *Clients who set goals and work toward meeting them are moving beyond considering themselves victims, and the victim game is an easy one to play.*
>
> 3. *Goal setting involves placing demands on themselves, and this can involve hard work and pain; client systems may not be grateful for the kinds of challenging that goes on in this phase.*
>
> 4. *Setting goals places limits on actions. By choosing to take one course, other possibilities are closed off. Some individuals and groups are reluctant to take action because of what they might miss. (pp. 225–226)*

Using different language, bell hooks (1993) in *Sisters of the Yam: Black Women and Self-Recovery* poses the question to other black women struggling with their issues, "Are you sure, sweetheart, that you want to be well?" (p. 14).

Goal Setting

Earlier in the book, we discussed our concerns about the concept of solution. Two unfortunate consequences of using the term "solution" are that people assume the end result is one correct solution, and that the goal is to find the correct final solution for the identified concerns. Instead, in many situations, what is desired is to manage the situation over time. Choosing and setting goals is a technical process. The role of the social worker is to model the skills associated with goal development. By learning to set goals, the client system can develop these capacities for use in managing the current concern as well as future concerns.

There are at least two types of goals. Some goals may be discrete, one-time actions or decisions ("I'm going to get a second job to pay off bills"). Ongoing goals relate to long-term management of issues and incremental efforts to reach a preferred outcome. "Examples of ongoing goals include managing conflict effectively, expressing feelings openly, asserting one's rights, setting limits with children, controlling anger, participating in group discussions" (Hepworth and Larsen, 1986, p. 302).

Guidelines for Goal Setting In *The Skilled Helper,* Gerard Egan (1994) writes about the difficulties that many client systems have with the term "goal setting" in that it seems too rational as well as technical. He suggests that workers use whatever language makes sense to the people with whom they are working. "Looking at what needs to be different and what needs to happen to get there" may sound less intimidating to some people. Regardless of the words, the following ten guidelines can be useful in the goal-setting process.

The first two guidelines are to be applied in selecting goals.

1. *Ensure that the goals the client system is setting are central to the concerns of the client system and will have real impact on the client system's situation.* Goals need to be set in areas that are central to the life situation and preferred reality of the client system, be it a community, group, person, family, or organization. This seems self-evident, but there are two compelling reasons to make sure that a goal that is being agreed on does in fact contribute in a significant way to making things different.

First, the more client systems can see that goal accomplishment will make a difference, the more effort they are likely to put into pursuing the goal. When the time comes for action, we discover how important a specific goal is. The more central to the concerns, the more likely the goal will produce ongoing action. Epstein (1980) remarks: "There is no way in the world to stretch a client's motivation, to maneuver him into a commitment for a personal change he does not want, does not see, does not accept. . . . Clients, however, eagerly seek help and value help that makes sense to them, is useful to their daily lives, gets or keeps them out of trouble" (p. 177).

Second, in the process of goal setting, goals that are important might be displaced by goals that are easy to reach. A single mother may feel out of control with money problems and a toddler whose behavior is unsettling and disruptive. The mother reports that she is watching an increasing amount of television to distract herself from her troubles. Setting a goal to watch less television may be useful, but it does not address the paramount issues.

2. *Work with the client system to determine which areas of concern have more potential impact on the current issues and which ones fit best with a preferred reality.* The following questions can be used to select goals for managing issues and identifying opportunities when considering a number of possible goals:

   a. Which issue seems to be causing the most pain for the client system?

   b. Which issue, if unresolved, will have the most adverse consequences?

   c. Which issue, if resolved or managed differently, will have the most desirable consequences for the client system?

   d. Which issue can be resolved or managed with only a moderate investment of time, effort, or other resources? Where do the benefits outweigh the costs?

   e. Which issue has the potential of the client system being successful and enhancing competency and mastery? (Egan, 1994; Sheafor, Horejsi, and Horejsi, 1994).

Once goals are selected, the client system and the social worker are ready to begin stating them in useful ways. Guides 3 through 5 enable the client system and the social worker to do this.

3. *Work with the client system to develop a goal statement that is as specific and measurable as possible.* There are real advantages to goal statements that are specific and measurable. When a family talks about getting along better or members of a community group agree that they need to improve race relations in the community, they are expressing ideas in generalities about a preferred reality. They are useful as starting points, as intents, but cannot be measured as stated. If the family decides that reducing the number of verbal fights by half is an appropriate goal, that is something that can be measured. The community group can decide to hold a "unity picnic" or some other event (a discrete goal) or keep working on what indicators they could use to measure improved race relations. It is not always possible to state goals in this fashion, but being specific makes it much easier for the worker and client system to determine movement.

For individuals, families, and groups, part of their sense of efficacy, that they can be successful in what they do, comes from past successes. Measuring success or progress can give the client system tangible information. In some cases, the client system can feel proud of what has been accomplished. When there hasn't been accomplishment, then the worker and client system can work from that point.

When the direction of change or movement toward goal achievement is different than intended or expected, exciting awareness and understanding can emerge. The experience of a student in field placement using a Goal Attainment Scale (discussed further in Chapter 8) to measure the movement of his work with a client who has developmental disabilities provides an illustration of the insight and understanding that can occur. Over a period of three weeks of keeping track of behaviors identified as necessary for the desired change, the client and the student social worker noted that the client's movement was regressive rather than in the preferred direction. As they explored this phenomenon together, they realized they had identified and specified a goal that was inappropriate for their work together. From this awareness, they were able to reframe a goal that was a better fit.

Though many goals are easy to measure, it is not necessary to use only goals that can be quantified. According to Egan (1994), "It is not always necessary to count things in order to determine whether a goal is reached, although sometimes counting is helpful" (p. 259). Scaling, which we describe later in this chapter, is one mechanism for measuring more subjective goals like staff morale or family communication. If a couple sets a goal of improving their communication, the worker can ask them: "On scale of one to ten, with one being the worst and ten being the best, how would you evaluate your communication this week?" and then compare this response with their answer at the start of the work. Doing this can give all of the participants in the change activity ideas about how well they are progressing toward achieving desired outcomes.

4. *Work with the client system to develop goal statements that are as realistic and attainable as possible.* Part of the skill in enabling client systems to develop goals is in making sure that the goals are realistic. There are a number of questions that can be asked to help shape goals in ways that are attainable:

- *How well does the goal have to be attained?* The adage "Anything worth doing is worth doing well" may have done more harm than good. Some goals can be reached with less than perfect results. A parent who wishes a child to have a room that looks better may negotiate with the child for the bed to be made up each day and no exotic life forms growing in the room. That's not spotless, but it may be sufficient.

- *What resources does the client system have that could be of assistance?* Using the strengths perspective, an expanded view of resources can include support systems, past successes in dealing with situations, and other personal capacities and informal community resources. For client systems with more resources, meeting ambitious goals may be less difficult than for client systems with fewer developed resources.

- *How much influence does the client system have for attaining the goal?* I (Jim) have worked with groups of men who are abusive. Often what they want to do in group sessions is to gripe about their wives or partners, or sometimes to worry about the substance abuse problems of someone in their family. What I have said in these groups is that you can't change another person. (I [Becky] concur with Jim; however, I believe that we can influence others' behaviors and attitudes by our actions and reactions.) In family or couples therapy, the issues identified by the men who abused spouses and partners that were associated with the interaction of the couple could be worked on (once the men had worked on some of their violence and power issues).

It's usually advisable for client systems to work on goals over which they can exercise some influence. If there is a major obstacle that could block the way, that also needs to be considered. "It does not do to leave a live dragon out of your calculations if you live near him" (Dyson and Dyson, 1989, p. 171).

- *Is this a goal that can be sustained?* For some goals, it can be easier to change them over a short period of time than over the long haul. If the goal involves major changes in such aspects as relationships, finances, or ways of managing conflict, can these changes be maintained over time? In the next phase, we will discuss the issue of maintaining goals in in greater detail.

- *Is the time frame realistic?* A time frame on meeting a goal should be neither too short to make the goal attainable nor so far in the future that there will be a tendency to put it off. Losing ten pounds by next Tuesday is not realistic for most people (unless you are pregnant and were due to deliver last month); on the other hand, saying that you will lose ten pounds by a year from Tuesday invites procrastination for months and months.

Hepworth and Larson (1986) write about situations in which the worker may want to assist the client system with setting realistic goals:

In most instances, clients possess the capacity to accomplish goals they set for themselves, and it is both appropriate and desirable to affirm the validity of their goals and to express belief in their capacity to attain them. Occasionally, you will encounter clients who are grandiose or who deny personal limitations that are obvious to others. In these instances, you can perform a valuable service by sensitively and tactfully assisting them to lower their aim to the upper range of what is realistically achievable. (p. 305)

And we would add: assisting them in a competency assessment enables them in deciding if acquiring the abilities it would take to meet the original goal could be an intermediate goal they wish to pursue.

For example, I (Barry) have always loved singing; however, I am blessed with a singing voice that not even my mother could love. While I may love to sing, I quickly learned that it was not always desirable to inflict my lack of talent on others, and so my finest singing performances remain very much private acts. So it may be for many of our clients—they may have dreams that do not fit well with their current talents or likely opportunities.

While we always respect the dream, our responsibility to the client system is to join in assessing existent competencies and in clarifying the capacities necessary for meeting the goal. With this information, the client system is able to make a determination about whether to acquire the capacities necessary to pursue the goal.

5. *State goals in positive language.* As we often use goals to address concerns and difficulties, we tend to think of goals that start with "As of now, I'm going to stop doing. . . ." Insoo Kim Berg (1992), who uses a solution-focused approach in family-based interventions for at-risk families, explains why it's preferable to state goals as positive, replacement behavior other than the absence of negative, undesirable behavior:

A client saying things like "I will never do it again," "I will never get mad," "I will never let him in," "I will never leave the child alone," is not enough. It is unrealistic to think that she will remember not to do all these things in the heat of anger or frustration. The more concrete, detailed options the client has, the better. Therefore, you need to clarify the goal with the client by asking "So what would you do instead of getting mad (getting drunk, leaving the child alone, etc.)?" The process of having to describe these alternatives forces clients to think out loud, and thus realistic choices can be made. . . . It is easier to recognize when a positive goal has been achieved than a negative one. That is, when the client does not *hit the child, it is difficult for her to know that she is not hitting. If she sets herself goals such as "I will count to 10," "I will send him to his room," "I will walk out of the house," she will know when she is achieving her goal. (p. 59)*

Working for change can be difficult. There are losses as well as gains associated with change and a number of actions associated with implementing the change effort. Guides 6 through 8 address these aspects of goal setting and planned change efforts.

6. *Ensure that the client system is aware of potential risks and implications as well as the benefits associated with pursuing the goal.* One of the major tenets of systems theory is that a change in one part of a system affects the entire system. In describing a preferred reality and pursuing goals toward that reality, it is important to be mindful of the possible or potential consequences as well as the intended outcomes.

> *Enhanced functioning sometimes entails growth pains and negative as well as [desired] consequences. Examples of the former include losing a job by being assertive with an unjust employer, being rejected by a person . . . when making social overtures, experiencing increased pressure and family conflict by going to work, and suffering from anxiety and discomfort by exposing painful emotions to family and group members. Clients have a right to be aware of potential risks, and you may be vulnerable to lawsuits if you neglect your obligation in this regard. (Hepworth and Larsen, 1986, p. 310)*

Bambera acknowledges another dimension of the potential risks associated with pursuing goals when she notes, "Just so's you're sure, sweetheart, and ready to be healed, cause wholeness is no trifling matter. A lot of weight when you are well" (cited in hooks, 1993). In pursuing wellness and wholeness there are losses as well as gains. Choices are altered from whether or not we *can* respond to whether or not we are *willing* to respond in specific situations.

One of the risks of change is that some actions, when done, cannot then be undone. I (Jim) have used the metaphor of burning bridges in working with client systems. I ask them to think about a major life choice they are contemplating as a wooden bridge over a road and whether or not the choice would burn the bridge. Even though the decision to burn the bridge may be a desired one, client systems are more aware of the potential losses associated with their choices and actions.

7. *Provide clarification and support about the hard work, the potential difficulties, and the duration of the change effort.* In their work with problem drinkers, Berg and Miller (1992) advocate stressing that goals involve hard work. It both promotes and protects a client system's sense of self-worth and dignity. A goal that is reached as a result of hard work is something of which to be proud, a boost to self-esteem. If the goal is not reached, it does not indicate that the client system is a failure, just that there is more work to be done.

Hepworth and Larson (1986) propose that an explanation similar to the following can provide a realistic picture of the change process:

> *We've talked about goals you want to achieve. Accomplishing them won't be easy. Making changes is seldom accomplished without a difficult and sometimes painful struggle. People usually have ups and downs as they seek to make changes. If you understand this, you won't become unduly discouraged and feel like throwing in the towel. I don't mean to paint a grim picture. In fact, I feel very hopeful about the prospects of your attaining your goals. At the same time, it won't be easy, and I don't want to mislead you. (pp. 320–321)*

8. *Work with the client system to be sure there is clarity as to who will do what by when.* As part of being specific, it can make sense to spell out responsibilities, specific actions, and timelines. These are important not only for the client system but for the worker/client relationship. Hepworth and Larsen (1986) identify one advantage of formal contracts in working with client systems:

Mutually formulating a contract is a vital process because it divests the helping process of mystery and clarifies for clients what they may realistically expect from the practitioner and what is expected of them; what they will be mutually seeking to accomplish and in what ways; and what the problem-solving process entails. Comprehending these factors is significant to the majority of clients, many of whom have lacked accurate information about what social workers do and have stereotyped fears of being analyzed or controlled by a "shrink." (p. 30)

The final two of our ten guides for the goal-setting process are intended to be used by social workers as they commit to working with client systems toward the identified goals.

9. *Ensure that you (the worker) have the skills and capabilities for enabling the client system to meet the identified goal(s).* Part of knowing yourself is knowing your own limitations. What a particular client system needs might be out of the range of your expertise and experience. I (Jim) don't have the background to work with people who sexually abuse others, and I won't work with such client systems until my knowledge and skill in this area is greater than it is now.

Knowledge of limitations requires self-awareness. Self-understanding enables Jim to understand that he may not be the best helper when the issue is sexual abuse. However, awareness and acknowledgment of limitations does not remove the ethical obligation to serve. Jim still needs to know where help for people who sexually abuse others may be found and to link client systems in need with the appropriate resource.

Other social workers may find that they cannot work with physical illness or the severely mentally ill. Again, what we do with these limits is important. If we are the only readily accessible social worker in a community or neighborhood, we may seek additional knowledge and training. If such training is not available, we might seek supportive networks with others on how best to proceed.

10. *Check to be sure that the goals under consideration are within legal limits and your ethical parameters.* Because of your own values, religious beliefs, or morals, you may not always be able to partner effectively with client systems who are pursuing goals that conflict with these beliefs. For example, I (Jim) am unapologetically child centered and would have a lot of trouble working with client systems who wish to give up custody of their children to follow their dreams.

In cases of conflict over values, Hepworth and Larsen (1986) suggest referring the client system to another professional who would be comfortable working with the client system toward the identified goal. They provide a sample explanation:

I'm sorry I can't join you in working toward that goal. You and I have different values, and mine would get in the way of giving you the help you're seeking. I'm not faulting you for being different from me. We're all different, and that's how it should be. I do want to help you obtain the service you need, however, and if it's agreeable with you, we can explore that together. (p. 307)

In cases where the social worker feels conflicted over a dilemma in values and morals, talking with a supervisor, coworker, or professional colleague can provide insight and perspective. If the worker is concerned about the legality of a proposed action, checking with the agency's legal counsel is advised.

While referral in this instance may be ideal, practice realities often preclude this possibility, especially if you are the appropriate professional as determined by your position or the only professional available to join with the client system in the planned change process. When this occurs, we recommend an honest discussion with the client system(s) of the potential barriers. If client systems wish to proceed, we believe social workers are obligated to go forward, with the understanding that they take care not to impose their values or views. This is the operating principle that enables us to work with client systems as they move toward their preferred reality.

Contracting

If goal setting proceeds in a useful manner, establishing a working contract will be much easier. We connect the idea of contracting with the goal-setting process because goals without commitment and action plans are more difficult to realize. A working contract between the client system and the social worker may be thought of as the agreement to proceed (and on how to proceed) in taking action to realize the preferred reality. In arriving at a working contract or agreement, several points are worth remembering.

- *The contract may either be oral or written.* In part this decision rests with the client system and the social worker; however, some agencies may require a written version. A hazard in relying only on oral contracts is that memory may be faulty about what was to be done and by whom when the process and issues are revisited at a later time.

- *It is important that contracts spell out the details of action.* Agreement is necessary between the client system and the social worker about such items as what will be the first steps, who will do what and when, and what contextual resources will be accessed.

- *An agreement about how the client system and the social worker will work together is a vital component of contracting.* Information that is necessary to accomplish this aspect of contracting includes: client systems sharing their preferences about how they work best in change activities and how the work together could proceed; and the social worker sharing the intervention approaches and strategies, tools and techniques he or she has competence in and is likely to use in working with the client system. For example, note taking during interactions may be distracting to the client system. On the other hand, some client systems may expect note taking as a sign the social worker is listening. To respect client system needs and preferences, the social worker needs to know what they are. Being clear about these kinds of details enables the work to move forward.

- *The social worker and the client system identify ways to monitor and evaluate progress toward the preferred reality.* It is important to know the means by which goal attainment will be assessed so the client system and the social worker can be aware of the progress being made in the change efforts.

Hepworth and Larsen (1993) note the difficulties in contracting with clients who are present in the change effort involuntarily. We agree that this an important area for social worker sensitivity. While client systems (for example, a family being investigated for abuse, a neighborhood faced with relocation for a road project, or a community facing a major plant closing) may be forced into a planned change process, we believe it is imperative for the social worker to find, respect, and incorporate the client system voice into how their work together is to proceed. Hepworth and Larsen (1993) suggest the following techniques as useful for engaging a reluctant client system in the change process:

- reframing the issue of concern so that some common ground for working together may be explored and identified,

- suggesting an alternative of working together to better understand the issues that may have forced them together if common ground is not found,

- working with the client system to address the issues that forced them together so that the client system can be rid of the reason for their work together being mandated, and

- discussing the option of agreeing to begin the work together around other issues the client system may see as more important than the issues that resulted in the mandate for intervention. By doing this, a productive relationship can be established to enable bringing into the process the mandated issues.

Values, Knowledge, and Skills for Describing a Preferred Reality

Values: Self-Determination Reaffirmed

There is an assumption that values become important only if they are threatened or in conflict with other values. As we stated in Chapter 2, self-determination in the abstract is easy to accept. It becomes hard to embrace when you are working with a community that has chosen not to take advantage of governmental funding resources because of the strings attached to government money. This refusal to apply for state or federal funding can be even more difficult to understand when there is solid evidence that the community could benefit greatly from such support.

In another example, operationalizing self-determination can be troublesome when working with a 26-year-old adult with schizophrenia who opts not to take his medications because he doesn't think he really needs them. In your work with this client, you have documented his progression toward his preferred reality and found that regression appears to occur during the periods when he discontinues his medication.

We believe, however, that the principle of self-determination holds, and we honor client system choices within ethical and legal limits. Knowing and understanding these limits can help us determine if we need to intervene with the community or with our 26-year-old. A reasonable test here would be the potential for harm to others by the decision made. We are also worried about the potential harm to the client system; yet we are not convinced that in every situation we should intervene to protect client systems from themselves.

I (Becky) worked with a young woman in her mid-thirties who had been a dialysis patient for an extended period of time. Her condition was worsening, and the likelihood that she would qualify for a kidney transplant was diminishing rapidly. She was married and had two children.

As her condition continued to deteriorate, she began talking about discontinuing the dialysis. She knew that once she stopped she would die within a period of about two to three weeks. Even though she included her husband, children, and close family in the decision-making process, deciding whether or not to end her dialysis was difficult. If the choice was to end dialysis, she was opting for both imminent death and control of the last days of her life. If the choice was to continue dialysis, she was electing prolonged life for an uncertain period of time, frequent and time-consuming treatments, and questionable quality of life.

Whether or not I agreed with her decision, my commitment to her was that I would support her and assist her in her journey, whichever path she chose. The question of whether to intervene to protect client systems from themselves is an ethical dilemma with which all social workers will be faced at some point in their careers. Our challenge is to work out for ourselves how we will manage that dilemma when the situation arises.

As we work with client systems to shape a preferred reality, it is important not to erode client system self-determination. As was outlined in Chapter 2, erosion of self-determination occurs under the following conditions: when interference with the actions or intentions of client systems occurs; when information that might clarify alternatives is withheld from client systems; when misinformation is deliberately disseminated; and when client systems are unduly influenced and manipulated to make choices that meet with worker approval.

It is vital in developing competencies and building on strengths that worker/ client system partnerships enhance the client system experience of self-determination. We do this when we encourage client systems to take action.

Knowledge

There are a number of knowledge areas that are applicable to shaping and working toward a preferred reality.

Knowledge about Resources and Possibilities   A single mother who's struggling in a dead-end, low-paying job can benefit from hearing about training programs and financial support for people who enroll in them. A private, nonprofit agency, which exists from month to month not knowing if it will continue to survive, might benefit from learning about foundation resources and grant options.

As stated above, ethical practice demands that we do not selectively share information with client systems. Thus, for example, in talking with a single woman who just found out that she is pregnant, the social worker shares information on all the alternatives for managing the unintended pregnancy and unwanted fetus whether or not the worker agrees with women's legal rights to an abortion.

Information about How to Pursue Alternatives It has been our experience that some of the most useful information for enabling client systems to believe they can pursue possibilities is to describe in detail the process involved and the capacities essential to attaining the alternatives. By doing this, people have the chance to mentally compare their experiences and background with what would be required of them if they chose to select a particular goal. In one of the examples cited above, the single mother had not finished high school. Understanding that there was a program for completing a high school equivalency degree (GED) and that others who had dropped out in their junior years as she had done could complete the program in about six months made this opportunity more real.

Learning from Others Learning from the experiences and viewpoints of others can happen in a general way and is applicable to both Phase One and Phase Two work. As we stated in Chapter 5, it helps many client systems to know that they are not the first to try to manage a given issue or concern. Parents who have a child who is schizophrenic or who have lost a child to leukemia often benefit from hearing that the range of emotions they are feeling is common and normal. Frequently, for this very reason, small group processes are the intervention of choice for adults who have experienced the trauma of childhood sexual molestation.

Beyond the value of understanding the universality of some experiences, it is often useful to hear how others have coped and managed as one is planning the next steps. People who are successfully navigating similar situations can be powerful models. For example, community representatives might visit a small town with similar demographics that has had encouraging results in developing and implementing substance abuse prevention programs for teenagers. Agency staff might attend state conferences to hear about how other agencies are implementing state policies and procedures.

We rarely tap into the expertise of client systems who have been successful in trying circumstances. As part of my ongoing work with families who are homeless, I (Jim) am collecting stories of how parents have survived (and in some cases, thrived) through adversity. One such story is of a family who was homeless from spring until fall one year, camping in an urban area.

The children reported that the camping experience had been an adventure. The mother had kept the children in the same school, they were involved in the same recreation activities and library programs in which they had participated during previous summers, and they continued to spend time during weekends at a grandparent's house. In the children's minds, all that had changed was where they were living.

During this experience of homelessness, the children did not suffer the sense of dislocation common to many children who are homeless. When other parents hear this story, they are able to use parts of the experience that are applicable to their own lives.

As we discussed in Chapter 2, how we experience our world has profound implications for whether we see a situation as expanding or foreclosing options. I (Jim) have met two women in the last year who refused to let physical conditions define their lives. One is living with AIDS and calls it "my dancing partner, and I lead." Another, in a wheelchair with multiple sclerosis, describes herself as having "mermaid syndrome"—she functions much better in water. Sharing these perceptions can be beneficial to client systems who seem to be locked into the limitations of a situation or experience.

Skills

As Egan (1994) states, setting goals is a no-formula approach. As you read this chapter, it should be clear that enabling client systems to envision a preferred reality and specify goals to get there requires skill. In addition to the skills identified for Phase One, skills useful in facilitating this phase include: creating an atmosphere for imagining, clarifying, reframing, offering feedback, mediating, and assisting in decision making.

Creating an Atmosphere Where People Feel Safe Enough to Dream   For many people, the experience of sitting down and thinking about how they would like things to be different—and having someone take them seriously—is an uncommon one. To risk dreaming and sharing your dreams with another or in a group is scary.

Creating a climate where people feel free enough to talk about things that are important to them is no small feat. It involves encouraging, stimulating, and modeling open sharing as well as exhibiting trustworthiness, empathy, nonjudgmental positive regard, and concern for those with whom you are working.

In working at the community level to design more responsive service delivery systems, collaborative strategies among agencies require forging a shared vision, joining the personal and organizational conceptions of a collective of people. Visions that are truly shared take time to emerge. They grow as a by-product of interactions of individualized visions.

Experience suggests that visions that are genuinely shared require ongoing conversation where the persons involved feel free to express their dreams *and* learn how to listen to the dreams of others. Out of this listening, new insights into what is possible can emerge (Senge, 1990).

Imagining preferred realities requires the ability to temporarily suspend actuality. One of the primary principles of the idle generation technique of brainstorming is to delay judgment about any of the ideas until all ideas are expressed. This holds true for engaging with the client system in identifying and describing a preferred reality. We do this by putting aside, momentarily, current reality and suspending judgment about the reality of a possibility until the vision or dream has been elicited. Withholding judgment is difficult to do. However, the degree to which we can delay making judgments about the feasibility of options encourages creativity and more options and, paradoxically, enhances the capacity to construct a reality that is possible. In Chapter 7, we will present the process of brainstorming in greater detail as a tool for identifying strategies for making plans and dreams real.

Clarifying Questioning and reflective responding are central to the skill of clarifying. It is through the process of clarifying that client systems shape planned change goals. If a goal is too limited, achieving it will not help the client system realize the preferred reality. If reaching the goal does not have the desired effect, the motivation for further action may be reduced.

As we work to enable client systems to think about a preferred reality and to set goals, there are some questions that might be useful:

- How would you like your situation (family, community, agency, group) to be different?
- What would this situation look like if you (or your family, community, agency, group) were handling it differently?
- What changes in your present interactions (lifestyle, communication, reactions) would make sense?
- What would you be doing differently with the people in your life?
- What patterns of behavior (interactions, relationships, communication) would be in place that are not currently in place?
- What would you have that you don't have now?
- What accomplishments would be in place that are not in place now?
- What would this opportunity look like if you (your family, your community, your agency, your group) developed it?
- If we succeed in our work together, how will you (your family, your community, your agency, your group) think and behave differently?
- So what do you (your family, your community, your agency, your group) need to do so that you'll feel better about yourself (yourselves)?
- What do you think it would take for you to convince others that you are serious about changing? (Berg, 1992; Berg and Miller, 1992; Egan, 1994).

Reframing Reframing is the term most often used by practitioners to express what we have discussed in Chapter 2 regarding cognitive restructuring. An example of how to apply this skill follows: During a workshop I (Jim) attended in Miami, a family therapist presented a session about the use of reframing with families. She had worked with a Cuban American family in which the father had very strict rules concerning his teenage daughter. She was not to go on dates when she was not chaperoned and she had to be in early. The daughter rebelled against rules that were so unlike those of her friends and was constantly running away and staying with families of friends.

At the start of the family therapy, both the father and the daughter wanted the therapist to take their respective sides. Instead, the therapist asked the father if he loved his daughter. He replied that he did. The therapist then asked the daughter if she loved her father, and the daughter replied that she did love him. The therapist then reframed the conflict as to how the father and daughter might live in the same house so that the bond of family love would not be permanently broken. As a result of the therapist's reframing the issue, the family was able to arrive at a compromise in family rules that all could live with in order to preserve the relationship.

Offering Feedback   Offering feedback is a skill that is useful throughout the planned change process as a means for building competencies, evaluating outcomes, and providing information about how the work together is progressing. Feedback is by definition neither exclusively positive or negative. Rather, it is about sending back information that enhances the client system's ability to engage in self-reflection and to refine the nature of change goals that are important.

Another common way to use feedback is to provide information to client systems about their performance as it relates to intervention strategies that have been employed during the planned change process, such as applying specific skills, learning from the rehearsal of new behaviors, or facilitating mastery. Gambrill (1983), Cormier and Cormier (1985), and Hepworth and Larsen (1993) provide some useful guidelines for offering feedback that enhance the opportunity for the feedback to be beneficial to the recipient. We have adapted these guidelines and added some of our own.

Feedback is most useful when:

1. *it is provided because of a desire to communicate respect for the goals and needs of, and to enhance interaction with, the recipient of the feedback.* We are more receptive to feedback when it comes from someone we believe cares about us and is concerned that we develop the capacities and competencies that will aid in our journey toward achieving our goals. Feedback that we as social workers present to fulfill our own purposes and needs without consideration of how the feedback will affect our relationship with the recipient is more likely to be destructive and less likely to be heard.

2. *it is a response to a solicitation from the receiver for feedback rather than forced or imposed on an unwilling recipient.* Feedback is most useful when the receiver is open to hearing it. Generally, this openness is demonstrated when the receiver asks for another person's impression or input regarding his or her attitudes and/or actions. An important caveat for this guideline is to remember that, just because a person or group solicits feedback from others, it does not mean that they are obligated to follow or use the feedback. Feedback is offered, not imposed. Respect and regard for self-determination is vital in the process of offering feedback.

Equally important, especially when working with involuntary client systems, is the recognition that it may be necessary to provide feedback that has not yet been solicited. For example, during child abuse investigations, the risk assessment may indicate a need for some action to protect the child. Even though it may not be requested (though often feedback is sought through such questions as "Why are you doing this?" or "I haven't done anything wrong. Why are you taking my children?"), providing feedback on the levels of risk found is important, to fully respect the rights of all parties to have available to them the fullest information possible about the issues and concerns that surface during the investigation.

3. *it addresses specific behaviors rather than general attributes.* Specificity is possible when feedback is based on observable behaviors. To learn that someone perceives your behavior as "intimidating" is not as useful as it could be if you were told "as I listen to your position about the decision we have before us, I get the feeling by your tone of voice and the words you use that I have no choice but to accept your position or risk being attacked if I don't."

4. *it focuses on behavior and attitudes over which the receiver has control.* The purpose of offering feedback is to provide receivers with information useful to their efforts in advancing the planned change process. The most beneficial feedback provides information about behaviors and attitudes that a client system can change.

5. *it is offered only if there has been an opportunity to observe the recipient's attitudes and behaviors.* Many times a person will ask for feedback about behaviors or attitudes about which the social worker has no knowledge. For example, a client system may want to know if they "did the right thing" when a specific decision was made or an action was taken. As a respondent, we might not have had an opportunity to observe the action or have knowledge of all the factors considered when the decision was made. In these circumstances, responding without clarification or understanding may mean that the recipient is provided with feedback that is related more to what he or she wants to hear than to information that might be useful in the change process.

6. *it is descriptive, neutral, and tentative rather than judgmental, evaluative, and intractable.* Descriptive, neutral, and tentative feedback is based on an "authentic" report (Hepworth and Larsen's language [1990]) of one's response in interaction with the other. As a result, the use of "I" statements couched in tentative language is desirable. For example, the response, "As *I* was listening to you talk about your conflict with your supervisor, *I* heard *what seemed to me to be* anger, hostility, and frustration through your words, voice, and body language," provides information the person may choose to use or not. The tentativeness of the feedback reduces the likelihood of a defensive reaction and creates the opportunity for the client system to address the accuracy of the worker's perceptions.

7. *the response is appropriately timed.* This guideline is associated with the concept of "when" presented in Chapter 1. Feedback offered as soon after the behavior or attitude has been observed—when the receiver is open and ready to hear it—and, equally important, within a context of privacy and respect is the most beneficial.

Public sharing of feedback is appropriate only when the purpose of the gathering is associated with the development of insights into and awareness of the effect participants have on others. The most common types of gatherings that fit this definition are treatment groups and some classroom settings. One benefit of offering feedback in these settings is the opportunity for both the receiver and the respondent to explore with other group or class members the accuracy of the feedback and whether or not the impression of the respondent is shared by other members of the gathering.

8. *the message received is equivalent to the message intended.* Central to this guideline is the recognition that messages are not always sent with the meanings intended and are not always received as they were sent. Because of this, a component of offering feedback should be to explore with the receiver what was heard and understood in an effort to ensure that the message received is comparable with the message intended.

Feedback is most likely to be beneficial to the receiver when:

1. *the receiver of the feedback is motivated to change;*

2. *the feedback provides an adequate, but not an excessive, dose of information; and,*

3. *the feedback helps the receiver to identify or implement other response alternatives. (McKeachie, 1976, p. 824, cited in Cormier and Cormier, 1985, p. 315)*

With a solid, trusting relationship established between the client system and the social worker, it will be more possible, when it is appropriate, to provide feedback that contains a professional evaluation or judgment regarding behaviors that have had a positive or negative impact on goal attainment.

Mediating We have chosen to place this section on mediation in Phase Two because of changing practice realities. Increasingly, social workers are sought out to assist a range of client systems in imagining a preferred reality and setting goals around issues and concerns that are conflictual in nature and tone. Mediation skills enable us to work more effectively within the framework of these realities. As with the majority of the skills we have described and will be presenting, mediation skills are useful in all phases of the planned change process (especially Phase Three, Making Plans and Dreams Real).

Conflict—the clash of ideas, principles, beliefs and/or interests—like change, is an inevitable, natural, and desirable part of life. Our appreciation for and comfort with conflict will affect our capacity and willingness to manage it in our work and in our lives.

From our experiences, being comfortable in conflictual situations is one of the greatest challenges people face. Conflict is a part of the human condition. Yet it is common that many of us lack the skills for managing conflict in a healthy way; otherwise, there wouldn't be so many workshops and groups available for teaching us the ways to engage in and manage conflictual situations.

Developing comfort with conflict involves a great deal of self-reflection, unlearning old patterns, and mastering new skills. I (Becky) have found that developing capacities in cognitive restructuring (or reframing) and assertiveness has enabled me to enhance my comfort level with and management of conflict.

As I (Barry) have grown older (and I hope somewhat wiser) I have come to better understand the need for addressing and dealing with conflict. In my earlier years, I would consciously work to avoid it and often found myself faced with communication barriers more difficult than if I had faced the conflictual issue much earlier.

Things that work for me to manage conflict include trying to be clear about my level of agreement or disagreement, recognizing the sources of the conflict, understanding and appreciating that there are multiple ways to see and experience an issue, and working to find a common ground for proceeding when conflict is present. It is not possible to always find common ground between disputing parties, yet it is possible to disagree and continue working productively together. Respect, acceptance, and commitment to both the process and outcomes help me function with conflict, which I am now able to view as a dynamic opportunity and challenge for growth.

Considering conflict as desirable may cause some of you to shudder. However, tension and conflict are real opportunities for learning and growth. Also, without challenges, many of which are in the form of conflict, our natural tendency as human and social systems is to move toward stagnation and entropy. The clash of ideas and beliefs are fodder for creative and synergistic processes and outcomes.

Just as we don't solve issues and concerns, we don't solve conflicts; we manage them over time. There are a number of ways to manage conflict: we might use our power in such a way as to force conformity with our ideas; we might choose arbitration in which a third party or a judge settles our dispute; or we might choose to reach integration through mediation. According to Mary Parker Follett, integration, rather than compromise, is the desired outcome of managing conflict (Davis, 1989). She defined integration as an outcome "in which both desires have found a place, that neither side has had to sacrifice anything" (Davis, 1989, p. 224–225).

Mediation differs from other forms of managing conflict in that the power and responsibility for managing the conflict remains with the people in conflict, not with the person who facilitates the process. Because of this, all parties involved in the dispute or conflict must voluntarily agree to participate in the mediation process (Community Relations Section, 1991). Thus, mediation fits well with strengths, empowerment, and competency-building perspectives.

Successful mediation requires that persons in the role of mediator be neutral, disciplined, attentive, focused, and empathic. The primary functions of the mediator are to respect the dignity and worth of all parties in the dispute and to structure and guide the process (Community Relations Section, 1991). This is accomplished by tuning in (listening and reflective responding), coming together (discovering the issues that are shared and needing work), working (taking action for change), and transitioning (moving on from the situation with the issues addressed) (Shulman, 1982).

Assessment is a vital component of mediation. It is through the assessment process that the mediator and the participants are able to understand participant perspectives, identify differences and underlying causes of conflict, discover a common ground among participants, identify participants' interests and willingness to contribute toward integration, and discover "positives" to share (Community Relations Section, 1991; Davis, 1985, 1989).

"Bringing the differences into the open," according to Mary Parker Follett, is necessary for reaching integration in the mediation process (Davis, 1989, p. 225). Identifying and clarifying the differences enables all parties to understand more fully the underlying roots of the conflict and thus focus on "interests, not positions" (Davis, 1989, p. 225). This point is best illustrated by Follett when she describes an experience she had in the Harvard Library.

> [I]*n one of the smaller rooms, someone wanted the window open, I wanted it shut. We opened the window in the next room, where no one was sitting. This was not a compromise, because there was no curtailing of desire; we both got what we really wanted. For I did not want a closed room, I simply did not want the north wind to blow directly on me; likewise the other occupant did not want that particular window open, he merely wanted more air in the room. (Davis, 1989, pp. 224–225)*

Discovering commonalities among the participants and positives to share in the mediation process is another basic principle of mediation. Identifying and reflecting commonalities provides a foundation on which to build a collaborative, cooperative relationship and create a joining together of participants to reach an integration.

Sharing an intense experience or a critical incident with strangers can create indelible bonds between the people involved. The same principle applies when managing conflicts. For example, parents fighting over the custody of children often share feelings of fear, hurt, anger, and grief. When we share common feelings, experiences, ideas, or beliefs, we have the basis for the development of a bond. Identifying and naming the ways in which the disputing parties share common feelings, ideas, experiences, or beliefs fosters this development; but the process is possible only if the disputing parties remain open to the discovery of these commonalities.

Effective mediation requires skill in listening, seeking concreteness and specificity, identifying and naming concerns and themes, checking perceptions and meanings, responding reflectively, summarizing, offering feedback, making instructions clear, clarifying, and confronting (Community Relations Section, 1991).

Listening, as we noted in Chapter 5, involves attending to, hearing, and remembering verbal and nonverbal communication. Davis (1985) notes that [l]istening like a mediator takes a great deal of energy and concentration. At the end of a mediation . . . , you may well be exhausted. You may also feel elated because active, empathic listening works so well to help the parties let go of their anger and defensiveness and to join together to design creative and collaborative agreements" (p. 1).

Seeking concreteness and specificity, clarifying, and checking perceptions and meanings are all aspects of asking questions. Properly done, these processes ground the communication in the present and in reality. When we are seeking concreteness and specificity, clarifying, and checking perceptions, we are inviting the participants to move "from the general and ambiguous to [the] particular and clear-cut" (Community Relations Section, 1991, p. 52). We facilitate this process by soliciting examples, illustrations, and details about a particular situation or event, with questions and statements such as: "For example?" "Tell me more about that," "How does this experience relate to . . . ?" and "What does it mean to you when you say (or hear) . . . ?"

We communicate our awareness and understanding of the participant's feelings, messages, and experiences through *responding reflectively.* Paraphrasing and empathic response are key skills associated with this process. Paraphrasing is the process by which we state in our own words the content of what we heard and understood the participant or client system to say. On the other hand, an empathic response is a statement that reflects our awareness of the emotions experienced by the participants or client systems, which may or may not have been voiced by them.

Developing skill in paraphrasing and empathic responding requires focus, attention, seeking clarification to ensure accuracy in reflecting the content of the words, and identifying and naming feelings. When responding reflectively, it is important that the social worker solicit and be open to receiving feedback from the client system as to whether or not he or she has misunderstood or misinterpreted the client system's message or the feelings being communicated.

As noted above, *identifying and naming concerns and themes* refers to the process of identifying and stating the concerns and interests presented for mediation. This is done initially to focus the mediation process. In addition, throughout the process, recurring themes or interests may emerge that will need identification and naming to ensure that all mediation participants have clarity and understanding about the nature and intensity of the conflict. Attending to emerging themes and concerns is especially significant in managing troublesome emotional differences. We can identify recurring themes and concerns by attending to and making mental notes of nuances, clues, and repetitions in verbal and nonverbal communication. We name them when we verbalize these awarenesses during the process.

A skill useful for maintaining focus, creating movement toward the desired objective, and closing the interaction is *summarization.* We summarize when we concisely review and connect together salient content, ideas, and feelings. "A . . . summary can assist in [reviving] a conversation which has stopped or [been] interrupted . . . as a way of getting back to work quickly" (Community Relations Section, 1991, p. 54). In closing a mediation, we recap by summarizing the points of agreement for managing the conflict.

During mediation, *offering feedback* is a useful skill for enhancing participant awareness of self and their contributions to or disruptions of the process. Generally, feedback is offered by the mediator to the participants. This differs from offering feedback in other situations in which the feedback may be offered by all parties involved in the change process, enabling both the social worker and the client system to learn and grow.

As mentioned previously, one of the functions of the mediator is to provide structure and guide the process. While the decisions are made by the participants, the mediator has a responsibility to create a nonthreatening environment; one way to accomplish this is by *making instructions clear.*

Some general rules of mediation include: only one person talks at a time, all participants will have an opportunity to present their concerns and respond to the presentation of other participants' concerns, mediators do not decide who is right or wrong nor do they decide the outcome, violence or threats of violence are not tolerated, and the mediator has the right and responsibility to stop the mediation process at any time. Being able to clearly state the rules, format, and expectations of the process is vital to the creation of a nonthreatening environment and a facilitative process.

According to Hepworth and Larsen (1990), *confrontation* is useful in enhancing self-awareness and promoting change, and "involves facing clients with some aspect of their thoughts, feelings, or behaviors that is contributing to or maintaining their difficulties" (p. 550). Skillful confrontation requires attending to the verbal and nonverbal communication patterns of the client system; caring for and concern about the client system; noticing discrepancies, contradictions, or inconsistencies in client system behaviors, feelings, beliefs, and thoughts; and empathically sharing the observations of the inconsistencies with the client system (Hepworth and Larsen, 1990).

We are reminded by Hepworth and Larsen (1990) that confrontations "embody consideration of clients' feelings that underlie obstacles and resistances to change. Because fears are generally involved in resistance to change, skill in relating with high levels of empathy is prerequisite to using confrontation effectively" (p. 550). They also caution that confrontation is a "tool" to be used sparingly.

> *Practitioners who make frequent confrontations generally have failed to master the facilitative conditions, as practitioners who use the latter skillfully foster* self-confrontation *by their clients as the helping process evolves. In other words, as clients gain expanded awareness of themselves and their problems through self-exploration, they tend to become aware of and to confront discrepancies and inconsistencies themselves. (Hepworth and Larsen, 1990, p. 550)*

In summary, the social worker as mediator seeks to create a nonthreatening environment, assess the dynamics and intensity of the conflict, and facilitate a process through which the participants can negotiate and collaborate in the development of an integration

> *which serves the best interests of each. . . . Mediation is not only a method of dispute resolution, but also an . . . [educational] process. Disputants learn about each other and are encouraged to see the other's point of view. The best mediations provide an opportunity for the disputants to learn new and better ways to manage conflict. (Community Relations Section, 1991, p. 5)*

Assisting in Decision Making Brown, Kahr and Peterson (1974) note that, after the 1960s, a general technology known as decision analysis emerged "for imposing logical structure on the reasoning that underlies any specific decision. . . . Decision analysis . . . assists individuals and organizations to make up their minds, by quantifying the considerations, however subjective, which enter into any decision" (p.5).

Reflecting on the objective and subjective components of the decision-making process, Etzioni (1992) observes that the majority of choices involve "no or little information processing but largely or exclusively draw on affective involvements and normative commitments" (p.91). Normative commitments are "prescriptive in nature" and are predetermined by the values and beliefs held by the person making the decision. A normative commitment might be based on the "shoulds" associated with specific cultural or religious tenets or doctrines. To illustrate, the option of abortion as a means for managing an unwanted pregnancy might not exist for many women because of specific cultural or religious beliefs.

According to Ivey (1994), it is the value or meaning of the factors or choices that is central to decision making. "Meanings run as deep as, or deeper than feelings. . . . Meanings are organizing constructs that are at the core of our being" (pp. 238, 248). It is through meaning that we make sense of "the world around us [which] is often complex and confusing. . . . All of us seem to have some system of ordering meaning, concepts, and judgments, but with varying degrees of clarity" (p. 240).

A significant component of setting goals in Phase Two is the skill to elicit and reflect meaning. Skills associated with eliciting and reflecting meaning are similar to exploratory questioning and reflective listening through paraphrasing and empathy. The difference is that we seek clarity about the meaning of experiences and options from the client system's perspective or frame of reference (Ivey, 1994).

Ivey (1994) proposes three key elements that must be present when exploring and reflecting meaning:

1.   *The behaviors, thoughts, and feelings need to have been made explicit and clear through attending behavior, client observation, and the BLS [basic listening skills]. A general understanding of the client is essential as a first step.*

2.   *Questions in which content is oriented toward meaning may be asked. For example:*
"What does this mean to you?"
"What sense do you make of it?"
"What values [beliefs] underlie your actions?" . . .

3.   *The key meaning and value words of the client are reflected. . . . Your task is reflecting meaning, values, and the way a client makes sense of the world. . . .*
A reflection of meaning is structured similarly to a paraphrase or reflection of feeling. . . . Simply change "You feel . . ." to "You mean . . . ," . . . "You value . . . ," . . . "Your intention was . . . ," . . . or "It sounds like you value. . . ."
. . . Closing with a checkout such as "Is that close?" or "Am I hearing you correctly?" may be helpful. (pp. 242–243, 248)

By operationalizing these skills, social workers enable client systems to explore and clarify the values and beliefs that provide a foundation for making decisions about preferred realities.

There are three primary approaches to decision making in groups or collectives of people: authority, majority, and consensus. Decisions made autocratically (independently) by an expert, an executive director, a social worker, or a subgroup of the whole fit in the authority category (Zastrow, 1989). Autocratic decision making is often necessary in situations of catastrophic crises, when there is neither time nor opportunity to gather staff or participants for discussion and decision making or when the decision does not affect staff or participants. When client systems, during interactions with a social worker, exercise self-determination in decision making, they are approaching the decision from an authority position.

Another component of autocratic decision making is when the decision is made by one person after soliciting input and feedback from the participants who will be affected, if only indirectly, by the decision. For example, a committee member has the responsibility of scheduling with a local radio station public service announcements about the organization's fundraising efforts. The specific times for running the announcements were not discussed during the committee's most recent meeting, and the announcements must run before the next meeting. The responsible committee member may solicit feedback individually from different committee members about ideal times for running the spots before contracting with the radio station.

The majority approach to decision making encompasses the use of democratic processes such as a simple majority vote, two-thirds or three-fourths majority vote, multiple voting, and averaging individual opinions (Zastrow, 1989). All of these mechanisms for selecting one option out of several viable alternatives are based on the premise that the majority rules.

One caution with this approach is that, by the very nature and structure of voting, winners and losers are created. Support in carrying out the decision may not be forthcoming from the people who voted for a different outcome.

When the process, outcome, and collective support of the decision are desired, decision making by consensus is the appropriate approach. Consensus is a collective opinion arrived at by a group of people in a climate in which there is open communication, support, and a fair chance for every member of the group to influence the decision.

When a decision is made by consensus, all members of the group understand the decision and are prepared to support it (Zastrow, 1989). When the decision that has to be made directly affects the group members, the consensus approach is the most desirable mechanism. Consensus decision making enhances the participation of all group members and generally reflects a synthesis of group members' thoughts and ideas.

Several principles apply when engaging in consensus decision making:

1. *Consensus decision making takes time.* Sufficient time for expression of ideas, feelings, and meanings associated with the decision is vital. Often, several meetings are necessary to ensure that all members of the group have provided input and to manage conflict and differences that surface as a natural part of the process.

Even though the central focus of consensus decision making is the *process* of reaching a collaborative decision, it does not mean that consensus decision making occurs without structure or timelines. We (Barry, Becky, and Jim) found the structure of having a publisher's deadline for submitting the manuscript for this text extremely helpful in facilitating consensus! Just as earlier we discussed the relationship of action to imagining preferred realities and goal setting, action can occur before a consensus is reached.

2. *Ensure that all members have opportunities for expressing their views.* Some members, because of cultural norms or personal qualities, may have difficulty expressing their views within the group. With understanding and sensitivity, the process facilitator can elicit input from these members.

3. *Identify commonalities in viewpoints as a foundation for working toward consensus.* As with mediation, building on the capacity for agreement is a fundamental component of consensus decision making. This foundation enables the group to develop a bond and a cohesiveness that aids in the creation of a climate in which conflicts and differences of opinion are more openly expressed, listened to, and utilized.

4. *Differences and conflicts in viewpoints are to be treasured.* Effective decision making by consensus is based on the synthesis of differing perspectives. Arriving at a consensus is not a competition—there are no winners or losers. Consensus decision making is an inclusionary process during which differing ideas and viewpoints are elicited to ensure that all sides of or perspectives on an issue are expressed.

Imagining a Preferred Reality in Different Contexts We have concentrated thus far on situations where the client system is actively charting the story and setting the direction. There may be situations, however, where the client system will not be as integrally involved in goal setting because of contextual or systemic constraints. In these situations, the social worker may serve in an advocacy role to ensure that needs and concerns are identified and voiced from the client system's perspective (not the institution's) and that the goals and plan of action are client system centered.

Client systems who enter into a relationship with a social worker involuntarily present another challenge for goal setting. We think the guidelines presented above apply, with one additional emphasis: the establishment of a climate that facilitates goal implementation. To create such an environment requires identification of the realities that obligate the client system to be present involuntarily in a service-receiving position. Honest discussion of the events (the story exploration in Phase One) that made it necessary for the client system and the social worker to work together can start the description of a preferred reality and the goal-setting process. Many child protective service workers tell us they use the idea of client systems working to get the social workers out of their family's life as a motivation tool.

Goals are set within the context of the client system's experience. The context influences who is describing the preferred reality, who is making decisions about what goals to set and the direction of the goals, and how opportunities, barriers, and resources are perceived. Within this process is the balance of respecting culture and human rights.

Once the preferred reality is known and agreed upon, the work of moving toward that reality begins. This aspect of social work practice takes us to Phase Three.

Summary

Phase Two centers the social worker and the client system on the exciting and challenging work of expressing the hopes and dreams associated with their issues and concerns. This is hard work, but critical to the planned change effort. At the heart of this phase is the belief that change is possible and that the capacities for change are within the client system. One challenge in this phase is the necessity for moving beyond the self-imposed limits that issues and concerns often present for the client system.

We have deliberately chosen the phrase "hopes and dreams" to help us think about our role with the client system. Until one can imagine a different future, one cannot set about realizing it. Often, given the reluctance within our society to prize help seeking, social workers meet people whose recent experiences may tell them that little can be achieved on their core concerns. Challenging that belief may be one of the most important contributions we make to this phase as we continue our work with the client system.

We have set forth some guides for facilitating the process of clarifying the specific goals most closely linked with the issue or concern. Key points for goal setting and clarification include the need for goals to be measurable, grounded in reality, stated positively, clear about the risks, legal, and within the social worker's ethical limits.

We have also described what we see as useful knowledge and skills for Phase Two of the model. Knowledge about resources, how to pursue alternatives, and learning from others is vital to the task of envisioning a preferred reality and setting goals for the work ahead. The nature of the process of Phase Two demands that social workers have skill in creating a safe atmosphere, clarifying, reframing, offering feedback, mediating, and assisting in decision making.

As you move on to learn about taking action for realizing hopes and dreams, please consider the following:

1. Think about a time when you wanted to do something new but found it rather frightening. How were you able to find a way to begin taking action?

2. How has the second phase of our model been consistent with your experiences with change? In what ways is it different?

3. How do you experience setting goals and thinking about making a change in your life circumstances?

4. Think about situations client systems may present with which you would find it difficult to work. What makes the situations difficult? Is this something you may wish to change so it could be less difficult?

5. Think about a time when you were forced to change. How did you find that experience? What lessons are there for times you may be working with involuntary client systems?

CHAPTER SEVEN

Phase Three: Making Plans and Dreams Real

Courage is not the absence of fear, but the capacity to go ahead in the very direction of which you're afraid.

M. SCOTT PECK
(1995, P. 399)

Introduction

Taking action with client systems requires the social worker to be grounded in professional values, knowledgeable about generalist practice, and skilled in a variety of helping roles. This chapter focuses on the action phase of our model as it relates to our description of the key aims of social work practice, presented earlier in the book.

A mother approaches a school social worker because she thinks her second grader is not seeing well and probably needs glasses. The school vision tests are not for another three months, and the mom doesn't have the money to pay for an eye exam or glasses. In this situation, the social worker adopts the broker role, setting out to find an optometrist who will do the exam and then contacting the Lions' Club (which has vision care as one of its missions) to pay for the needed glasses. The social worker may be in contact with this parent on other issues, and in more complicated cases, will start more fully with the client's telling the story and imagining a preferred reality. In this instance, however, the social worker starts with action and the added credibility and trust of having been able to meet an immediate need for the parent.

The process we have outlined in previous chapters is a common one. It is necessary to tell the story well and completely for both the social worker and client system to understand the current reality. It is also important to consider how the situation might be different and to set goals so that actions are based not on the perception of difficulties but on an image of a preferred reality that leads to greater commitment to action. Given that we believe the decisions that are associated with the story are those of the client system, we understand that on some occasions we will enter the process at Phase One, on others at another phase. The point is that understanding the phases and their tasks will help us know how to better connect with the issues at hand, as well as the nature of the relationship that may need to be developed to realize the tasks.

We see the generalist planned change process unfolding like hypertext, the operating system on the World Wide Web. Pursue a certain issue in Phase One and you go immediately to Phase Three, or some other phase in the model. Additionally, as the process of work evolves, we imagine it as moving along a spiral path where both client system and social worker find understanding on a new plane as the work is realized and the relationship grows.

As we continue with the metaphor of the story, Phase One (Telling and Exploring the Story) describes the present situation in context, and Phase Two (Describing a Preferred Reality) identifies the outcomes and direction for the work. Depending on the situation and the goals of the client system, there are a variety of paths the client system may take as well as a variety of ways the social worker might work with the client system as they enter the next phase.

To say that the social worker can utilize a variety of ways or approaches might give the impression of an unorganized grab bag of tools. This is not the case at all! Rather, we ground our interventions in selective knowledge and skills that are compatible with the values and ethics of social work, especially as expressed within the aims and purposes of the social work profession. These aims are important anchor points for taking action in Phase Three.

As we work with client systems on making plans and dreams real, we refer back to our depiction of the five aims of social work. We believe that social workers

- facilitate the effective functioning of client systems and work toward preferred realities in their context;
- link client systems with needed resources from the context through providing information, brokering, and advocacy;
- support client systems by working with them to strengthen their social supports and social network;
- work with client systems and with others to alter the social, economic, and political structures of the context so that they are more responsive to the needs of persons, families, groups, and communities and more conducive to social justice; and
- carry out these aims in ways that strengthen the competencies of and increase the options for client systems.

Hopps, Pinderhughes, and Shankar (1995) found that client systems presenting concerns that required change external to their system were often being treated with interventions that were focused on changes internal to the system. If we are limited in the nature and number of tools we have to manage a concern, our tendency is to perceive the concern in a way that makes it possible to use the tools we have. The challenge and opportunity facing the social worker is to fit the strategy for influencing change to the needs and concerns as identified and voiced by the client system.

The interventions that support action for making plans and dreams real are organized around the aims of social work practice as we have identified them above and around the values, knowledge, and skills an effective social worker needs to apply the interventions. However, the sequence of use of these interventions across phases is not linear. Instead, the social worker needs to be flexible in freely moving with the client system between phases as called for and as the client system is ready to act on issues of concern.

For purposes of illustration, Figure 7.1 demonstrates the social worker/client system partnership as they move through the planned change process. The same kind of process can occur whether the practitioner is working with a person, a family, a group, a community, or an organization with these systems simultaneously.

After working with the social worker to explore the story and decide about the direction of change efforts, the client system has a number of options, some of which can be pursued simultaneously in different arenas. In our discussion of Phase One, we introduced a situation in which a group of low-income women started with learning more effective parenting behaviors. Their concerns about

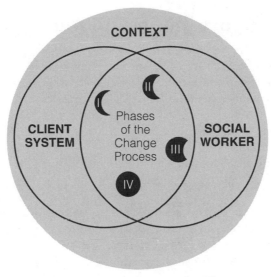

Figure 7.1 Primary Partners in the Change
Process

the quality of their children's education led to a successful class action suit against the Board of Education, which ultimately benefited the city's children.

Our experiences suggest that the most common way in which the simultaneity of working with multiple systems is put into practice is in those circumstances where the social worker experiences a singular case challenge and, as a result, identifies an unmet community, contextual need. I (Becky), as the rookie staff member in a community mental health facility, was routinely assigned the more "interesting" cases. Within a period of two weeks, I received three different referrals of young men of high school age, all with the presenting concern of exhibiting themselves in public. With the second referral, I started wondering why I had gotten two referrals for similar behaviors in a short period of time. When I received the third referral, I began to recognize that there might be something systemic occurring.

All the young men with whom I talked did not display any other patterns of behavior or ideation that would lead me to believe there were more severe issues or concerns. Upon further exploration of their story, I discovered that they all belonged to a club, not sanctioned by the high school, that had as an initiation requirement exhibiting oneself in public.

These young men were not disturbed; they were engaging in rituals associated with belonging. Unfortunately, the consequences of their behaviors were more than they had intended. Through interaction among high school personnel, the youth and their parents, and community leaders, we were able to create community and school-sanctioned activities that met the needs of the young men without the unintended consequences.

When client systems achieve success, they are more likely to try again and be willing to take on even greater challenges.

Values that Support Taking Action

While the focus of this phase is on implementing strategies to achieve client system goals, it is important to understand that, as in the previous phases, professional values play a central role in guiding the process of working and in the behaviors exhibited by the social worker. Loewenberg and Dolgoff (1966) note that "Professional values that do not provide guidance and direction are only of limited value" (p. 20).

The Curriculum Policy Statement of the Council on Social Work Education (1992) summarizes important professional values that social work educators are expected to address throughout the professional curriculum. We paraphrase them and add others of our own that we think are useful guides for taking action. These values are not presented in any preferred order.

- Belief in the respect for and contributions of diverse populations in a pluralistic society
- Belief in the capacity of people to self-determine, engage in process, and change
- Belief in competency and the existence of resources
- Belief in belonging
- Belief in acting to affirm dignity
- Belief in the client system's right to service and society's responsibility to its members
- Belief in the responsibility of the members of a society to act in ways that reflect a respect for the rights and responsibility of the other members of the society
- Belief in the process
- Belief in addressing the needs of the spirit
- Belief in acting for social and economic justice

There are three primary foci of these beliefs. One is a focus on client system ownership of behaviors; for example, belonging, self-determination, and incumbency to act in ways that reflect responsibility to self, to others, and to society. The second is the focus on those behaviors of which the social worker has primary ownership; for example, acting to affirm dignity and competency, affirming client system rights to service, and embracing the role of process in influencing change. Finally, the remaining beliefs are most appropriately shared with others; for example, respecting and appreciating the contributions of diverse populations, acting for social and economic justice, and addressing the needs of the spirit. We examine each of these beliefs in more detail below.

Ethnorelativism is the ideology that supports the *belief in the respect for and contributions of diverse populations*. Bennett (1986) proposes a continuum for

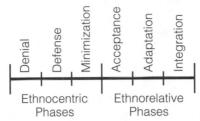

EXPERIENCE OF DIFFERENCE

Development of Intercultural Sensitivity

Figure 7.2 Movement from Ethnocentrism to Ethnorelativism [*Source:* Bennett (1986, p. 32).]

examining the movement from an ethnocentric experience of diversity (denial of difference or the existence of other cultures) to ethnorelativism and the synergistic, integrative effects of the interaction of a culturally diverse society. This continuum is illustrated in Figure 7.2.

In Bennet's illustration, ethnocentrism is characterized most definitively by the isolation and separation associated with the *denial* of differences. *Defense* is an awareness of diversity characterized by denigration (the negative evaluation and stereotyping of difference), superiority (a we/they orientation with the "we" being superior), and reversal (embracing other cultures and denigrating one's own (Bennett, 1986, pp. 37–41). Most of the "isms" and phobias linked with diversity (e.g., racism, ageism, sexism, homophobia) are associated with the placement of negative value on the other person or culture.

Minimization and *acceptance* are the border phases between ethnocentric and ethnorelative experiences of difference. The concept of a melting pot society, in which cultural identities and differences diminish, is associated with the phase of minimization. Whereas minimization emphasizes the similarities of acknowledged differences, acceptance is a recognition of acknowledged differences.

According to Bennett, the next phase is *adaptation*. However, I (Becky) prefer what I believe to be a more accurate label: appreciation. When we appreciate diversity, we can move beyond acceptance and begin to cherish and celebrate differences and develop empathy with those who are different from us.

Appreciation is associated with the concept of a pluralistic society in which diverse populations simultaneously sustain cultural identities and join with and become part of the whole. According to Bennett (1986), "[p]luralism *may* be a development beyond empathy. It is a development in the sense that cultural difference is respected as highly as one's self, since it is intrinsic to the self" (p. 55). As a participant noted in a workshop I (Becky) led on diversity, appreciation in relation to the experience of diversity is like a smorgasbord. All the foods maintain their own unique qualities and characteristics and yet when eaten together blend to provide a celebration of colors, smells, textures, and tastes.

The final state in Bennett's continuum is *integration.* Integration is characterized by an ethnorelative identity whereby difference is incorporated into "the meaning of life" and "difference . . . becomes integral to identity" (Bennett, 1986, p. 58). Bennett (1986) notes:

> [t]he state of integration represents a development beyond adaptation because, in Adler's words [1977], "the multicultural person . . . is not simply the person who is sensitive to many different cultures, rather, he is a person who is always in the process of becoming a part of and apart from a given cultural context." . . .
> In the model discussed here, the term "pluralism" was used to indicate "sensitivity to many cultures." The key to being "in process" is not simply being pluralistic; it is having integrated the skill of defining cultural context into one's ongoing sense of self. (p. 58)

As referenced in the quote above, included in the state of integration is the ultimate development of the capacity to be both part of and apart from cultural boundaries. In this sense, the experience of difference is subjective and "relative"; the multicultural person is continually in the process of constructing a reality that is inclusive of and transcends identification with a specific culture (Bennett, 1986).

The second item on our list of beliefs and values, the *belief in client systems' rights to self-determination and their capacity for change,* is at the core of professional beliefs, as presented in Chapter 2. We include them here to reinforce the point that the social worker's ability to communicate this belief may be an important source of support to the client system in taking action.

We chose to combine the ideas of competency and resources in our list of professional values and beliefs because we see being competent as one important resource client systems possess, although in times of crisis the memory of these competencies may be less available. Resources may be thought of as anything of value that can be used to address client systems' issues or concerns (Siporin, 1975). *Affirming that client systems possess competence and that the context has useful resources* facilitates acting from strength.

Belief in belonging may be thought of as meeting a basic human need experienced by all people in all cultures. Being connected with others who provide social support can be an important variable in taking action. The greater the degree of isolation—whether physical, social, or emotional—the more difficult acting can be. Social workers recognize this and act with client systems to strengthen their social supports.

Affirming one's dignity is an important experience for taking action. The degree to which dignity is denied weakens the opportunity to work well in the pursuit of goals. The loss of dignity and respect raises serious challenges to the client system's sense of competence and capacity to act. Social workers need to be mindful of the messages, both verbal and nonverbal, they send regarding their belief in and respect for the dignity and worth of client systems.

Social work has a long history of *belief in the client system's right to service and in the client system's responsibility to use those resources effectively.* This value gets at the reciprocal nature of the relationship of the society and its members. The social work profession prizes this relationship and works to enhance society/member interaction so members' issues and concerns can be more fully addressed within the societal context.

The society/member interaction is not solely dependent upon either the government or the private sector. Rather, we see a healthy society as one that actively works to create the kind of opportunities and resources its members need to address their issues and concerns. It is further understood that the members of the society have a *responsibility to act in ways that reflect the rights and responsibilities of the other members of the society.*

Nowhere is this relationship between society and its members more apparent than in the debate during the 1990s about the role of work. In the United States, work is valued as the primary means for acquiring the monetary resources needed for living. Yet, citizen access to jobs that are supportive of other citizen goals—being able to live in a small town as opposed to a metropolitan area or vice versa—is not always available. This becomes more troublesome when we consider that the economic structure of the United States is based on a supply-and-demand market economy that requires a minimum unemployment of a given percentage in order to survive.

An economist might suggest that unemployment is transient in nature, moving from one employer to the next. However, in the modern economy, as skills become obsolete, people face extended, if not permanent, conditions of unemployment. Also, people whose unemployment benefits have been exhausted and who have stopped looking for work are not counted in the unemployment statistics. If these populations were counted, we estimate that the percentage rate for current unemployment would be two to three percentage points higher.

We seem to trust employers who create jobs at places of their choosing and leave workers to figure out how to find the jobs and relocate. The requirement of a minimum level of unemployment and the demand for relocation to find jobs create difficult realities that strain the relationship between society and its members.

Throughout this book, we have noted that social work practice is both process and outcome oriented. We believe that *valuing the planned change process* equally with outcomes is vital for acting in ways that are consistent with the aims and purposes of the social work profession. It is in the process of our work with client systems that much of the mutual learning necessary for responsible action takes place. An effective change process should contribute to the empowerment and enhanced awareness of the capacities and competencies of both client systems and social workers.

One function of the social worker and, at times, of members of support groups is to help the client system reflect on what was learned that was of value from trying out a new behavior or approach. I (Jim) do a lot of work with parenting groups and tell the parents with whom I work to actively practice what they are learning in groups—techniques such as linking the children's behavior with consequences and talking directly with children, using statements that disclose the parents' feelings and expectations. "We can talk about how it worked next week," I say, "because as a parent, if it doesn't work today, you'll always have another chance tomorrow."

As we discuss in Phase Four of our model, the learning realized from an effective process can be reused and exchanged between the client system and the social worker. I (Barry) was involved in a panel a few years ago where one of my students, currently employed in a social work role, included a person with whom she was working as part of the panel. As the person spoke of her relationship with the social worker and the social worker's effective case management practice, it was clear that both she and the social worker had learned much from one another. The person had come to more fully discover her voice and the ways she could use it to seek the resources she needed, and the social worker had discovered the value of seeing competency in others.

In Chapter 2, we discussed at some length the value of and issues associated with *spirituality* and religion. In part we have included spirituality in our discussion of values because of its potential as a resource and also because there is a spiritual side to the human condition that is often part of our issues and concerns. Taking action may mean using spiritual resources in some instances and it may mean enabling the client system to link more clearly with that side of the human condition in others.

Jim Wallis (1994) envisions the spiritual needs of people as closely aligned with issues of having hope. Grounding his work in theology, he sees hope as "the engine of change" and "the energy of transformation" (p. 238). As we take action to make plans and dreams real, hope is an important part of the process. Understanding and valuing spirituality and hope enables us to be sensitive to the challenges and potentialities these forces hold for taking action.

The last value found on our list addresses our belief in action for *social and economic justice.* Historically, social and economic justice has been an important goal for the social work profession. Much of the energy of the profession has been directed, with varying degrees of success, at addressing these concerns. We believe that they are so important that, as we contemplate taking action with client systems, we need to be clear about the way our acts advance the cause of economic and social justice in our society.

We are not suggesting that all issues and concerns brought by client systems will be about social and economic justice. However, when there are people in our society living in poverty or in areas of declining economic opportunity, or who face obstacles and barriers because of their gender, race, sexual orientation, cultural context, or disability, then we need to act in ways that address these issues.

To see poverty or oppression only as a personal issue is to miss the systemic change obligations of the social work profession. To see issues only as personal concerns continues the history of blaming the victim—all too often a part of client systems' experiences (as you recall from Chapter 1).

The core values we have reviewed here are intertwined with the five aims, outlined earlier, that we have set forth for the social work profession. These aims of social work guide our actions when working with client systems toward making their plans and dreams real. The remainder of the chapter will help us think more carefully about the knowledge and skills that inform the interventions associated with these aims.

Knowledge and Skills That Support Taking Action

We organize our discussion of the knowledge and skills for taking action around our five aims and purposes of social work. The categories are organized about a common objective of the actions of client systems and social workers necessary to realize the goal. The aims, as we have identified them, are designing strategy, linking with resources, providing social support, influencing the social, economic, and political context, and increasing client system competence and capacity.

Facilitating the process of making plans and dreams real is based on the foundation of a relationship characterized by respect, dignity, genuineness, and integrity. Modeling, self-awareness, and the conscious use of self in relation to the other; awareness of and appreciation for the experience of the other (empathy); and encouragement and development of the capacities of the client system are necessary components of all strategies for influencing change. The challenge for the social worker is to bring to the partnership with the client system a competency in consciously using self, in appreciating the experience of the other, and in encouraging and building on client system capacities as the work progresses toward desired realities.

AIM ONE:
Facilitate the effective functioning of client systems and work toward preferred realities in their context

One measure of quality in social work practice is our ability to enable client systems to design strategies for achieving goals and desired outcomes that have a high probability of success. Much of what applies to contracting and goal setting in the discussion of Phase Two also applies here.

Knowledge

Two areas of knowledge that are indispensable for professional practice are the knowledge of human behavior and the social environment and the knowledge of change processes. Knowledge about human behavior and the social environment necessary for influencing change includes knowledge of social, economic, and political systems and structures; cultural diversity, human growth, and development; human biology, oppressed populations, and populations at risk; and the arts, humanities, and sciences.

At first reading, this list of human behavior knowledge appears to be what any social worker may need to know about human behavior, and we agree that it is. This is intentional in that our challenge with the change process is basically to understand the dynamics of this process, the dynamics of human behavior at various levels (world, nation-state, community/neighborhood, family, person), and the effective ways to influence change within the context of the client system's reality and perception of preferred reality. Thus, our challenge as social workers is to enable and support client systems as they engage in change processes *in ways that are possible within their context.*

In Chapters 1 and 4, we discussed the process of change. Knowing how change processes work and are experienced is vital. When we understand the change process, we realize that it is not linear; it spirals and occurs with stops, starts, and detours.

We also realize that, when there is change that leads to realizing goals or dreams, there are losses as well as gains and some grieving that goes along with things being different. A man who has quit drinking relishes his improved health and work performance but still misses the slightly out-of-control excitement of inebriation. A couple who have worked on their communication issues find that they are getting along better but still in some ways miss the old days when they weren't working so hard on mutual understandings. The community working on prevention of substance abuse within their adolescent population might be excited that they have pulled together but still miss the time when they were not so aware of the issue or so frightened by the consequences of the prevalence of teenage substance abuse in their locality.

A major premise of this book is that the specific context in which the social worker and the client system work shapes the change process. Therefore, the specific knowledge that is needed to facilitate client systems' effective functioning and working toward preferred realities in their context varies from situation to situation. Books and journal articles can be resources for advancing our knowledge about context- and situation-specific information to inform our work with client systems. It is our professional responsibility to keep up with new findings in the field. Besides being ethically necessary, keeping current with the professional literature and engaging in continuing education activities enables us to enhance and add to our competencies for and effectiveness in practice.

I (Becky) shared earlier my association and experience with creating the Family Violence Prevention Program in a community where I lived and worked. One of the cofounding members of the program, a dear friend and social worker, and I conducted workshops throughout the state on the dynamics of and intervention strategies for working with families experiencing violence in the home. This was in the middle 1970s before much was known about family violence and the ways to work with families experiencing violence.

Five years later (I had moved away to work on my doctorate and then returned to the community), my colleague and I were preparing for a workshop we were to present on women in transition. There was some material from our family violence presentations we thought might be relevant for the workshop we were preparing. We were horrified when we realized how little we had known then about family violence compared to what had been researched and discovered during the five years that had passed. None of the materials from the earlier workshop were usable because they were so out of date.

Today, with the explosion of knowledge, it is even harder to keep current with new findings and understandings about our world and our experience in it. There is no way one person can know all there is to know about human behavior and social, political, cultural, and economic systems. Thus, skill in critical thinking and information retrieval is absolutely vital for social work practice today and in the future (Bloom, 1975).

In Phase Two, our emphasis was on dreaming about and selecting goals that contribute to preferred realities. There's a tendency for client systems (and social workers at times) to consider that, having set clear goals and reasonable strategies, the rest won't be that difficult. When we believe this way, we're underestimating the power of Murphy's Law—if anything can go wrong, it will!

Shortly after graduating from college, I (Jim) spent two years working through the Peace Corps in the Municipal Community Action Department in the capital city of a Central American country. Although much of our work was strictly community development, we participated indirectly through the community groups with which we were working in the first land invasion in Central America. In land invasions, large numbers of people without places to live squat on uninhabited land all at once and hope that the military won't evict them by force. The logistics for this invasion were impressive, and on the night in question, 3000 people descended on a plot of land in 45 minutes.

The Peace Corps volunteers who worked with the community groups stayed away the night of the invasion, and the next day when we visited (the army hadn't intervened), we marveled at the order of the instant neighborhood. However, in the days to come, difficulties surfaced, as the planning group had not thought out issues of water, hygiene, and support for those group members who had quit their jobs to coordinate things full-time.

Skills and Techniques

Similar to professional knowledge and values, skills and techniques are important resources for effective social work practice. However, although these words are often used interchangeably, skills and techniques are not the same thing. We think of skills as the social worker's capacities and competencies, while techniques are specific tools (for example, genograms, ecomaps, brainstorming) that can be useful in all phases of the change process. Techniques may or may not be used skillfully.

In the sections that follow, we will present the skills of teaching and offering advice as well as some techniques that social workers may find useful in working with client systems. The techniques described below are useful for facilitating learning and learning transfer, developing client system skill, monitoring movement toward goal achievement, and generating options, alternative strategies, and skills necessary for making plans and dreams real.

Teaching Teaching is both a role and a skill associated with generalist social work practice. As a role, teaching is one of the many hats we wear as we are fulfilling the purpose and aims of social work by joining with client systems in planned change processes. We are teaching when we empower client systems by assisting in the acquisition of skills, knowledge, and information.

The skill of teaching encompasses all the skills we discussed previously in Chapters 5 and 6. It can take many forms and look very different, depending on the context, the concern, and the nature and size of the client system. For example, our client system may be a group of teenage mothers seeking knowledge and skills in caring for their children. One primary form the teaching may take in this case is modeling.

Modeling is a powerful teaching tool. So often we tend to forget that, as the saying goes, our actions speak louder than words. The psychological theory of social learning expands the theories of B. F. Skinner and his predecessors on behaviorism and behavior modification, the application of behaviorism in practice. The major premise of social learning theory is that we can learn novel behaviors—behaviors that are not a part of our existing repertoire—and that learning can occur even though the behavior is not immediately performed. Thus, learning can result by observing and/or imitating the behavior of another person or model (Bandura, 1969).

We model respect, worth, dignity, and appreciation for difference by how we respond to the teenage mothers seeking child care skills. We model healthy management of conflict and frustration by how we relate to the mothers when these situations occur. We model child care principles and processes by how we relate to the mothers' children when the children and mothers are together. We model in the grocery store by how we respond to our own children. Opportunities to teach through modeling abound!

The concern about what children and adolescents are learning by watching television comes from an understanding that children frequently imitate what they have seen others do. Adolescents and adults may either imitate the behaviors of others or may gradually acquire the mannerisms and habits of the people who are significant to them or who they admire. The best illustration of this phenomenon comes from watching people who have been living together awhile or who are long-term best friends or colleagues. It is very common for them to use the same phrases in their speech and to develop very similar patterns of behaviors.

Think about your own habits and mannerisms. Are there any mannerisms you can identify that you picked up from someone you admire, a family member, or a good friend? What about the people to whom you are significant? Do they ever display any mannerisms or patterns of speech that they learned from you?

Generally, we don't pay much attention to the mannerisms we pick up from or model for others unless the habits we have acquired or transmitted are troublesome. I (Becky) recall very vividly an experience when I was visiting a field instructor and student. I noticed that the field instructor was using the phrase "you know" much more frequently than I had ever heard her use it before. When I mentioned my observation to her, she acknowledged that this in fact was the case, as her student used the phrase repetitively. Early on in the field placement process, the field instructor had discussed with her student the concern she had about the repetitive use of "you know" and how it might affect the student's presentation of self with client systems, resources, and colleagues. In spite of the discussion, the student continued to use the phrase. The field instructor had not realized that she too had picked up the habit until her husband brought it to her attention.

We model behaviors in everything we do, personally and professionally. This presents us with a challenge of how we conduct ourselves both on and off the job. I (Becky) experienced most of my teen years as a preacher's kid (PK). My brothers, sisters, and I were repeatedly reminded to "watch our P's and Q's" whenever we left the house, as we were to "set an example" for those around us.

Just as it can be very difficult to constantly be in the spotlight as a teenager, so too it can be frustrating to know that, as social workers, we are under the public microscope. This is especially true in small communities and rural areas. How we conduct ourselves in our personal lives is as important as how we function and behave as professionals.

Two other skills associated with teaching are coaching and role playing or behavior rehearsal. Coaching is a method of instruction in which the teacher and learner are engaged together in the step-by-step process of learning a skill, acquiring new knowledge, or carrying out a task. As children, we learned many of our skills of self-care through both modeling and coaching.

Think about how you might teach a child to tie a shoe or brush his or her teeth. Until the child has developed enough to have the muscle control and dexterity to accomplish these tasks, we model the behaviors while we are brushing the child's teeth or tying his or her shoes. Eventually, the child will want to take over the task and do it unassisted. This is when we begin coaching.

In the example of brushing teeth, while we are standing by the sink together, we may have to remind the child ("Before we start brushing, it is important to put toothpaste [or baking soda, or tooth powder] on the brush [or the finger]. Do you remember how this is done?") or model the behaviors first (the child does not remember how to put toothpaste on the brush, so we slowly explain as we demonstrate each step before asking the child to do the same thing we just did).

One way of coaching is through role playing, which provides an opportunity to apply and practice behaviors in a safe place before facing the challenge of using them in a new experience or difficult situation. To prepare a woman who has been severely battered by her spouse to give testimony at a public hearing for a bill before the legislature, the social worker may want to role-play the situation with the woman, especially if there may be questions from legislators present at the hearing. In this situation, because of the social worker's knowledge of the process, the social worker would play the role of a legislator and the woman providing the testimony would play herself. In other situations, the social worker might play the role of the person wanting to learn new behaviors, and the person would play the role of the person with whom he or she is experiencing difficulty or conflict. In this role-play situation, the worker first models the behaviors before the client system is asked to use them in the role play.

Using role-playing and behavior rehearsal techniques enables client systems to identify and face anxieties and fears often associated with change. Just as social workers need the combination of values, knowledge, and skills to carry out their roles successfully, so do client systems.

Rehearsal activities incorporate aspects of doing with those of thinking and feeling. Involving more than talk alone, these activities constitute practice of the action step itself. Engaging several dimensions of experience (e.g., thinking, feeling, doing) in the rehearsal activity, the client moves closer to what will be necessary in the real-world context where the change must take place. Rehearsing the action step decreases the anxiety associated with the idea of taking the action, increases the probability that the activity will be undertaken, and enhances the idea that the action step will be successful. (Cournoyer, 1991, p. 271)

Coaching is often the way in which new staff of an agency learn about paperwork or how to fill it out. It can also be a beneficial way to assist client systems new to an agency in filling out required paperwork. For example, we might begin by saying:

"This is the form we use for determining eligibility for our services. The top section is for identifying information, such as name, address, phone, income, and insurance. As you read it over, let me know if you have any questions about what fits where or why the information is being requested. . . .The second section is asking about what is happening in your family, agency, community, or life that you decided to talk with someone about it. What fits here for you? . . .That's exactly what is being asked for here. It's okay to fill in that spot before we proceed to the next section. . . ."

Another example of ways in which coaching might be used is in various types of groups. Teachers often coach in the classroom. Coaching is invaluable in assertiveness and self-defense training groups. And, finally, coaching is an excellent way to teach socialization skills in groups.

Another program of the inner-city neighborhood mental health center where I (Becky) worked was a socialization group for people who were recently discharged from mental health institutions after being hospitalized for an average of 20 years. The mass discharge of residents from these mental health facilities was the result of state legislation requiring community mental health services to be the primary client system care resource and mental health institutions to serve as a "last resort" for crisis intervention and stabilization until return to the community was possible. As often happens, the state law went into effect before sufficient discharge planning could be done at the institutions or before there were sufficient community programs to handle care and case management.

Our mental health center responded very quickly to the need by creating supervised housing and socialization groups for the discharged residents. We did a lot of coaching in these groups to teach group members self-care—how to shop, ride the bus, and develop skills to make a contribution in the community.

One of the highlights of the experience with this socialization group was a trip to Radio City Music Hall that was funded by the group members' making and selling arts and crafts, doing light housework or janitorial work, cooking, house-sitting, or providing other services in the community for pay. Also, many of the group members made new clothes for the trip. All of the skills and techniques associated with the role of teaching were utilized to enable the group as a whole and each of its members to accomplish their goals.

As forms of instruction, modeling, coaching, and role play fit our model best because they rely on the processes of engaging in activities together with client systems. When we apply these skills and techniques, we are in partnership with the client system in the teaching/learning process.

Some situations, contexts, and client systems may require a more formal approach to providing knowledge and information. I (Becky) have a very dear friend and social work colleague who was the mental health consultant for our area Head Start program. Frequently, while present in a Head Start setting to observe children and assist in assessment and referral, she would spend time with the teachers and aides, sharing her knowledge and wisdom about child developmental processes and clues to understanding inappropriate behaviors.

Realizing that the teachers and aides were asking many of the same or similar questions, she organized some workshops and seminars for teachers and aides to discuss and share knowledge about common topics and interests. In the workshop setting, her teaching was much more structured (didactic presentations, use of handouts, structured discussion, and/or role play), but she continued to be informal and unstructured when a teacher or aide engaged her in conversation about specific needs.

In some contexts, the primary method of teaching is through ritual, narrative, and storytelling. As we mentioned and illustrated in Chapter 3 in our discussion of the context of practice, rituals, narratives, and storytelling are effective means for transmitting knowledge and information. In many cultures, rituals, narratives, and storytelling are the primary ways in which history, culture, and traditions are taught.

Offering Advice　Social workers are generally taught never to advise client systems, in that advising compromises client system self-determination. However, research evidence indicates that client systems not only desire advice but benefit from it (Davis, 1975). For example, many Asian American client systems who come to see helpers are seeking clear directions and advice (Uba, 1994, p. 19).

There are several important guidelines to follow in offering advice. Generally, the relationship with the client system is defined by degrees of engagement, nurturance, sustenance, and transformation; and the farther along you are in the helping process with a client system, the more effective offering advice will be. Novice social workers, beginning to learn practice skills through role play, often respond to the initial description of a concern with "Have you ever thought of doing. . . ?" It is not until much later in the process of change that the reasoned opinion of the worker can be very valuable.

When a client system asks for advice and you don't think it is appropriate to give it, offer an explanation and something else instead. Recently, a woman in a parenting group I (Jim) was leading asked me what to do about her 2-year-old who bites a lot. I told her that I didn't know her son well, and I wanted to know more about when he bites, what leads up to his biting, and her reactions when he bites. What started out as a request for advice turned into a group discussion about how to get young children to take naps (which was the precipitating event for the biting). The mother didn't get advice from me, but she came away from the group with support for her situation and with some ideas and options for managing it differently.

When we do decide to offer advice, it makes sense to do so within context. When client systems ask, "What would you do if you were me?" the first response is to empathically relate to their frustration or discouragement; before proceeding with any advice, we need to relate that our life experiences are different and, thus, what might fit for us won't necessarily fit for them. Another principle for offering advice is to be certain that the advice is framed as an "I" statement and couched in tentative language. For example, one might respond to the question posed above, "As I listen to you talk about your situation, one option for consideration might be. . . ." After putting the circumstances in context, then advice can be more accurately interpreted by the client system.

Finally, while we do not rule out offering advice, we do think that it is best to ensure that more than one option is provided. Identifying choices and options for client systems to consider enables them to think about alternatives they might not have otherwise imagined.

Identifying Practice Activities In working with persons or groups where the focus is on building and applying skills, engaging client systems in practicing the skills in the natural environment can be effective. When client systems are seeking to acquire new skills, the social worker and client system can identify opportunities and activities that may be carried out between meetings and then reported during the next meeting for review and evaluation.

If client systems practice, then one of two desirable outcomes is likely. The technique they are practicing may be successful ("I counted to ten when my supervisor criticized me, and then I wasn't defensive"), which reinforces the client system's sense of self-efficacy. Or it may not be successful, in which case this can be a fruitful topic for the next session.

Keeping Track of What Goes Well in Life Berg and Miller (1992) suggest that solution-oriented therapists use a different kind of homework assignment, one in which client systems are encouraged to focus on successful strategies instead of troubling behaviors. When a client system is asked between meetings to "keep track of what you do when you overcome the urge to yell," the idea that the client system knows what to do, can do it, and that the social worker is confident about his or her capacities is reinforced.

Tracking what is going well focuses the attention of client systems on the successful strategies they might not have been aware they were already applying. Once the awareness of their capacities has been raised, then these capacities can be consciously employed.

Support groups also are helpful to client systems in keeping track of how they are doing. Such groups as Alcoholics Anonymous, parenting groups, and Weight Watchers have realized success in tracking movement as well as helping client systems take action through the use of support.

Using Scaling to Monitor Movement toward Desired Outcomes As we discuss in greater detail in Chapter 8, one useful tool to help client systems and the social worker monitor the progress of moving toward preferred realities is the use of scales. Scales are tools that can enable us to know what degree of change has been realized and in what direction the change has taken. Obvious examples are measuring weight loss, periods of sobriety, or the number of family outings or shared play experiences.

These tools, including Goal Attainment Scales and self-anchored ratings by the client system, can be helpful allies in focusing on how the work is unfolding. Often, change is hard, and feedback that illustrates movement toward the desired outcome is an important source of motivation to "keep on keeping on" with the work.

Brainstorming Brainstorming, invented by Alex Osborn (1963), is a technique that can be used with client systems to come up with as many ideas as possible on a given topic. The ideas are written down and then evaluated later. While it can be used in the other phases of the change process, brainstorming may be especially useful in the search for and identification of strategies to reach goals. Osborn's ground rules, as outlined in Davis (1981), are useful for ensuring the effectiveness of the brainstorming process. They are as follows:

- *Try to come up with as many ideas as possible.* At this point in the process, the goal is quantity, not necessarily quality. Encourage the person or group with whom you are working to keep thinking of more strategies and not to consider at this point those strategies that have already been suggested.
- *Crazy ideas are fine.* Strange and off-the-wall answers serve at least two functions. They can free up people to think broadly. (A woman who is trying to figure out how to afford to go back to school says, with a smile, "I could knock off a liquor store." The worker replies: "That might get you some money; what else?") And it also may be that one of the crazy ideas could be the seed of an idea that is useful.
- *"Piggyback" on ideas that are suggested.* An idea that a person comes up with may lead that person, or another in a group, to think of a similar idea. I (Jim) was working with a community group that was trying to figure out how to turn a vacant lot into a playground. After one member suggested getting a civic group to pay for a piece of playground equipment, there was a torrent of ideas by other group members of other groups or businesses that might be willing to chip in for other equipment.
- *Avoid evaluating or criticizing ideas as they emerge.* It is almost impossible to be both creative and critical at the same time. In a group setting, it only takes one comment—"That's a dumb idea" or "Yes, but . . ."—to throw cold water on the free flow of ideas. People who are brainstorming can't keep the ideas coming if they stop to consider each one.

After the group or person has come up with as exhaustive a list as possible, then the ideas can be considered in relation to their applicability and feasibility in making plans and dreams real.

Identifying Possible Resources and Strategies Later in this chapter, we discuss the ways that information can be used as part of the brokering process. Similarly,

Egan (1994) suggests that it can be useful to ask client systems to think of other people or organizations that may be associated in some way with the client system's preferred reality and the goals established to reach that reality. These can include:

- *Persons.* Who does the client system know who has done the kinds of things the client system wants to accomplish, and how have they done it? What specific people could help the client system reach its goals?

- *Communities or groups.* What groups or communities of people are there through which the client system could work toward a preferred reality? (We will address this more later in the chapter.)

- *Organizations or programs.* Are there programs out there that could help? If the client system and/or social worker do not know of the programs, how can they find out?

Identifying Skills Necessary for Reaching Goals   It may be that client systems need to learn communication skills, conflict resolution skills, skills in understanding the way governmental bodies make decisions, or such, before they can proceed (Egan, 1990). At the time that the client system is searching for options, the social worker can be of great assistance by sharing relevant data. According to Shulman (1992), relevant data are "facts, values, ideas, and beliefs that are related to the client's immediate task at hand" (p. 158). As long as the information provided is related to the working contract and fits with the issues of concern the client system has identified, sharing this information is appropriate. Shulman (1992) imparts a caution about sharing data:

> *A problem is created when the worker wants to "teach" something indirectly to the client and uses the interchange to "slip in" personal ideas. This mistaken sense of function on the worker's part is rooted in a model in which the worker can "change" the client by skillfully presenting "good" ideas. The problem is that the client soon senses that the worker has a "hidden agenda"; instead of using the worker as a resource for his or her agenda, the client must begin to weigh the worker's words to see what is "up his (or her) sleeve." (p. 158)*

AIM TWO:
Link client systems with needed resources from the context through providing information, brokering, and advocacy

Knowledge

When securing resources for client systems, social workers are fulfilling the broker role. Knowledge of both formal and informal resources is indispensable in order for social workers to act as brokers. Social workers who are new to a locality or just beginning their careers should visit community resources to determine the services, eligibility criteria, intake or admission processes, characteristics, and the appropriate contact people of the resource (Kirst-Ashman and Hull, 1993). Some social work educators we know have students visit one another during field placement to learn about other resources and to experience walking through another agency's door.

Knowledge of available formal resources is important, especially for persons who are dealing with crises. Gerard Egan points out that some clients need only to know what the available resources are and they can proceed on their own. For others, knowledge of the existence of some formal benefit or resource can be useful in reducing the level of stress—just knowing that help is available can be a relief—as well as in addressing the current concern. Some people might need to know about available resources just to be able to consider a preferred reality—a woman in an abusive relationship without knowledge of shelters and other potential supports for battered women may find she has new options with the knowledge of those resources.

Knowing how formal resources actually operate is invaluable. In Chapter 9, we discuss the ways that discretion on the part of agency workers and officials can lead to improved services in some situations and to discrimination against some kinds of client systems in other situations. When both social workers and client systems who are trying to access the resources are familiar with the policies and regulations, it is much harder for client systems to be treated unjustly.

Similarly, understanding the structures and procedures of bureaucracies in general and of local and regional agencies in particular can help with determining whether or not a request for assistance is appropriate. Living and working in a state that has a great diversity of American Indian tribes, I (Becky) have had to learn about the policies, structures, and organizational realities of the tribes and of the Bureau of Indian Affairs because of their differences.

It is important to know that some resources are finite, some are more elastic. Finite resources are those that are limited. Some programs in the United States have nonentitlement funding, meaning that people who are eligible for the services can receive them until the money runs out for that month or year. The Women, Infants, and Children Nutrition Program (WIC) and Head Start are examples of this. There are also limits on the amount of time social workers have for providing services. Even with short lunch hours and leaving late, the social worker can see only a finite number of people during a normal workweek.

However, there are tangible resources available outside of the formal helping system that might be more elastic in nature. Often, money and other in-kind benefits and services are available from churches, civic clubs, and other voluntary organizations. Seldom are these resources listed in community resources directories; therefore, it is vital for social workers to know who does what in a community in order to access these resources. Generally, there is not a fixed amount of money or services available from these sources (although usually what they do have is not infinite!), and the act of asking can sometimes increase the level of support.

Another example of nonfinite resources is in the use of self-help groups. In self-help groups, the person seeking help is also a resource to others. In Alcoholics Anonymous, for example, every person who comes to a meeting for the first time is a potential sponsor for another person in the future, once his or her own drinking is under control. Because there is only limited staff time involved in setting up and maintaining most self-help groups, they do not depend as much on the availability of professional staff as do organizations that provide direct services.

Skills

The skills associated with linking client systems to needed resources include brokering and advocacy.

Making Referrals: Carrying Out the Broker Role I (Jim) was one of three social work representatives in a multidisciplinary conference on working with children with special needs in the age range from birth to three years. In this conference, each discipline met to identify what it could contribute to effective service to this population and what the other professions (medicine, nursing, and physical therapy in this context) needed to do well. It was a consensus among the other professionals that social workers were the ones who could connect people with resources and work with families.

This role is especially important in the United States where social services are so fragmentary. In much of western Europe, social services are provided primarily through the federal government, and residents of the north of France receive services similar to residents who live in the south of France. In the United States, services and programs are delivered by state, county, and federal governments as well as through a variety of not-for-profit and for-profit organizations, some of which receive government funds. (As noted above, civic groups, voluntary organizations, and charities also have resources that are useful in certain situations.)

Providing information about and linking client systems with resources are connected functions. A particular emphasis of social work among the helping professions is to assist persons to relate more effectively with their contexts. Like a real estate or insurance broker, the social worker identifies, in partnership with the client system, the client system's needs and concerns and helps the client system gain access to appropriate resources (for example, social provisions such as housing/public assistance or social services and funding sources such as foundations and corporations). In order to effectively broker resources, we have adapted the following principles (and added some of our own) from Hepworth and Larsen (1993) and Weissman (1976), as cited in the Hepworth and Larsen text.

1. *Referral is client system centered.* The referral is made because the client system has an issue or concern that can best be addressed elsewhere. Client system needs are paramount.

2. *Referral requires joining with the client system to assess the situation, needs, concerns, and readiness for referral.* The social worker needs to be skilled at assessing such factors as the client system's vulnerability, culture, resources and competencies, esteem, interaction patterns, and commitment to change.

3. *Referral options are explored mutually.* This requires that social workers be familiar with:

    a. local and regional services and resources (informal as well as formal). A knowledgeable social worker is familiar with resource guides and directories, and knows who to call to find out unfamiliar information.

    b. policies and procedures of resources, including the strengths of, barriers in, and processes for accessing them;

    c. the quality and nature of services or assistance provided by resources;

    d. personnel associated with the resources; and

    e. assessment of the fit, in partnership with the client system, between the client situation and the resource. Depending on the ability and motivation of the client system to follow through and the receptivity of the resource to provide services, the social worker will be more or less active.

Informing client systems of the existence of services is often not enough, unless we are sure that they will follow through with little structure or encouragement. In making referrals, we are creating an opportunity for client systems to manage one (or more) of their critical concerns. To increase the likelihood that the referral is successful (after being sure that the resource being brokered is the best possible fit for the client system), the following steps can be beneficial:

1. *Write out the necessary information regarding the resource (names, phone numbers, addresses, hours available, restrictions, requirements) for the client system.* It is important to provide the client system with the name of a specific contact person. Describe the resource contact person to the client system in terms of the worker's function as well as job title; personalize the contact person whenever possible.

2. *Explore with client systems if they want you to initially contact the resource or if they want to initiate contact with the resource.* If a client system prefers that you initiate the contact, it is preferable to do so in the presence of the client system. If the client system opts to contact the resource, it can sometimes be beneficial, with the client system's permission, to contact the resource in preparation for the client system's contact.

3. *If the reason for referral is complex, it may be advisable for the worker and client system to work together to write a statement detailing the nature of the concern and the service needed.*

4. *Client systems who are apprehensive may wish to be accompanied to the initial meeting with the resource contact person.* Explore alternatives with the client system.

5. *Client systems who are ambivalent about taking advantage of another resource may find it beneficial to talk with the resource contact person in the presence of the worker.*

6. *Follow up to ensure that the referral met client system needs.* Ask the client system to let you know how the contact went after the initial meeting with the resource person, *and* ask for permission to contact the client system. Following through with the client system enables the social worker to monitor the effectiveness of the referral.

Acting as a Cultural Broker or Translator Ethnic minority groups tend not to use existing physical and mental health services as much as would be expected, given their size in the general population. This is especially true for Asian Americans (Uba, 1994) and Mexican Americans (Devore and Schlesinger, 1991). Reasons for this underutilization include: stigmas within some groups in admitting mental health concerns, limited knowledge about available resources, and language barriers (Devore and Schlesinger, 1991; Flaskerud, 1990; Tung, 1985).

A cultural broker can improve communications between formal resources and members of ethnic minority groups, especially recent immigrants and refugees. To the degree that social workers are bilingual, bicultural, and connected to both formal and informal resources in a community, they can serve as a bridge and a translator between potential client systems and organizations. Also, they can serve to explain to apprehensive persons and groups the ways social services and other resources might be relevant to their situations and aspirations. At the same time, social workers are ethically bound to work with and within agencies and institutions to modify the services provided and the interventive strategies utilized so that they are more culturally responsive and effective (Green, 1982).

Enabling Client Systems to Connect with Appropriate Resources in Faith Communities In Chapter 2, we introduced a series of open questions about where people find meaning and hope:

- What's your source of strength?
- On what is your hope based?
- What gives meaning to your life?
- What do you value most?

For people whose responses indicate that they find support in churches and faith communities, we are brokering when we assist them in making the connections they wish.

One social worker reported that a depressed client gained a great deal of help from attending many church services every week. It is also true that churches are open on the weekends, when mental health and other agencies are often closed.

Another social worker writes about her experience with making referrals within the realm of religion and spirituality when working with battered women:

> *We have a list of clergy and other spiritual leaders who are knowledgeable about domestic violence. While counseling, I ask if there is someone else my client would like to speak with about the abuse in the family. From the Christian perspective, many battered women have difficulty leaving a marriage without feeling disapproved of by their faith. It is essential that I provide these women with the appropriate resource to relieve spiritual fears. Otherwise, the person may not seek safety. (Shook, 1996, p. 2)*

In working with clients who have non-Western belief systems, forging a link between traditional services and religious leaders can be essential. A social worker writes of her experience with Cambodian clients in a midwestern city:

When I started working with them, I noticed their lackluster efforts in participating in traditional western therapy methods. Once the western social workers and psychiatrists were able to collaborate efforts with indigenous Cambodian healers and monks, the therapy program was more successful. Not only did the indigenous healers understand their particular cultural beliefs but they also transcended spiritual and religious beliefs and gave legitimacy to the healing process. (Hilliard, 1996, p. 2)

Advocacy   In Chapter 4, we introduced the idea that generalist social work practice demands that the worker practice not only across roles but also across a continuum from nonpolitical to political. Advocacy efforts are at the political end of that continuum.

In its literal sense, advocacy means to speak for people (*ad* meaning "for" and *voca* as in "vocal"). We are called to advocacy, or choose to advocate for people, at times when other approaches are not working. Examples of situations that call for advocacy include the following:

A couple who have a child in foster care have been cleared to get the child back from the county protective services department as soon as they get a three-bedroom apartment (a requirement when there are both boys and girls in the home). The couple complains to a social worker they are seeing about parenting issues that, when one of them visits an apartment, they are often told that there shouldn't be a concern. When the other of them comes to look over the apartment and meets the landlord, it is (suddenly) not available. This is in a rural community, and the couple is biracial.

A renter in an urban area who is responsible for his water bill receives a bill for $189 for a three-month period ($40–60 is average). The city water department refuses to look into the possibility of a leak when the renter calls.

Case and Cause Advocacy   In situations such as those outlined above, what may be called for is activity on behalf of a single case: a person, family, or small group. We also refer to cause advocacy—actions to address an issue of concern to a client system group or some part of the community (Kirst-Ashman and Hull, 1993). Both types of advocacy present themselves as needs in practice.

Previously, we stated that social workers are the helping professionals who are expected to know about and have access to needed resources. Social work's concern for the social, economic, political, and cultural conditions of society as well as the psychosocial functioning of people has shaped its practice.

There is another reason for social workers at times to engage in advocacy: in the intersection between utilitarianism and social justice. In most cases, the process of linking client systems with resources is a nonpolitical one; if the resources are available and the client system meets the requirements, the brokering is successful. However, far too often, racism, homophobia, or other "isms" are present, leading to discrimination.

In the first vignette in this section, a biracial couple was looking for an apartment. It took several phone calls to the Housing Authority and the threat of legal action before a landlord rented to this couple.

An outreach worker for an AIDS support network in a rural area complains

*that referrals are not routine with clients with HIV and AIDS. A dentist refused
to treat a patient with HIV because he didn't have protective clothing (he wanted
the agency to buy him the equivalent of a space suit). Home health agencies
routinely don't return phone calls when it's known that the applicants have
AIDS. It becomes my job to go and explain to the agency what they legally have
to do. (Fox, 1994)*

Often, advocacy is based on the law or regulations (make sure you know the
law well!), on what is "right" (an appeal to justice or morality), or on the harsh
light of public opinion.

There are many occasions for advocacy. It can be appropriate when an agency
or organization is operating in such a way that its practices or attitudes
disenfranchise people or lead to people not receiving services or benefits to which
they are entitled (for example, through practices of discrimination, concealing
information, and/or applying governmental or agency policy in punitive ways). It
is also appropriate when the affected people are too uninformed, too powerless,
or too overwhelmed to advocate for themselves; or when costs are involved from
a person's self-advocacy (for example, possibility of losing a job, being harassed,
or other reprisals).

Guidelines for successful advocacy include:

1. ensuring that the situation is one that necessitates action, that the locus of the
   difficulty is within the external system. I (Becky) am reminded of the training
   I received when in law enforcement—the "shoot, don't shoot" exercises for
   developing skill in speedy judgment as to whether or not the target is an actual
   threat. Without careful exploration, the person, agency, organization, or
   community may be inappropriately identified as the source of the obstacle.

2. ensuring that advocacy is really necessary by examining the source of the
   difficulty (for example, a lack of communication or information or a policy
   that may be restrictive).

3. ensuring that you have the permission of the client system to initiate the
   advocacy.

4. discussing the complaint first with the contact person within the external
   system from whom the client system has been unsuccessful in receiving the
   desired services. If that doesn't produce results, then go to someone higher
   up. (Going to a supervisor without talking to the contact person first rarely
   works.)

5. being assertive—not aggressive or passive—and actively listening (for example, listen to the agency worker to be sure you are understanding and being
   heard, for possible useful information, and for possible courses of resolution).

6. ensuring success by

   a. clearly stating the concern;

   b. affirming the opportunity for the agency (or organization or community)
      representative to respond to stated concerns;

    c. affirming the opportunity for the representative to come up with a solution or think of one that saves face for the agency (or organization or community); and

    d. having a contingency plan.

7. watching out for self-righteousness or righteous indignation. The goal is to help the client system, not to shame a worker or agency (organization, community).

Whenever possible, we advocate *with* client systems instead of advocating for them. As Si Kahn (1991) reminds us, advocacy can lead to "non-empowerment" if the people for whom we are advocating don't participate in the process and it doesn't change the way they relate to each other or to power structures. Successful legal or other advocacy may make real improvements in people's lives, but it may do little to change the relationship of power between these institutions and the people who deal with them.

Aim Three:
Support client systems by working with them to strengthen their social supports and social network

There are two related parts to this aim. One is the recognition that moving toward a preferred reality is a process, not an event. The other is the significance of enhancing client systems' social supports and networks and gaining support from these resources for the change effort.

    Many (if not most) of the difficulties we face are not solved once and for all. In a relationship, one of the persons cannot say, "We've solved our communication problems." They may have identified some barriers to communication and ways of communicating that were troubling, adopted new styles of talking, and found places and times to communicate with each other, but this does not mean that the couple's issues are finally solved. As things change in their lives, they will find new challenges on which to work to maintain healthy communication. And continuing to work on issues over time can be more difficult than making the initial progress.

    The belief in ultimate solutions may also interfere with another client system right; that is, the right to say when there has been enough change. Sometimes partial achievement of a desired goal is enough, and the client system is ready to move on to other issues.

    From another perspective, being able to say "enough is enough" can be vital in relation to the quality of life of someone who is dying. I (Becky) have a dear friend and colleague who shared with me her experiences as a home health social worker with a client who was dying. Some health professionals were pushing this client into more and more life-sustaining treatments that were diminishing his quality of life. In talking with the client, she discovered that he did not want to continue treatments until he died; he wanted to stop them but didn't know when. In order to enable him to reach some clarity about when enough was enough, she asked him questions about the frequency of treatments and when he would say no: "Will you continue receiving treatments when they are scheduled weekly? What about twice a week? Three times a week? Four times . . ." By the time she had gotten to four times a week, the client emphatically said "NO!" Then the client laughed with relief, as finally he had figured out how far he would go with treatments before refusing them.

In Phase Two, we introduced the concept of hard work to achieve goals. It is important to affirm with client systems that movement toward desired outcomes is a challenge and that not to succeed does not imply their failure as a person (people).

When I (Jim) work with parents, I tell them that substantial changes in their children's behaviors can take a month for each year of their child's life (seven months for a 7-year-old, for example). Their initial reaction is usually one of shock, and then they realize that habits formed over a long period of time can take a while to change.

In gaining support for reaching goals and beyond, the social worker may be far less important than others in the client system's life. In *The Empowerment Tradition in Social Work,* Simon (1994) writes:

> *The work of empowerment-oriented social work, now and in the future, is to assist clients and their communities in fully attending to those things that matter most to themselves. Empowerment-oriented social work is also the art and science of being expert at helping clients to trust themselves and the "natural helping networks" or social supports that sustain their daily lives. Central to empowerment practice is the imperative of aiding clients to assess, tap, and contribute to the constructive friendships, family connections, links with neighbors, and community resources that they have built up long before as well as during the period of engaging a social work professional's help. (p. 187)*

Knowledge

There is abundant evidence that the existence of social supports is important in people's lives. Studies of families that are abusive and neglectful show that they have far less social support than comparable families (McLoyd, 1990). In the case of child neglect, this is largely unintentional. As Garbarino, Kostenly, and Dubrow (1983) state, "[p]arents who maltreat children prefer to solve problems on their own" (p. 183).

Social support networks, according to Garbarino et al. (1983), "are interconnected relationships, durable patterns of interaction, and interpersonal threads that comprise a social fabric. They provide enduring patterns of nurturance and contingent reinforcement for efforts to cope with life on a day-to-day basis" (p. 5). People find support in their families, churches, volunteer associations, neighborhoods, and through friendships and service contacts. Whitaker (1983) refers to these as "mediating structures"—structures that generate and maintain values and sustain us when we need help.

People and groups vary as to the composition and degree of their informal supports. In many communities, including a large number of African American ones, the church is a major source of support. Many Latinos live in extended family relationships, which enable families to pool their limited resources. Among

Latinos, fictive kin such as *compadres* (godparents) are more significant than they are in many other groups (Becerra, 1992).

Increasingly, as has been noted earlier in this chapter, people are finding support in mutual aid groups. In these groups, people share relevant concerns and ideas, and begin to experience others in the same boat moving through the same turbulence.

> *As they confided, shared and move into taboo areas, they feel less singled-out, their concerns . . . become less unique, less unusual, and often less pathological. By its very nature the group mutual aid system universalizes people's problems, reducing isolation and stigma. . . . This unleashes a group's inherent potential for "multiplicity of helping relationships," with all its members invested and participating in the helping process. (Lee and Swenson, 1986, p. 350)*

In *Sisters of the Yam,* bell hooks (1993) writes of strategies that she and other black women have used to heal their lives in support groups and other settings. She explains the importance of these, as they can replace other structures that are not as common at present:

> *Often when I tell black folks that I believe that the realm of mental health, of psychic well-being, is an important arena for black liberation struggle, they reject the idea that any "therapy"—be it in a self-help program or a professional therapeutic setting—could be a location for political praxis. This should be no surprise. Traditional therapy, mainstream psychoanalytical practices, often do not consider "race" an important issue, and as a result do not adequately address the mental-health dilemmas of black people. Yet these dilemmas are very real. They persist in our daily life and they undermine our capacity to live fully and joyously. They even prevent us from participating in organized collective struggle aimed at ending domination and transforming society. In traditional southern black folk life, there was full recognition that the needs of the spirit had to be addressed if individuals were to be fully self-actualized. In our conventional religious experience we sang songs that posed profound questions like "Is it well with your soul? Are you free and made whole?" Psychological problems were not ignored back then. (pp. 15–16)*

According to Lee and Swenson (1986), there are four kinds of self-help groups:

- *those stressing enhancement of self-control or conduct reorganization (for example, Alcoholics Anonymous);*
- *those offering mutual support to deal with situations and stresses common to the participants (for example, groups of parents with severely disabled children);*
- *those supporting and advocating for the well-being of people who are often discriminated against (Gay Pride groups);*
- *those with a personal growth or spirituality focus. (p. 370)*

We would add to this list groups who "help" themselves by acting to create and nurture their communities (for example, area development associations, co-ops, volunteer fire departments, Rails to Trails committees, Habitat for

Humanity, and 100 Black Men). While not normally seen as self-help groups, these groups provide opportunities for their members to discover new competencies, achieve belonging in the community, and share talents with others.

In *Sharing the Journey: Support Groups and America's New Quest for Community,* Wuthnow (1994) writes that a central purpose of the small group and mutual aid movement from its inception has been to provide people with a sense of community. There is a widespread assumption that a sense of community is evaporating, leaving many people alone. In support groups, where people have a chance to swap stories, there is an occasion for "rounding off the rough edges of our individuality, transforming us into communal beings" (p. 293).

Wuthnow warns, however, that small groups provide communities that are more tenuous than real communities. People show up when they want to, and often, there are not bonds of reciprocal support outside the groups. Support groups may also at times "merely provide occasions for individuals to focus on themselves in the presence of others" (p. 6).

Garbarino, Kostenly, and Dubrow (1983) also offer cautions about social support networks:

> Social support networks offer no panacea or quick solution to the problems faced by human service practitioners. Social networks can be destructive as well as supportive, and an improper infusion of professional expertise can quickly eliminate what is most vital in all social support strategies: their informality, mutuality, and reciprocity. (p. xii)

The caution for social workers is not to intervene in social support networks without being aware of the potential risks for undoing them. Interventions ill thought out often block the group's effectiveness by our efforts at professionalizing them.

Skills

Two skill areas that are particularly relevant to strengthening the client system's social supports and social network are process skills and task skills. Our discussion and illustration of these skills reflect their application for working with persons, families, groups, organizations, and communities.

Process Skills   Process skills are crucial to the role of the "enabler" in generalist social work practice. The process skills we are presenting in this section are in actuality *skill clusters*. As the planned change process becomes more complex, so does the nature of the skills necessary to influence movement within and between the phases of the process. Skill clusters are the "sum of the parts" when specific skills are combined. Many of the skills that have been presented throughout this book are components of the skill clusters useful in making plans and dreams real.

Process skills are social worker behaviors and attitudes that enable the client system to feel the support necessary to take desired actions. The intent is to communicate a belief in the capacity and competency of the client system to take effective action.

While taking action is a challenging goal at times and often follows a rocky path, the message communicated by the social worker who makes sound use of process skills helps to create a work environment that is safe, challenging, nurturing, and encouraging.

Key process skills include:

- *creating a safe place for naming and sharing feelings, experiences, attitudes, and thoughts.* The notion of having a safe place to share is about having trust. The social worker and the client system have enough trust to be able to share with the confidence that the sharing will not be used to harm. Also, each understands that the right to share will be supported even when the content, ideas, and feelings shared may be unpleasant to hear or experience and open to challenge by either party.

- *inviting the naming and sharing of thoughts, feelings, attitudes, and experiences.* This skill is about using the climate to invite active sharing when the client system may be blocked or otherwise unable to share. Sometimes a simple, but real, invitation to share will open the process so that both the client system and the worker can proceed.

- *focusing.* This skill is about helping maintain the focus on working toward the outcomes that were named by the client system during Phase Two. Working can be hard, tiring, and even boring. It may be necessary to refocus the client system on the tasks at hand by asking the client system to revisit and reevaluate the goals. Other times, it may be necessary to use a direct challenge or confrontation about perceived changes in the focus, with an invitation for the client system to return to the processes and tasks identified.

- *objectifying the subjective.* This skill is helpful in grounding in external realities client systems' feelings, attitudes, and beliefs about their own capacities and competencies that may have been internalized as a product of their past or current struggles. It is accomplished by assisting client systems with cognitive reframing, where new meanings and understandings of objective events are used to replace the subjective interpretations that have been associated with them.

To illustrate, a client system may be playing a negative message of "We can't do anything" because of past messages the client system has received (for example, "We are a rural, hick community where no one would want to relocate or bring a business"). The worker may engage the client system in thinking about the external evidence that challenges this thinking so that other messages, including one of competence, may emerge (for example, "Small rural communities are becoming attractive to many people and businesses because of quality of life, tax structures, and less congestion. Also, new technology makes it possible to be connected with the world without leaving the community").

A caution in using this skill is to be clear about what feelings or attitudes may need to be objectified. This requires the capacity to differentiate between subjective responses that are grounded in reality and those that are not.

- *encouraging.* The intent of this skill is to recognize that client systems carry within themselves the seeds for growth and positive change associated with their hopes and dreams. The social worker—by listening, clarifying, affirming, and responding reflectively—provides client systems with the inspiration and support for taking action. This skill goes beyond the routine "I know you can do it" to engaging client systems in considering to take action that may stretch their capacities in ways that help them acquire new competencies.

Recall some experiences in your life when you were faced with challenges that seemed distasteful, overwhelmingly difficult, or frightening to you. What message did you receive from the people around you about yourself and your capacities for meeting these challenges? Generally, the responses we get are punishment, rewards, praise, or encouragement.

Punishment, the direct application of some form of unpleasantness, has the possible consequences of inviting retaliation, teaching that might and power "make right," and affecting change in behaviors or attitudes only momentarily.

Similarly, rewards, the actions associated with providing external reinforcement for desired behaviors and attitudes, may have the consequences of reinforcing this externalized (rather than internalized) motivation for exhibiting appropriate behaviors only when external gains are present and perpetuating a power differential between the participants (Marlin, 1983).

Surprisingly, the possible consequences of praise, the expression of glorification and favorable judgment, are very similar to those of both punishment and rewards: reinforcement of a power differential, externalization of the motivation for behaving appropriately, and loss of credibility of the person doing the praising, particularly if the receiver of the praise doesn't feel deserving (Marlin, 1983). These consequences are especially likely to occur when the praise is generalized and not specific.

Often, praise is used in an attempt to share with another an appreciation for his or her behaviors, feelings, and/or beliefs. Sharing appreciation for another person is a form of offering feedback and, thus, principles associated with offering feedback are applicable: communicating the appreciation out of respect and regard for the person, using "I" statements, being specific, referring to observable and observed behaviors, and timing the expression appropriately.

In contrast to punishment, rewards, and praise, encouragement is a response that inspires and stimulates "courage" for action (Marlin, 1983). Encouragement is compatible with a strengths orientation, in that we encourage when we show confidence, build on strengths, value the worth and dignity of the person, stimulate a willingness to use the person's "own abilities and efforts, and . . . contribute those abilities cooperatively to working, playing and associating with others" (Popkin, 1990, p. 58).

Task Skills Task skills are the specific actions negotiated between the worker and the client system that facilitate movement toward achieving outcomes. In this instance, the action is to realize the goals of the planned change process of Phase Three and the aim of strengthening supports and social networks.

One key task skill is that of facilitating access to information, knowledge, and skill enhancement. To illustrate, in helping a group of single mothers start a day care center, the worker might arrange for a small business expert to come and meet with them on how to handle their tax issues and contracts for space. One of the mothers might agree to arrange for meeting space and to call others to remind them about the meeting. Yet another might arrange for transportation. The point is that these concrete tasks need to be named and assigned to move the work in a productive way.

Aim Four:
Work with client systems and with others to alter the social, economic, and political structures of the context so that they are more responsive to the needs of persons, families, groups, and communities and more conducive to social justice

If your view of social justice encompasses Walzer's thesis (1986) that a society has to have a healthy economic, social, and cultural infrastructure, a viable safety net, equality of opportunity, and a strong democracy, then our society at present may not measure up well. When we look at a society where, currently, almost 25% of the children are poor and often lacking adequate supports like health care, it seems that we are not living in the best of all possible worlds.

The following definition works well in reminding social workers of the need for the profession to be involved with community development:

> *Community Development refers to efforts to mobilize people who are directly affected by a community condition (that is, the "victims," the unaffiliated, the unorganized, and the nonparticipating) into groups and organizations to enable them to take action on the social problems and issues that concern them. A typical feature of these efforts is the concern with building new organizations among people who have not been previously organized to take social action on a problem. (Rivera and Erlich, 1992, p. 3)*

Historically, the social work profession has attempted to influence the context and achieve social change and social justice through the use of intervention models like locality development, social planning, and social action (Rothman and Tropman, 1987). Additionally, the work of Alinsky (1971) and Freire (1989) have been influential in presenting a more radical view of the role of organizing in the community. They rightly focus, just as does the social action model, on the imbalances of power relationships and resource allocation. In working with social issues at the community and policy levels, social work comes closest to addressing its interests in social justice, yet such professional activity is not done without risks.

Most of us will be employed to provide direct services to persons, families, and small groups, or to manage their delivery. As such, efforts at social change are not always well received, especially when they might attract negative publicity to our employer. While this risk can never be fully removed, it can be managed. I (Barry) attended a meeting of a human service association where we reminded ourselves that part of the value of the association was that, through it, we could advocate for children's needs while hiding behind the veil of its stated mission of education, research, and advocacy for human service issues.

Sometimes having a place to carry out the social change role is necessary and important to fully realizing social justice goals. We will have more to say about this subject in Chapter 10.

Perhaps it is the nature of the work involved in enabling the context to be more responsive, but the distinction between knowledge and skills is not as clear to us here as it is with the other aims. Consequently, we combine the discussion of essential knowledge and skills for this issue.

In working with persons, families, and small groups, the client system's perspective emerges as part of the work. In larger system change, the voices of those most affected by a situation are often discounted. When community development corporations come into distressed neighborhoods, they focus almost entirely on a product, such as housing or bringing in a business incubator for small businesses; their planning is not resident driven. They are based in the community, not community based (Medoff and Sklar, 1994).

For most of you, efforts to alter the social context will be either things that you do as part of your job, using the knowledge you acquire through your work to influence public policy, or things you do outside of work. Given this reality, many social workers who involve themselves in community change have less background and training in this area than in other aspects of their professional lives. We believe that Rivera and Erlich's advice (1992) for organizers working in communities is applicable for others working to alter the context: "Organizers and the community need to view each other as subjects rather than objects, as learners, and as equals. No organizer should enter a community with a sense that she or he has 'the' answers for it" (p. 16).

This section not only discusses the knowledge and skills necessary for practicing in this arena but also provides sources for obtaining more specific information. With this information, social workers are less likely to try to reinvent the wheel, or reinvent the pothole (Shimkus and Winship, 1977).

Knowledge and Skill in Organizing

Veteran community and labor organizer Si Kahn (1995) has a simple definition of organizing: "people working together to get things done" (p. 5). Given that most poor and middle-class people have little power individually, the most effective way to exert power to alter the social context lies in joining with others.

Kahn (1995) also believes that there are other long-term benefits to organizing:

> Through organizing, people learn something new about themselves. They find dignity in place of mistreatment. They find self-respect instead of a lack of self-confidence. They begin to use more fully the skills and abilities that they possess: to work with other people to influence, to speak up, to fight back. (p. 10)

Organizers who have worked in organizing communities and mobilizing people have identified processes and techniques that are applicable in varying situations. Knowledge and skills related to entering communities, setting up meetings, devising strategies, and dealing with conflict within groups can be found in Kahn's *Organizing: A Guide for Grassroots Leaders* (1991), Rivera and Erlich's *Community Organizing in a Diverse Society* (1995), and Burghardt's *The Other Side of Organizing* (1982).

Economic and Community Development In many communities, social woes can be linked to a diminishing economy or community infrastructure. Economic development and community development have been artificially separated in the educational system and in professional practice. Economic development has been viewed as the province of the professions of business, economics, and planning, and the planning that is usually done by economic developers does not consider community involvement or human development (Pantoja and Perry, 1995). In *Promoting Community Change: Making It Happen in the Real World,* Mark Homan (1994) provides an inclusive approach to community development.

Mobilizing Scarce Resources Resources can be thought of as essentials for influencing change. In this era of diminishing governmental support for social services, agencies and organizations need to be able to bring in additional funds to support their work. In addition to money, other resources can include volunteers and specialized services such as foster homes, contracted family preservation services, and rest homes for the elderly.

Social workers can assist with the development of such resources through the generalist practice role of mobilizing. This role involves working to modify or create new resources designed to facilitate movement toward preferred realities as named by the client system. Social workers use skills in enabling, negotiation, mediation, advocacy, data collection, grant writing, and networking to influence the desired modification or creation of the needed resource. Often, success in this role means that others may also benefit. Once a modified program or new resource is in place in the community, others may access it as well (Kurzman, 1995).

To illustrate, I (Barry) recall during my first year of graduate school working with another graduate student to link children from low-income families who were attending a day care center in an inner-city neighborhood with the day care program at my field placement agency, located in a more affluent community. In doing so, we modified our existing day care program so that its resources could be shared with a more vulnerable population group with which it had not previously been associated.

Fundraising Fundraising can provide a wide range of benefits for an organization or agency. The money raised can be used for a wide variety of purposes, unlike funds from governmental sources that usually have strings attached—provisions about the ways the money can and cannot be spent.

Successful fundraising provides an indication to local governments, United Way agencies, and foundations that the work of the agency has local support. In choosing among competing organizations and agencies, this local endorsement of the agency's work can tilt a funding decision in its favor.

Many foundations and other funding sources demand that funding recipients have other sources of funds to match those provided by the funder. These matching funds for grants are often acquired through fundraising efforts (Flanagan, 1977).

In addition to the actual money raised and the gain in community support, there are other benefits to fundraising. In raising money, you are also raising the community's awareness of your services, which can lead to even greater community support and volunteer assistance. A shelter for people who are homeless in a small midwestern community sets up a booth to sell pasta at the county fair each year. In addition to raising almost 10% of their budget through this effort, they also let people know the existence and value of their service and are effective in recruiting volunteers as they sell breadsticks and pasta. It may even be, as one public relations professional and researcher believes, that fundraising is essentially public relations (Kelly, 1991).

Organizations and agencies can raise money in a variety of ways. Staging benefits, holding a raffle or an auction, holding a crafts fair, carnival, or rodeo, and sponsoring "fun runs" are just a few of the strategies used. Good sources of knowledge and skill in this area include Gordon's *The Fundraising Manual: A Step-by-Step Guide to Creating the Perfect Event* (1993) and Flanagan's *The Grassroots Fundraising Book* (1977).

Recruiting Volunteers In the United States, volunteerism is seen as important for fulfilling two needs. First, it provides citizens with a way to contribute their time and energy to enterprises that enhance the well-being of the nation and its members. And second, people who are seeking opportunities to live their values and beliefs, to learn, and to grow can generally find them through volunteering (Schindler-Rainman and Lippitt, 1977).

On a less abstract level, volunteers enable agencies to carry out tasks that they would otherwise not be able to do. Volunteers can provide mentorship for children, companionship for older adults, and transportation for people without cars, as well as offer a variety of specialized skills, such as financial consultation, legal services, and public relations assistance.

It requires skill to recruit, train, and utilize volunteers in ways that help people feel their efforts are worthwhile—that they are contributing to the community and getting something out of the activity—without overburdening them. The following literature explains ways to effectively work with volunteers: Wrobleski's *The Seven Rs of Volunteer Development: A YMCA Resource Kit* (1993), Wyant and Brooks's *The Changing Role of Volunteerism* (1993), and Schindler-Rainman and Lippitt's *The Volunteer Community* (1977).

Knowledge and Skill in the Political Arena

Using Our Special Knowledge in the Public Arena Social workers have an important role to play in the legislative debate and process. As Briar and Briar (1982) observe: "Practitioners are in a unique position to discern the impact of policies both on client problems and on their own practice effectiveness, but many are reluctant to make such connections explicit to their clients" (p. 47).

Most lawmakers and much of the public have a very limited understanding of the complex and varied situations that, for example, contribute to families and persons becoming homeless or to family violence and the difficulties many face in becoming more self-reliant. Those who work with people experiencing homelessness or violence in the family on a daily basis can communicate the ways in which these families are like most other families, not a breed apart.

If, as the author Sam Keen (1991) writes, "Kindness is the recognition of kinship" (p. 167), the accounts of families' adversities and the ways they cope with them can help to achieve a greater level of understanding and a sense of connectedness in the general public. A practitioner working with women who are homeless writes: "You cannot feign blindness when your eyes have been etched with indelible images" (Ferrill, 1993, p. 17). Getting some of these images to the public and to legislators can serve to interrupt contempt for persons who are poor and homeless.

Beyond advancing a greater general understanding, social workers, other service providers, advocates, and client systems can testify as to how actual public policies help or hinder families who are struggling to achieve economic security and well-being and how proposed policies are likely to affect vulnerable people. Carefully drawing portraits of the ways policies and programs impact families can be of great value.

The efforts of a few people to become more politically active in educating legislators and influencing policy is best illustrated by an organization that is in its infancy. A social work undergraduate student in field placement is in the process of joining with and organizing people who are both survivors and victims of domestic violence to give voice to their concerns, traumas, and needs in the political arena. The organization is called SAVE, Survivors Advocating for Victim Equality.

The idea for the organization occurred when the social work student and one of the women clients with whom she was working had the opportunity to testify at a state hearing regarding a victims' rights bill. Both left the experience feeling extremely empowered and energized, with a vision of doing more. On the long ride home from the state capital, the idea was conceived of starting an organization that had as its purpose advocating for victim rights and equality. Though they are in the beginning stages of developing the organization, I (Becky) believe that they will be able to make their dreams real because of their passion, courage, energy, and capacities. Others are joining them in voicing the needs of survivors of family violence.

The goal of being active in the political arena is to inform the current policy debate with other voices, less grounded in ideology and more grounded in people's life experiences. Social workers' testimony, and those of their client systems, can change the perspective from thousands of feet up to ground zero.

Research knowledge and skill can be an important ally in this process. A colleague and I (Barry) are currently interviewing public assistance recipients about barriers they face in achieving their hopes and dreams. The goal of the study is to use their voices in educating legislators and other decision makers about ways to move forward on welfare reform that help client systems realize hope and dreams rather than punishing them for being poor.

Policy practice requires specific skills and knowledge; yet, it is an area that we can work within effectively. Iatridis (1995) notes that policy practitioners usually engage in one or more types of practice—legislative, administrative, or judicial—designed to change undesirable social conditions.

Jansson (1994) summarizes the skills and tasks commonly associated with policy practice. These are familiar skills and tasks that social workers have used or become acquainted with in providing services for persons, families, and small groups; what is different is the context and issues to which they apply. The primary skill clusters include:

- analytic skills—used to identify policy choices, evaluate their merit, and make recommendations,

- political skills—used to assess feasibility, identify power resources, and create a strategy for achieving the policy,

- interactional skills—used to make contacts, create support and action networks, identify other networks important to the issue, build personal relationships, and create coalitions and committees, and

- value-clarification skills—used to place the policy choices within a moral context and assess how that can be used to achieve support for a recommended course of action (pp. 9–10).

Jansson (1994) also identifies some core tasks associated with policy practice. He suggests six primary tasks, including:

- setting agendas—this task involves the acts necessary to get a policy issue on the agenda of the appropriate decision-making body (that is, legislative, administrative, or judicial);

- identifying and defining concerns—this task is used to connect policy with a social need and to define it clearly;

- making proposals—this task involves the investigation and examination of policy choices and the selection of a specific policy proposal;

- enacting policy—this task focuses on developing a strategy to get the policy adopted;

- implementing policy—these tasks are associated with the actual placing of the adopted policy into practice and evaluating and modifying the policy as needed; and

- assessing policy—this task is used to evaluate the policy impacts and decide what changes may be needed if there have been negative consequences.

Many of the analytical models that most social workers learn about in policy classes are helpful in carrying out these tasks. The point is that, if we want to improve our community, our agency, and our world, we need to be able to enter actively into the policy arena at the local, state, and federal levels.

Testifying at Public Hearings One of the ways we can put this special knowledge to effective use is by testifying at public hearings. This section is designed to help social workers become more skilled at testifying before the state legislature; it can be used at county and city levels as well. (The writings of McInnis-Dittrick (1994) and Sharwell (1982) were very useful to us in this section.)

In state legislatures, after a bill is introduced, it is referred to a committee. Committees have public hearings on some bills before they vote on whether to send the bill to the whole assembly. At these hearings, the legislators have the opportunity to hear how affected persons, organizations, and the general public feel on important and controversial issues. Perhaps now more than ever, our voices and those of the people we serve need to be heard.

We are living in a time when there are swift-moving societal currents that are buffeting many of the most vulnerable in society. The movement of jobs from the cities (and in some cases, the country) has contributed to unemployment rates in central cities and isolated rural areas that are far higher than for the society at large. Wages for working people in real dollars (taking inflation into account) have declined 10% over the past 25 years, and during this same time period, the value of public assistance benefits has decreased by over 40% in real dollars (Wilson, 1996).

At the same time when an increasing number of people are worse off, less secure, and less hopeful for their future, legislators are increasingly passing laws that weaken the safety net for those in need and that remove their "handrails"—programs that help people who are stumbling so they don't fall. Part of the rationale behind the attack on social welfare programs is expressed something like this: "Well, we've tried social programs for the past 30 years, and they haven't solved the problems. Doing something different or doing less (or even doing nothing) can't be any worse than what we're doing now!" While the debate about where to locate the safety net (federal, state, or local level) may be worthwhile, the idea that society bears responsibility for creating such a net is beyond question from the perspective of the social work profession.

A jet pilot dropping bombs at thousands of feet above the earth doesn't see the damage to real people from the bombs, and legislators are often unaware of the impact their legislation has on those affected. The voices of those who do know the situation and the impact of changes need to be heard.

Combining Stories and Reasoned Data The psychologist Jerome Bruner (1990) believes that human beings process information and make decisions in two parallel channels. One is a rational, problem-solving one and the other is through stories. We tend to remember stories far longer than we remember a string of figures.

Both the general public and legislators use stories that they hear about specific situations as they form ideas about how things are and the way programs work. This can lead to government by anecdote. It is not uncommon for some politicians to collect newspaper clippings and pull out a story that best represents the point they wish to make about legislation up for consideration. (One of the favorite stories used to illustrate perceived waste in public assistance programs is of the welfare recipient driving her Cadillac from public assistance office to public assistance office to pick up checks.)

The stories that people hear have an impact, and too many of the stories are not representative of the real situations of people who are struggling or in need.

What can be done in testimony (and in other public education efforts) is to present the stories and the context in which they occur. Data from an agency database or from other official sources can illustrate the big picture (for example, the increase in children who run away from home). However, when we talk about the issue and use several actual anecdotes or have a person in that situation present, the listener is much more likely to understand and remember.

Arranging to Testify at a Legislative Hearing If there is a bill that has been introduced that affects you and the people with whom you work, find out to which committee the bill has been referred. Call the committee staff and ask when the hearing is, and ask to testify at the hearing. You need to ask to be scheduled to present testimony and for a commitment that you will be placed on the agenda. This gives some recognition to your organization and also means that you are less likely to face the kinds of time pressures placed on those who testify later.

Doing Your Homework Testimony before a legislative hearing is more complicated than merely showing up and voicing your opinion. Your goal is *purposeful communication* that will have an impact. For that to happen, you need to:

- *know the legislation*—you need to understand what the legislation would do, what law or laws it would replace. Tailor what you're saying to what the legislators are considering; testimony on a specific bill before a specific committee is not a soapbox to talk about other concerns.

- *know the legislative process*—you need to understand where the bill is in the legislative process, who's supporting it and who's opposing it, and what its chances are for success. These factors will influence how you craft your testimony.

- *know your audience*—in a given legislative committee, it is important to understand who may be supportive of your position, who will definitely oppose it, and (most importantly) which legislators are receptive if not supportive. Crafting your remarks to reach the people in the receptive middle is solid strategy; if possible, examples from their legislative district should be used.

Preparing a Written Statement Testimony before committees is oral testimony. However, providing a written statement may be just as important. Reasons for providing a committee with a written statement in addition to oral testimony include:

- communicating to the legislators more than a casual and passing interest in the legislation;

- forcing the organization to thoroughly think through the issues and to have consensus about its stand on the issue;

- ensuring that the committee record of the testimony is accurate;

- making the oral presentation to the committee more effective by supplementing it with written material;

- permitting the person testifying to say all that needs to be said in the written statement while still being able to meet the time restraints often imposed on oral testimony;

- creating flexibility so the person testifying can highlight a portion of the written testimony in the oral remarks, knowing that the written statement will cover all of the desired points; and

- providing greater assurance that media coverage of the testimony will be fuller and more accurate. Getting to the hearing room early and distributing copies of the written statement to media representatives enables them to read the statement before the hearing starts, reinforcing the impact of later testimony. Copies of the statement can also be distributed to news organizations that do not attend the hearing (McInnis-Dittrick, 1995; Sharwell, 1982).

These guidelines may be useful in preparing a written statement:

- Write the statement so that it stands on its own and doesn't need the oral testimony to be understood.

- Limit the written statement to between 1500 words and 2500 words. Any technical material and supporting data or statistics should go in an appendix or appendices.

- Avoid jargon (except in appendices). Use shorter rather than longer words.

- Focus the statement on the proposed legislation; this is not the opportunity to raise larger issues and societal concerns.

- Avoid hostility in any form, even when it is difficult to see anything besides mean-spiritedness or a compact with the devil as a reason for proposing the legislation (McInnis-Dittrick, 1994; Sharwell, 1982).

Delivering Oral Testimony   Generally, reading your written testimony will not be as effective as oral testimony that is based on the written statement but does not repeat it (that's pre-Gutenberg [pre-printing press] communication in a post-Gutenberg age).

You will want to start with brief introductory remarks—your self-introduction, a description of the organization that you represent, and an expression of appreciation for being allowed to testify. From there, you can take several approaches. If your testimony follows that of a client system or a person who is experiencing the difficulty addressed by the legislation, you may want to concentrate on drawing the connections between that person's testimony and the legislation. You are helping the legislators put the story in context.

If you are testifying in opposition to a bill, you can use the "sandwich" method: start with a positive, end with a positive, and in the middle make the criticism of the proposal. One example of this could be to start with, "I applaud the legislature's commitment to examining this issue. There is near-total agreement that what we are doing now is not the best approach. However, . . ." Then you explain, with stories and data, the flaws in the proposal, and conclude with a thank-you to the committee for allowing you to speak.

If you are testifying in favor of a piece of legislation, you want to make a limited number of points. The old rule for preachers on Sunday morning was "no more than three points to the sermon," and the same can apply to spoken testimony. Use your personal experience, data, and others' stories to make a limited number of points and to make them well. Remember that it's not what you say, but what the legislators and media representatives come away with, that counts.

After your testimony, it's a nice touch to send letters of appreciation to the legislators and committee staff. Most of what legislators receive are not letters of appreciation, and a piece of mail that is neither criticizing the legislator nor asking for something is often appreciated.

Use of Data and Information in the Policy Process

One can make a distinction between data (raw facts and numbers) and information (data that has been interpreted to give it meaning). Both are somewhat useful in the policy process.

If the policy-making process were more rational, data and information would be more useful. However, this is not the case for a number of reasons. For one, few social values are generally agreed on. Values influence how people and society frame a situation (for example, why certain behaviors such as teenage pregnancy are seen as a concern and what it is about the concern that is troubling), and how an issue is defined influences the way it is addressed. Many conflicting costs and values cannot be compared or weighed, and policy makers cannot accurately forecast consequences of policy alternatives.

Added to this is the political aspect of policy development. Policy makers are not necessarily motivated to make decisions on the basis only of rationality and data; the way their constituents respond to the policy may be more important. Still, solid data is useful. Without data, we have no defense against the anarchy of my opinion being as good as yours—all versions of reality have equal merit.

We can make data more useful by creating a context for the raw numbers. This can be done by using ratios, such as identifying the percentage of heavy drug users who are ages 18 to 24 when we don't know how many people in that age range live in the state. We can use ratios as a way to compare groups of data (age groups, other geographical regions, other years) or for comparison against a standard or established benchmark (for example, low birth weight is defined as less than five and a half pounds). We can also present the information in graphical form (bar charts or pie charts) so the data is more understandable.

Given their familiarity with the context in which numbers and data about situations and client systems are derived, social workers can interpret the information to others. Numbers in and of themselves may indicate a concern but cannot explain causation. Interpretation involves studying and explaining the rationale behind the information or drawing inferences about its meaning. Analysis of numerical data is used to explain why the numbers are the way they are, to forecast what the numbers might look like in the future, to evaluate whether the numbers are positive or negative given a clear set of policy goals, and to prescribe a public policy based on the conclusions drawn from explaining, forecasting, and evaluating.

Groups outside the power structure can also use data to make their points and presence felt. In a southeastern city, a management information system (MIS) was developed to track students in the school system. The City Manager commented: "In attempting to influence the school system and other bureaucracies, YFA's most powerful tool has been its MIS. Data documenting the disproportionate and consistent failure rates of black males, for example, backed up YFA's call for a task force to look at the plight of the black male student. You can't keep ignoring that data" (Melaville and Blank, 1993, p. 116).

The Task Force for the Homeless in Atlanta and the National Coalition for the Homeless have developed a computerized information and referral system for people experiencing homelessness. When people call into a centralized location, they are asked a series of questions and then referred to an appropriate shelter or service. In the process, information about the person's situation is entered into a database, where it can be used for policy and advocacy purposes. In Atlanta, the task force has used this information to document the rise in the numbers of families that are homeless, and nationally the system is being used to assess the effects of the changes in public assistance on families.

It should be noted that data and information can also be used to inhibit change and slow down the policy process. A common tactic for stalling public pressure for change is for governmental bodies to appoint a commission to study an issue and bring back recommendations in hopes that there will be less public concern for altering the status quo by the time the committee makes a report.

Community Awareness and the Media

The special knowledge social workers have about the social conditions that client systems face and the strategies they use to cope and survive can be utilized in more than just the political process. The media provide another tool social workers can use for community awareness of issues, for prevention messages, and for public relations for human service agencies and organizations.

Edward Brawley (1995) implores professionals to adapt to a changing reality in which the media increasingly influence public perceptions:

Clearly, human service personnel need to devote greater attention than they have in the past to providing the kind of information to the public that will support people's coping capacities and will educate the public about important individual and community problems and constructive responses to those problems. In the process they will demonstrate to the public precisely what they stand for and what they do in their efforts to address people's needs and problems. The media provide ample and incomparable opportunities to engage in this public education effort. Those human service professionals who engage in public communication efforts through the media will find the work challenging and at times frustrating but if they persevere, they will also find it an invigorating and rewarding opportunity to enrich their professional horizons and areas of expertise. (p. 328)

In some areas, the League of Women Voters and the United Way provide guides on working with media. Excellent source books on working with the media are Brawley's *Human Services in the Media* (1995) and his *Mass Media and the Human Services: Getting the Message Out* (1983).

Group Process and Teamwork

Throughout the book, we have discussed the ways in which a concern for process and teamwork is indispensable. In altering the social context, much of the work for change happens in large meetings, in small groups, in task forces, and in committees. In these settings, knowledge of group process and skills for facilitating group progress are essential.

In a struggle with city government, an organizing effort, or a political campaign, I (Jim) have had the experience that people tend to focus almost exclusively on the tasks to be done and pay little attention to the process—to relationships and to hurt feelings. People get burnt out, offended, or marginalized, and so they drop out, often at times when their ideas and contributions are needed most.

In his study of housing cooperatives in a diverse section of southern California, Heskin wrote of the difficulty and importance in sustaining these groups. His work is generalizable to other groups, especially similar ones in which oppressed people are participating:

> *many people will rally when a threat is presented, but I have also seen people participate because of the fullness they feel in the good times when community is achieved. Any scheme to assist cooperatives will need to explore how to organize in the good times as well as the bad. The populist approach which I know has only one real tool to achieve these moments of community. In the Route 2 project it is called "keeping the process open." (Heskin, 1991, p. 164)*

AIM FIVE:
Carry out these aims in ways that strengthen the competencies of and increase the options for client systems

The last of the aims of social work practice is to carry out these missions in ways that enhance client systems' competencies and increase their options. This brings us back to the question of how social workers approach their tasks and roles.

As we have stated throughout our practice model, there is a dual focus to how we work: the outcomes we work toward and the process through which we work to realize the outcomes. This last aim reminds us of the importance of the learning and opportunities available for the social worker and the client system that emerge from careful attention to the process of work.

A well-managed process, one that attends carefully to relationship issues, interactional patterns, and the cognitive, spiritual, cultural, and affective components of the people involved (as discussed in Chapter 4), provides the participants with new learning, understanding, and competencies. We (Barry, Becky, and Jim) have come to treasure our work together over the years in large part because of what it has taught us about the importance of process. Working together, we have come to understand how difference—whether of viewpoint, style, or knowledge—is a powerful and necessary resource for goal attainment.

Equally important has been the way we work together, which is to affirm, challenge, confront, encourage, nurture, and respect the differences each of us brings to our work. What has emerged from this is that we each better understand and actively use the strengths we have, realize more clearly our limits, work not to be overwhelmed by these limits, and have an increased sense of competence in ourselves.

Knowledge and Skills

We will not introduce new knowledge and skills for realizing this aim. This is because we feel that the model we are presenting is in fact grounded within the intents of this aim.

In Chapter 2, we discussed key concepts that inform our view of effective social work practice. Relevant to this discussion are the concepts of respect for human dignity, respect for human diversity, belief in hopes and dreams, commitment to practicing within a strengths orientation, and commitment to working in an empowering way.

Ethnic-Sensitive Approaches

In their book on ethnic-sensitive social work practice, Devore and Schlesinger (1991) argue for an approach that gives recognition to the part that membership in varying groups plays in shaping people's lives. In working with client systems to select strategies for meeting goals, they suggest a set of questions that might be asked:

- Does the approach give recognition to the part that membership in varying groups plays in shaping people's lives?

- Is the approach based on narrow, culture-bound perspectives on human behavior, or is it sufficiently fluid and broad based so as to generate interpretations of behavior that are consonant with world views and outlooks that differ from those most prevalent in mainstream America?

- Have interventive procedures been proposed that guide practitioners in their use of knowledge concerning the different world view of various groups? (p. 122)

A variety of approaches have been suggested for working with members of ethnic minority groups that fit within the framework of Devore and Schlesinger. For American Indians struggling with alcoholism, sweat lodges have been used successfully. Talking circles, an American Indian ritual, have been successfully adapted on several reservations to confront the issue of domestic violence.

Longres (1991) agrees that cultural differences play a major role with recent immigrants and refugees. He also sounds a cautionary note in assuming that there are vast cultural differences between the Anglo majority and African, Asian, Indian, Mexican, and Puerto Rican Americans born and raised in the United States. He writes:

> *I found that Puerto Rican women—women who were quite isolated from mainstream Anglo-American culture—were likely to abandon the use of folk medicine once exposed to public school education. In a recent study, Van Oss, Padilla, and De La Rocha (1983) interviewed a non-random sample of low income Hispanics—the sector where these beliefs might be expected to be widespread—and found that 20% had used a sobrador, 12% a midwife, 10% a botanica, 9% a curandero, and 6% a home/folk remedy for serious medical symptoms (p. 49).*

Longres concludes the article by noting that, for people who have been in this country for significant periods of time and are of minority group status, their lack of power and status in an encounter with a social agency may be far more significant than cultural differences.

Summary

We began this chapter with the observation that taking action, the work of Phase Three of the model, is grounded in the aims and purposes of the social work profession. These aims and purposes, along with our professional values and ethics, are the lens through which interventions are selected that best fit with the issues and concerns named by the client system. The aims and purposes help us stay focused on important social work outcomes, such as enabling client systems to improve competence, access resources, strengthen social networks, and work toward increased social justice in contexts.

We have presented some of the key areas of knowledge and skills for taking action as well as the professional values that reinforce the use of selected knowledge and skills. Several of the ideas we discussed included: the importance of being able to act as a generalist through simultaneous attention to both external and internal change goals; the importance of formal and informal resources and social supports in the planned change process; the commitment to taking action that recognizes both the processes and the outcomes of change; and the roles of broker, advocate, mobilizer, and enabler in achieving hopes and dreams. We ended the chapter with a discussion of working to change our contexts, as we believe the social justice objectives of the profession remain priorities for our work.

Our last phase in the model is about evaluating outcomes and transitioning as we look at how our work with client systems has been done. As you ready yourself for that phase, please think about the following questions:

1. Think about the times you have received help. What differences have you experienced when you have been enabled to do as opposed to receiving help by others doing for you?

2. Think about taking action to achieve social justice. What does this phrase mean to you? What might you be willing to give up so others in our society could have enough?

3. Think about what it is about being a social worker that appeals to you. How is your motivation more or less associated with helping others change? How is it associated with helping society change? How do you account for your views?

4. Think about times when you have faced a challenge. How was having or not having a social support network important in how you approached that challenge?

5. How do you see the knowledge gained in social work courses like human behavior, social welfare policy, and research and in liberal studies courses such as the social, political, economic, biological, sociological, and psychological sciences, arts and humanities, and math and statistics as supportive of being able to take action?

CHAPTER EIGHT

Phase Four: Evaluating Outcomes and Making Transitions

I try to learn as much as I can because I know nothing compared to what I need to know.

MUHAMMAD ALI
(1991)

Introduction

Social work practice has been presented in this book as having both a process and a product. We have argued that both are essential for effective practice in that the process, or the road traveled to realize desired outcomes, is valuable for the lessons we learn, and that the products (outcomes) are valued achievements for both the client system and society. The lessons of process are learned through effective social work intervention and are then available for use by the client system and the social worker in achieving new outcomes in future situations. Both means and ends do matter; to think that they are separate and unequal components of social work intervention misses the obvious opportunity for practicing in a way that achieves real and desired results while enhancing the competencies of the client system via the learning opportunity that effective intervention represents.

This view of practice leads us to the last phase of our model. For both the social worker and the client system, Phase Four focuses on more fully owning the results and lessons of working together, measuring movement toward the desired reality, and transitioning—preparing to move on from this specific episode of social work intervention.

The fourth phase of our model involves the learning that both the social worker and client system gain from their interaction and the transition that takes place in the client system/social worker relationship. The common perception is that these events occur late in the helping process. In reality, from the beginning of their work together, the social worker and client system are learning from their interactions as well as making transitions toward ending their change effort.

To the degree to which the client system is aware of the movement toward the preferred reality, learning is a part of the transition. Learning is what stays with us when the formal change process has served its purpose. Therefore, evaluating outcomes is a necessary component of process development.

Evaluating Outcomes

We attach importance to the evaluation of practice for several reasons. First of all, evaluation of both the process of work and the results of working together provides client systems and social workers with valuable feedback about what they have learned from their work. The evaluation of the extent to which the preferred reality has been realized facilitates client systems' awareness of how well the issues have been addressed as well as the competencies identified and developed during the process. Social workers learn about how well they have carried out their professional roles and applied their knowledge, further clarifying their own practice competencies.

Evaluation is more than just outcome measurement: it is equally about knowledge transmission and ownership of the competency associated with having knowledge. Awareness of our competence, an important product of practice evaluation, prepares us better for the next struggle.

When we speak of evaluation of practice, we are speaking of a number of approaches to gain information. This information can be useful for accountability, gauging the effectiveness of the agency or program, measuring the movement of the client system toward identified outcomes, and evaluating the quality of the social worker's practice.

Summative evaluations measure results or outcomes. These are most commonly used to compare the results of practice interventions at the program level across kinds of client systems and across a number of workers. Well-done summative evaluation can be generalized to other settings.

Formative evaluations are ways to monitor movement toward a goal or outcome and to provide feedback to the client system and the social worker throughout the process. They also provide feedback to the client system and the social worker about the extent to which goals have been realized. Much of what is written in this section is based on our view that social workers need to incorporate practice evaluation in all of their practice activities and that formative evaluation is the strategy that best supports this principle, with tools for the social worker and client system to better understand what is happening.

The approaches discussed here may or may not be useful for larger-scale program evaluation, but their primary purpose is for the immediate worker/client system interaction. Social workers will at various points in their careers be called upon to participate in program evaluation activity. We value those opportunities and hope that agencies routinely pursue them. However, we will not be giving much attention to that research activity in this book. Practitioners who would like to know more about strategies for program evaluation, that is, research that can tell us about program effectiveness, are referred to the work of Chambers, Wedel, and Rodwell (1992), Royse (1992), and Tripodi (1983).

Evaluating our practice is essential for the following reasons:

1. *It provides a mechanism for the social worker and the client system to measure movement occurring during the change process.* In many situations, neither social workers nor client systems are skilled at being able to "name and claim" what has been accomplished. Norman Polansky (1975), the noted writer on child neglect, tells of doing a consultation with a child welfare agency in western North Carolina. The workers who had been engaged with parents who were neglectful and abusive were discouraged about their work, as they reported little progress with the client systems. Polansky said that when he reviewed the case records, it was clear to him that the families were changing in a variety of ways, but no one was perceiving or acknowledging the progress.

2. *It enhances client system competency.* One of the ways competency and mastery are enhanced is by understanding how movement in managing an issue or concern occurs. Monitoring change throughout the interventive process is a way to add to understanding that can be transferred to other times and situations.

3. *It provides an opportunity for social workers to get better at what they are doing.* Enhancing our competencies is an ongoing process, and evaluating our own practice can give us information that we can use to be more effective. I (Jim)

believe the old motto "Practice makes Perfect" is incomplete. A more desirable way to state it would be "Practice plus Feedback plus Consultation and/or Reflection makes Perfect." While this is a harder motto to memorize, it better reflects the intent of practice and the professional obligation for continuing growth.

As Donald Schon (1987) states in *Educating the Reflective Practitioner,* the issues that professional practitioners face are rarely straightforward and clear. They are frequently complex and lack "right answers." Often, they cannot be solved solely by drawing on theories or skills learned in school. Schon notes that "[t]he indeterminate zones of practice—uncertainty, uniqueness, and value conflict—escape the canons of technical rationality and [are] central to professional practice" (p. 5). A conscious and ongoing process in which practitioners reflect on how they manage and approach the complex, "sticky" situations provides them with insight into how they make decisions and the competencies they might develop to enhance the process.

Evaluation of each practice intervention is successful or useful when:

1. *the social worker and client system have clearly identified what is to be different as a result of the intervention.* One can only evaluate the success of an intervention based on agreed-upon goals. The saying "If you don't know where you're going, any road will get you there" could be modified to "If you don't know where you're going, you can't say if you got there."

2. *there is careful articulation from the start, in which measurable and specific goals are stated and baseline information on the issues of concern is collected.* A 10% decrease in abusive or self-abusive behaviors may mean major progress, but it would be difficult to measure if the client system does not have good baseline information from which to proceed. While establishing a baseline may not feel quite right to many, having such information will help make movement and change toward the desired goals clearer for all the parties involved.

3. *the social worker and the client system have discussed the meaning of meeting, partially meeting, or not meeting the goals.* If client systems do not fully meet goals, it does not necessarily mean that they have not made progress in managing the issue of concern. From the effort may come information about the barriers to change and the client system's own strengths and resources that can be helpful when the client system tries again. Such a discussion also helps the client system and social worker better understand what degree of change will be "good enough" in moving toward goal attainment. This becomes important when we come to understand that final solutions to issues of concern are rare in any intervention experience.

Social Work Values and Evaluating Outcomes

Central values associated with Phase Four of our practice work include respect for human dignity, self-determination, societal responsibility to protect human subjects, and social worker responsibility to conduct research ethically.

One need look no further than the NASW Code of Ethics to find support for these principles as they relate to encouraging the involvement of social workers in the research process. The role of the social worker in the research enterprise is referenced in Standard 4, section 4.01 (c) [Competence] and Standard 5, sections 5.01 (d) [Integrity of the Profession] and 5.02 (a–p) [Evaluation and Research]. The Code of Ethics clearly supports the need for social workers to engage in practice-focused research, both in the evaluation of their practice or program outcomes and in knowledge building; that is, helping to discover the best practices associated with an issue or concern.

Also, the Code of Ethics is useful in thinking about how to conduct research in a manner that affirms other important professional values. Grinnell (1988) notes that NASW has established a set of six guidelines that should be used by all social workers in planning and conducting research. The guidelines address issues that may be encountered either at the level of personal practice evaluation or at the level of program evaluation or study. These guidelines are:

- consider the possible consequences for human beings
- ensure that client system participation is based upon voluntary and informed consent
- protect the client system from physical and mental harm
- share the results of research only with those with a legitimate professional reason to know
- protect client system confidentiality
- take credit only for the work done, and credit the contributions of others to the study (Grinnell, 1988, p. 67).

Hoffman & Sallee (1994) note that ethical considerations, that is, the needs of client systems versus the needs of the research, are frequently present in any practice episode. They place client system needs first, and so would we; however, we would argue that many of the dilemmas associated with doing research and evaluation can be addressed by having an agreed-upon plan in place from the beginning. In fact, the similarities between effective social work process and the evaluation research process are so great, it can be argued that practice evaluation opportunities exist by definition.

We think the need for building evaluation into our practice is also associated with other ethical principles. By bringing our best efforts to our practice out of respect for those we serve and by carrying out our professional roles and responsibilities in ways that build our mastery and competency, we also fulfill our ethical responsibilities to client systems (Standard 1, section 1.04) and the profession (Standard 4, section 4.01).

Knowledge and Skills for Practice Evaluation

In Chapter 3, we shared the story of the man searching for his lost keys by the lamppost because the light was better there (even though he had lost them somewhere else). In relation to knowledge and skills for practice evaluation, this story reminds us that practice evaluation can be a powerful tool in providing us with light about what has been effective and to what degree, as we work with client systems. In the following paragraphs, we share our thoughts and experiences about what has been useful for us in helping ourselves, our colleagues, and our students get better at what we do.

The Use of Feedback As was discussed in Chapter 6, a primary knowledge and skill area is the use of offering, receiving, and acting upon feedback as the social worker and client system move through the four phases of practice. Feedback can be used in a formative evaluative sense to provide information about how the work between the social worker and the client system has progressed and to what extent or degree the outcomes have been achieved.

With a solid, trusting, helping relationship established between the client system and the social worker, it becomes possible to provide feedback that gives a professional evaluation or judgment about behaviors that have had a positive or negative impact on goal attainment. Such feedback may be provided by either party in the helping process, thus enabling both the social worker and the client system to grow.

I (Barry) recall discovering the importance of soliciting feedback from my own days as a graduate student. I was working with a senior citizen discussion/support group in a public welfare setting, and we had decided to have a luncheon celebration as we approached our termination as a group. We had been discussing how to do this over a period of a few weeks, and I had noticed that every time the subject was raised, one woman in the group would make statements about hoping that we would do the luncheon soon as she feared she would not be around to join us.

In talking about this message with my supervisor and recalling my human behavior content on aging and the death and dying issues that might come up for the elderly, we determined that when this group member brought the issue up again I should use it as an opportunity to raise the death and dying concern and see if that was a discussion topic the group wished to put on its agenda. Feeling somewhat proud that I had been using my listening skills to pick up on an important issue, I was armed to raise the topic at the next group session if presented with the chance.

When given the "open door" by the woman at the next group session, I acknowledged that as we grow older we sometimes become concerned about our own mortality and asked if the group wished to discuss this issue more fully at a future meeting. Imagine my dismay when she looked surprised at my question and said, "Oh no, dear, that's not what I'm worried about—I'm planning a trip to visit my daughter and hope we can have our luncheon while I'm still in town!"

Getting and giving feedback is central to practice evaluation in that it helps to clarify both the effectiveness of the practice process and the degree of goal achievement. Also, the above experience reminds us that making assumptions is dangerous. It is vital that we explore with client systems the accuracy of our assumptions and interpretations.

The Use of Research While there is general agreement throughout the professional social work community on the value of feedback, another source of knowledge has been more controversial. This is the knowledge of research methods and tools and their use in social work practice. While the debate about the place of research in social work practice is beyond the scope of this book, it is important to note that such a debate exists. We do not wish to enjoin the discussion about how best to do research in social work; rather, we think it is more important that the social work practitioner come to the position of valuing research knowledge as a foundation for practice. Knowledge that has utility will be applied by most ethical practitioners for desired ends. Admittedly, this is a faith statement, but it is grounded in our understanding of how mature professional social workers think about knowledge and its use.

Whether we should focus our research around quantitative or qualitative research methods is for us a moot question. Pragmatically, we would argue for both, and the tools and methods presented below illustrate this view. Our position is supported by the work of other colleagues in the way they frame important questions associated with social work practice.

For instance, Berlin and Marsh (1993) discuss the role of thinking in clinical social work practice. They note at least four key types of thinking associated with understanding and intervening, including reasoning, problem solving, creativity, and metacognition (pp. 16–31). These abilities require capacities and skills that are not unrelated to the characteristics of a scientific social worker as defined by Gibbs (1991) and build upon the classic science paradigm.

Holmes (1992) identifies a series of research assumptions that support the empowerment paradigm. These assumptions focus on the theme that research acts taken by social workers should have utility, respect the client's voice, have empowerment as the goal, and add to the understanding of client system strengths and coping abilities. The point is that, whether one is guided by quantitative models or qualitative models, research efforts draw upon a set of skills and a knowledge base not unfamiliar to most social workers. What may be new or different for social workers, as well as for many social service agencies, is to think about themselves as being involved with research activity.

Tools and Methods for Evaluation   Many strategies, research methods, and tools may be useful to the social worker and the client system as they reflect upon and discuss what has been realized in their work together. The following methods (the specific plan used to do the evaluation) and tools (the specific knowledge and techniques used to collect and interpret the data) are but a few of the choices available to the social worker:

- Goal Attainment Scale (GAS)
- Single-subject design
- Measurement scales for client system outcomes
- Case study analysis
- Reflective questions
- Journaling by the social worker
- Client system satisfaction survey

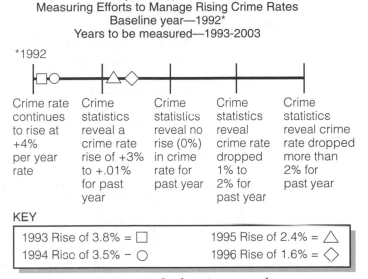

Community Development Committee
Measuring Efforts to Manage Rising Crime Rates
Baseline year—1992*
Years to be measured—1993-2003

*1992

| Crime rate continues to rise at +4% per year rate | Crime statistics reveal a crime rate rise of +3% to +.01% for past year | Crime statistics reveal no rise (0%) in crime rate for past year | Crime statistics reveal crime rate dropped 1% to 2% for past year | Crime statistics reveal crime rate dropped more than 2% for past year |

KEY

| 1993 Rise of 3.8% = □ | 1995 Rise of 2.4% = △ |
| 1994 Rise of 3.5% – ○ | 1996 Rise of 1.6% = ◇ |

Figure 8.1 Goal attainment scale

These tools and methods may be used independently or in some combination to assist the social worker and the client system in better understanding what has been accomplished through the change effort. It is important to note that the science of our practice has not advanced to a level where we can know with absolute validity and reliability the causal links between what we do and what is achieved; however, we argue that we do have methods and tools, from our understanding of the science of research, that can help us better understand what has been achieved, even if we may not be absolutely certain what the links are. Below are very brief summaries of each tool listed above and leading sources for learning more about them:

Goal Attainment Scale (GAS) The Goal Attainment Scale, devised by Kiresuk and Sherman (1968), is especially useful in tracking goals. See Figure 8.1 for an example.

This process involves collecting information, designating areas of concern, predicting the outcomes on a scale from the most unfavorable to the most favorable, and taking a follow-up measure at some predetermined point in the future after the intervention has been implemented. Bloom, Fischer, and Orme (1995) provide an expanded discussion of this tool as a means for practice evaluation.

One benefit of the Goal Attainment Scale is that it provides the client system and social worker with perceptual evidence of goal attainment against a preset scale of achievement. The midpoint of the scale, known as the expected level of success, is established first and then the remaining parts of the scale are defined behaviorally. In the example above, the expected level of success is no rise in crime rate. Thus, the initial goal was to stop the pattern of rising crime rates.

One advantage of identifying the midpoint of the scale as the expected level of success is that it enables client systems, with the support of the social worker, to name expected levels of change. We like to think of this as naming what is enough achievement to satisfy the issue of concern.

By adding the other categories, client systems are encouraged to think about what going beyond the expected outcome might look like, as well as what not getting to the expected outcome might mean. The example above illustrates the ideal of dropping crime rates and the possibility that, if the pattern of rising crime rates cannot be stopped, there still can be change in the degree to which crime rates rise.

Once this understanding has been agreed upon, both the client system and the social worker are committed to making some evaluation of effort and achievement as the work of the change process unfolds. The evaluation feedback becomes a data source for additional decisions about goal attainment once the assessment of achievement has been made.

Single-Subject Design Bloom, Fischer, and Orme (1995) have devoted much attention to the role of single-subject design research in social work practice. They note that this design has sufficient rigor to provide valid empirical feedback to the social worker and client system about what was achieved in the practice effort.

This design, commonly known in its simplest form as the AB design, assumes that the social worker and client system establish a baseline that defines the current behavioral level associated with the issue of concern, the "A" in the formula; the "B" in the formula is the indicator of behaviors that occur during and after the intervention process. The key idea behind this approach is that the comparison is between the baseline information and the information collected after the intervention has begun for the same client system at a specified period in time. The differences found, if any, are presumed to be the result of the intervention.

In using the single-subject design, it is important that the social worker be able to state clearly and operationally the type and nature of the intervention, or combination of interventions, to be used. Otherwise, it becomes difficult to know when the intervention begins and how to collect the data that will allow for some measurement of effect or outcomes realized.

Equally important is the selection of data collection tools that will be used throughout the study process, from establishing the baseline information to the follow-up collection during and after the intervention phase. The greater the reliability and validity of the instruments, the greater confidence one can have in the results discovered from data analysis.

Measurement Scales for Client System Outcomes Measurement scales are designed to assist client systems and social workers in establishing baseline information and later quantifying the direction and degree of change. They can be found in a variety of forms, from simple one-question client system satisfaction surveys to complex tests with strong records of reliability and validity.

For example, in working with a particular family, we may ask scaling questions like, "on a scale from one to ten, with ten meaning that you feel great about how much support you find for your family within your community, how would you rate the support you feel?" At the beginning of our work with this family, we may learn that they would rate the support as a "three"; three months later we may ask this question again and learn that they would say "six." A discussion of what had changed to impact this rating would then take place so that both the client system and worker could better name the gains that had been made and better understand the meanings this achievement might hold for future use by the client system.

Social workers can create their own scaling questions and combine them into instruments for repeated use, or they can take advantage of existing ones. The advantage of using an existing scale is that, if it is done well, you have increased confidence in the results while not having to expend the energy necessary to create it. On the other hand, existing tools may not be as sensitive to the specific information that a particular client system may need. This is a judgment call that the social worker and client system can make together.

The value of the technique of scaling is that the numbers can show the direction of change toward realizing goals. Through discussion, it is possible to learn what has changed and to enable the client system to discover what new information, skills, and/or capacities they have added while working through the planned change process.

Case Study Analysis The case study method of evaluation is designed to provide the client system and the social worker with a detailed description of the intervention process and the outcomes realized. Yin (1984) devotes an entire monograph to this particular research technique, with an emphasis on its use with program or organizational levels. He notes that this strategy is useful when questions of interest are concerned with the how and why of a contemporary event over which the researcher has or can exercise little control (p. 20).

Bloom, Fischer, and Orme (1995) note that the case study has been a common tool used by clinicians; however, Bloom et al. do not see this tool as a powerful one. They do acknowledge that case study analysis offers certain advantages, including giving immediate feedback on how an intervention theory is working and helping workers refine their skills by the close linkage between practicing the skills and feedback. Case studies can help in refining questions that can be studied with other research methods that are seen as having more experimental rigor.

However, Bloom, Fischer, and Orme (1995) believe that the limits of case study analysis are such that they identify it as a design of last resort. The question of rigor with this design is an important one, and Yin (1984) notes that in using case study analysis, the practitioner could address the issue of experimental rigor by designing a carefully constructed research protocol and closely following the protocol. This procedure requires a considerable investment of time and careful record keeping using a standardized recording process that, under analysis, may be useful in discovering just what has taken place within the service intervention effort.

Reflective Questions In Chapter 6, we introduced the use of reflective "miracle" questions as a means of enabling client systems to imagine a preferred reality. Family therapists, such as Berg (1992), utilize this technique to explore movement in realizing desired realities. Social workers can take advantage of this tool to facilitate the client system's reflection on the degree of progress and change associated with the helping experience.

The relationship of asking miracle or reflective questions to evaluating outcomes is very similar to encouraging dreaming, but the way the questions are framed is different. The questions that yield exploration of the nature, degree, and direction of change would focus on what the "fairy godmother" would actually see and experience if she were to visit the client system now. The response to this question can then be compared with the initial vision as well as with the difficulties, experiences, and concerns the client system identified at the beginning of the work together.

While the use of reflective questions to evaluate outcomes is viewed as weak evidence in the traditional science paradigm, such questions are valid in the sense that they provide useful feedback about the real benefits and gains from the helping process. Holmes (1992) argues that research design should

> *reflect the recognition that those under study have authority over their own lives and possess abilities to express that authority in some way—that they have strengths. Research should focus on eliciting, understanding, and developing these strengths; on how these individuals and groups have surmounted difficulties and coped. . . . Research should be planned and conducted in such a way that those under study can perceive that empowerment is the goal of the research. (pp. 159–160)*

Reflective questions do this.

Journaling by the Social Worker The technique of keeping a journal, which has been used as a therapeutic and an educational tool, also can be a powerful form of self-evaluation for the social worker. Journals have been used in a wide variety of ways, from teenagers who chronicle their years in personal diaries to professionals who keep daily records of their careers. We have chosen to include this technique here in the hope that more will consider it.

Well-constructed journals that include reflective content about one's practice, novel insights about what may have worked well or not so well, and common themes encountered in practice provide the social worker with the opportunity to become a self-reflective practitioner. Developing the capacity for self-reflection supports professional practice, including the concept of being more responsible for and responsive to the need for ongoing growth.

Client System Satisfaction Survey A survey generally takes the form of a series of questions presented most often in a yes-or-no format or sometimes in the form of a scale. It is commonly used by agencies to measure client system satisfaction with the programs and services of the setting. Depending upon the quality of the instrument, these surveys can provide much useful information about how the client system views its involvement with the agency.

A drawback to many consumer satisfaction survey efforts, however, is the overuse of yes-or-no questions. Such questions really tell us little and enable agencies to collect data, often of an "are you happy with" nature, that may give the agency a false sense of the client system's voice without really hearing it. If this approach is used, and we think it can be valuable, then care needs to be taken in selecting the information to be sought.

Questions that get at the meaning of the experience for client systems and their sense of achievement are preferable. Such information fed back to the agency and the client system give both a chance to evaluate the worth of the effort, as well as to have information that can be supportive of future change goals. Box 8.1 is an illustration of a client satisfaction survey.

The tools that we have described in this section can be used for assessing both process and outcomes. Some, like single-subject design and client satisfaction surveys, are more often used to measure outcomes. Others, like journaling and case study analysis, are tools for looking at the process. However, given the style of the social worker and the nature of the situation, these tools can all be used for either purpose.

Making Transitions

Termination or transition? The phase and process of ending work with a client system has traditionally been labeled "termination." Hellenbrand (1987) summarizes this phase as taking multiple forms. For example, the planned change process may come to a natural conclusion as goals are achieved, it may end because the client system no longer wishes to continue the work, or it may end because circumstances change with the social worker.

The choice of the word *transition* instead of termination is important. Termination carries with it the connotation that the work has been finished. As we have discussed, from the point of view of the client system, what might have changed is the relationship with the social worker and the agency, but concerns or issues are rarely solved. Or what may be occurring is that the client system has had enough for now and needs to move on with other life issues.

Having had enough is not intended to be a negative expression. It may be that the client system feels that the issue of concern has been addressed sufficiently. It could also mean that the issue has changed in important ways and the help of a social worker or agency is no longer appropriate for the work to continue. The important point is that the concept of termination may suggest an inappropriate view of what has taken place; that is, that a permanent solution has been realized.

Transition in the planned change process may be thought of as engaging the client system in a timely way, with planning and acting on managing the issue(s) and concern(s) and with making plans and realizing dreams as the change process evolves. The transition process begins with the initial contact and is visited and revisited throughout the experience. As the work begins to move toward closure, transitioning may involve less contact between the social worker and the client

Big Brothers/Big Sisters of Northern Arizona Family Feedback Form

We invite you to provide us with feedback about your experience with our agency. Please answer the following questions and return the form in the enclosed envelope.

Part I—Information about you and your children.

1. How many children live in your home? _____ How old are they?

2. How many of your children have had Big Brothers? _____ Big Sisters? _____

3. How long have your children participated in our program? _____

4. How long did you have to wait to be linked with a Big Brother or Big Sister for your child? _____ children? _____

Part II—We would like you to tell us how satisfied you have been with your experience with our program. Using the following scale, please rate your experiences with our program and volunteers:

> NA = no experience
> 1 = very unsatisfied
> 2 = unsatisfied
> 3 = satisfied
> 4 = very satisfied

1. How satisfied are you with: (circle the one best answer)

    a. the Big Brother/Big Sister(s) paired with your child(ren)? NA 1 2 3 4

    b. the influence the Big Brother/Sister has on your child(ren)? NA 1 2 3 4

system: for example, occasional or "booster shot" sessions with the social worker, or the end of formal contact with the client system.

Preparing for Transition

The time for the social worker to begin preparing for transitions and planning for evaluation of processes and outcomes is during the initial contact and engagement with the client system. It is similar to when a financial counselor conducting

c. the kind of activities your child(ren) and the Big Brother/Sister(s) do together?   NA   1   2   3   4

d. the support provided by the agency when you express concerns about your child(ren)'s Big Brother/Sister(s)?   NA   1   2   3   4

2. Have you had any issues or concerns about the quality of the Big Brother/Sister(s)?
_____ No _____ Yes. If yes, please explain _____

3. **Please complete this rating for each child paired with a Big Brother/Sister.**
How would you rate your child's progress in the following areas since she or he began with his or her Big Brother/Sister? Please use the following scale:

NA = no change needed
1 = worse
2 = no change
3 = improved
4 = greatly improved

School Grades	NA	1	2	3	4
School Attendance	NA	1	2	3	4
Relations with Teachers	NA	1	2	3	4
Relations with Friends	NA	1	2	3	4
Relations at Home	NA	1	2	3	4
Feelings about Self	NA	1	2	3	4

[Repeat of question 3 variables for additional children have been omitted for inclusion in this book.]

Please feel free to write any additional comments about your experience with our agency. You may continue on the back of this page if you need more space.

Thank you for your feedback. Please return this form in the enclosed envelope.

a workshop speaks of people with money woes because "Christmas sneaks up on them—year after year!"

The relationship between the social worker and the client system will inevitably change, and looking ahead to that point is part of the beginning work and the work throughout the process. Preparing for the ending of the relationship, at least in the formal sense of working together toward goal attainment, is an important part of transitioning.

I (Barry) recall my experience in my first graduate field placement. I had spent the year working in a Jewish community center, and one of my roles had been to staff a sixth-grade boys' group that had focused on social skills development via a range of cultural and recreational activities. As I entered the end of the placement, I found myself experiencing a sense of loss as I realized that I would no longer be working with these boys.

I came down with a virus and was not able to make the last formal activity I had planned with the group. (I will leave it to the psychodynamically inclined to wonder about the timing of the illness!) Two of the boys had become quite close to me and we had been talking about how we could stay in contact with one another after I returned to my home state.

One day in the week following the meeting that I was unable to attend, these two boys came by the center and found me in the rec room. They asked how I was feeling, let me know that they were concerned that I had been ill, and asked if we could shoot some pool. I agreed, and as we spent some time around the pool table, it became apparent that they were sad to see me leave. In fact, they had come by to say good-bye and let me know how important I had been to them. I shared my honest feelings of sadness at leaving as well. After we had talked about this a bit, they each gave me a paper with their addresses, asked for mine, and we agreed to keep in touch over the summer. As it came time for them to leave for home, each shook my hand and indicated how glad they were that we had a chance to see one another before I left.

As I was driving home that evening, I reflected on how the need for some closure had been important to these boys—and to me—and how, by missing the last meeting, I failed to bring the group (which had six active participants in it) to a successful closure and transition. The two members who sought me out needed to know how I saw them and our time together. We were able to process some of that, but to this day I regret missing that last meeting, and I admit that I still have trouble sometimes letting go in the helping context.

The lesson I learned from this experience was that it is important to review and acknowledge with the client system achievements and the meaning of important work together so both the client system and the social worker can leave the change process with a clearer sense of achievement, of harmony, and of the future.

As Gerard Egan (1990) points out, in clinical sessions it is important early in the change process to decide with the client system what degree of progress or change is sufficient for transition. Egan refers to the work of Maholich and Turner (1979) and their questions useful for enabling client systems to decide when it is time for transition:

- *Have initial concerns been reduced, eliminated, or managed?*
- *Has the original stress been dissipated or reduced?*
- *Is the client system coping better with concerns?*
- *Does the client system understand itself better?*
- *Has the client system's sense of competency been increased?*
- *Is the client system relating more effectively with other systems?*
- *Is the client system going about the tasks of everyday life reasonably well? (Cited in Egan, 1990, pp. 404–405)*

The use of questions such as these not only provides the social worker and client system with a mutually identified ending point but also helps in shaping goals and providing some benchmarks for how progress (or the lack of it) may be unfolding during the working phases of the process. We would note that the idea of defining how much achievement is enough applies to all levels of intervention and with all client systems, from the person to the family, group, organization, and community. The capacity to name what is enough in and of itself is an empowering experience, as it affirms the right of the client system to name and exercise control to the maximum extent feasible.

I (Barry) recall a cartoon I once saw in an assertiveness training manual where a person labeled "meek" posed a question to God. The question went something like, "But do I really have to inherit the whole thing?" The strength to say "I have worked enough" or "This is better to the point of being okay" is an important expression of client system right and competency and facilitates the transitions of living.

Attending to Transitions

An integral part of the transition (which may involve either less contact with the client system or the end of formal contact with the client system) is the opportunity for the client system to reflect on and claim accomplishments and learning. In their efforts with the social worker, client systems may or may not have been successful in managing concerns and working toward a preferred reality. In all cases, however, client systems have learned some things that can be helpful down the road. It is important to be able to claim that learning as a sense of accomplishment.

Also, the social worker is provided with a similar opportunity to learn more about his or her practice. Soliciting and hearing evaluative feedback strengthens our practice base for future use. However, this activity must be planned for from the beginning and scheduled into the work at various points along the way. We fear, if this is not done, that the opportunity can be lost to both the client system and the social worker in the pressures of day-to-day events that surround the change process.

The social worker bears a special obligation to facilitate planning for the transition and evaluation of the change process. Building these steps into the service plan is one effective way to meet this professional responsibility.

Sometimes, client systems may need to be encouraged to track their movement toward goals, as the progression may be very subtle and covert. In other situations, progress may be very clear. In reflecting on the work that has been done, client systems may experience an increased sense of mastery from the ability to meet the challenges and demands of internal and external realities. This can be empowering, as client systems have a greater sense of their own competence and power while the relationship with the worker becomes less intensive.

Transition, then, can be a time of affirmation of competence realized and identification of roads remaining to be traveled. Even when the results may not be realized in a way that was originally envisioned, this reflection process provides client systems with the opportunity to learn from the experience. Just as we regularly remind our students that there are no dumb questions—except those not asked—there are no worthless efforts in planned change processes, even though there may be some that work more effectively than others.

Attending to transitions in the change process can be a time for marshaling resources for the future, when client systems can ask questions such as:

- How do we need to strengthen our support system?
- What behaviors do we need to change for well-being?
- Where can we get support for maintaining efforts that have been realized?
- How can we as a community ally with others to achieve systemic goals?
- Where do we wish to go next with our concerns?

The point of these questions is that they enable client systems to think about the next steps they may wish to take as well as to realize that, while there are always challenges, opportunities, and struggles, they are better equipped to address them.

Summary

In this chapter, we have presented the final phase of our practice model, focused upon evaluating outcomes and making transitions. Key ideas include valuing the process of learning how well the work went and being clear about what goals were realized. We identify methods and tools for conducting practice-level and, to some degree, program-level evaluations. We also review the importance of research knowledge as it supports our practice and key skills, such as seeing links between events, setting up the practice process so that evaluation is a natural part of it, and providing useful feedback.

We describe a number of tools and methods for practice evaluation, including Goal Attainment Scaling, single-subject design, case study analysis, client satisfaction surveys, measurement scales for outcomes, and reflective questions. Journaling, a technique that is helpful with self-evaluation, is also discussed. Each of these has been presented as a way that the social worker and the client system together can look at what was achieved in their work as well as identify concerns and issues still to be addressed. Before moving on to learn about working and influencing change in the organizational context, please reflect on these questions:

1. Recall the times when you were actively involved in change processes (for example, planning a wedding, preparing for college, seeking employment, talking with a school counselor or social worker, or helping a friend manage the loss of a friendship). What did you learn from the experience? How were the work and outcomes evaluated? If they weren't evaluated, as you reflect back on the experience, what might have been different for you in terms of

your memory of and learning from the experience if the process and outcomes had been evaluated?

2. Think about the ways you have experienced evaluation. What feelings do you recall? Are there ways we can evaluate and attend to the anxiety it might create?

3. Think about the ways research and social work practice are similar. How comfortable does being in a research role feel to you?

4. What is your reaction to the use of the concept of transition to describe the last phase of providing services to others? Think of the transitions in your life as terminations. How does this affect your reaction to the change that took place?

5. How does what you have learned about people and social processes fit with the model for influencing change that we have outlined in this book?

CHAPTER NINE

The Organization and Social Work Practice

*I know things are tough right now,
but just remember every flower
that ever bloomed had to go through
a whole lot of dirt to get there.*

FROM A PICTURE PAINTED BY ADOLESCENT RESIDENTS
ASPEN HILL HOSPITAL, FLAGSTAFF, ARIZONA

Introduction

In an article that has come to be viewed as a classic, Robert Pruger (1973) notes that "[i]f social workers must be bureaucrats—and they must—they might as well be good ones" (p. 26). Pruger was addressing one of the three functions that he saw professional social workers performing: the helper function, the organizational function, and the bureaucratic function. It is noteworthy that two of these functions are associated with the organizational context in which the social worker is employed.

A more recent trend in the social work profession has been the growth of professional social workers entering some form of private independent or private group practice: 16.8% of NASW members listed private practice as the primary setting for their practice in 1991 (Gibelman & Schervish, 1993). This trend is somewhat analogous to what is happening in the fields of medicine and law; yet, even with this growth, a large majority of social workers still find their practice taking place within formal organizations.

Given that we still find the majority of social workers employed within some type of organizational structure, it is worthwhile to consider how this contextual reality shapes the practice of social work. This chapter is designed to help us think about being members of organizations as we carry out our professional functions and about how we might use our professional capabilities to influence our organizations to become better at what they do; that is, to deliver programs and services in a way that supports the competencies of those who use the programs and of the staff who deliver the services.

One could ask why we see social workers as having a need to participate in organizational change. That is a valid and important question, and we return to the Code of Ethics (NASW, 1996) for part of the answer. Standard 3, sections 3.09 (b), (c), (d), and (e) [Commitments to Employers] and Standard 6, sections 6.01 [Social Welfare] and 6.03 (a), (b), and (d) [Social and Political Action] are guides for professional behavior associated with enabling social work organizations to be more accessible and effective. Inherent in this challenge is a reflection of the need for creating effective organizations that build staff capabilities so staff can support more fully the competencies of those they serve.

I (Barry) conducted a job satisfaction study for the National Association of Social Workers chapter in West Virginia a few years back and discovered that the workers perceived themselves to be under extreme stress on the job, with little support in their agencies. In such circumstances, it is difficult for workers to have a sense of power, and as Simon (1994) notes, "[t]he deterioration of the conditions under which social workers deliver services endangers directly their capacity to assist client empowerment" (p. 190).

The idea that we need to pay attention to our work climate and organizational practices is not new; however, it has taken on a new urgency, as our society is in the midst of major changes in the way the economy and the jobs associated with it are managed. Newspapers and newsmagazines regularly report on the anxiety felt in the workforce about job security and on employment trends that suggest employees entering the work force are likely to experience three to four distinct careers in their lifetimes.

In a climate of uncertainty, which is also changing the nature of social service delivery and social work practice, being able to sort through complex organizational issues and have the flexibility to manage change and meet new demands will be requisite skills for effective social workers. For example, mental health agencies and hospitals in many states have been laying off social workers and other providers as Medicaid program costs are brought under greater controls and limits.

As we thought about these issues, we were drawn back to the phases of our practice model. We think they have relevance, especially when coupled with the questions presented in Chapter 3 (understanding the context of the locality), in helping us as social workers to become better able to work well in our employing organization.

Phase One: Telling and Exploring the Story

In our practice model, we named the first phase Telling and Exploring the Story. For social workers entering into a new place of employment or assuming a new function with a current employer, this phase has aims similar to that of our work with client systems and service consumers. We need to understand our organization in order to tell its story in our communities, as we deliver its services and struggle with common dilemmas that arise when organizations lose sight of their mission or vision.

Telling and exploring the story of the organization includes understanding key components that shape the way social workers, who are part of the organization, practice. Some of these key components include organizational structure, funding base, internal and external power relations, and organizational climate and culture. Organizational theory can be one tool for aiding social workers in understanding how their agency may operate.

Holland (1995) notes four common theoretical perspectives that define how organizations function: open-systems, behavioral, economic, and cultural.

Open-Systems Perspective—this view holds that organizations are sets of related parts interacting with one another and the external environment such that changes in any one component stimulate corresponding modifications in other parts. The agency is understood as a dynamic whole, and any impacts on any part of its elements, including external events, influence the behavior of the agency.

To illustrate, the universities where we practice are publicly supported and must compete with other public programs for tax revenues. Over the past years, as health care costs have risen and more and more state citizens have been forced to use the Medicaid program to meet their health needs, more tax revenue has been allocated to this program. At some of our institutions, we have witnessed the loss of public revenue as more has been shifted to support Medicaid. The competition for scarce dollars has meant that higher education may lose some funds that go instead to a valuable social service program. This dilemma of scarce resources cannot be fully understood without some appreciation of the other demands for public dollars.

Behavioral Perspective—this orientation focuses on the actions and choices of the people in the organizations. The belief is that people have goals but organizations do not, and that people will act to maintain stability and minimize disruption to existing relationships and agreements.

This view suggests that what people see as important and what they do determines what the organization will be. This perspective may help to explain one of the disturbing tendencies of many organizations to move away from their original purposes. Known as goal displacement, the energy and efforts of the organization and its employees become directed more toward self-maintenance than toward quality service delivery.

Goal displacement is the phenomenon where the original purpose of a policy or program gets displaced (the way a body in a tub displaces water). This happens when:

1. the means become the ends—an organization measures how many clients are seen or programs are run instead of looking at the impacts of the program(s).

2. the appearance becomes more important than the reality—according to one account of the development of services for people who are homeless in New York, one administrator remarked that "merit in decision making" was not important. What was important was how policy decisions played in the press and how good the governor looked (Funiciello, 1993).

3. the needs of the organizational members become paramount—some social agencies are open only from 8:30 a.m. to 4:30 p.m., the same working hours of many service consumers (which means that the consumers have to take time off to be served). Often, hours are not adjusted (to 10:00 a.m. to 6:00 p.m., for example) because staff members prefer to keep regular hours.

Many agencies structured as bureaucracies have experienced goal displacement. In performing the organizational function of practice, social workers can assess organizational practices and address them if goal displacement is a concern.

Economic Perspective—this view holds that organizations use rational decisions to maximize optimal outcomes. Cost-benefit analysis is a useful tool for assessing the relationship of the costs and the gains associated with the provision of the service. The key is to maximize the utility of outputs or to produce the greatest good that available resources permit.

The economic perspective continues to have considerable influence in social service agencies, often a result of outside pressures for accountability. We are not opposed to accountability as a goal; however, we are not fully convinced that financial patterns are the best or only measure of accountability. Often, agencies need to consider other variables in arriving at decisions about the efficiency and effectiveness of organizational outputs.

I (Barry) recall serving on a small non-profit family agency board of directors when we were given the option of becoming a case management agency for home health services to the elderly in our region. To do so at the time would have required us to stop providing direct home health services. As the only certified

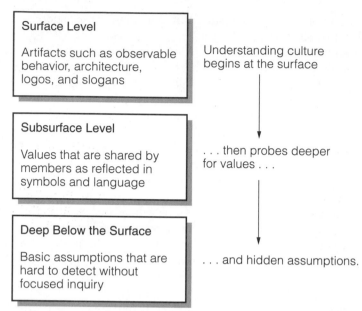

Figure 9.1 Levels of Awareness of Organizational Culture
[*Source:* Robey and Sales (1994, p. 365).]

provider of these services to the low-income elderly, we chose not to pursue the more financially lucrative program, as our current client systems would not have had the options to receive the home-based aid they needed to function and live more independently.

The most rational economic decision would have been to become the case management agency, yet the board felt it could not abandon the client systems currently being served. While the call to accountability and "cutting back" is strong, using only the economic model may increase the number of vulnerable people who fall through the holes of the safety net. As social workers, we must face these challenges in our day-to-day work within our employing agency.

Cultural Perspective—this view assumes that human behavior is guided by cultural patterns and that organizations develop norms and patterns as well. The organization's culture is defined as the constellation of values, beliefs, assumptions, and expectations that drive organizational behavior. We all know or have heard about the corporate identity and the organization person. These labels come out of the cultural context of the organization.

Organizational culture is a pattern of assumptions and behaviors that enables the members of the organization to construct meaning, define rules for internal functioning, and relate to others outside the organization (Robey and Sales, 1994). Much of what we consider to be culture is not easily seen or understood and may not be noticeable to many of the organization's members.

Robey and Sales (1994) describe organizational culture as a multilevel arrangement that can be well understood only after much observation, discussion, and open-minded analysis. Figure 9.1 illustrates a conceptualization of the complexity of organizational culture.

Symbols and artifacts are the most obvious manifestation of the organizational culture. Unlike large corporations, where the building can be designed to reflect the leader's vision of the organization, few social service agencies design the buildings in which they operate. However, the way the waiting room is furnished, what kinds of paintings or posters are on the wall, or how the offices are arranged can provide clues to the culture.

While symbols can be designed and controlled by management, the *stories* of the organization that are shared by its members reveal basic assumptions about the organization held by the people working there (Boje, 1991). I (Jim) have a sister-in-law who works for Electronic Data Systems (EDS), the management information firm that Ross Perot founded (and later sold to General Motors). When Perot owned the company, he once paid a million dollars to aid in the escape efforts of two EDS employees from a prison in Iran, when negotiations to get them out of prison failed. EDS employees would tell that story, which demonstrates the commitment of that employer to his employees.

The opposite of an employer's commitment to employees is illustrated by the story of a human services agency where a popular new worker was fired right before the end of her probationary period. While the worker did many things well, she was slow to get the paperwork done. Management's concern about her timely completion of paperwork had been communicated to her, but it was not clear to her or to the other staff that this was a job-threatening concern. This story is told as a warning to staff and possibly to communicate that management can't be trusted.

Organizations can be said to have strong cultures when there is much consensus as to the purpose and values of the organization and the artifacts, stories, and rites/rituals reinforce these purposes and values. I (Jim) worked for a settlement house in Ohio that had served the neighborhood where they were located for over a hundred years. Workers were generally proud of the long-standing commitment to the area. Photos that showed well-baby clinics from the 1890s and stories about events held in the 1930s served to reinforce the sense of mission. This is an example of a strong culture that is positive.

However, agencies can also have strong cultures (much consensus as to the purpose and values of the organization) in organizations that are not client centered. Goal displacement takes place in some organizations, as we noted earlier. When goal displacement occurs and the organizational culture is strong, we refer to this as a strong culture that is negative.

While much of the social contract between the employer and the employee is undergoing rapid change, social workers who wish to be effective within the organizational context need to understand the culture that drives the organization's responses to internal and external demands and opportunities. Understanding the culture is fundamental to knowing the organization and how it is likely to respond to challenges and opportunities. We think this is generalizable to all settings.

The perspectives outlined above may be used as one explanation for how organizations come to structure themselves and carry out their roles within the community and society. Organizations often draw upon each of these perspectives to define themselves at any point in their story, and we would do well to consider all four perspectives in coming to better understand our own agency.

Agency Structure

Another way to understand the organization is by its governance structure. Sheafor, Horejsi, and Horejsi (1994, pp. 473–474) identify four governance models that may be found in social service: bureaucratic, collegial, project-team, and mixed-matrix.

Traditionally, recalling Pruger's point at the beginning of this chapter, social service organizations have governed themselves by the *bureaucratic,* hierarchical approach. In this approach, everyone has a supervisor to whom to report, and there are several decision-making levels through which communication must flow. A common dilemma for social workers, supported by the ideal of professionalism, is practicing with autonomy within the organizational constraints of the structure and policies.

The *collegial* structure is positioned at the other end of the continuum from the bureaucratic and assumes that all persons in the organization are of equal status and fully independent in their approach to tasks. This model, while it sounds appealing, raises important questions about the efficient use of resources and accountability.

In the *project-team* structure, members of the organization are brought together to work on a common task. They usually have a team leader to facilitate the project and to handle regular communication to the larger organization, of which the team is but one part. This structure is favored by many organizations today for its flexibility and the creativity found in teams working together on a common task. There can be difficulties with accountability and quality if, initially, the project is not well defined.

Finally, the *mixed-matrix* model attempts to use the benefits of both teams and bureaucratic structures. Teams are formed to take advantage of members' skills but are placed clearly under the supervision of the organizational leadership structure so that communication and accountability are maintained. For example, it is common to set up ad hoc committees in social service agencies to plan or demonstrate a new service program. The team generally works on the task under the leadership of an agency supervisor or manager for accountability purposes. Teams can be quite effective, yet often are threatening to the organization.

I (Barry) recall working in a public agency charged with providing child protection services, along with many other programs. The agency was set up as a classic bureaucracy, with clear lines of authority and communication processes delineated.

Several veteran employees in child welfare investigation, all but one with master's degrees in social work, approached the management team with the idea of working without a direct supervisor and reporting directly to the manager of all social service programs in the region. The management team, after much debate, agreed to try out the new unit and see how it worked.

To our surprise, the newly structured unit worked quite well. Referrals were quickly followed, and the team used all of its members in deciding how best to proceed with child abuse and neglect complaints. One positive outcome was the deflection from the formal system of the complaints that were not appropriate, often enabling families to get help with needs without being charged as neglectful parents.

The agency's chief administrator was so pleased with how the unit was working that he wrote it up in one of his monthly reports to the state office. What followed was a classic organizational response from the bureaucracy. They required that the unit be assigned a supervisor, as it was not appropriate for staff not to be directly supervised. We did so and, over the next several months, watched as solid, professional social workers left to find other opportunities where their professional roles and abilities were better respected.

The message is clear that governance structures shape and influence the way social workers work. We need to understand this reality and be comfortable with the dominant structure if we are to be effective. Even where the structure may be more rigid than we like, we can work to influence change, and professional colleagues can be a sound source of support. However, nothing replaces solid knowledge about how the organization defines its mission and governance and about how to work effectively within that context for needed change. Pruger (1973) suggests several survival strategies. In this context, *survival* refers to maintaining a sense of professional integrity and competence while working in the bureaucracy. These strategies are presented a little later in this chapter.

Agency Funding

Just as structure shapes practice, so does the source and amount of financial resources available to the organization. Social services tend to be funded in two ways: public funds and private funds. Many agencies access both sources in providing their programs.

Public dollars most often come from the general revenue accounts of government at the local, state, or federal levels. One important debate that gained momentum after the 1994 elections was the role of the federal government in supporting public social services programs. A public consensus emerged in the late 1990s that the federal government should be smaller and leaner. The growth in nonentitlement spending slowed or stopped, and there have been cuts in programs serving poor and marginalized people.

Private sector sources of funding take a variety of forms, from fees for services provided to private foundation grants for selected programs. Much of the debate around reducing the amount of public dollars suggests that the private sector will make up any potential loss of funds. However, reviews of foundation giving and interests suggest that programs designed to address poverty and other risk factors have not been a priority area for private philanthropy. There are notable exceptions in the health care arena: both the Kellogg and Robert Woods Johnson Foundations make substantial grants to support health care delivery; and regional foundations have been established to better the overall quality of life in specific geographical areas.

Understanding the impacts of the sources of funding on the agency and its programs can enable social workers to better appreciate the relationship of funding to their practice. The advent of managed care models in the delivery of community mental health services illustrates the impact funding resources may have on practice.

Our colleagues in mental health agencies regularly report how managed care plans, which have the authority to control insurance payments for services provided to client systems of the insurer, shape the way they do practice. For example, many providers of mental health services report that the practice model preferred by managed care plans is some form of brief therapy, often limited to three sessions, which has obligated the mental health professionals to change the way they work with their client systems in order to meet these constraints. Also, many managed care plans do not pay for collateral contacts—contacting other professionals or community persons to more effectively address client systems' issues.

Similarly, public sector funds tend to flow through specific, and often narrowly defined, categories. Services, then, are available to those who meet the specific eligibility criteria established by the funding category.

Social workers are often challenged with providing what the client system is eligible for rather than what the client may need. For example, a family may qualify for public assistance benefits because they don't have transportation to a job, yet assisting them in purchasing a car when no other form of public transportation is available is beyond the scope of the program.

Another impact of funding is on educational opportunities and the preparation of social workers. Recently, some social work programs have lost field placement opportunities because the need to generate revenue through patient or client system contact is so great that the agency did not feel it could provide the time for field instruction or supervision. Should this become widespread, finding ways to provide quality field placements could become more difficult.

Agency Relations

The way organizations structure themselves influences the internal relationships among social work staff and their consumers. Effective social workers take stock of the power relations in the organization and attempt to use them to serve the needs and desires of the consumers of the agency's program(s).

Many sources of power, both formal and personal, exist within the organization. Formal power emerges most often from the official positions assigned. For example, the title administrator carries certain power and authority, as does the title social worker or secretary. The more traditional the structure, the more likely power differentials are seen as important in terms of professional functions and positions.

Visionary leaders have often used their formal positions of power as an impetus for change. To illustrate, in 1995, we (Barry and Jim) attended the 20th annual National Institute on Social Work and Human Services in Rural Areas. At this meeting, the history of the effort around this conference was reviewed; what had emerged over the years was that a few social workers saw a need and began to respond to it, often using their professional positions to legitimate the effort. In the past two decades, we have seen a considerable body of literature and professional policy statements created that attempt to speak to the interests of social workers in small towns and rural areas. This development would most likely not have moved as far without visionary leaders who used their positions within the social work profession and within their organizations to advocate for the needs and issues of social work in rural areas.

Another major source of power is found at the personal level. Personal power characteristics include charisma, knowledge, expertise, reputation, social status, and personal traits like integrity and trustworthiness. These sources of personal power often place people in positions of influence within the organization.

Personal power is also associated with the informal structure that exists in any organization. In one of our universities, the records clerk has been there for a long time, has always been very student oriented, and is well respected by all students. In our senior seminar, we have students do an organizational analysis assignment that shows both the formal and informal decision-making structures as they see and experience them. The formal chart always has the dean and program directors at the top of the governance structure. However, the informal chart often has the records clerk at the top. When asked about this, the students rightly identify the records clerk as the person that keeps them on track and the one to whom they can go for information.

Social workers need to pay attention to power structures and dynamics within their organization. Getting on the wrong side of a powerful staff person, even if the person reports to you or your equivalent within the organization, can create barriers to effective practice.

A related area in agency relationships has to do with the competing perspectives that various staff members may have of the agency mission and what they get out of being employed there. One of the tensions that sometimes surfaces in social service agencies is the conflict that occurs between staff who see themselves in a career position and other staff who see themselves as having a job. While generalization is always risky, part of the tension may express itself around issues of loyalty, commitment, and a willingness to extend oneself beyond the official job description for the position held. Often, staff who see themselves as employed in a job may not be as willing to extend themselves beyond their job description and see the organization only as providing them with a way to make a living—one that is often felt to be inadequate.

On the other hand, the ethics of most professions suggest that services cannot be limited to the official working hours or only to the job description if something more is called for to achieve the desired practice outcomes; one's career obligation demands this orientation. Regardless of orientation, however, the story of the agency can be fully understood only by considering the differing perspectives held by its staff.

Street-Level Bureaucrats in Organizations

Street-level bureaucrats (SLBs), according to Michael Lipsky (1981), are the frontline workers in public service: social workers, eligibility workers in governmental agencies, police officers, teachers, and those who have direct contact with the public. In essence, the way SLBs implement governmental policies *is policy* to members of the public. If state troopers do not pull you over unless you are going over seven miles an hour over the speed limit, the real speed limit on the highways is 72, not 65.

Street-level bureaucrats have a great deal of power, in that the expectations about their job performance are often ambiguous and/or contradictory and often job performance is hard to measure and is not linked to compensation. Additionally, because of civil service and union provisions, some public employees are difficult to sanction and fire.

They have also a great deal of discretion, in that they are being asked to implement often contradictory rules in situations that are too complicated, with too many variables, to reduce to a "cookbook." In order to get the volume of work done, SLBs need to simplify and routinize procedures; they devise and use shortcuts.

For example, police officers in most places do not give tickets to people who jaywalk (crossing streets where there are no stoplights or crosswalks). Although there are laws that make this an offense, police officers realize that they have other priorities that are higher. However, jaywalking might be one of the charges issued if someone were crossing a street very slowly in order to slow traffic down or create a scene.

Another area in which street-level bureaucrats have a great deal of power is in their relations with client systems. Client systems who are involuntary, who are ordered by a court or protective services to be consumers of the agency, have difficulty voting with their feet. They often do not have other options of where to go for services. Persons using governmental social services also have few ways to influence the workers—if they don't come back, that may be seen as a positive sign, especially in public welfare agencies that are trying to reduce the number of recipients. In situations where client system cooperation (having all the necessary information, being polite, not asking too many questions) makes the work go smoother from the point of view of the worker, client systems who do not accept that role may be treated less responsively than more conforming client systems.

Workers can reward client systems by giving them information not shared with all service consumers, by devoting more time to their situation, and by using their discretion in allocating resources. To illustrate, some years back, welfare officials in a southeastern state were informing most, but not all, applicants of their rights to apply for assistance. As another example, public housing officials in a large northeastern city were coaching elderly applicants in how to apply for emergency housing status, which, if approved, would put them at the top of a long waiting list. By selectively sharing information with some clients and not with others, some clients are favored, and obviously some are worse off than they would have been if there had been no special treatment. SLBs often use their own values and preferences in deciding how to implement policies and procedures (Lipsky, 1981).

Worker discretion is not always undesirable, however. It's far better for trained workers to make decisions in complex situations full of ambiguity and complexity than to rely on inflexible policies. As Handler and Hasenfeld (1992) point out, "as long as government and large-scale agencies are serving and regulating the disadvantaged, then the consequences of unfair power in the exercise of discretion must be addressed" (p. 24).

Social workers can be mindful of their power and their discretion. How they use them can foster the enhancement of client systems' use of their own power in interactions with organizations and institutions.

According to Hasenfeld (1984), client systems (especially low-income clients) are at a power disadvantage in working with agencies, especially those agencies that have a monopoly on services. Four principal ways that client systems can gain power over their social services environment are by (1) reducing their needs for specific resources and services, (2) increasing the range of alternatives through which they can meet their needs, (3) increasing their value to those agencies whose services/resources they need, and (4) reducing the available alternatives to those whose services and resources they need (that is, making it harder for agencies not to serve "less desirable" clients).

Social workers can also increase client systems' power resources, by doing the following:

- providing clients with greater information about the agency, its resources, and particularly about client systems' entitlements;
- affirming and training client systems to assert and claim their legitimate rights in the agency;
- increasing client systems' knowledge and expertise in handling their needs;
- increasing client systems' resources through their own collective actions;
- linking client systems with a supportive social network that can add resources, reduce dependence on the agency, and help to better negotiate the context; and
- using social workers' own resources (information, expertise, and legitimacy) to obtain needed benefits and services for client systems (Hasenfeld, 1984).

Organizations and Dignity

Another key concept that is gaining more and more attention in organizational thinking is dignity and how the organization either affirms or assails the dignity experience of both client systems and employees. In review, possessing and experiencing dignity means having one's essential humanity affirmed and recognized, apart from the social roles the person assumes. It is one thing to communicate respect to the president of an organization, quite another to communicate and affirm dignity to a person who is homeless and seeking service from an agency. The capacity to affirm dignity, both at the interpersonal level and at the organizational level, is one key way we think mature and professional organizations express themselves.

In Chapter 2, we discussed at some length our views about the importance of dignity. Here we wish to highlight the ways in which dignity is especially important to affirm in our day-to-day activities in the practice setting. The areas where dignity becomes an important issue in the organizational experience are in the way people are treated by the organization (for example, are they treated as people who are important or unimportant?) and in the way issues of power, autonomy, competence, social participation, and inclusion are addressed. Some primary concepts that can have an influence on these two areas of concern are listed below.

•   The atmosphere of the organization, in relation to both consumers and employees, can affect people's sense of dignity. Does the climate suggest to people that they have worth or lack worth? To illustrate, the waiting rooms of many public agencies are rather spartan and depressing places. There may be no place for staff to gather, eat a quiet lunch, or rest. Often, the unspoken message is that people who come to the agency or work in the agency do not count for much.

•   The way we receive our client systems may tell them important things about who has power and control. We (Barry, Becky, and Jim), in making field visits to students in field placement, have been troubled by how client systems are received in many human service settings. It has not been uncommon to watch employees come to a doorway of the waiting room, shout out for client systems, tell them to follow, and turn away. The typical response is for the persons to look around with embarrassed expressions and to shuffle off with their heads down. It does not cost the social worker or organization any more to extend a warm and friendly greeting, yet the price the client system pays for not getting that greeting seems very high.

•   Likewise, programs that are delivered in a way that instructs the client system what to do and when can take away dignity and power. While there are always rules, the way we present and utilize them can facilitate a sense of hope and competency by working in partnership with the client system in making decisions and selecting options.

•   Dignity understood as a source of hope is a powerful expression in the helping experience. While we hesitate to label it as a tool, social workers who have a fundamental commitment to the concept of dignity move a long way down the road to success as they communicate this commitment through their actions and interactions with others.

•   Finally, as implied in the first point, the message to the client systems that use our agencies is also a message to the employees. We have all heard negative comments made about public employees, and we have known dedicated and effective social workers in the public sector who have felt so devalued that they begin to question their own competence and ability. Once this becomes real to them, they are at risk of fulfilling that view, known as self-fulfilling prophecy. That is why we need to work to create caring work climates for employees as well as client systems.

Phase Two: Describing a Preferred Reality

The second phase of our model, as it was applied to working with client systems, focused on describing a preferred reality and naming the goals necessary to work toward desired outcomes. As we carry out our professional social work roles in our agencies, there is also the need to discover a preferred reality for our agency and the programs it delivers.

Asking questions about what the organization could be like, routinely taking the organizational pulse, and working to increase the organization's cultural competence are important tasks and efforts that can assist an agency at being better at what it does. Bailey (1995) notes that "naming the world can become a model for changing the world" (p. 1662). We think this fits well with the task of organizational change toward a preferred reality.

Organizations, as dynamic systems, need a strong and effective feedback mechanism or they face the risk of becoming closed systems that are no longer viable. Systems theory assumes that some form of feedback and energy exchange between the agency and its environment is necessary for organizational well-being.

Often, one challenge is how to ensure energy exchange in light of the tendency of many leaders to take care of troubles behind closed doors. While at times this is appropriate, all too often becoming closed off from one's environment places the agency at risk of losing support or resources when they are most needed.

There are several techniques for engaging in energy exchange and soliciting input regarding agency structure, functioning, and services. Many of these techniques were identified and described in Chapter 8, where we discussed the need for practice and program evaluation.

An effective way of securing regular feedback involves creating feedback tools (for example, surveys, focus groups, and interviews) to use with consumers, staff, and key informants from the external context. The point to creating these mechanisms is to provide the organization with safeguards against potential entropy, goal displacement, program or climate drifts toward less effectiveness, and shifts in consumer need that make the current program obsolete.

As has been referred to earlier, in a 1988 study, I (Barry) found that most of the respondents to a work climate survey perceived themselves to be under extreme stress at work and that their employing organization was not doing much, if anything, to help them address the stressful environment. Beyond reporting that finding, I also approached the professional continuing education director for the School of Social Work at my university and asked that, for the next several years, at least two workshops on stress management tools be offered throughout the state. These workshops proved to be very popular with social work professionals. Social service administrators were also advised of the findings of the study and encouraged to support staff in better managing the stress as well.

Soliciting and then acting upon feedback is a key strategy for enabling agencies to develop their story toward an improved reality. Lest we appear overly optimistic, we acknowledge that there are real constraints on what can be done to improve programs and services; yet, we are persuaded from our personal experiences and discussions with other colleagues that, often, positive change of a small nature (for example, seeking client system feedback on how to make a program better and acting on the feedback) goes a long way in strengthening the agency and its position within the community.

In an increasingly diverse society, we believe that all organizations face the issue of becoming more pluralistic and culturally competent. Bailey (1995) presents an argument for creating leaders who can help organizations achieve increased sensitivity to the contributions of diversity in the workplace. She defines these leaders as those who have the ability to "celebrate the new arrivals to the table, actively support their rights to full expression of ideas and perspectives, facilitate their access to all needed resources, and, most important, ensure equity of power in the pluralistic organization" (p. 1659). The "new arrivals" at the table are those women and people of color who have not historically had a place in the decision-making process. We would add that the idea of cultural competence should be extended to all groups who are oppressed and need to have a voice within the organizational context.

A typology to help organizations take a look at how well they address the need for increased sensitivity to diversity has been developed by the Equity Institute. They define the following four levels of organizational awareness:

- *Level 1—the token equal employment opportunity organization. Minorities are hired because of EEO guidelines and are rarely found in positions of power.*

- *Level 2—the affirmative action organization. Minorities are actively recruited and hired; however, power and status are only acquired by adopting the Anglo-Western male ideology.*

- *Level 3—the self-renewing organization. The organization actively reviews its culture (espoused and enacted values, systems, strategy, staffing, and structure) to evaluate how well it supports pluralism and multiple perspectives.*

- *Level 4—the pluralistic organization. This organization prohibits all forms of discrimination, prescribes governance and management policies and practices that support the value of pluralism, and develops a workforce composed of individuals and groups who subscribe to multiple cultural perspectives. (Equity Institute [1990] as cited in Bailey, 1995, pp. 1659–1660)*

While achieving either level 3 or 4 is a daunting task, we think that goal is certainly embraced by the NASW Code of Ethics (1996), and social workers are in a unique position to help their agencies work toward this preferred reality as a matter of social justice.

As social workers find themselves in leadership roles and management positions, they may wish to take advantage of principles of pluralistic management. Bailey (1995) notes that

Nixon and Spearmon (1991) delineated several principles of pluralistic management, which can be summarized in the following managerial actions:

- *recognize that skill in pluralistic leadership that uses the human resource . . . potential of everyone in the workplace is central to managerial competence and critical to pluralistic organizations;*

- *valuing one's own cultural heritage and that of others through ensuring the availability of resources for empowering the work force;*

- *changing the organizational culture (values, attitudes, behaviors, and symbols) to accommodate differences in style, practices, and worldviews. (p. 1660)*

Phase Three: Making Plans and Dreams Real

It has been said that hope or faith without action is meaningless. As we think about working effectively in organizations, that advice is central to the change process. None of us, or our agencies, have arrived at a state of optimal or fully effective functioning. Action is necessary; yet the key is to take worthwhile actions, especially when one is working within bureaucratic structures. What follows are some ideas about tools and techniques that can be useful to the social worker who desires to work well within the organizational context.

Working Well within Organizational Contexts

Robert Pruger (1973) wrote about being a good bureaucrat. While that may sound like an oxymoron of the highest order, his intent was to suggest ways that social workers could set about meeting professional goals and remain connected with bureaucratic organizations. His advice still has currency for the practice challenges we are faced with today. Pruger (1973, pp. 26–32) identifies the following tactics that help social workers become good bureaucrats in meeting their primary functions as helpers, organizers, and administrators:

1. *Understand legitimate authority and the organizational enforcement of it.* This understanding enables the social worker to discover that much room for professional autonomy and its use remains within the legitimate authority limits of the organization. For example, as educators, we must meet the curriculum standards set forth by the Council on Social Work Education. However, the way we do this and the emphasis we use in teaching our classes leaves considerable autonomy for us in the classroom.

2. *Conserve personal energy.* The idea is to know what issues are worth fighting over and where to put our energy. Carefully choosing our battles can assist in avoiding burnout and in feeling empowered about our choices. The Serenity Prayer fits here: "God, grant me serenity to accept the things I cannot change, courage to change the things I can, and wisdom to know the difference." Often what we do need is courage to act!

3. *Acquire a competence needed by the organization.* This goes beyond our professional degree and encourages social workers to find areas where their professional knowledge and skill can be especially useful for the organization. I (Barry) have a friend and colleague who for years has worked in the public sector. One thing that sets this friend apart is his ability to see trends and new knowledge needs in whatever program he is involved with at the time. When block grants came along in the 1980s during the Reagan administration, he began to study this new way of funding programs. When the governor needed someone to take the lead in working on this new source of funding in West Virginia, my friend's name came up. He played a key role in early efforts to organize the public sector's response to block grants.

4. *Don't yield unnecessarily to the requirements of administrative convenience.* The challenge here is to be able to differentiate between tasks that further the organizational mission and tasks that merely serve the organization. Another way of thinking about this is in the way we as social workers seek to stay focused on planned change goals—ideally set with the client system—and not get caught up in goal displacement.

Staying focused on organizational mission and client system goals involves some risk taking on the part of the social worker, but taking risks becomes easier if we are clear about our position and are well grounded theoretically and professionally. Also, the challenge is made easier if we are not overly concerned with winning our viewpoint. On some issues, we will carry the argument and debate, and on others, we will not. Regardless of the outcome, being a good bureaucrat demands that we face up to challenges and not lose sight of the agency mission and client system goals in our delivery of services and programs.

In a later work, Pruger (1978) developed his thinking about working in the bureaucracy as a social work skill. Central to his argument is the idea that most social workers are unprepared for organizational life. While we have learned many things over the past 15 to 20 years, we still think this theme rings true for many as they begin their professional careers. According to Pruger (1978, pp. 151–164), some of the key things social workers need to know about the bureaucracy include:

- understanding the capacity bureaucratic systems have for continuing apathetic, alienated employees. This knowledge forewarns workers to depend upon themselves, and not on the system, if they are really concerned about not ending up as one of the burned-out group.

- possessing bureaucratic skills that help the worker develop the means to be more self-directed within the organization.

- understanding the ideological opinion that being a professional *and* a bureaucrat are incompatible roles and seeing the difficulty this ideological opinion presents by creating unnecessary tension for the social worker.

    For those who work in formal organizations, it is both unrealistic and unproductive to think of bureaucracy simply as an evil to overcome. Rather, it can be understood as a complex milieu within which private and collective purposes are pursued—purposes that are easily lost because the skills necessary for dealing with that complexity are often lacking. (Pruger, 1978, pp. 156–157)

- realizing that discretion in the ways we carry out roles and responsibilities is always present, even though we may not believe it. The important knowledge and skill is understanding how much social workers can do to create their own reality in the organization. Conflict tolerance and management are also important skills.

- knowing that dealing with organizational change requires more than being in favor of change. Change is a given and, as a continuous process, provides social workers with influence opportunities if we can tune our eyes to see them.

- understanding the importance of remaining an actor rather than becoming an object acted upon. Given the slow pace of most organizational change, social workers who hang in and maintain their independence of thought can make a difference in the life of the organization if they so choose.

Surviving and Influencing Organizational Change

Others have also thought about the issue of surviving well within the organizational context and helping its story change in positive ways. In a quite humorous approach, Knopf (1979) offers several tips of how to survive as an HP (helping person) in the BS (bureaucratic system). While no effort will be made to reproduce his entire work here, there are several points we think are worth sharing. They include his super six tips for surviving the bureaucratic system:

- *A working knowledge and awareness of the bureaucracy.*
- *A working knowledge and awareness of specific HP helping skills.*
- *Self-awareness and personal growth.*
- *Creative problem-solving using opportunities within the bureaucratic system (BS).*
- *Physical activities.*
- *Active (doing) responses and individual survival techniques. (p. 76)*

Many of Knopf's tips complement Pruger's work. Having a knowledge and awareness of the bureaucracy (agency) for which we work is critical if for no other reason than that knowledge is power. Having such power leads to a sense of professional and personal competence within a place of employment.

Important knowledge areas are understanding organizational behavior; knowing your organization's view of structure and leadership and its management of hidden agendas; being aware of the secret rules of your organization; and understanding the words and language of the organization. Each of these points reflects our position that we should take the time to get to know our place of employment as fully as possible.

While knowing the organization in which we practice may seem obvious, many social workers don't do this. Comments such as, "Oh, I don't pay much attention to rules around here, I am too busy helping my clients," are at best naive and often fatal to one's long-term effectiveness.

In addition to knowing the organization, staying current within the profession is equally sound advice. Not only does this enable social workers to perform their professional roles with competency, it also enables us to be in better positions to influence change in our agencies and to know about the best practices within program areas at any particular time. Social workers who know how to listen really well, who take advantage of quality continuing education activities, and who know their competency areas will be in a better position not only to survive in their place of employment but to thrive as well.

Taking care of one's personal self, including the use of physical activity, is a vital part of being professionally competent. This message is often neglected by helpers of all sorts, including social workers. Yet, if we cannot manage the stress that is a part of our daily professional lives, burnout and other negative experiences are likely to emerge, with unhelpful consequences for the consumers of our services.

Taking care means knowing your personal limits and limitations and not setting yourself up for failure by ignoring them. It also includes knowing what you can influence and what you can't—avoiding the saving-the-world trap. Especially important is knowing how to manage stress with physical activity and play. We cannot serve our client systems or take care of the organization and help it change if we are too tired and overwhelmed on a personal level.

Assessing Risks and Liabilities   Another important way we take care of ourselves professionally, as well as personally, is through the careful assessment of risks and liabilities associated with our professional roles and responsibilities. By risks, we mean those instances and practice contexts where the potential for harm may be present.

A most obvious instance for potential harm is in child welfare, especially in child abuse and neglect investigations. I (Barry) recall a home visit to work with a family on reunification. The father of the family tried to take my life and the life of a graduate student who was with me. Had either of us been alone, we likely would not have survived the attack. The fact that we went to the home at the same time had nothing to do with our awareness of the potential for harm. However, this experience taught me, as well as the agency with whom I was employed, that we needed to pay more attention to the risks associated with our work so staff were not routinely placed in harm's way.

Since social workers continue to be involved with issues of protection of vulnerable children and adults, the risks associated with this role cannot be fully eliminated. We need to pay attention to the potential for harm and ask for backup support when we believe it is warranted. We (Barry, Becky, and Jim) caution our students to trust their gut feelings. If they feel threatened, they need to review their concerns with their supervisors and have a plan in place before proceeding.

Another kind of risk is associated with legal liability and professional malpractice. Social workers, like other helping professionals, have found themselves under ever-increasing threats of lawsuits charging malpractice. Often, such suits are associated with acts of commission or omission in the following areas:

- Inaccurate assessment, diagnosis, or treatment. In this circumstance, the social worker makes an error of judgment resulting in inappropriate intervention (for example, treating a biologically based issue as a psychologically based one).
- Allegations involving fraud. The social worker is charged with acts of fraud (for example, charging for services not rendered).
- Allegations of personal impairment. The social worker is perceived to be impaired (for example, by alcohol) to the extent that he or she cannot carry

out expected professional roles and responsibilities. To continue to practice is seen as engaging in unethical conduct.

- Allegations of engaging in sexual misconduct. In these instances, the social worker is charged with sexual misconduct involving his or her client system. Most often this is associated with engaging in some form of sexual relations or sexual harassment, a clear violation of the NASW Code of Ethics (1996; see Appendix for complete document).

- Failure to warn. As we mentioned in Chapter 1, these are situations when the social worker has failed to warn another person or other people of the client system's intention to harm them. Having such knowledge requires that the social worker act on the information from the client system as if the social worker has reason to believe (suspicion) the threat is real.

- Violation of confidentiality. The social worker is charged with violating the client system's confidence. It is the responsibility of the social worker to be clear about the privacy laws of his or her state and to discuss with client systems the restrictions or reporting requirements regarding confidential information (Kurzman, 1995).

Each of the above issues can in part be addressed by the use of risk management practices. *Risk management* is an assessment process that examines the level of liability risk associated with any business or professional activity, including the provision of social services. A solid assessment can minimize risks, although, as stated above, in some positions and circumstances, they cannot be fully eliminated. For example, social workers who work with adolescents are often trained in how to conduct themselves to avoid misconduct, especially regarding sexual misconduct or harassment. Taking care to conduct interviews jointly, or at least in visible spaces, can be professionally prudent.

Another way in which social workers may protect themselves from the expenses and losses associated with being sued is to make sure they purchase malpractice insurance. A benefit associated with membership in NASW is the availability of professional malpractice insurance. Such protection has become increasingly necessary as the members of our society become more litigious in nature. Finally, the NASW Code of Ethics is intended to be used as a guide for practice.

A last point that could be made here is that it is important not to make your ego satisfaction, actualization, or harmony dependent upon your agency. The agency cannot meet these needs nor is it designed to do so. We must carry responsibility for meeting our needs and, hopefully, we can all create work environments that we find positively challenging and rewarding.

Nevertheless, providing rewarding and challenging jobs is not the primary mission of the agency. In fact, I (Barry) have observed agencies that are not very effective at serving client systems; however, workers speak glowingly about how the administration cares about them and how much they enjoy being a part of the agency system. When this kind of goal displacement occurs, our client systems suffer.

Using Creativity Thinking creatively about the issues and challenges faced in the agency and in day-to-day practice is a key survival skill. Creativity confronts the tendency to become stale and burned out. Social workers who can meet issues head-on with comfort and competence, and most certainly with a sense of humor, will come to be valued members of the agency and the profession.

Creativity means taking risks. "Behold the turtle: it never makes progress without sticking its neck out!" Taking risks involves the potential to be wrong. The ability to be wrong, learn from the experience, and move forward is an important skill in helping ourselves and our agency improve at what we do. Part of this is also knowing when to leave.

I (Barry) recall the decision to leave my job in public social services to serve as a university faculty member. The decision was in part influenced by the comment of a graduate student who observed that maybe I had been at my agency too long and had lost some of the power and influence of my voice. Thinking on that, I concluded he was probably correct and moved on to a new challenge. Sometimes accepting new challenges is necessary; it is more desirable to leave from a position of strength.

Recently, many business organizations and governmental agencies have advocated the use of the principles of total quality management (TQM) as a strategy to improve the capacity of the organization to serve customers more effectively. While the tools associated with this orientation are useful, two central ideas are especially worthwhile: the use of teams and the teamwork process, and the recognition that any specific agency, business, or public organization has multiple customers, including those that consume the product or service and those that deliver it or otherwise provide support for it.

Teamwork is becoming increasingly important as a way of working, in that it offers special resources (group creativity, energy, support, synergy) that are useful in providing services that often go beyond the best efforts of a single person. Additionally, teams that work well together use the process of teaming to build ownership of the program in which they are working, which helps the team work toward better futures for the program.

The idea of multiple customers being associated with any program of service is an important one for managers and social workers to remember. Organizations that lose sight of either the service consumer or service provider are more likely to be less effective in meeting their mission. In part, this is associated with the reality that influencing change is a partnership and if any of the key members (that is, the consumer or the provider) feel devalued by the program delivery process, outcomes are likely to be negatively impacted.

TQM practices require that the multiple consumers and team members be empowered to bring their voices to the story of the organization in an effort to make it more effective. Organizations can do a lot to address the needs of these differing constituents. For instance, efforts that support day care in the workplace make it possible for many single parents to work or for two wage earners to take care of their day care needs more securely. Similarly, flexible work hours and business hours can meet the needs for access in ways that most service agencies have yet to acknowledge. The way in which services are delivered sends powerful messages about how important consumers are to the providers.

Human Diversity and Social Service Organizations

While we raised the issue of pluralism and the workplace earlier in the chapter, we think it is important to return to issues of human diversity and social service organizations. The social work profession embraces diversity as something to value and as a policy issue that requires monitoring and addressing when discrimination and oppression present barriers to opportunity.

As we move to an increasingly diverse and pluralistic society, the U.S. Census Bureau predicts that, by the year 2050, the percentage of minority group members (approximately 48%) in the United States will approach that of the white population (approximately 52%) (Rainie, 1995). Social service organizations need more than ever to be culturally competent, to act in ways that are effective and useful for diverse populations. Box 9.1 outlines the ways in which organizations can be structured and function to reflect cultural competence.

Feminist theory is one knowledge system that can be helpful in addressing gender issues within the organizational context. Kirst-Ashman and Hull (1993) present a solid overview of gender issues and generalist social work practice. Issues in the organization that often need attention include such practical concerns as access to equitable salary (it often isn't), child care, flexible working hours, child care leave (we now have some limited federal policy for family leave), and quality part-time employment with benefits. In a profession that is dominated by women, as social work is, we have a long way to go to create supports for these practical concerns.

For many reasons, these issues are probably best thought of as family issues—not in the so-called traditional family concept (which is not the reality for many families in the United States) but in the broader sense of how we support families to enable them to carry out their roles more effectively.

At another level, it is important to understand the philosophy behind practice at the organizational level as it has been informed and influenced by feminist theory. Drawing upon the work by Brandwein, Kirst-Ashman and Hull (1993, p. 440) note that there are four key themes in how feminists approach practice issues with communities, organizations, and other larger systems. These themes represent the way we have learned from and incorporated feminist theory into our practice:

- valuing the role of process in how things are accomplished,
- adopting a "win-win" view rather than a "win-lose" view in addressing and managing issues,
- valuing human relationships over time as opposed to forming them only for immediate short-term goals or needs, and
- valuing human diversity and prizing difference in the organization.

Many of these principles are counter to much of what has been classic organizational thinking, yet they are very consistent with the value base of the profession as well as the competency-building orientation that we think needs to be at the core of our practice.

BOX 9.1

Characteristics of Culturally Competent Human Service Agencies

Human service agencies display cultural competence when they:

1. target their interventions at more than one level.

- In *The Power to Care* (Hopps, Pinderhughes, and Shankar, 1995), the authors found agency efforts were often isolated and linear, working to change only one system at a time. When a family member is shot, therapy to manage grief, loss, anxiety, and fear is important—but the person still returns to violent streets.

- In working with overwhelmed client systems, addressing multiple levels and units (for example, the person, family, and/or neighborhood; employment opportunities; substance abuse) is necessary.

2. develop programs based on building competency rather than service delivery.

- Often, human service agencies have looked at situations from the framework of "How is this a personal problem that a credentialed professional can treat?" rather than looking at a difficult situation as an opportunity for persons, groups, and communities not only to manage an issue but also to gain a greater sense of their own capacities and competencies.

3. base their programs and policies on current demographic realities.

- Understand the demographic realities of the service area; know on an ongoing basis what ethnic, racial, or cultural minorities live in the service area and the size of the population in each group; and know about the human service agencies, informal supports, and natural helpers that the minority populations tend to use.

- Incorporate this knowledge as an integral part of the agency's service delivery (otherwise it is seen by minority groups as token efforts touted in an annual report).

4. integrate their services with other efforts in the community.

- Develop working relationships with the human service agencies, informal supports, and natural helpers that the minority populations tend to use.

- Do joint programming with and accepting referrals from the human service agencies, informal supports, and natural helpers that the minority populations tend to use.

- Reach out to and involve in decision making (service on boards or committees) important groups and people in minority populations—

ministers/religious leaders, advocacy groups, tribal or cultural organizations, and/or natural healers.

- Serve on committees and boards of agencies that are already providing culturally specific services (such as National Refugee Association, Hispanic Alliance, and Urban League).

5. are neighborhood/community based whenever possible.

- Transportation problems, health concerns, familiarity with the local area, and fear of the unfamiliar combine to make local services and sites more utilized.

- Senior citizens especially are more likely to use services if the persons providing the services look and talk as they do. For example, seniors using home health aides are more likely to reject the use of the service if service providers are of another race (U.S. Commission on Civil Rights, 1982).

- Neighborhood/community-based services can be more easily adapted to cultural preferences than more centralized services. For example, congregate meal sites in ethnically homogeneous neighborhoods can serve foods people prefer to eat.

6. in consultation with members of the community, focus the agency's efforts on ethnic strengths and strongly held values.

- Ethnicity and cultural background can be a source of strength as well as a source of struggle; Tlingit (Eskimo) programs for youth draw on the people's long history of surviving through adversity in helping adolescents cope with pressures (Carroll, 1986).

- Programs for family support in Latino neighborhoods start with the commonly held desire for intact, strong families, and work on ways to strengthen the bonds between couples and between parents and children.

7. reach out to minority populations in a variety of ways to make the services more accessible.

- When appropriate, produce brochures and agency materials in languages other than English and/or create minority-specific brochures with minorities depicted on the brochures.

- Out-station staff in high-density minority areas.

- Consult with minority group members on physical plant location and interior design.

8. recruit, hire, and promote from within the minority populations.

- Actively seek minorities for both key managerial positions and for positions that have potential for gaining the experience and skills for career advancement, such as project director. Too often, minority group members are selected for positions such as community relations coordinator or director of affirmative action—positions that do not generally lead to promotions to the top.

- Establish career ladders that illustrate how to progress from paraprofessional to professional positions, so that talented persons without professional qualifications can follow paths leading to better jobs.

Continued

9. pay attention to both societal injustices and the quality of their own services.

- One frequent criticism of mainstream agencies is that neither the programs nor the workers are aware of or sensitive to the way in which racism affects minority populations in many aspects of their daily lives—jobs, getting credit, and/or the ways minority populations are treated by others.

- Agencies (and workers) need to be involved in combating the trend of wanting to write off poor people and to dehumanize and forget about others.

- Too often, branches of agencies in minority communities have the least experienced staffs and smaller budgets than in more affluent, whiter areas. Worker expectations of client systems may also be lower.

In a related view, organizations that wish to be successful at becoming pluralistic need to be supportive of a multicultural approach to practice. Multicultural practice is based upon the idea that one's cultural heritage, including both race and ethnicity, is prized in order to work effectively with those different from ourselves. Kirst-Ashman and Hull (1993) identify ten barriers to effective multicultural practice. Box 9.2 highlights these barriers.

The essential point behind many of these barriers is that it is important for the social worker to take the time and interest to learn how cultural difference may influence the helping relationship. At the organizational level, this also holds true. Administrators need to think about how well their agencies support difference. Often, the problem of retention of minority professionals is in part associated with a lack of understanding in this area.

One of the reasons the social work profession has been so supportive of affirmative action policy is a recognition of these contextual barriers. We need to create opportunities for our minority colleagues to become part of our agencies at a variety of professional levels. Having role models at the highest levels sends important messages about our commitment to multicultural practice. In addition, organizations can be most helpful in their work within a multicultural environment by evaluating what orientations they use.

Social workers tend to learn about other cultures the same ways most people do—through the media and popular literature. Additionally, our perceptions from our experiences with client systems can give us a sample of a population that magnifies the difficulties in functioning and underplays the strengths of the culture. Terry Cross (1996) of the Indian Child Welfare Association lists these steps for learning more about a culture:

- *First, spend more time with strong, healthy people of that culture.*
- *Second, identify a cultural guide—that is, someone from the culture who is willing to discuss the culture, introduce you to new experiences, and help you understand what you are seeing.*

Multicultural Practice Barriers

- Accepting the "myth" of the "melting pot."
- Assuming all newcomers to the U.S. are happy to be here.
- Only seeing a people's behavior as defined by their culture or race.
- Attempting to be "color-blind" in thinking about a person and their behavior.
- Assuming that words used by all cultures have the same meaning.
- Assuming that all people with whom we interact think as we do.

- Assuming that different cultures all understand social work roles the same way.
- Our own lack of self-awareness of our cultural history.
- Lacking sound multicultural intervention skills.
- Lacking knowledge of the specific cultures likely to be encountered in our practice.

Source: Kirst-Ashman and Hull (1993, pp. 402–403).

- *Third, spend time with the literature. Reading articles by and for persons of the culture is most helpful. Along with the professional literature, read the fiction. This is an enjoyable way to enter the culture in a safe, nonthreatening way. Find someone with whom you can discuss what you have read.*
- *Fourth, attend cultural events and meetings of leaders from within the culture. Cultural events allow you to observe people interacting in their community and see values in action. Observing leadership in action can impart to you a sense of the strength of the community and help you identify potential key informants and advisors.*
- *Finally, learn how to ask questions in sensitive ways. Most individuals are willing to answer all kinds of questions, if the questioner is sincere and motivated by the desire to learn and serve the community more effectively. (p. 27)*

As we have noted above, in thinking about the story of any service agency, it is important to remember that change is a constant companion. The greater the clarity the social worker has about the mission and purpose of the agency, the more likely there will be opportunities to influence the change process in professionally desirable ways.

Phase Four: Evaluating Outcomes and Making Transitions

Just as social workers and their client systems need to take time to assess how they have been doing in working toward preferred realities and the goals associated with them, so too does the organization. The brief discussion of practice evaluation research as a tool in Chapter 8 fits with this phase of organizational experience. Social workers need to support effective program-level evaluation, especially as it is done to provide feedback about program effectiveness, efficiency, and achievement.

Our experience tells us that the record with program evaluation is spotty at best. Unless there are external requirements or pressures, program evaluation does not seem to be something many administrators appear willing to invest scarce resources in doing. While potentially short-sighted, this tendency is understandable. However, some organizations face the challenges of accountability, and the tools of evaluation research can be helpful in providing some information about how well programs have been delivered.

Seidl (1995) makes a worthwhile point about the differences between program evaluation and evaluation research. Evaluation research is grounded in the theory of social science research and is more comprehensive and encompassing than program evaluation, which he identifies as the formative study of programs. In this sense, formative study is the level of research designed to provide feedback on how to make immediate changes in the program so that it is better at meeting its intent.

We think this is an important distinction because of the difficulty most social service organizations have in meeting the expectations of scientific research methods. We are not arguing against science, rather, noting that services to human beings involve complex and messy conditions that are not easy to control (in the "research" sense of control) and therefore always have the challenge of study limitations to address.

It is not our intent to review all of the mechanics of program evaluation. However, it is important to note the value of such activity for the organization. Evaluation studies can take several forms, and the use of multiple data collection techniques is probably well advised. There are many models available to help with evaluation study. Refer to the work of Chambers, Wedel, and Rodwell (1992), Posavac and Carey (1985), and Royce (1992) for excellent descriptions of the evaluative process and its use with social service programs.

The important thing for social workers to remember in evaluating programs is to collect data in a way that supports rigor, either qualitatively or quantitatively, and to report the limitations of the data collection process and analysis fairly and thoroughly. For example, it is common for agencies to report consumer/client system satisfaction data as one measure of program effectiveness.

While we agree that consumer satisfaction data is worth collecting, unless a clear link can be established between satisfaction and program outcomes, the use of such data as a justification of the program is at best tenuous. We take this position in part because many client system satisfaction surveys focus on the feelings of the client systems as they used the agency and not on the outcomes realized. Client systems who are well received, extended respect, and given a chance to tell their story (all important things that social workers need to do) may feel good about the experience in a relationship sense, but may not have moved very far toward changing the issues that brought them to the agency in the first place. The point is that we need to make a good faith effort to do program evaluation in a way that lets us know if the program intent is being realized. It may seem obvious, but here the goodness of fit between the agency mission and the consumer's experience is of central importance.

Most program evaluation interests are associated with three types of variables: input, throughput, and outcome (Seidl, 1995). Input variables refer to the agency resources, including its mission and context. Throughput variables are associated with the process consumers experience in using the agency and include the services available and the methods of practice used to deliver them. Finally, outcome variables are associated with what was achieved in providing the services. Program evaluation can focus on any or all of these variables. Questions can be generated about the adequacy of resources and demand for services, the efficiency of one service method over another (for example, managed care in mental health appears to prize brief therapies over long-term ones), or the level of community awareness of and support for a specific program.

Seidl (1995) notes that most program evaluation efforts tend to look at the input and throughput variables. One potentially unfortunate consequence of the omission of outcome variables is that external stakeholders often are frustrated with the lack of evidence about outcomes achieved. While there are many reasons for the continuing debate over welfare reform and other social service expenditures, the lack of clear data about what works has not been helpful in building support.

In the spring of 1995, three students in a master's degree program for social work interviewed a number of families receiving welfare in southern West Virginia. One of the persistent themes that came up was the desire to be treated with respect and dignity as they sought help from agencies. As we have thought about this and related it to the previous discussion of dignity, we have begun constructing a tool to look at how client systems might be received in our agencies. Box 9.3 shows a draft of this tool, which we are calling a "dignity impact assessment."

While the instrument needs additional work, we share it here because we are of the opinion that one good way we as social workers can help both our client systems and our employers is by taking the pulse of our agency on how well client system self-worth is affirmed, how dignity and respect for client systems are expressed, and to what extent the dignity and worth of staff is affirmed. As we help our organizations improve, we think that keeping dignity and respect as core concepts will be important for the competency-building paradigm.

The dignity assessment tool can serve as a model for thinking about other ways to assess the organization or agency. A "self-determination assessment" or a

BOX 9.3

Dignity Assessment and Human Services Guide

Below is a set of elements that we think can be useful for social service managers, providers, and educators in thinking about the degree to which current organizational or professional practices may assail or affirm human dignity.

I. *Persons seeking services from my agency are more likely to experience:*

_____ a poorly maintained waiting room

_____ a warm and well-furnished waiting room

_____ a place to sign in and be told to take a seat

_____ a courteous and personal greeting

_____ having their name called out and being told to "follow me"

_____ being personally met and invited to the office

_____ nonverbal cues from the staff that they are a bother

_____ nonverbal cues that suggest we are glad they are here

_____ treatment that says "you are another case"

_____ treatment that says "you are a person"

II. *Persons seeking services in my agency are more likely to be:*

_____ treated as problems that need to be solved

_____ treated as partners in a mutual process of deciding how to proceed

_____ given treatment based on the "medical model"

_____ provided treatment based on a competency model

"respecting and cultivating strengths assessment" could also be developed to provide valuable information to agencies about the degree to which they are serving and working with people or merely processing cases.

Another way organizations may wish to learn about the climate they present is through the planned use of job and client satisfaction information. While there are limits to the use of this data, as we suggested above, systematic efforts at collecting and, when appropriate, acting upon this information are consistent with TQM concepts. When an agency cares enough to collect and make use of this kind of data, the participants feel empowered in the process, and the agency is often seen in a more positive light. This facilitates the kind of self-regulating behaviors supportive of professional practice.

_____ seen as problems	_____ seen as people with issues and needs
_____ seen as needing an expert	_____ seen as the expert

III. _Employees within my setting are more likely to experience:_

_____ getting written memos about new changes	_____ being asked for input about new changes
_____ being on the firing line alone	_____ being supported in their roles
_____ wishing for another job	_____ joy in coming to work
_____ feeling like their consumers are not important to the agency	_____ feeling their consumers are important to the agency
_____ feeling like they are a drain to the community	_____ feeling like they are a resource to the community
_____ feeling unimportant to the agency	_____ feeling important to the agency
_____ lack of respect for other employees	_____ respect for other employees

IV. _My experience with the context tells me that:_

_____ respect for human diversity is ignored	_____ respect for human diversity is valued
_____ membership in the community is blocked to those who are different	_____ membership in the community is open to all
_____ social services are at best tolerated	_____ social services are willingly supported

Summary

In this chapter, we have raised some of the important issues associated with providing effective social work services within the organizational context of practice. Our intent is to remind social workers that, regardless of our specific theory or practice orientations, a primary definer of what we do is the agency or organization in which we are employed. The recent trend of many graduate-level social workers entering private practice may in fact be associated with the perceived limits of working within organizations; however, the fact remains that most social workers are employed by agencies and most new social workers start their careers there. While frustrating at times, the need for social workers to take seriously the challenge to improve the organizational structure, climate, and delivery of programs remains an important professional responsibility. We have provided some ideas for the ways in which we can approach understanding the organizational context, looking at how well our programs and services work, and influencing the organization. We have also discussed how to foster cultural competence within organizations.

Client systems in all settings report frustration with the accessibility and delivery of services. As a society, we still have a hostile attitude toward social services in general, and specifically toward poor persons. If we are to become more effective and enhance the competencies of our consumers, this attitude must change. As we work within our organizations, we must also work within our community. We end the book by thinking about this topic.

As you prepare to read Chapter 10, please consider the following questions:

1. Think about social service agencies you know something about. How does the general population's view of the agency influence who might seek help there?

2. Think about an agency you have experienced that is a bureaucracy. What was your experience like in approaching the setting?

3. How was the way you were received similar to how you hoped to be received? How was it different?

4. Review the dignity assessment tool we included in this chapter. What do you find useful there? How are your experiences with organizations reflected in this document?

5. How did you react to the point made by Pruger that if social workers must be bureaucrats, they might as well be good ones? Identify ways that you have experienced meeting "good" bureaucrats.

CHAPTER TEN

Living and Working Well in a Changing Community and World

Service is the rent you pay to room on this earth.

SHIRLEY CHISHOLM
(1995)

Introduction

David Cox (1995), in a plenary address to the annual program meeting of the Council on Social Work Education, observed:

> *The message is that at the center of a fulfilling life for most people must stand healthy communities. Of course healthy individuals can contribute to healthy communities, but you do not build healthy communities simply by fostering healthy individuals. Similarly, healthy communities are facilitated by the existence of a healthy society as their broader context, but they neither depend on such nor do they derive automatically from such. Indeed, both an emphasis on individual pursuits and an emphasis on building strong centralist societies are as likely to be at the expense of community as they are to be to its benefit. Strong societies require a large measure of decentralization, at the political, economic and social levels; otherwise they serve the needs of but a favored minority. At the same time, strong individuals need to be rooted in community if they are to continue to grow and be productive in a full sense. (pp. 6–7)*

We share the view that social workers, both as professionals and as citizens, need to be concerned with supporting and working to build more healthful communities and societies. Everywhere we turn today, we see calls for more caring communities and the need for people to get involved.

It is not uncommon on most college and university campuses to find service learning opportunities that are designed to help students, regardless of major, find a way to give back to the community through some kind of volunteer service. Over the years large national programs have been created, including the Peace Corps, VISTA (Volunteers in Service to America), and, most recently, AmeriCorps. Additionally, our society has encouraged the development of volunteer social service networks, such as the United Way, Big Brothers and Big Sisters of America, Girl and Boy Scouts, and the Red Cross, that have provided important benefits at the local community level.

However, things do not appear to be in such good shape with most modern communities. Evening newscasts, admittedly not always representative, are full of the concerns of living in a modern society (for example, crime and violence, unemployment, drugs, and homelessness), leaving persons and families with the feeling that all is not well on the streets of the towns and cities across the United States. Bellah and his colleagues (1985) note: "There is a widespread feeling that the promise of the modern era is slipping away from us" (p. 277). This feeling is partly caused by our unease with the change in the communities in which we live and by the way we live in those communities.

In 1990, 72% of the people in the United States did not know their neighbors, and over the past 20 years, the number of people who say that they never spend time with their neighbors has doubled (Pipher, 1996). Where we work and where we live are increasingly unconnected. Membership in a chat room on the Internet, while intellectually stimulating, does not substitute for a friendly relationship with a neighbor. The person you know on the Internet won't feed your cat or watch for suspicious characters while you're away on vacation.

Robert Putnam, a professor of government at Harvard, believes that we are less likely to be members of groups of any kind. He illustrates this with the example of bowling; while more people bowl now than ever before, membership in bowling leagues is down 40% since 1980 (Putnam, 1993).

Along with the global economy, the United States is experiencing a modern economic plague, politely called "downsizing." For those who have dedicated their lives to working in the same company, and the company is "rightsizing" so they are no longer needed, the experience is anything but polite.

When the stock in companies that are downsizing goes up, the stockholders are pleased. However, in surveying the human damage, one is left wondering if we have taken the idea of self-interest too far. Bellah and his colleagues (1985) sum up their work on individualism and community in the United States by observing:

> *Perhaps life is not a race whose only goal is being foremost. Perhaps true felicity does not lie in continually outgoing the next before. Perhaps the truth lies in what most the world outside the modern West has always believed, namely that there are practices of life, good in themselves, that are inherently fulfilling. Perhaps work that is intrinsically rewarding is better for human beings than work that is only extrinsically rewarded. Perhaps enduring commitment to those we love and civic friendship toward our fellow citizens are preferable to restless competition and anxious self-defense. Perhaps common worship, in which we express our gratitude and wonder in the face of mystery of being itself, is the most important thing of all. If so, we have to change our lives and begin to remember what we have been happier to forget. (p. 295)*

Rediscovering who we are and where we may wish to be, at least for us, involves revisiting the concept of community. We are convinced that the United States needs to actively embrace community as a means of securing more fully the freedoms we have associated with being a democratic society.

As social workers, we carry many professional roles. This is equally true for us as private persons. In our professional lives, we may be a provider of direct social services, a member of a planning committee for the local United Way, and a provider of training workshops on domestic violence for our colleagues. We wear many hats. As private persons, we may be a parent, a spouse or partner to another, a family member, a neighbor, and a citizen. The list could go on, but the point is that we have both private and professional lives.

Often, the personal and the professional intermingle; it is our view that we should seek ways to use our professional talents in our private citizen roles to help our communities become healthier, as expressed in the quote from David Cox at the beginning of the chapter. The remainder of this chapter is devoted to thinking more about our place in our communities, with the hope that each of us will be challenged to think about ways to become more active in our citizenship behaviors, not only because it is a good idea but because it is the professional and morally right thing to do.

The Goal: A Just Society

In our model, communities as well as persons and families are challenged to think about and name preferred realities. The extent to which community exists in the United States is an open debate and one we will address shortly. First, we think it is important to consider the goal of social justice and the idea of creating a just society as the preferred reality.

Part of the way we can address the need to create and support a just society is through an informed and active debate and action within our towns and communities. The losses that people and communities continue to experience, as well as the fears and anxieties that accompany them, are too great to ignore. Dialogue about a preferred reality, one we would build on social justice for all, is the first step toward that reality. To do this requires that each of us as a citizen care enough to take responsibility for being involved with the effort.

Part of the challenge lies in our tendency to think of being involved in community change as overwhelming—that one person can't make much of a difference. Yet, Lappé and DuBois (1994) provide many stories of the very real differences people across the United States are making in practicing a living democracy. Their book, *The Quickening of America,* is highly recommended reading for all social workers who hold a vision of working toward a better future, especially at the local community level.

Mutually Supportive Interdependence

We think that social justice as a societal goal, as opposed to only maximizing self-interest (as suggested by the economics of capitalism), can best be approached through what we call the goal of *mutually supportive interdependence.* We define this as a system of social, economic, and political policies, procedures, and supports that promotes the well-being of all of a society's members. We are not suggesting that all be treated the same, as same treatment does not take into consideration the uniqueness of persons and social systems. We do suggest, however, that one mechanism for promoting well-being is to ensure and actively support equal access to opportunity structures. We think that equal access is maximized in healthy communities, as suggested by Cox (1995).

In part, this goal of mutually supportive interdependence comes from our increasing awareness that well-being for all is tied together in ever-increasing and interdependent ways. Martin Luther King observed: "Before you finish breakfast this morning, you've depended on more than half the world. This is the way our universe is structured" (1986, p. 119). We aren't going to have peace on earth until we recognize the interrelated nature of all reality.

Understanding the role, obligations, limits, and benefits of community is important for the social worker who wishes to work toward healthier communities. Martinez-Brawley (1995) discusses the traditional ways that community has been viewed in much of the Western world. In a structural sense, community is often seen as the mechanism to link the person and the state, as well as a political entity used to deal with personal and state relations.

In a sociopsychological sense, the work of Töennies (1957) has been most influential. He provides us with the definitions of the social continuum of the local community (gemeinschaft) and the larger-scale society (gesellschaft). Community is understood to include such important concepts as mutuality, close bonds, common destiny, and the rewards and obligations associated with close relationship patterns. Society is seen as the arena in which market forces dominate and rational choices that maximize self-interest take place. It is at the societal level that economic downsizing in corporate America is applauded, while it is in the community that the job losses and the real grief of such decisions are felt.

Lappé and DuBois (1994) would argue that we have come to emphasize the gesellschaft end of the continuum in modern society, with a loss of the local community; but they are nonetheless hopeful that we can rebuild our communities. Mermelstein and Sundet (1995) argue that rural social workers need to rethink the notion of community and its role for much of the rural United States. Their thinking is that many rural areas have come to reflect the alienation and anomie that has traditionally been associated with urban life.

Regardless of how one sees the issue, the message is clear: people need the social and psychological benefits of healthy communities if they are to be fully whole. As we discussed in Chapter 3 on understanding the context of our practice arena, the social worker needs to take the time to discover how the local community works, the ways people are included or excluded, and what cultural norms are prized or devalued. With such understanding, the social worker—both as a professional and as a citizen—may be more competent to act in ways that facilitate the community to go beyond acting as a market or political entity and to embrace the goal of creating a just community through supporting mutuality and healthy interdependence.

What You Can Do in Your Job

We take the general welfare charge found in the NASW Code of Ethics (1996), Standard 6, section 6.01 (Social Welfare) quite seriously. Social work as a profession must find ways to commit its resources, at least in part, to the pursuit of social justice within an empowerment and competency tradition. Cox (1995) makes the argument convincingly when he notes:

> *The key message of this paper is that social work has to change. For the sake of our world and the integrity of our profession it has to change. Most important, it has to change in the U.S., for those social workers in the U.S. tend to be the banner-bearers of this profession. Within the U.S. are the profession's best and best-known social work educators. The world looks to the U.S. for leadership,*

and it is the American social work literature that everywhere guides the next generation of social workers. (p. 2)

He further observes:

The key assumption on which this article is based is that social work has a mission to respond to the situations of the world's poor and oppressed. If one accepts that proposition, then one must take seriously the implications that flow from it. If one does not accept it, then let us stop being so hypocritical as to continue to state that this is a key element of our professional mission. (p. 2)

As social work educators, we are both humbled and troubled by the implications that the world looks to us for leadership. Yet, we are energized and encouraged by the opportunity behind Cox's challenge. The social work profession, if it so chooses, can make an important contribution to our communities as we address issues of oppression and to the world as we share our experiences and learning.

Cox's vision (1995) of the opportunity that awaits us is that of the professional rediscovering the knowledge, skills, and tools of social and community development. We wholeheartedly agree! These competencies become an important part of what we can do in our jobs to make our community and the world a better place for all of us.

Paradigms for Community Practice

Traditionally, the social work profession has approached community practice within the three models of locality development, social planning, and social action (Rothman and Tropman, 1987). In Box 10.1, we have outlined our view of the key elements associated with each of these strategies that influence how social workers might approach their work with communities.

These three models have informed much of what we do as social workers in community practice; however, as Martinez-Brawley (1995) notes, there is another promising model that has been used extensively in the United Kingdom, namely, community social work. This model assumes that professional social workers provide their services in conjunction with the full range of resources, both formal and informal, to be found within the context. In such a partnership, the emphasis moves away from a professional dependence toward the greater use of informal supports and other natural helping networks. In the United States, we have recently encountered similar thinking in the strengths and empowerment movements. The English model of community social work reflects many of the processes within the locality development and social action models outlined in Box 10.1.

Weil and Gamble (1995) summarize models for influencing change in the community by breaking them down into the following types: neighborhood and community organizing, organizing functional communities, community social

BOX 10.1

Community Development Approaches

Locality Development

- focused on self-help processes
- change involves a broad cross section of community members
- change tactics focus on consensus building and group process
- the social worker is seen as a teacher, enabler, and coordinator
- the power structure is seen as a collaborator in the change process
- change is assumed to focus on shared and reconcilable concerns and issues
- the beneficiaries are viewed as citizens
- the client role is seen as a participant in the change process

Social Planning

- focused on task achievement to solve community problems
- change involves data collection and choosing the most rational acts
- change tactics tend to emphasize authoritarian decision making and conflict management
- the social worker is seen as a data collector, analyst, and program implementer
- the power structure is seen as the employer and sponsor of change efforts
- change is assumed to focus on manipulation of formal organizations
- the beneficiaries are viewed as consumers of product
- the client role is seen as a consumer or recipient

Social Action

- focused on shifting power base and institutional change
- change involves organizing people to act against an external enemy
- change tactics focus on conflict, direct action, and negotiation
- the social worker is seen as an advocate, broker, partisan, and negotiator
- the power structure is seen as the oppressor and target to be changed
- change is assumed to focus on political processes and manipulation of mass organizations
- the beneficiaries are viewed as victims
- the client role is seen as the employer or constituent

Source: Rothman and Tropman (1987).

and economic development, social planning, program development and community liaison, political and social action, coalitions, and social movements. The value in this approach is that client system groups served by the different models, as well as the shared and distinct professional roles likely to be carried by the social worker, become more clearly distinguished. The most hopeful part of our review of their work is that the social work roles are ones quite familiar to social workers trained in the generalist tradition, of which our model is one example, and include broker, teacher, enabler, advocate, mobilizer, and mediator (BTEAMM*). The point is that social workers have something to offer our communities if we have the will to do so.

Using these models where one is employed can be a challenge. Often, employers become rather rule-bound and attempt to restrict the definition of social work intervention to that of direct service delivery. However, in such circumstances, the social worker may wish to point out the advantages of community work in generating new resources that may have benefits for client systems, as well as the potential gains, if any, of forming partnerships within the community. The more likely it is that the change tactics will lead to efforts at social action, or involve social movements, the greater the resistance the social worker may encounter with the employer, especially if the agency is heavily supported by public funds or by local powerful supporters of other funding sources like the United Way. In these instances, the social worker may choose to use a strategy we call "doing social work at night," which we discuss later in this chapter.

Other ways that social workers can use their day-to-day jobs to foster the development of healthier communities include:

- engaging in community education about issues, needs, and opportunities and fostering the commitment to care and work toward health,

- expanding our knowledge, capabilities, and competencies and going beyond the limits of our best practices by being creative and open to new ideas and responses, and

- working to ensure that consumers and community persons have access to our agencies and fostering a climate of openness within them.

These ideas are not new, nor do they exhaust the possibilities; yet these recommendations are likely to be supported because they attend to important principles of democratic societies, such as education, access, and the use of the best available knowledge. To illustrate, in many communities it is common practice for agencies to network and do communitywide projects like social service fairs and wellness programs in local malls or community centers. Such events take advantage of the opportunity to educate the community about potential services they might wish to use; however, a related side benefit is that, in the planning of such events, social workers often come to discover one another and common concerns they share. Working together in these planning efforts

---

* The acronym BTEAM (for broker, teacher, enabler, advocate, and mediator) was created by Arleta Lebrun-Owens, BSW, MSW while she was an undergraduate student in the Northern Arizona Social Work Program.

often results in other collaborative projects or at least facilitates interest in working together to better serve the community. We would encourage social workers to seek such opportunities routinely and to reach out to involve other elements of the community with them.

Another way to foster the development of healthier communities is through conscious acts of volunteerism. The executive director of the regional Community Action Agency, in the community where the university in which I (Barry) work is located, requires the agency staff to volunteer at another social agency in the region at least one working day per month. While requiring volunteering appears contradictory, the payoff for the agency and the community it serves can be valuable.

Social Work Practice and Policy Practice

In Chapter 7, we discussed the knowledge and skills necessary to inform policy makers and influence policy. Policy informs social work practice; therefore, if we as social workers desire to get better at what we do, we will need to work with the policy issues that parallel practice.

The links between public policy and issues of social justice are straightforward. For too long, the policy supports for social welfare programs in the United States have carried a residual orientation that often views the client system of those programs, especially those of the public sector, with contempt. We think that it is way past time for this society to face up to this degradation and to actively move toward a competency and opportunity orientation that holds real hope for the citizens of a multicultural society.

It is easier said than done, however, to alter orientations and beliefs. It cannot be accomplished without significant numbers of citizens, including social work professionals, standing up and naming this residual orientation as an issue in need of change.

Jansson (1994) writes about policy practice as social justice. We agree that one important tool for achieving a more just society is influencing social policy so that it attends more fully to social justice goals. An important way of creating a just world is to change the rules, that is, public policies, so that they are more fair. The fact that women could not vote until 1920, with the passage of the Nineteenth Amendment, is just one example of why policy practice is important.

If one reviews major policy changes at almost any level, the power of community education strategies becomes evident. Change without education is rare, either at the personal or community levels.

While legislative policy is an important arena for work, it is not the only one. Agency and community policy are important focal points for possible intervention as well. Local agencies and governments often operate in ways that limit access; by encouraging agencies and governments to be more responsive to the needs of client systems and citizens, we make the community a healthier place for its members.

While we believe that social workers need to be active policy shapers, we also realize that often this is an area about which it is hard to generate much excitement. However, we are convinced that the risks of noninvolvement are far too high for the profession and the citizens we serve.

Leaving the welfare reform debate (or any social issues debate, for that matter) exclusively to special interest groups all but ensures that our client system's voices, as well as our own, will not be heard. Whenever I (Barry) get overly frustrated by what I see in the public arena, I remind myself that persons can and do make a difference if they stick with the courage of their convictions. My youngest sister became a rather well-known, if not always liked, environmental activist out of her concern for her children's health. She was able to find the courage to stand up and speak her informed mind in front of the community and the state legislature, with the ultimate result being that the community was able to keep a toxic waste incinerator from being built in their locality. She came to this task out of her discovery that she had a public life.

Thinking that political work is somehow dirty and beneath our professional life is not a viable position for us. We can understand how one might wish to draw that conclusion; yet, as Lappé and DuBois (1994) remind us, we each have a public life that we need to embrace. We agree, and hope that, for many social workers, just as it has done for so many others, this will lead us into efforts at shaping and influencing social policy.

Social Work at Night — The Challenges of Citizenship

Several years ago I (Barry) had a colleague who liked to post questions to students on the school bulletin board. During the first term of President Reagan when he was aggressively cutting social spending, this faculty member posed a question to the students about how they planned to have social work careers when so much funding was being cut for programs. One student responded in a way that got me thinking about the ways we do social work. The student noted that he planned to have a "day job" and "do social work at night." We think this student was wise about part of our professional functions, opportunities, and responsibilities in that, regardless of where we may find ourselves employed, we can find ways to work toward preferred and desired professional goals and community realities independent of our employment. For us, part of being an effective social worker in our communities involves doing social work at night.

There are many ways that social workers can contribute to community betterment. The May 29, 1995, issue of *Newsweek* was devoted to recognizing persons they called everyday heroes. Three of those singled out were named as social workers. While it was not clear that they all held social work degrees, what was clear was that they had gone beyond the expectations of their employment.

One of those featured in the article was a medical social worker who had built a successful social service program for children with AIDS. The other two social workers started a program of rehabilitating abandoned housing that now serves over 300 formerly homeless tenants. While we are proud that three of our colleagues were identified for these awards, the really important point is the idea that social workers have positive contributions to make in our communities. These stories suggest an important kind of understanding: that committed persons, singly and in collectives, can make a difference in the quality of life for the community in which they live and serve.

There are specific understandings, beyond commitment, that are necessary for social workers who desire to work effectively within their communities. Lappé and DuBois (1994) provide some helpful thoughts on this, even though their work is targeted to an audience much larger than just social workers. They suggest that there are ten myths that get in the way of working well at the community level:

- *Public life is what someone else—a celebrity or big shot—has.*
- *If I'm not a celebrity, public life is unappealing and unrewarding.*
- *Public life involves a lot of ugly conflict.*
- *Public life competes with—even detracts from—a satisfying private life.*
- *We must learn to squelch our self-interest for the common good.*
- *For most people, public life is really about pursuing their own selfish interests.*
- *Power is a dirty word.*
- *There's only so much power to go around, so I have to fight for what's mine.*
- *Power is a one-way force; if I've got it, I can make others do my bidding.*
- *Power is about winning victories today, now! (p. 12)*

If you review this list carefully, you will note that many of the myths have to do with the idea of a public life. We think this idea is important enough that all social workers need to think about and actively use our public lives, to seek out and carry a range of roles in our work, our community, and its institutions, that help us contribute toward creating healthier communities.

For us, actively using our public lives is part of doing social work at night. The ethical dictates regarding our professional obligation to be concerned about the general welfare of society bring us to this position, and we hope the reader will come to embrace this view as well. Bellah and his colleagues (1985) also affirm this need:

> *Our concern is that if we are going to be the kind of persons we want to be, and live the kind of lives we want to live, then attention and not distraction is essential. Concerns that are most deeply personal are greatly connected with concerns that are global in scope. We cannot be the caring people whom our children need us to be and ignore the world they will have to live in. (p. 275)*

To illustrate one way of engaging in public life, a few years ago the scanning network of which I (Barry) was a member was involved in an effort to better track and respond to emerging social issues in West Virginia. While this network was hard to maintain as members found they could not devote the necessary time, it did prove to be effective in bringing some issues to the attention of state political leaders and citizens for education and debate. For example, realizing that the welfare bashing that was occurring around the country would likely come to West Virginia, the association created a "Welfare Myths" pamphlet that was used as part of a public education campaign to counter the common myths that exist about welfare and public assistance.

Not all efforts need to be focused at a statewide level; many social workers carry out their public lives by serving on local agency boards. Others volunteer at church or in civic groups, and still others are good neighbors who are called upon informally to help people, outside of their formal professional roles.

Being a part of the natural, informal helping network can be tricky, in that sometimes you may be asked to render a professional opinion about a social issue (say, child abuse) that is outside your area of professional practice or your knowledge and information base. In such instances, the ethical response is not to attempt to provide a professional answer but to help the person or group seeking the information link with someone who has the needed knowledge. The important point is that we can make useful contributions to needs and issues within our communities, and we need to feel empowered to do so.

As we review the myths identified by Lappé and DuBois (1994), we are challenged to think about issues of power and control and how we see them. If we see power only in a limited and finite way (that is, there is only so much power, and if we attempt to share any, we may diminish ourselves; or if we don't have much power, we have to take it from others, which will diminish them), then we miss the key concept of empowerment. Miley, O'Melia, and DuBois (1995) make this point when they suggest: "Acquiring power does not necessitate a power struggle or relinquishment of power by one group in favor of another. Empowerment is geometrically expansive rather than a zero sum commodity" (p. 69). Admittedly, this understanding is not all that common in Western society, especially in our economic and political institutions where the emphasis is almost exclusively on winners and losers. Yet, we would argue that it must become more common if our communities are to be recreated in ways that nurture healthfulness and build on the competencies of their citizens.

It is tempting to say, "Here are the skills and knowledge that will enable us to recreate our communities in desirable ways." Fortunately, we are not in a position to do this any more than we felt we could provide the "cookbook" for how to best work with a specific client system. We say "fortunately" because there is no one best way, and the challenge for professional social workers is to continually assess and reassess what works for them and what they do particularly well.

Certainly, there are useful tools and views that can support us in doing effective social work at night (that is, being effective as citizens beyond our officially defined roles), including taking full advantage of the four-phase model previously presented in this book. Congruent with our approach are the findings of Lappé and DuBois (1994) on working effectively in communities across the United States.

- *The most effective decision making depends on the ingenuity and experience of those who are directly affected, from patients and welfare clients to students, teachers, and employees.*
- *The best decisions arise from the interplay of diverse experiences and viewpoints.*
- *The best decision making is an ongoing process, not an end point. It is always evolving in response to new information and new insights.*
- *To be successful, problem solving must actively involve those who must ultimately implement the decisions. (p. 17)*

Even though these points do not provide us with a specific skill set, they do lead us to a process of partnership with others, as opposed to the classical view of doing for and to others. These observations are consistent with effective social work practice as we learned it and have attempted to express it here. The fact that the profession may have lost in its recent history part of its tradition of working well within the community does not mean we cannot recapture it, as we set about the challenge of working with others committed to rebuilding community.

Addressing National and Global Issues

While the majority of social workers carry out their professional roles by providing direct services, most often to persons and families, we think that it is also necessary to think about the larger issues that challenge any society and community. If we were to take a poll (and we won't since so many others do), we would imagine that the following issues would find a place on it:

- how to improve economic security
- how to support and foster families
- how to reduce violence and crime
- how to improve health care access and control costs
- how to make our schools work better
- how to generate respect for human and cultural diversity
- how to strengthen the environment

You may have other issues you would add, and we would encourage you to do so and talk with your colleagues about them. We think a public dialogue about these kinds of issues is critical to understanding them and to creative thinking about desirable ways to address them. Working on the big issues, as we call them, involves more than personal helping. Personal helping (working with people and their issues one at a time) is useful for the parties involved; yet it rarely reaches the root causes in a way that is preventative.

Lappé and DuBois (1994, p. 239) identify ten arts of democracy. We place them here because we think they can help us with our work in the community and because they clearly demonstrate the use of knowledge and skills that we have already reviewed as part of effective social work practice. We have used their names for the arts and modified the definitions to fit our thinking. They include:

- *Active listening*—listening that encourages the speaker and helps us to understand meanings;
- *Creative conflict*—challenging others and ourselves in ways that produce growth and change;
- *Mediation*—supporting processes that enable people in conflict to "really hear and understand" one another in order to reach a mutually satisfying agreement;
- *Negotiation*—working to turn win-lose situations into ones more like "win-win" situations where all parties get some key interests met;
- *Political imagination*—describing preferred realities for our communities and dreaming how to create them;
- *Public dialogue*—encouraging, facilitating, and participating in public talk about issues and concerns within the community;
- *Public judgment*—arriving at public decisions that require citizens to choose and acting to implement those choices;
- *Celebration and appreciation*—publicly expressing joy for what has been learned and achieved by public acts;
- *Evaluation and reflection*—thinking critically about both the how and the what of achievement; and,
- *Mentoring*—actively sharing with others the learning from our involvement with the arts of democracy.

As presented in our four-phase model, the knowledge, values, and skills in each phase support many of the points above. Social work practice, as we envision it, is very much about active involvement with democratic life. While this view may not be fully supported within our profession or within our communities, we are convinced that our modern society demands this of us.

Before moving on, we think it is important to look more carefully at the use of mediation, negotiation, and mentoring as social work skills for working in the community context. Social workers who work with community-level issues will find that mediation skills, as discussed in Chapter 6, are necessary for moving the process toward desired ends.

Sometimes we will not be able to take the more neutral position of mediator and will find ourselves in the role of negotiator. In this role, the social worker has a clear interest and preferred position. The position may be a personal one as a citizen or a professional one as a client system advocate. What changes with negotiation is the desire to achieve a specific position while not creating a lasting enemy. Negotiation is similar to mediation in that the focus of the negotiation process is that the parties involved feel, for valid reasons, that they got something they wanted out of the process.

Strategies that, instead, clearly define losers may not serve the community well over the long haul. I (Barry) was recently at an athletic event and noticed someone wearing a T-shirt with the message, "If you don't win, don't bother coming home—No Rules." While this may appear to be a cute message, when it is used to guide our lives, we all are poorer for the experience.

Fisher and Ury (1983) identify four principles in the negotiating process: keeping the issue and the personalities separate, focusing on mutual interests, finding options that benefit all parties, and enabling all parties to agree on *objective criteria* for deciding the issue. We emphasize the idea of objective criteria to stress that agreement on the criteria is the important goal.

Finally, we like the idea of social workers serving as mentors to one another and to our fellow citizens. Being a mentor involves sharing one's knowledge by modeling what works, by challenging ourselves and others to stretch our visions and talents, by actively teaching about the change process, and by forming partnerships between newcomers and seasoned veterans. Mentoring is a positive way of thinking about work and helping within our communities.

Each of us can look back and identify someone—a teacher, a neighbor, a minister, a colleague—who helped us master a task or a way of working. I (Barry) recall with great fondness a former neighbor who became a dear friend. This gentleman taught me much about life as we both pursued our interests in gardening. He had always gardened using the organic approach and avoided overuse of artificial chemicals. As I came to understand how to garden in a more natural way, I was struck by how my ideas about healthy living and the world came to change. This former neighbor (whom I have been remiss in visiting) will probably never fully know just how much he influenced the way I think and how that in turn has shaped my work with Jim and Becky in writing this book. In the greatest sense, this man was my mentor. There have been others, and the point is that we need them for our own well-being and, ultimately, the well-being of our community.

As we move on, we would urge social workers not to lose sight of the opportunity to work with our client systems and communities on the big issues. Client systems have much to contribute to this process, including naming from their perspective the desired realities and outcomes that are necessary to address these issues.

We need to get beyond thinking only about government, corporations, and communities as good or bad and come to understand that, within most issues, there is a common ground from which useful dialogue can emerge. As we come together to envision a preferred reality, a major challenge is that the vision must be truly and freely shared before we can begin to think about the ways to get there. The key is not to discount the visions of others for a preferred reality nor close off the need to work together. For us, both the process of discovering that vision and the outcomes that make it real are equally important.

Our Challenges for the Social Worker and the Profession

While it is always risky to discuss the future as if it were a certain place, we do think there is value in creative speculation about what lies ahead. Today it is easy to become pessimistic about the future of the society and the world. While we are concerned, we remain hopeful that humankind can find ways to live better with one another on the fragile planet we call home. For this to be possible, we will need to be visionary and take actions that encourage each of us, social workers and citizens alike, to reach our potential.

We would like to share some developments and issues currently being addressed that make us hopeful:

1. *An increasing questioning of the medical model and the concept of clienthood in the human services.* We think the idea of moving from being clients who are cared for by the experts, to citizens competent to act on issues and concerns in ways that make sense to the people or community naming them, needs to be embraced more fully by the social work profession.

Lappé and DuBois (1994) speak of the shift from being clients to becoming citizens. The social work profession needs to think carefully about how our practice models fit this world view. We think the way we have attempted to describe the process of working through the four phases of the story reflects this rediscovered understanding.

2. *The debate over dependence and independence in how we deliver programs and services.* All helping professions, including social work, teaching, law, and medicine, need to take stock of the ways that what they do works to empower and build the competencies of people. If our programs leave those who need to use them less able, then we need to change them.

This perspective should not be misunderstood as a desire to get rid of social programs. To the contrary, with many issues such as health care, job development, and education, we would advocate for greater funds from government for effective programs. What is needed is the recognition that how we do our work is important and that we are all interdependent.

Being interdependent is not the same as being dependent to the point of losing one's legitimate voice and influence. Interdependence does not suggest a "bootstraps mentality," where we assume that hard work and personal effort alone are sufficient to meet human need.

3. *The desire and need to rediscover a sense of community.* While our streets remain all too violent and far too many of our citizens live in conditions that are not okay given the wealth of this society, people who care are making a difference. Things that work appear to do so in part because they are done within the context of a caring community—one that is not defined solely by geography.

People discover their capacity to influence as they work together on shared issues and concerns. Volunteerism and giving back are becoming important concepts for many. Recently, I (Becky) attended a series of training sessions on hospice care. The most common reason given by the participants for enrolling in the training was to give back to the community what they had experienced with the hospice program while caring for a loved one who was dying.

As our experiences move away from doing for toward doing with, a sense of community is created that will serve us well. Social work needs to be at the forefront of this discovery, not because we should lead it but because we can learn so much from being associated with it.

4. *The debate over the role of government and public policy.* We include this issue not because we are optimistic, but rather to challenge us not to lose sight of important goals the social work profession has said it holds for public policy. If we leave our voices and the voices of those most vulnerable out of the policy debate, then we are likely to be worse off than we currently are.

Schorr (1986) offers five principles for creating policies that support and affirm community. They include the ideas of fair shares (a way of redistributing resources within a society to reduce poverty), mainstreaming (creating policies that are inclusive rather than exclusive or based on narrow means tests), full employment (policies that would help people have access to adequate wages and a sense of participation in the life of the community), selective decentralization (policies that facilitate community control and influence over those areas best addressed at the local level), and integration (policies that affirm the value of diversity and support the full participation of all members of our society in its life). We think this set of principles is worthy of our support and use as social workers. It is consistent with the democratic underpinnings that have informed the belief system, at least as expressed in principle if not in specific acts, of the United States.

Summary

We have included this chapter in part as a call to action. We believe that the social work profession continues to have a role in creating better communities that often calls for efforts beyond the officially defined roles of agency job descriptions. Our intent here is to challenge each of us to hear and see the national and global issues that are often present in the issues and concerns brought to us by client systems and experienced in our communities.

Throughout the book, we have suggested ways that we can work more effectively within the context of community. This chapter reminds us of the need for continuing work toward creating a more just society through the use of such processes as locality development, social planning, and social action. Additionally, we discussed the importance of working to influence social policy in the public and private sectors.

We also discussed the opportunities to practice as professionals and contribute as citizens, using the phrase "doing social work at night." We did this to remind aspiring social workers that the aims and purposes of the social work profession often demand that we go beyond the professional roles as defined by our employers and agencies.

As you have reached the end of this particular journey with us, please think about the following questions:

1. Think about times you may have volunteered in your community. What motivated you to do so? What motivated others you may have worked with to get more involved with their community?

2. How does our idea about having important roles to carry out beyond those of the job description strike you? How does this fit with your understanding of being a professional?

3. Reflect on the entire book now that you have reviewed it carefully. How do the concepts, principles, and processes fit with the career interests and desires that brought you to the profession of social work?

4. What was not addressed in the book that you expected to find in it?

5. What have you learned from reading this book that has the most meaning for you? How will that influence you in your career as a social worker?

Epilogue

If you have arrived at this point of the book and are still searching for answers, that is wonderful and desirable. If you are still hopeful that we will provide them, then in part we have failed in achieving our preferred reality for creating this book.

This book is not about answers so much as it is about recognizing the validity of hopes and dreams, and the professional commitment we have as social workers to work toward realizing them. Certainly we (Barry, Becky, and Jim) have our dreams for the future, both for the social work profession and for the communities in which we live. However, we hope that each generation of social workers somehow will go beyond the limits of our vision or the visions of their teachers and colleagues. This is absolutely necessary if the social work profession is to fulfill its mission of service to our society.

We know this sounds like a commencement address and that's okay. For the hopes and dreams of people to be more fully realized, it is necessary for future colleagues of any profession or academic discipline to go beyond our best knowledge and learn more about ways to enhance our practice and advance our profession. As you develop your knowledge, we challenge you to pass your learning on to the next generation.

The creators of the popular movie and television series *Star Trek* understood this concept when they spun off the first sequel. It was called *Star Trek: The Next Generation* for understandable reasons. The series built on its past but continued to discover its present and shape its future. We think this is a valid way for thinking about the social work profession and our hopes for you, the readers of this book.

As you move forward with your social work careers, we hope you take the time to dream with client systems and citizens. We hope that you actively work with your community to create a better world and society, and that you understand the importance of arriving at a preferred reality in partnership with those you serve and with the members of your community.

Thinking about social work practice in the closing years of the 20th century and at the start of the next millennium, we return to the metaphor of story to close the book. The nation's story can be seen as having previous chapters, the past; a present, where we are in the story; and a future that is still to unfold. As the saying goes, "The best way to predict the future is to create it." As social workers and citizens, we can play active roles in creating and living the future.

Appendix
Code of Ethics of the National Association of Social Workers (1996)

Overview

The National Association of Social Workers Code of Ethics is intended to serve as a guide to the everyday professional conduct of social workers. This code includes four sections. Section one, "Preamble," summarizes the social work profession's mission and core values. Section two, "Purpose of the Code of Ethics," provides an overview of the Code's main functions and a brief guide for dealing with ethical issues or dilemmas in social work practice. Section three, "Ethical Principles," presents broad ethical principles, based on social work's core values, that inform social work practice. The final section, "Ethical Standards," includes specific ethical standards to guide social workers' conduct and to provide a basis for adjudication.

Preamble

The primary mission of the social work profession is to enhance human well-being and help meet basic human needs of all people, with particular attention to the needs and empowerment of people who are vulnerable, oppressed and living in poverty. An historic and defining feature of social work is the profession's focus on individual well-being in a social context and the well-being of society. Fundamental to social work is attention to the environmental forces that create, contribute to, and address problems in living.

Social workers promote social justice and social change with and on behalf of clients. 'Clients' is used inclusively to refer to individuals, families, groups, organizations, and communities. Social workers are sensitive to cultural and ethnic diversity and strive to end discrimination, oppression, poverty, and other forms of social injustice. These activities may be in the form of direct practice, community organizing, supervision, consultation, administration, advocacy, social and political action, policy development and implementation, education, and research and evaluation. Social workers seek to enhance the capacity of people to address their own needs. Social workers also seek to promote the responsiveness of organizations, communities, and other social institutions to individuals' needs and social problems.

The mission of the social work profession is rooted in a set of core values. These core values, embraced by social workers throughout the profession's history, are the foundation of social work's unique purpose and perspective:

- Service
- Social justice
- Dignity and worth of the person
- Importance of human relationships
- Integrity
- Competence

The constellation of these core values reflects what is unique to the social work profession. Core values, and the principles which flow from them, must be balanced within the context and complexity of the human experience.

301

Purpose of the Code of Ethics

Professional ethics are at the core of social work. The profession has an obligation to articulate its basic values, ethical principles, and ethical standards. The NASW Code of Ethics sets forth these values, principles, and standards to guide social workers' conduct. The code of ethics is relevant to all social workers and social work students, regardless of their professional functions, the settings in which they work, or the populations they serve.

This NASW Code of Ethics serves six purposes:

- The code identifies core values on which social work's mission is based.

- The code summarizes broad ethical principles that reflect the profession's core values and establishes a set of specific ethical standards that should be used to guide social work practice.

- The code of ethics is designed to help social workers identify relevant considerations when professional obligations conflict or ethical uncertainties arise.

- The code provides ethical standards to which the general public can hold the social work profession accountable.

- The code socializes practitioners new to the field to social work's mission, values, ethical principles, and ethical standards.

- The code articulates standards that the social work profession itself can use to assess whether social workers have engaged in unethical conduct. NASW has formal procedures to adjudicate ethics complaints filed against its members.*
  In subscribing to this code social workers are required to cooperate in its implementation, participate in NASW adjudication proceedings, and abide by any NASW disciplinary rulings or sanctions based on it.

This code offers a set of values, principles, and standards to guide decision making and conduct when ethical issues arise. It does not provide a set of rules that prescribe how social workers should act in all situations. Specific applications of the code must take into account the context in which it is being considered and the possibility of conflicts among the code's values, principles, and standards. Ethical responsibilities flow from all human relationships, from the personal and familial to the social and professional.

Further, the code of ethics does not specify which values, principles, and standards are most important and ought to outweigh others in instances when they conflict. Reasonable differences of opinion can and do exist among social workers with respect to the ways in which values, ethical principles, and ethical standards should be rank-ordered when they conflict. Ethical decision making in a given situation must apply the informed judgment of the individual social worker and should also consider how the issues would be judged in a peer review process where the ethical standards of the profession would be applied.

Ethical decision making is a process. There are many instances in social work where simple answers are not available to resolve complex ethical issues. Social workers should take into consideration all the values, principles, and standards in this code that are relevant to any situation in which ethical judgment is warranted. Social workers' decisions and actions should be consistent with the spirit as well as the letter of this code.

In addition to this code, there are many other sources of information about ethical thinking that may be useful. Social workers should consider ethical theory and principles generally, social work theory and research, laws, regulations, agency policies, and other relevant codes of ethics, recognizing that among codes of ethics social workers should consider the NASW Code of Ethics as their primary source. Social workers also should be aware of the impact on ethical decision-making of their clients' and their own personal values, cultural and religious beliefs, and practices. They should be aware of any conflicts between personal and professional values and deal with them responsibly. For additional guidance social workers should consult relevant literature on professional ethics and ethical decision making, and seek appropriate consultation when faced with ethical dilemmas. This may involve consultation with an agency-based or social work organization's ethics committee, regulatory body, knowledgeable colleagues, supervisors, or legal counsel.

---

* For information on NASW adjudication procedures, see *NASW Procedures for the Adjudication of Grievances.*

Instances may arise where social workers' ethical obligations conflict with agency policies, relevant laws or regulations. When such conflicts occur, social workers must make a responsible effort to resolve the conflict in a manner that is consistent with the values, principles, and standards expressed in this code. If a reasonable resolution of the conflict does not appear possible, social workers should seek proper consultation before making a decision.

This code of ethics is to be used by NASW and by other individuals, agencies, organizations, and bodies (such as licensing and regulatory boards, professional liability insurance providers, courts of law, agency boards of directors, government agencies, and other professional groups) that choose to adopt it or use it as a frame of reference. Violation of standards in this code does not automatically imply legal liability or violation of the law. Such determination can only be made in the context of legal and judicial proceedings. Alleged violations of the code would be subject to a peer review process. Such processes are generally separate from legal or administrative procedures and insulated from legal review or proceedings in order to allow the profession to counsel and/or discipline its own members.

A code of ethics cannot guarantee ethical behavior. Moreover, a code of ethics cannot resolve all ethical issues or disputes, or capture the richness and complexity involved in striving to make responsible choices within a moral community. Rather a code of ethics sets forth values, ethical principles and ethical standards to which professionals aspire and by which their actions can be judged. Social workers' ethical behavior should result from their personal commitment to engage in ethical practice. This code reflects the commitment of all social workers to uphold the profession's values and to act ethically. Principles and standards must be applied by individuals of good character who discern moral questions and, in good faith, seek to make reliable ethical judgments.

Ethical Principles

The following broad ethical principles are based on social work's core values of service, social justice, dignity and worth of the person, importance of human relationships, integrity, and competence. These principles set forth ideals to which all social workers should aspire.

VALUE: *Service*
Ethical Principle: *Social workers' primary goal is to help people in need and to address social problems.*

Social workers elevate service to others above self-interest. Social workers draw on their knowledge, values, and skills to help people in need and to address social problems. Social workers are encouraged to volunteer some portion of their professional skills with no expectation of significant financial return (pro bono service).

VALUE: *Social Justice*
Ethical Principle: *Social workers challenge social injustice.*

Social workers pursue social change, particularly with and on behalf of vulnerable and oppressed individuals and groups of people. Social workers' social change efforts are focused primarily on issues of poverty, unemployment, discrimination, and other forms of social injustice. These activities seek to promote sensitivity to and knowledge about oppression, and cultural and ethnic diversity. Social workers strive to ensure equality of opportunity, access to needed information, services, resources, and meaningful participation in decision making for all people.

VALUE: *Dignity and Worth of the Person*
Ethical Principle: *Social workers respect the inherent dignity and worth of the person.*

Social workers treat each person in a caring and respectful fashion, mindful of individual differences and cultural and ethnic diversity. Social workers promote clients' socially responsible self-determination. Social workers seek to enhance clients' capacity and opportunity to change and to address their own needs. Social workers are cognizant of their dual responsibility to clients and to the broader society. They seek to resolve conflicts between clients' and the broader society's interests in a socially responsible manner consistent with the values, ethical principles, and ethical standards of the profession.

VALUE: *Importance of Human Relationships*
Ethical Principle: *Social workers recognize the central importance of human relationships.*

Social workers understand that relationships between and among people are an important vehicle for change. Social workers engage people as partners in the helping process. Social workers seek to strengthen relationships among people in a purposeful effort to promote, restore, maintain, and enhance the well-being of individuals, families, social groups, organizations, and communities.

VALUE: *Integrity*
Ethical Principle: *Social workers behave in a trustworthy manner.*

Social workers are continually aware of the profession's mission, values, ethical principles, and ethical standards, and practice in a manner consistent with them. Social workers act honestly and responsibly and promote ethical practices on the part of the organizations with which they are affiliated.

VALUE: *Competence*
Ethical Principle: *Social workers practice within their areas of competence and develop and enhance their professional expertise.*

Social workers continually strive to increase their professional knowledge and skills and to apply them in practice. Social workers should aspire to contribute to the knowledge base of the profession.

Ethical Standards

The following ethical standards are relevant to the professional activities of all social workers. These standards concern: (1) social workers' ethical responsibilities to clients, (2) social workers' ethical responsibilities to colleagues, (3) social workers' ethical responsibilities in practice settings, (4) social workers' ethical responsibilities as professionals, (5) social workers' ethical responsibilities to the profession, and (6) social workers' ethical responsibilities to the broader society.

Some of the standards that follow are enforceable guidelines for professional conduct and some are more aspirational in nature. The extent to which each standard is enforceable is a matter of professional judgment to be exercised by those responsible for reviewing alleged violations of ethical standards.

1. Social Workers' Ethical Responsibilities to Clients

1.01 Commitment to Clients

Social workers' primary responsibility is to promote the well-being of clients. In general, clients' interests are primary. However, social workers' responsibility to the larger society or specific legal obligations may on limited occasions supersede the loyalty owed clients and clients should be so advised. (Examples include when a social worker is required by law to report that a client has abused a child or has threatened to harm self or others.)

1.02 Self-Determination

Social workers respect and promote the right of clients to self-determination and assist clients in their efforts to identify and clarify their goals. Social workers may limit clients' right to self-determination when, in their professional judgment, clients' actions or potential actions pose a serious, foreseeable, and imminent risk to themselves or others.

1.03 Informed Consent

a. Social workers should provide services to clients only in the context of a professional relationship based, when appropriate, on valid informed consent. Social workers should use clear and understandable language to inform clients of the purpose of the service, risks related to the service, limits to service because of the requirements of a third-party payor, relevant costs, reasonable alternatives, clients' right to refuse or withdraw consent, and the time frame covered by the consent. Social workers should provide clients with an opportunity to ask questions.

b. In instances where clients are not literate or have difficulty understanding the primary language used in the practice setting, social workers should take steps to ensure clients' comprehension. This may include providing clients with a detailed verbal explanation or arranging for a qualified interpreter and/or translator whenever possible.

c. In instances where clients lack the capacity to provide informed consent, social workers should protect clients' interests by seeking permission from an appropriate third party, informing clients consistent with their level of understanding. In such instances social workers should seek to ensure that the third party acts in a manner consistent with clients' wishes and interests. Social workers should take reasonable steps to enhance such clients' ability to give informed consent.

d. In instances where clients are receiving services involuntarily, social workers should provide information about the nature and extent of services, and of the extent of clients' right to refuse service.

e. Social workers who provide services via electronic mediums (such as computers, telephone, radio, and television) should inform recipients of the limitations and risks associated with such services.

f. Social workers should obtain clients' informed consent before audiotaping or videotaping clients, or permitting third party observation of clients who are receiving services.

1.04 Competence

a. Social workers should provide services and represent themselves as competent only within the boundaries of their education, training, license, certification, consultation received, supervised experience, or other relevant professional experience.

b. Social workers should provide services in substantive areas or use intervention techniques or approaches that are new to them only after engaging in appropriate study, training, consultation, and/or supervision from persons who are competent in those interventions or techniques.

c. When generally recognized standards do not exist with respect to an emerging area of practice, social workers should exercise careful judgment and take responsible steps—including appropriate education, research, training, consultation, and supervision—to ensure the competence of their work and to protect clients from harm.

1.05 Cultural Competence and Social Diversity

a. Social workers should understand culture and its function in human behavior and society, recognizing the strengths that exist in all cultures.

b. Social workers should have a knowledge base of their clients' cultures and be able to demonstrate competence in the provision of services that are sensitive to clients' culture and to differences among people and cultural groups.

c. Social workers should obtain education about and seek to understand the nature of social diversity and oppression with respect to race, ethnicity, national origin, color, sex, sexual orientation, age, marital status, political belief, religion and mental or physical disability.

1.06 Conflicts of Interest

a. Social workers should be alert to and avoid conflicts of interest that interfere with the exercise of professional discretion and impartial judgment. Social workers should inform clients when a real or potential conflict of interest arises and take reasonable steps to resolve the issue in a manner that makes the clients' interests primary and protects clients' interests to the greatest extent possible. In some cases, protecting clients' interests may require termination of the professional relationship with proper referral of the client.

b. Social workers should not take unfair advantage of any professional relationship or exploit others to further their personal, religious, political, or business interests.

c. Social workers should not engage in dual or multiple relationships with clients or former clients in which there is a risk of exploitation or potential harm to the client. In instances when dual or multiple relationships are unavoidable, social workers should take steps to protect clients and are responsible for setting clear, appropriate, and culturally sensitive boundaries. (Dual or multiple relationships occur when social workers relate to clients in more than one relationship, whether professional, social, or business. Dual or multiple relationships can occur simultaneously or consecutively.)

d. When social workers provide services to two or more persons who have a relationship with each other (for example, couples, family members), social workers should clarify with all parties which individuals will be considered clients and the nature of social workers' professional obligations to the various individuals who are receiving services. Social workers who anticipate a conflict of interest among the individuals receiving services, or who anticipate having to perform in potentially conflicting roles (for example, when a social worker is asked to testify in a child custody dispute or divorce proceedings involving clients), should clarify their role with the parties involved and take appropriate action to minimize any conflict of interest.

1.07 Privacy and Confidentiality

a. Social workers should respect clients' right to privacy. Social workers should not solicit private information from clients unless it is essential to providing service or conducting social work evaluation or research. Once private information is shared, standards of confidentiality apply.

b. Social workers may disclose confidential information when appropriate with a valid consent from a client, or a person legally authorized to consent on behalf of a client.

c. Social workers should protect the confidentiality of all information obtained in the course of professional service, except for compelling professional reasons. The general expectation that social workers will keep information confidential does not apply when disclosure is necessary to prevent serious, foreseeable, and imminent harm to a client or other identifiable person or when laws or regulations require disclosure without a client's consent. In all instances, social workers should disclose the least amount of confidential information necessary to achieve the desired purpose; only information that is directly relevant to the purpose for which the disclosure is made should be revealed.

d. Social workers should inform clients, to the extent possible, about the disclosure of confidential information and the potential consequences and, when feasible, before the disclosure is made. This applies whether social workers disclose confidential information as a result of a legal requirement or based on client consent.

e. Social workers should discuss with clients and other interested parties the nature of confidentiality and limitations of clients' right to confidentiality. Social workers should review with clients circumstances where confidential information may be requested and where disclosure of confidential information may be legally required. This discussion should occur as soon as possible in the social worker-client relationship and as needed throughout the course of the relationship.

f. When social workers provide counseling services to families, couples, or groups, social workers should seek agreement among the parties involved concerning each individual's right to confidentiality and obligation to preserve the confidentiality of information shared by others. Social workers should inform participants in family, couples, or group counseling that social workers cannot guarantee that all participants will honor such agreements.

g. Social workers should inform clients involved in family, couples, marital, or group counseling of the social worker's, employer's, and/or agency's policy concerning the social worker's disclosure of confidential information among the parties involved in the counseling.

h. Social workers should not disclose confidential information to third party payors, unless clients have authorized such disclosure.

i. Social workers should not discuss confidential information in any setting unless privacy can be assured. Social workers should not discuss confidential information in public or semi-public areas (such as hallways, waiting rooms, elevators, and restaurants).

j. Social workers should protect the confidentiality of clients during legal proceedings to the extent permitted by law. When a court of law or other legally authorized body orders social workers to disclose confidential or privileged information without a client's consent and such disclosure could cause harm to the client, social workers should request that the court withdraw or limit the order as narrowly as possible and/or maintain the records under seal, unavailable for public inspection.

k. Social workers should protect the confidentiality of clients when responding to requests from members of the media.

l. Social workers should protect the confidentiality of clients' written and electronic records and other sensitive information. Social workers should take reasonable steps to ensure that clients' records are stored in a secure location and that clients' records are not available to others who are not authorized to have access.

m. Social workers should take precautions to ensure and maintain the confidentiality of information transmitted to other parties through the use of computers, electronic mail, facsimile machines, telephones and telephone answering machines, and other electronic or computer technology. Disclosure of identifying information should be avoided whenever possible.

n. Social workers should transfer or dispose of clients' records in a manner that protects clients' confidentiality and is consistent with state statutes governing records and social work licensure.

o. Social workers should take reasonable precautions to protect client confidentiality in the event of the social worker's termination of practice, incapacitation, or death.

p. Social workers should not disclose identifying information when discussing clients for teaching or training purposes, unless the client has consented to disclosure of confidential information.

q. Social workers should not disclose identifying information when discussing clients with consultants, unless the client has consented to disclosure of confidential information or there is a compelling need for such disclosure.

r. Social workers should protect the confidentiality of deceased clients consistent with the preceding standards.

1.08 Access to Records

a. Social workers should provide clients with reasonable access to records concerning them. Social workers who are concerned that clients' access to their records could cause serious misunderstanding or harm to the client should provide assistance in interpreting the records and consultation with the client regarding the records. Social workers should limit client access to social work records, or portions of clients' records, only in exceptional circumstances when there is compelling evidence that such access would cause serious harm to the client. Both the client's request and the rationale for withholding some or all of the record should be documented in the client's file.

b. When providing clients with access to their records, social workers should take steps to protect the confidentiality of other individuals identified or discussed in such records.

1.09 Sexual Relationships

a. Social workers should under no circumstances engage in sexual activities or sexual contact with current clients, whether such contact is consensual or forced.

b. Social workers should not engage in sexual activities or sexual contact with clients' relatives or other individuals with whom clients maintain a close, personal relationship where there is a risk of exploitation or potential harm to the client. Sexual activity or sexual contact with clients' relatives or other individuals with whom clients maintain a personal relationship has the potential to be harmful to the client and may make it difficult for the social worker and client to maintain appropriate professional boundaries. Social workers—not their clients, their clients' relatives or other individuals with whom the client maintains a personal relationship—assume the full burden for setting clear, appropriate and culturally sensitive boundaries.

c. Social workers should not engage in sexual activities or sexual contact with former clients because of the potential for harm to the client. If social workers engage in conduct contrary to this prohibition or claim that an exception to this prohibition is

warranted due to extraordinary circumstances, it is social workers—not their clients—who assume the full burden of demonstrating that the former client has not been exploited, coerced, or manipulated, intentionally or unintentionally.

d. Social workers should not provide clinical services to individuals with whom they have had a prior sexual relationship. Providing clinical services to a former sexual partner has the potential to be harmful to the individual and is likely to make it difficult for the social worker and individual to maintain appropriate professional boundaries.

1.10 Physical Contact

Social workers should not engage in physical contact with clients where there is a possibility of psychological harm to the client as a result of the contact (such as cradling or caressing clients). Social workers who engage in appropriate physical contact with clients are responsible for setting clear, appropriate, and culturally sensitive boundaries that govern such physical contact.

1.11 Sexual Harassment

Social workers should not sexually harass clients. Sexual harassment includes sexual advances, sexual solicitation, requests for sexual favors, and other verbal or physical conduct of a sexual nature.

1.12 Derogatory Language

Social workers should not use derogatory language in their written or verbal communications to or about clients. Social workers should use accurate and respectful language in all communications to and about clients.

1.13 Payment for Services

a. When setting fees, social workers should ensure that the fees are fair, reasonable, and commensurate with the service performed. Consideration should be given to the client's ability to pay.

b. Social workers should avoid accepting goods or services from clients as payment for professional services. Bartering arrangements, particularly involving services, create the potential for conflicts of interest, exploitation, and inappropriate boundaries in social workers' relationships with clients. Social workers should explore and may participate in bartering only in very limited circumstances where it can be demonstrated that such arrangements are an accepted practice among professionals in the local community, considered to be essential for the provision of service, negotiated without coercion and entered into at the client's initiative and with the client's informed consent. Social workers who accept goods or services from clients as payment for professional services assume the full burden of demonstrating that this arrangement will not be detrimental to the client or the professional relationship.

c. Social workers should not solicit a private fee or other remuneration for providing services to clients who are entitled to such available services through the social workers' employer or agency.

1.14 Clients Who Lack Decision-Making Capacity

When social workers act on behalf of clients who lack the capacity to make informed decisions, social workers should take reasonable steps to safeguard the interests and rights of those clients.

1.15 Interruption of Services

Social workers should make reasonable efforts to ensure continuity of services in the event that they are interrupted by factors such as unavailability, relocation, illness, disability, or death.

1.16 Termination of Services

a. Social workers should terminate services to clients, and professional relationships with them, when such services and relationships are no longer required or no longer serve the clients' needs or interests.

b. Social workers should take reasonable steps to avoid abandoning clients who are still in need of services. Social workers should withdraw services precipitously only under unusual circumstances, giving careful consideration to all factors in the situation and taking care to minimize possible adverse effects. Social workers should assist in making appropriate arrangements for continuation of services when necessary.

c. Social workers in fee-for-service settings may terminate services to clients who are not paying an overdue balance if the financial contractual arrangements have been made clear to the client, if the client does not pose an imminent danger to self or others,

and if the clinical and other consequences of the current non-payment have been addressed and discussed with the client.

d. Social workers should not terminate services to pursue a social, financial, or sexual relationship with a client.

e. Social workers who anticipate the termination or interruption of services to clients should notify clients promptly and seek the transfer, referral, or continuation of services in relation to the clients' needs and preferences.

f. Social workers who are leaving an employment setting should inform clients of appropriate options for the continuation of service and their benefits and risks.

2. Social Workers' Ethical Responsibilities to Colleagues

2.01 Respect

a. Social workers should treat colleagues with respect, and represent accurately and fairly the qualifications, views, and obligations of colleagues.

b. Social workers should avoid unwarranted negative criticism of colleagues with clients or with other professionals. Unwarranted negative criticism may include demeaning comments that refer to colleagues' level of competence or to individuals' attributes such as race, ethnicity, national origin, color, age, religion, sex, sexual orientation, marital status, political belief, mental or physical disability, or any other preference, personal characteristic, or status.

c. Social workers should cooperate with social work colleagues and with colleagues of other professions when it serves the well-being of clients.

2.02 Confidentiality with Colleagues

Social workers should respect confidential information shared by colleagues in the course of their professional relationships and transactions. Social workers should ensure that such colleagues understand social workers' obligation to respect confidentiality and any exceptions related to it.

2.03 Interdisciplinary Collaboration

a. Social workers who are members of an interdisciplinary team should participate in and contribute to decisions that affect the well-being of clients by drawing on the perspectives, values, and experiences of the social work profession. Professional and ethical obligations of the interdisciplinary team as a whole and of its individual members should be clearly established.

b. Social workers for whom a team decision raises ethical concerns should attempt to resolve the disagreement through appropriate channels. If the disagreement cannot be resolved social workers should pursue other avenues to address their concerns, consistent with client well-being.

2.04 Disputes Involving Colleagues

a. Social workers should not take advantage of a dispute between a colleague and employer to obtain a position or otherwise advance the social worker's own interests.

b. Social workers should not exploit clients in a dispute with a colleague or engage clients in any inappropriate discussion of a social worker's conflict with a colleague.

2.05 Consultation

a. Social workers should seek advice and counsel of colleagues whenever such consultation is in the best interests of clients.

b. Social workers should keep informed of colleagues' areas of expertise and competencies. Social workers should seek consultation only from colleagues who have demonstrated knowledge, expertise and competence related to the subject of the consultation.

c. When consulting with colleagues about clients, social workers should disclose the least amount of information necessary to achieve the purposes of the consultation.

2.06 Referral for Services

a. Social workers should refer clients to other professionals when other professionals' specialized knowledge or expertise is needed to serve clients fully, or when social workers believe they are not being effective or making reasonable progress with clients and additional service is required.

b. Social workers who refer clients to other professionals should take appropriate steps to facilitate an orderly transfer of responsibility. Social workers who refer clients to other professionals should disclose, with clients' consent, all pertinent information to the new service providers.

c. Social workers are prohibited from giving or receiving payment for a referral when no professional service is provided by the referring social worker.

2.07 Sexual Relationships

a. Social workers who function as supervisors or educators should not engage in sexual activities or contact with supervisors, students, trainees, or other colleagues over whom they exercise professional authority.

b. Social workers should avoid engaging in sexual relationships with colleagues where there is potential for a conflict of interest. Social workers who become involved in, or anticipate becoming involved in, a sexual relationship with a colleague have a duty to transfer professional responsibilities, when necessary, in order to avoid a conflict of interest.

2.08 Sexual Harassment

Social workers should not engage in any sexual harassment of supervisees, students, trainees, or colleagues. Sexual harassment includes sexual advances, sexual solicitation, requests for sexual favors, and other verbal or physical conduct of a sexual nature.

2.09 Impairment of Colleagues

a. Social workers who have direct knowledge of a social work colleague's impairment which is due to personal problems, psychosocial distress, substance abuse, or mental health difficulties, and which interferes with practice effectiveness, should consult with that colleague when feasible and assist the colleague in taking remedial action.

b. Social workers who believe that a social work colleague's impairment interferes with practice effectiveness and that the colleague has not taken adequate steps to address the impairment should take action through appropriate channels established by employers, agencies, NASW, licensing and regulatory bodies, and other professional organizations.

2.10 Incompetence of Colleagues

a. Social workers who have direct knowledge of a social work colleague's incompetence should consult with that colleague when feasible and assist the colleague in taking remedial action.

b. Social workers who believe that a social work colleague is incompetent and has not taken adequate steps to address the incompetence should take action through appropriate channels established by employers, agencies, NASW, licensing and regulatory bodies, and other professional organizations.

2.11 Unethical Conduct of Colleagues

a. Social workers should take adequate measures to discourage, prevent, expose, and correct the unethical conduct of colleagues.

b. Social workers should be knowledgeable about established policies and procedures for handling concerns about colleagues' unethical behavior. Social workers should be familiar with national, state, and local procedures for handling ethics complaints. These include policies and procedures created by NASW, licensing and regulatory bodies, employers, agencies, and other professional organizations.

c. Social workers who believe that a colleague has acted unethically should seek resolution by discussing their concerns with the colleague when feasible and when such discussion is likely to be productive.

d. When necessary, social workers who believe that a colleague has acted unethically should take action through appropriate formal channels (such as contacting a state licensing board or regulatory body, NASW committee on inquiry, or other professional ethics committees).

e. Social workers should defend and assist colleagues who are unjustly charged with unethical conduct.

3. Social Workers' Ethical Responsibilities in Practice Settings

3.01 Supervision and Consultation

a. Social workers who provide supervision or consultation should have the necessary knowledge and skill to supervise or consult appropriately and should do so only within their areas of knowledge and competence.

b. Social workers who provide supervision or consultation are responsible for setting clear, appropriate, and culturally sensitive boundaries.

c. Social workers should not engage in any dual or multiple relationships with supervisees in which there is a risk of exploitation of or potential harm to the supervisee.

d. Social workers who provide supervision should evaluate supervisees' performance in a manner that is fair and respectful.

3.02 Education and Training

a. Social workers who function as educators, field instructors for students, or trainers should provide instruction only within their areas of knowledge and competence, and should provide instruction based on the most current information and knowledge available in the profession.

b. Social workers who function as educators or field instructors for students should evaluate students' performance in a manner that is fair and respectful.

c. Social workers who function as educators or field instructors for students should take reasonable steps to ensure that clients are routinely informed when services are being provided by students.

d. Social workers who function as educators or field instructors for students should not engage in any dual or multiple relationships with students in which there is a risk of exploitation or potential harm to the student. Social work educators and field instructors are responsible for setting clear, appropriate, and culturally sensitive boundaries.

3.03 Performance Evaluation

Social workers who have the responsibility for evaluating the performance of others should fulfill such responsibility in a fair and considerate manner, and on the basis of clearly stated criteria.

3.04 Client Records

a. Social workers should take reasonable steps to ensure that documentation in records is accurate and reflective of the services provided.

b. Social workers should include sufficient and timely documentation in records to facilitate the delivery of services and to ensure continuity of services provided to clients in the future.

c. Social workers' documentation should protect clients' privacy to the extent that is possible and appropriate, and should include only that information that is directly relevant to the delivery of services.

d. Social workers should store records following the termination of service to ensure reasonable future access. Records should be maintained for the number of years required by state statutes or relevant contracts.

3.05 Billing

Social workers should establish and maintain billing practices that accurately reflect the nature and extent of services provided, and by whom the service was provided in the practice setting.

3.06 Client Transfer

a. When an individual who is receiving services from another agency or colleague contacts a social worker for services, the social worker should carefully consider the client's needs before agreeing to provide services. In order to minimize possible confusion and conflict, social workers should discuss with potential clients the nature of their current relationship with other service providers and the implications, including possible benefits or risks, of entering into a relationship with a new service provider.

b. If a new client has been served by another agency or colleague, social workers should discuss with the client whether consultation with the previous service provider is in the client's best interest.

3.07 Administration

a. Social work administrators should advocate within and outside of their agencies for adequate resources to meet clients' needs.

b. Social workers should advocate for resource allocation procedures that are open and fair. When not all clients' needs can be met, an allocation procedure should be developed that is non-discriminatory and based on appropriate and consistently applied principles.

c. Social workers who are administrators should take reasonable steps to ensure that adequate agency or organizational resources are available to provide appropriate staff supervision.

d. Social work administrators should take reasonable steps to ensure that the working environment for which they are responsible is consistent with and encourages compliance with the NASW Code of Ethics. Social work administrators should take reasonable steps to eliminate any conditions in their organizations that violate, interfere with, or discourage compliance with the Code of Ethics.

3.08 Continuing Education and Staff Development

Social work administrators and supervisors should take reasonable steps to provide or arrange for continuing education and staff development for all staff for whom they are responsible. Continuing education and staff development should address current knowledge and emerging developments related to social work practice and ethics.

3.09 Commitments to Employers

a. Social workers generally should adhere to commitments made to employers and employing organizations.

b. Social workers should work to improve employing agencies' policies and procedures, and the efficiency and effectiveness of their services.

c. Social workers should take reasonable steps to ensure that employers are aware of social workers' ethical obligations as set forth in the NASW Code of Ethics and their implications for social work practice.

d. Social workers should not allow an employing organization's policies, procedures, regulations, or administrative orders to interfere with their ethical practice of social work. Social workers should take reasonable steps to ensure that their employing organizations' practices are consistent with the NASW Code of Ethics.

e. Social workers should act to prevent and eliminate discrimination in the employing organization's work assignments and in its employment policies and practices.

f. Social workers should accept employment or arrange student field placements only in organizations where fair personnel practices are exercised.

g. Social workers should be diligent stewards of the resources of their employing organizations, wisely conserving funds where appropriate, and never misappropriating funds or using them for unintended purposes.

3.10 Labor-Management Disputes

a. Social workers may engage in organized action, including the formation of and participation in labor unions, to improve services to clients and working conditions.

b. The actions of social workers who are involved in labor-management disputes, job actions, or labor strikes should be guided by the profession's values, ethical principles, and ethical standards. Reasonable differences of opinion exist among social workers concerning their primary obligation as professionals during an actual or threatened labor strike or job action. Social workers should carefully examine relevant issues and their possible impact on clients before deciding on a course of action.

4. Social Workers' Ethical Responsibilities as Professionals

4.01 Competence

a. Social workers should accept responsibility or employment only on the basis of existing competence or the intention to acquire the necessary competence.

b. Social workers should strive to become and remain proficient in professional practice and the performance of professional functions. Social workers should critically examine, and keep current with, emerging knowledge relevant to social work. Social workers should routinely review professional literature and participate in continuing education relevant to social work practice and social work ethics.

c. Social workers should base practice on recognized knowledge, including empirically-based knowledge, relevant to social work and social work ethics.

4.02 Discrimination

Social workers should not practice, condone, facilitate, or collaborate with any form of discrimination on the basis of race, ethnicity, national origin, color, age, religion, sex, sexual orientation, marital status, political belief, or mental or physical disability.

4.03 Private Conduct

Social workers' should not permit their private conduct to interfere with their ability to fulfill their professional responsibilities.

4.04 Dishonesty, Fraud, and Deception

Social workers should not participate in, condone, or be associated with dishonesty, fraud, or deception.

4.05 Impairment

a. Social workers should not allow their own personal problems, psychosocial distress, legal problems, substance abuse, or mental health difficulties to interfere with their professional judgment and performance or jeopardize the best interests of those for whom they have a professional responsibility.

b. Social workers whose personal problems, psychosocial distress, legal problems, substance abuse, or mental health difficulties interfere with their professional judgment and performance should immediately seek consultation and take appropriate remedial action by seeking professional help, making adjustments in workload, terminating practice, or taking any other steps necessary to protect clients and others.

4.06 Misrepresentation

a. Social workers should make clear distinctions between statements made and actions engaged in as a private individual and as a representative of the social work profession, a professional social work organization, or of the social worker's employing agency.

b. Social workers who speak on behalf of professional social work organizations should accurately represent the official and authorized positions of the organizations.

c. Social workers should ensure that their representations to clients, agencies, and the public of professional qualifications, credentials, education, competence, affiliations, services provided, or results to be achieved are accurate. Social workers should claim only those relevant professional credentials they actually possess and take steps to correct any inaccuracies or misrepresentations of their credentials by others.

4.07 Solicitations

a. Social workers should not engage in uninvited solicitation of potential clients who, because of their circumstances, are vulnerable to undue influence, manipulation, or coercion.

b. Social workers should not engage in solicitation of testimonial endorsements (including solicitation of consent to use a client's prior statement as a testimonial endorsement) from current clients or from other persons who, because of their particular circumstances, are vulnerable to undue influence.

4.08 Acknowledging Credit

a. Social workers should take responsibility and credit, including authorship credit, only for work they have actually performed and to which they have contributed.

b. Social workers should honestly acknowledge the work of and the contributions made by others.

5. Social Workers' Ethical Responsibilities to the Social Work Profession

5.01 Integrity of the Profession

a. Social workers should work toward the maintenance and promotion of high standards of practice.

b. Social workers should uphold and advance the values, ethics, knowledge, and mission of the profession. Social workers should protect, enhance, and improve the integrity of the profession through appropriate study and research, active discussion, and responsible criticism of the profession.

c. Social workers should contribute time and professional expertise to activities that promote respect for the value, integrity, and competence of the social work profession. These activities may include teaching, research, consultation, service, legislative testimony, presentations in the community and participation in their professional organizations.

d. Social workers should contribute to the knowledge base of social work and share with colleagues their knowledge related to practice, research, and ethics. Social workers should seek to contribute to the profession's literature and to share their knowledge at professional meetings and conferences.

e. Social workers should act to prevent the unauthorized and unqualified practice of social work.

5.02 Evaluation and Research

a. Social workers should monitor and evaluate policies, the implementation of programs, and practice interventions.

b. Social workers should promote and facilitate evaluation and research in order to contribute to the development of knowledge.

c. Social workers should critically examine and keep current with emerging knowledge relevant to social work and fully utilize evaluation and research evidence in their professional practice.

d. Social workers engaged in evaluation or research should consider carefully possible consequences and should follow guidelines developed for the protection of evaluation and research participants. Appropriate institutional review boards should be consulted.

e. Social workers engaged in evaluation or research should obtain voluntary and written informed consent from participants, when appropriate, without any implied or actual deprivation or penalty for refusal to participate, without undue inducement to participate, and with due regard for participants' well-being, privacy and dignity. Informed consent should include information about the nature, extent, and duration of the participation requested and disclosure of the risks and benefits of participation in the research.

f. When evaluation or research participants are incapable of giving informed consent, social workers should provide an appropriate explanation to them, obtain the participant's assent, and obtain consent from an appropriate proxy.

g. Social workers should never design or conduct evaluation or research that does not use consent procedures, such as certain forms of naturalistic observation and/or archival research, unless rigorous and responsible review of the research has found it to be justified because of its prospective scientific yield, educational, or applied value and unless equally effective alternative procedures that do not involve waiver of consent are not feasible.

h. Social workers should inform participants of their rights to withdraw from evaluation and research at any time without penalty.

i. Social workers should take appropriate steps to ensure that participants in evaluation and research have access to appropriate supportive services.

j. Social workers engaged in evaluation or research should protect participants from unwarranted physical or mental distress, harm, danger, or deprivation.

k. Social workers engaged in the evaluation of services should discuss collected information only for professional purposes and only with persons professionally concerned with this information.

l. Social workers engaged in evaluation or research should ensure the anonymity or confidentiality of participants and the data obtained from them. Social workers should inform participants of any limits of confidentiality, the measures that will be taken to ensure confidentiality, and when any records containing research data will be destroyed.

m. Social workers who report evaluation and research results should protect participants' confidentiality by omitting identifying information unless proper consent has been obtained authorizing disclosures.

n. Social workers should report evaluation and research findings accurately. They should not fabricate or falsify results and should take steps to correct any errors later found in published data using standard publication methods.

o. Social workers engaged in evaluation or research should be alert to and avoid conflicts of interest and dual relationships with participants, should inform participants when a real or potential conflict of interest arises, and should take steps to resolve the issue in a manner that makes participants' interests primary.

p. Social workers should educate themselves, their students, and colleagues about responsible research practices.

6. Social Workers' Ethical Responsibilities to the Broader Society

6.01 Social Welfare

Social workers should promote the general welfare of society, from local to global levels, and the development of people, their communities, and their environment. Social workers should advocate for living conditions conducive to the fulfillment of basic human needs and promote social, economic, political, and cultural values and institutions that are compatible with the realization of social justice.

6.02 Public Participation

Social workers should facilitate informed participation by the public in shaping social policies and institutions.

6.03 Public Emergencies

Social workers should provide appropriate professional services in public emergencies, to the greatest extent possible.

6.04 Social and Political Action

a. Social workers should engage in social and political action that seeks to ensure that all persons have equal access to the resources, employment, services, and opportunities that they require in order to meet their basic human needs and to develop fully. Social workers should be aware of the impact of the political arena on practice, and should advocate for changes in policy and legislation to improve social conditions in order to meet basic human needs and promote social justice.

b. Social workers should act to expand choice and opportunity for all persons, with special regard for vulnerable, disadvantaged, oppressed, and exploited persons and groups.

c. Social workers should promote conditions that encourage respect for the diversity of cultures and social diversity within the United States and globally. Social workers should promote policies and practices that demonstrate respect for difference, support the expansion of cultural knowledge and resources, advocate for programs and institutions that demonstrate cultural competence, and promote policies that safeguard the rights of and confirm equity and social justice for all people.

d. Social workers should act to prevent and eliminate domination, exploitation, and discrimination against any person, group, or class on the basis of race, ethnicity, national origin, color, age, religion, sex, sexual orientation, marital status, political belief, mental or physical disability, or any other preference, personal characteristic, or status.

References

Abromovitz, M. (1993). Should all social work students be educated for social change? Pro. *Journal of Social Work Education, 29*(1), 6–13.

Adler, P. (1977). Beyond cultural identity: Reflections upon cultural and multicultural man. In R. W. Brislin, Editor, *Culture learning concepts, application and research.* Honolulu, HI: University of Hawaii Press.

Ali, Muhammad. (1991). Quote. In D. Riley, Editor, *My soul looks back, 'less I forget: A collection of quotes by people of color,* 237. New York: Harper-Collins.

Alinsky, S. D. (1971). *Rules for radicals: A pragmatic primer for realistic radicals.* New York: Vintage Books.

American Psychiatric Association. (1994). *Diagnostic and statistical manual of mental disorders,* fourth edition. Washington, DC: American Psychiatric Association.

Anderson, E. (1994). The code of the streets. *Atlantic Monthly,* May, pp. 81–94.

Anello, E. (1992). Should social workers use the DSM III? Yes. In E. Gambrill and R. Pruger, Editors, *Controversial issues in social work,* 140–145, 154–156. Boston: Allyn & Bacon.

Arizona Chapter, NASW. (1996). *NASW Newsletter, Arizona Chapter.* June, p. 1.

Bailey, D. (1995). Management: Diverse workplaces. In R. Edwards, Editor-in-Chief, *Encyclopedia of Social Work,* nineteenth edition, 1659–1663. Washington, DC: NASW Press.

Baldwin, J. (1995). Quote. In V. Johnsen, Editor, *Heart full of grace: A thousand years of black wisdom,* 46. New York: Fireside.

Bandura, A. (1969). *Principles of behavior modification.* New York: Holt, Rinehart & Winston.

Barlett, D. L., and Steele, J. B. (1992). *America: What went wrong?* Kansas City, MO: Andrews and McMeel.

Barnet, R., and Cavanagh, J. (1994). Global dreams. In R. C. Longworth, The world of work. *Chicago Tribune,* September 4, Section 4, p. 1.

Bartlett, H. M. (1970). *The common base of social work practice.* Washington, DC: National Association of Social Workers, Inc.

Basso, K. (1986). *The Cibecue Apache.* Prospect Heights, IL: Waveland Press.

Becerra, R. M. (1992). Mexican American families. In J. M. Henslin, Editor, *Marriage and family in a changing society,* fourth edition, 66–75. New York: Free Press.

Begley, S. *Annual editions of race and ethnic relations.* Guilford, CT: Dushkin Publishing.

Belenky, M. F., Clinchy, B. M., Goldberger, N. R., and Tarule, J. M. (1986). *Women's ways of knowing.* New York: Basic Books.

Bellah, R. H., Madsen, R., Sullivan, A. S., Swidler, A., and Tipton, S. M. (1992). *The good society.* New York: Alfred A. Knopf.

Bellah, R. H., Madsen, R., Sullivan, A. S., and Tipton, S. M. (1985). *Habits of the heart: Individualism and commitment in American life.* New York: Harper & Row.

Bennett, M. J. (1986). Towards ethnorelativism: A development model of intercultural sensitivity. In R. M. Paige, Editor, *Cross cultural orientation, new conceptualizations and applications,* 27–69. Lanham, MD: University Press of America.

Berg, I. K. (1992). *Family-based services: A solution-focused approach.* Milwaukee, WI: Brief Family Therapy Center.

Berg, I. K., and Miller, S. D. (1992). *Working with the*

problem drinker: A solution-focused approach. New York: W. W. Norton & Company.

Berlin, S. B., and Marsh, J. C. (1993). *Informing practice decisions.* New York: Macmillan Publishing Company.

Berthold, M. S. (1989). Spiritism as a form of psychotherapy: Implications for social work practice. *Social Casework, 70*(6), 502–509.

Beverly, D. P., and McSweeney, E. A. (1987). *Social welfare and social justice.* Englewood Cliffs, NJ: Prentice Hall.

Biestek, F. (1957). *The casework relationship.* Chicago: Loyola University Press.

Billingsley, A., and Caldwell, C. H. (1991). The church, the family, and the school in the African American community. *Journal of Negro Education, 60*(3), Summer, 427–440.

Bloom, M. (1975). *The paradox of helping: Introduction to the philosophy of scientific practice.* New York: John Wiley & Sons.

————. (1990). *The drama of social work.* Itasca, IL: F. E. Peacock Publishers.

Bloom, M. Fischer, J., and Orme, J. G. (1995). *Evaluating practice: Guidelines for the accountable professional,* second edition. Boston: Allyn & Bacon.

Boehm, W. W. (1958). The nature of social work. *Social Work, 3* (April), 10–18.

Boje, D. (1991). The story telling organization: A study of story performance in an office supply firm. *Administrative Science Quarterly, 36* (March), 106–126.

Brawley, E. A. (1983). *Mass media and the human services: Getting the message out.* Beverly Hills, CA: Sage Publications.

————. (1995). *Human services in the media: Developing partnerships for change.* Luxembourg: Harwood Academic Publishers.

Briar, K. T., and Briar, S. (1982). Clinical social work and public policies. In M. Mahaffey and J. Hanks, Editors, *Practical politics: Social work and political responsibility,* 45–54. Silver Spring, MD: NASW Press.

Brown, D., and Brooks, L. (1991). *Career counseling techniques.* Boston: Allyn & Bacon.

Brown, J. C. (1933). *The rural community and social case work.* New York: J. J. Little and Ives Company.

Brown, L., Editor. (1993). *The new shorter Oxford English dictionary.* New York: Oxford University Press.

Brown, R. (1989). Are rural communities dying? *Janesville (Wisconsin) Gazette,* August 12, pp. 1, 8.

Brown, R. V., Kahr, A. S., and Peterson, C. (1974). *Decision analysis: An overview.* New York: Holt, Rinehart & Winston.

Bruner, J. S. (1990). *Acts of meaning.* Cambridge, MA: Harvard University Press.

Brunner, J. (1996). Student paper: Spirituality and religion. Unpublished document.

Burghardt, S. (1982). *The other side of organizing.* Cambridge, MA: Harvard University Press.

Burns, D. D. (1980). *Feeling good, the new mood therapy,* first edition. New York: Morrow.

Canda, E. R. (1988). Spirituality, religious diversity, and social work practice. *Social Casework: The Journal of Contemporary Social Work, 69*(4), April, 238–247.

————. (1989). Religious content in social work education: A comparative approach. *Journal of Social Work Education, 25*(1), Winter, 36–45.

Caplan, G. (1974). *Support systems and community mental health: Lectures on concept development.* New York: Behavioral Publications.

Carlson, P. (1992). West Virginia mountain paradox. *Washington Post Magazine.* November 22, pp. 9–27.

Carroll, M. (1986). The carrier role of social work: Learning from Alaskan Native Americans. *Social Casework: The Journal of Contemporary Social Work, 67*(3), 180–184.

Carson, J. (1989). *Stories I ain't told nobody yet.* New York: Orchard Books.

Carter, S. (1993). *The culture of disbelief: How American law and politics trivialize religious devotion.* New York: Basic Books.

Cates, J. (1996). Student paper: Spirituality and religion. Unpublished document.

Caudill, H. (1963). *Night comes to the Cumberlands: A biography of a depressed area.* Boston: Little, Brown & Company.

Chambers, D. E., Wedel, K. R., and Rodwell, M. K. (1992). *Evaluating social programs.* Boston: Allyn & Bacon.

Chapin, R. K. (1995). Social policy development: The strengths perspective. *Social Work, 40*(4), July, 506–514.

Chisholm, S. (1995). Quote. In V. Johnsen, Editor, *Heart full of grace: A thousand years of black wisdom,* 91. New York: Fireside.

Coles, R. (1990). *The spiritual life of children.* Boston: Houghton Mifflin.

_____ . (1992). The human context of homelessness. In G. Giamo and J. Grunberg, Editors, *Beyond homelessness: Frames of reference,* 162–183. Iowa City: University of Iowa Press.

Collier, K. (1978). Education for rural social work practice: The Saskatchewan experience. In E. B. Buxton, Editor, *2nd National Institute on Social Work in Rural Areas reader,* 83–93. Madison, WI: University of Wisconsin-Extension.

Community Relations Section. (1991). *Attorney general mediation training manual.* Phoenix: Civil Rights Division, Arizona Attorney General's Office.

Conrad, A. (1988). Social justice—present dilemma and future potential: A student/field instructor comparison. Paper presented at the annual program meeting of the Council on Social Work Education, Atlanta, GA.

Coopersmith, S. (1967). *The antecedents of self-esteem.* San Francisco: W. H. Freeman.

Corcoran, K. and Videka-Sherman, L. (1992). Some things we know about effective clinical social work. In K. Corcoran, Editor, *Structuring change,* 15–27. Chicago: Lyceum Press.

Cormier, W. H., and Cormier, L. S. (1985). *Interviewing strategies for helpers,* second edition. Pacific Grove, CA: Brooks/Cole Publishing Company.

Cornett, C. (1992). Toward a more comprehensive personology: Integrating a spiritual perspective into social work practice. *Social Work, 37*(2), March, 101–102.

Coser, L. A. (1967). *Continuities in the study of social conflict.* New York: Free Press.

_____ . (1977). *Masters of sociological thought: Ideas in historical and social context,* second edition. New York: Harcourt Brace Jovanovich.

Council on Social Work Education. (1992). *Curriculum policy statement.* Alexandria, VA: Council on Social Work Education.

_____ . (1994). *Handbook of accreditation standards and procedures.* Alexandria, VA: Council on Social Work Education.

Cournoyer, B. (1991). *The social work skills workbook.* Belmont, CA: Wadsworth Publishing Company.

Cousins, N. (1981). *Anatomy of an illness as perceived by the patient.* New York: Bantam Books.

Cox, D. (1995). Social development and social work education: The USA's continuing leadership in a changing world. *Social Development Issues, 17* (2/3), 1–18.

Cross, T. (1996). Developing a knowledge base to support cultural competence. *The Prevention Report, 5*(1), 27–30.

Danielson, P. (1995). Personal communication, July 9.

Davidson, B. P., and Jenkins, P. J. (1989). Class diversity in shelter life. *Social Work, 34*(6), November, 491–495.

Davis, A. M. (1985). Mediation training: When the parties talk . . . mediators listen to . . . . Boston, MA: Massachusetts District Court Mediation Project.

_____ (1987). Mediation training: When mediators talk . . . they speak to . . . . Boston, MA: Massachusetts District Court Mediation Project.

_____ (1989). An interview with Mary Parker Follett. *Negotiation Journal,* July, pp. 223–235.

_____ (1991). Mediation training: Ten tips on asking questions. Boston, MA: Massachusetts District Court Mediation Project.

_____ (1993). Mediation training: Moving from story to settlement in mediation. Boston, MA: Massachusetts District Court Mediation Project.

Davis, G. A. (1981). *Creativity is forever.* Cross Plains, WI: Badger Press.

Davis, I. (1975). Advice giving in parent counseling. *Social Casework: The Journal of Contemporary Social Work, 56,* 343–347.

Decker, L. (1995). Including spirituality. *Clinical Quarterly: National Center for Post Traumatic Stress Disorder, 5*(1), 1, 3.

Denton, R. T. (1990). The religiously fundamentalist family: Training for assessment and treatment. *Journal of Social Work Education, 26*(1), Winter, 6–14.

Descartes, R. (1958). *Descartes' philosophical writings.* New York: Modern Library.

de Shazer, S. (1991). *Putting difference to work.* New York: W. W. Norton & Company.

Devore, W., and Schlesinger, E. G. (1987). *Ethnic-sensitive social work practice,* second edition. Columbus: Merrill Publishing Company.

_____ . (1991). *Ethnic sensitive social work practice,* third edition. Boston: Allyn & Bacon.

Dewey, J. (1933). *How we think,* revised edition. New York: Heath.

Doyle, W. L. (1993). *Fundraising ideas for all nonprofits: Charities, clubs, churches, etc.* New York: American Fund Raising Institute.

Duncombe, P. (1982). Rural churches and rural networks: Implications for service delivery. In G. M.

Jacobsen, Editor, *Nourishing people and communities through the lean years,* 22–31. Iowa City: University of Iowa Printing Service.

Dyson, B., and Dyson, E. (1989). *Neighborhood caretakers: Stories, strategies, and tools for healing urban communities.* Indianapolis, IN: Knowledge Systems, Inc.

Easton, A. (1976). *Decision making: A short course for professionals.* New York: John Wiley & Sons.

Egan, G. (1990). *The skilled helper: A systemic approach to effective helping,* fourth edition. Pacific Grove, CA: Brooks/Cole Publishing Company.

———. (1994). *The skilled helper: A problem-management approach to helping,* fifth edition. Pacific Grove, CA: Brooks/Cole Publishing Company.

Epstein, L. (1980). *Helping people: The task-centered approach.* St. Louis, MO: Mosby.

Etzioni, A. (1992). Normative-affective factors: Toward a new decision-making model. In M. Zey, Editor, *Decision making: Alternations to rational choice models,* 89–111. Newbury Park: Sage Publications.

Fenby, B. L. (1978). Social work in a rural setting. *Social Work, 23*(2), 162–163.

Ferrill, L. (1993). *A far cry from home: Life in a shelter for homeless women.* Chicago: Noble Press.

Fisher, R. (1987). Community organizing in historical perspective: A typology. In F. Cox, J. Erlich, J. Rothman, and J. Tropman, Editors, *Strategies of community organization,* fourth edition, 387–397. Itasca, IL: F. E. Peacock Publishers.

Fisher, R., and Ury, W. (1983). *Getting to yes: Negotiating agreement without giving in.* New York: Penguin Books.

Flanagan, J. (1977). *The grassroots fundraising book: How to raise money in your community.* Chicago: The Swallow Press.

Flaskerud, J. (1990). Matching client and therapist ethnicity, language, and gender: A review of research. *Issues in Mental Health Nursing, 11*(4), 321–336.

Flora, C. B., Flora, J. L., Spears, J. D., and Swanson, L. E., with Lapping, M. B., and Weinberg, M. L. (1992). *Rural communities: Legacy and change.* Boulder, CO: Westview Press.

Flowers, B. S., Editor. (1989). *Bill Moyers: A world of ideas.* New York: Doubleday.

Fost, D. (1995). American Indians in the 1990's. In J. Kromkowski, Editor, *Race and ethnic relations: Annual edition,* 99–103. Guilford, CT: Dushkin.

Fox, D. (1994). Personal communication, spring semester.

Frankl, V. (1963). *Man's search for meaning.* Boston, MA: Beacon Press.

Franklin, B. (1924). *Poor Richard's almanac.* New York: Rimington Hooper.

Freedberg, S. (1989). Self-determination: Historical perspectives and effects on current practice. *Social Work, 34*(1), January, 33–38.

Freire, P. (1989). *Pedagogy of the oppressed.* New York: Continuum Publishing Company.

Freud, S. (1957). *The future of an illusion.* Garden City, NY: Doubleday.

Friedlander, W. A., Editor. (1976). *Concepts and methods of social work practice,* second edition. Englewood Cliffs, NJ: Prentice Hall.

Fulghum, R. (1991). *Uh-oh: Some observations from both sides of the refrigerator door.* Canada: Ballentine Books.

Funiciello, T. (1993). *Tyranny of kindness: Dismantling the welfare state to end poverty in America.* New York: Atlantic Monthly Press.

Furman, L. (1994). Personal communication, June 25.

Galagher, W. (1993). *The power of place.* New York: Poseidon Press.

Galston, W. (1986). Equality of opportunity and liberal theory. In Frank S. Lucash, Editor, *Justice and equality: Here and now,* 89–107. Ithaca, NY: Cornell University Press.

Gambrill, E. (1983). *Casework: A competency-based approach.* Englewood Cliffs, NJ: Prentice Hall.

Garbarino, J., Kostenly, K., and Dubrow, N. (1983). Social support networks: Rx for the helping professionals. In J. Whitaker and J. Garbarino, Editors, *Social support networks: Informal helping in human services,* 3–28. New York: Aldine.

———. (1991). *No place to be a child: Growing up in a war zone.* Lexington, MA: Lexington Books.

Garreau, J. (1981). *The nine nations of North America.* New York: Avon Books.

Gates, H. L. (1994). *Colored people: A memoir.* New York: Alfred A. Knopf.

Gergen, K. (1985). The social constructionist movement in modern psychology. *American Psychologist, 40*(3), 266–275.

Germain, C. (1981). The ecological approach to people-environment transactions. *Social Casework,* June, 323–331.

Germain, C., Editor. (1985). *NASW National Conference on Clinical Social Work Practice: Excellence for the 1980's.* Silver Spring, MD: National Association of Social Workers.

Germain, C. B. (1991). *Human behavior in the social environment.* New York: Columbia University Press.

Gewrith, L. (1982). *Human rights: Essays on justice and its applications.* Chicago: University of Chicago Press.

Gibbs, L. E. (1991). *Scientific reasoning for social workers: Bridging the gap between research and practice.* New York: Macmillan Publishing Company.

Gibbs, P. (1991). Confidentiality. *BSW field manual.* Morgantown, WV: West Virginia University School of Social Work.

Gibelman, M., and Schervish, P. H. (1993). The glass ceiling in social work. *AFFILIA: Journal of Women and Social Work, 8940,* winter, 442–455.

Giddings, P. (1984). *When and where I enter: The impact of black women on race and sex in America.* New York: Bantam Books.

Gillespie, E., and Schallas, B., Editors. (1994). *Contract with America: The bold plan by Rep. Newt Gingrich and Rep. Dick Armey and the House Republicans to change the nation.* New York: Times Books.

Gilligan, C. (1982). *In a different voice.* Cambridge: Harvard University Press.

Ginsberg, L. H. (1976). *Social work in rural communities.* New York: Council on Social Work Education.

Goldani, C. (1993). Quote. In R. Andrews, Editor, *The Columbia dictionary of quotations, 93.* New York: Columbia University Press.

Goldberg, G., and Middleman, R. (1974). *Social service delivery: A structural approach to social work practice.* New York: Columbia University Press.

Goldstein, H. (1984). *Creative change: A cognitive-humanistic approach to social work practice.* New York: Tavistock Publications.

————. (1992). If social work hasn't made progress as a science, might it be an art? *Families in Society, 73*(1), January, 48–55.

Gordon, M. (1993). *The fundraising manual: A step-by-step guide to creating the perfect event.* Boston: Fig Press.

Gorman, J. (1993). Postmodernism and the conduct of inquiry in social work. *AFFILIA: Journal of Women and Social Work, 9*(3), fall, 247–264.

Gosline, G. (1993). Personal communication, June 26.

Governors State University. (1993). *Korean Americans in Chicago.* (Video recording). Chicago: Governors State University.

Graber, L. (1992). Critique of problem terminology. Salem, OR: State Office of Services for Children and Families.

Graber, L., and Nice, J. (1991). The family unity model: The advanced skill of looking to and building on strengths. *The Prevention Report,* fall, pp. 3–4.

Green, J. (1982). *Cultural awareness in the human services.* Englewood Cliffs, NJ: Prentice Hall.

Greenwood, E. (1957). Attributes of a profession. *Social Work, 2*(3), 45–55.

Grinnell, R. (1988). *Social work research and evaluation,* third edition. Itasca, IL: F. E. Peacock Publishers.

Guralick, D. B., Editor-in-Chief. (1978). *Webster's new world dictionary of the American language,* second college edition. New York: William Collins + World Publishing Company.

Gutheil, I. A. (1992). Considering the physical environment: An essential component of good practice. *Social Work. 37*(5), 391–396.

Gutierrez, L. M. (1990). Working with women of color: An empowerment perspective. *Social Work, 35*(2), March, 149–153.

Hammond, K. R., McClelland, G. H., and Mumpower, J. (1980). *Human judgment and decision making: Theories, methods, and procedures.* Boulder, CO: Praeger.

Handler, J., and Hasenfeld, Y. (1992). *The moral construction of poverty: Welfare reform in America.* Newbury Park, CA: Sage Publications.

Hanton, S. (1978). A case for the generalist social worker: A model for service delivery in rural areas. In B. L. Locke and R. A. Lohmann, Editors, *Effective models for the delivery of services in rural areas: Implications for practice and social work education,* 192–201. Morgantown, WV: West Virginia University School of Social Work.

————. (1980). Rural helping systems and family typology. *Child Welfare, 59*(7), 419–426.

Hardman, D. G. (1975). Not with my daughter, you don't. *Social Work, 20*(4), 278–285.

Hasenfeld, Y. (1984). Analyzing the human service agency. In F. Cox, J. Erlich, J. Rothman, and J. Tropman, Editors, *Tactics and techniques of community practice,* 14–26. Itasca, IL: F. E. Peacock Publishers.

Haynes, K. S., and Mickleson, J. S. (1991). *Affecting change: Social workers in the political arena,* second edition. White Plains, NY: Longman Publishing Group.

Hearn, G. (1958). *Theory building in social work.* Toronto: University of Toronto Press.

————. (1969). Introduction. In G. Hearn, Editor, *The general systems approach: Contributions toward an holistic conception of social work,* 1–4. New York: Council on Social Work Education.

Hellenbrand, S. C. (1987). Termination in direct practice. In A. Minahan, Editor-in-Chief, *Encyclopedia of social work,* eighteenth edition, 765–770. Silver Spring, MD: NASW Press.

Hepworth, D. H., and Larsen, J. A. (1982). *Direct social work practice: Theory and skills.* Chicago: Dorsey Press.

————. (1986). *Direct social work practice: Theory and skills,* second edition. Chicago: Dorsey Press.

————. (1990). *Direct social work practice: Theory and skills,* third edition. Belmont, CA: Wadsworth.

————. (1993). *Direct social work practice: Theory and skills,* fourth edition. Belmont, CA: Wadsworth.

Herman, T. L. (1992). *Trauma and recovery.* New York: Basic Books.

Heskin, D. A. (1991). *The struggle for community.* Boulder, CO: Westview Press.

Hilliard, L. (1996). Student paper: Spirituality and religion. Unpublished document.

Hilman, J., and Ventura, M. (1992). *We've had a hundred years of psychotherapy and the world's getting worse.* San Francisco: Harper & Row Publishers.

Hodgkinson, H. (1989). *Demographic trends in education.* New York: American Federation of Teachers.

Hoffman, K. S., and Sallee, A. L. (1994). *Social work practice: Bridges to change.* Boston: Allyn & Bacon.

Holland, T. P. (1995). Organizations: Context for social services delivery. In R. Edwards, Editor-in-Chief, *Encyclopedia of social work,* nineteenth edition, 1787–1794. Washington, DC: NASW Press.

Hollis, F. (1972). *Casework: A psychosocial approach.* New York: Random House.

Holmes, G. E. (1992). Social work research and the empowerment paradigm. In D. Saleeby, Editor, *The strengths perspective in social work practice,* 158–168. New York: Longman Publishing Group.

Homan, M. (1994). *Promoting community change: Making it happen in the real world.* Pacific Grove, CA: Brooks/Cole Publishing Company.

hooks, b. (1993). *Sisters of the yam: Black women and self-recovery.* Boston: South End Press.

Hopps, J., Pinderhughes, E., and Shankar, R. (1995). *The power to care: Clinical practice effectiveness with overwhelmed clients.* New York: Free Press.

Howard, G. (1991). Culture tales: A narrative approach to thinking, cross-cultural psychology, and psychotherapy. *American Psychologist, 46*(3), 187–197.

Human Service Alliance. (1972). *Touching the soul.* (Video recording). Braintree, MA: Horizon Media.

Iatridis, D. S. (1995). Policy practice. In R. Edwards, Editor-in-Chief, *Encyclopedia of social work,* nineteenth edition, 1855–1866. Washington, DC: NASW Press.

Irey, K. (1980). The social work generalist in a rural context: An ecological perspective. *Journal of Education for Social Work, 16*(3), 36–42.

Ivey, A. E. (1994). *Intentional interviewing and counseling: Facilitating client development in a multicultural society,* third edition. Pacific Grove, CA: Brooks/Cole Publishing Company.

Jackson, J. (1995). Quote. In V. Johnsen, Editor, *Heart full of grace: A thousand years of black wisdom,* 154. New York: Fireside.

Jackson, S. (1996). Student paper: Spirituality and religion. Unpublished document.

Jacobsen, G. M. (1980). Rural communities and community development. In H. W. Johnson, Editor, *Rural human services: A book of readings,* 196–202. Itasca, IL: F. E. Peacock Publishers.

Jansson, B. S. (1994). *Social policy: From theory to policy practice,* second edition. Pacific Grove, CA: Brooks/Cole Publishing Company.

Johnson, H. W. (1980). *Rural human services: A book of readings.* Itasca, IL: F. E. Peacock Publishers.

Johnson, L. (1992). *Social work generalist practice.* Boston: Allyn & Bacon.

Kahn, S. (1991). *Organizing: A guide for grassroots leaders.* Washington, DC: NASW Press.

————. (1995). *How people get power.* Washington, DC: NASW Press.

Kant, I. (1964). *The metaphysics of morals: The doctrine of virtue.* New York: Harper & Row Publishers.

Keen, S. (1991). *Fire in the belly: On being a man.* New York: Bantam Books.

Keith-Lucas, A. (1972). *Giving and taking help.* Chapel Hill: University of North Carolina Press.

Kelly, K. S. (1991). *Fund raising and public relations: A critical analysis.* Hillsdale, NJ: Lawrence Erlbaum Associates.

Kieffer, C. (1984). Citizen empowerment: A developmental perspective. *Prevention in Human Services, 3*(2–3), 9–36.

Kilpatrick, A. C., and Holland, T. P. (1995). *Working with families: An integrative model by level of functioning.* Boston: Allyn & Bacon.

King, M. L. (1986). *The portable Martin Luther King, Jr.* New York: St. Martin's Press.

Kiresuk, T. J., and Sherman, R. E. (1968). Goal attainment scaling: A general method for evaluating comprehensive community mental health programs. *Community Mental Health Journal, 4,* 443–453.

Kirk, S., and Hutchins, H. (1992). Should social workers use the DSM III? No. In E. Gambrill and R. Pruger, Editors, *Controversial issues in social work,* 145–154. Boston: Allyn & Bacon.

Kirkland, J., and Irey, K. (1978). Confidentiality: Issues and dilemmas in rural practice. In E. B. Buxton, Editor, *2nd National Institute on Social Work in Rural Areas reader,* 142–150. Madison: University of Wisconsin-Extension.

Kirst-Ashman, K. K., and Hull, G. H. (1993). *Understanding generalist practice.* Chicago: Nelson-Hall Publishers.

Knopf, R. (1979). *Surviving the BS: A handbook for HP's.* Wilmington, NC: Mandala Press.

Kotlowicz, A. (1991). *There are no children here: The story of two boys growing up in the other America.* New York: Doubleday.

Kozol, J. J. (1995). *Amazing grace: The lives of children and the conscience of a nation.* New York: Crown Press.

Kretzmann, J. P., and McKnight, J. L. (1993). *Building communities from the inside out: A path toward finding and mobilizing a community's assets.* Evanston, IL: Center for Urban Affairs and Policy Research.

Kreutziger, S. S. (1995). Spirituality in faith. *Reflections, 1*(4), fall, 28–35.

Kromkowski, J., Editor. (1995). *Race and ethnic relations: Annual edition.* Guilford, CT: Dushkin.

Kübler-Ross, E. (1969). *To live until we say good-bye.* New York: Macmillan Publishing Company.

Kurzman, P. A. (1995). Professional liability and malpractice. In R. L. Edwards, Editor-in-Chief, *Encyclopedia of social work,* nineteenth edition, 1921–1927. Washington, DC: NASW Press.

Labao, L. (1990). *Family and industry structure and socioeconomic conditions.* New York: State University of New York Press.

Lamb, R. K. (1977a). Suggestions for a study of your hometown. In F. M. Cox, J. L. Erlich, J. Rothman, and J. E. Tropman, Editors, *Tactics and techniques of community practice,* 17–23. Itasca, IL: F. E. Peacock Publishers.

_____ . (1977b). Utilizing community resources. In F. M. Cox, J. L. Erlich, J. Rothman, and J. E. Tropman, Editors, *Tactics and techniques of community practice,* 35–42. Itasca, IL: F. E. Peacock Publishers.

Lappé, F. M., and DuBois, P. M. (1994). *The quickening of America. Rebuilding our nation, remaking our lives.* San Francisco: Jossey-Bass.

Lee, J. A. B., and Swenson, C. R. (1986). The concept of mutual aid. In A. Gitterman and L. Schulman, Editors, *Mutual aid groups: Vulnerable populations,* 361–380. New York: Columbia University Press.

Lichtenstein, A. (1996). Student paper: Spirituality and religion. Unpublished document.

Lipsky, M. (1981). The welfare state as workplace. *Public Welfare, 39*(3), 22–27.

Locke, B. A. (1995). *Case description.* Unpublished.

Locke, B. L. (1988). *Role expectations for social work in small towns and rural areas.* Unpublished dissertation.

Locke, E., and Latham, G. (1984). *Goal setting for individuals, groups, and organizations.* Chicago: Science Research Association.

Loewenberg, F. M., and Dolgoff, R. (1966). *Ethical decisions for social work practice,* fifth edition. Itasca, IL: F. E. Peacock Publishers.

Loganbill, C., Hardy, E., and Delworth, U. (1982). Supervision: A conceptual model. *The Counseling Psychologist, 10*(1), 3–42.

Longres, J. (1991). Toward a status model of ethnic sensitive practice. *Journal of Multicultural Social Work, 1*(1), 41–55.

Lorde, A. (1993). There is no hierarchy of oppressions. In V. Cyrus, Editor, *Experiencing race, class, and gender in the United States,* 102. Mountain View, CA: Mayfield.

Lum, D. (1996). *Social work practice and people of color: A process-stage approach,* third edition. Pacific Grove, CA: Brooks/Cole Publishing Company.

Mahedy, W. (1995). Some theological perspectives on PTSD. *Clinical Quarterly: National Center for Post Traumatic Stress Disorder, 5*(1), 6–7.

Markowitz, L. (1994). The cross-currents of multi-culturalism. *The Family Therapy Networker, 18*(4), 18–24.

Marlin, K. (1983). Punishment • rewards • praise • encouragement. *Practical parenting,* 1–4. Columbia, MI: Practical Parenting Publishers.

Martin, S. (1996). Student paper. Spirituality and religion. Unpublished document.

Martinez-Brawley, E. E. (1990). *Perspectives on the small community: Humanistic views for practitioners.* Silver Spring, MD: NASW Press.

————. (1995). Knowledge diffusion and transfer of technology: Conceptual premises and concrete steps for human services innovators. *Social Work, 40*(5), September, 670–682.

Maslach, C. (1982). *Burnout—the cost of caring.* Englewood Cliffs, NJ: Prentice Hall.

Maslow, A. H. (1968). *Toward a psychology of being,* second edition. New York: D. Van Nostrand Company.

McCall, N. (1994). *Makes me wanna holler: A young black man in America.* New York: Random House.

McDermott, F. E. (1982). Against a pervasive definition of self-determination. In H. Rubensen and M. H. Block, Editors, *Things that matter: Influences of helping relationships,* 77–88. New York: Macmillan.

McGoldrick, M. (1994). Foreword. In M. P. Mirkin, Editor, *Women in context: Toward a feminist reconstruction of psychotherapy,* xiii–xv. New York: Guilford Press.

McInnis-Dittrick, K. (1994). *Integrating social welfare and social work practice.* Pacific Grove, CA: Brooks/Cole Publishing Company.

McIntosh, P. (1993). White privilege: Unpacking the invisible knapsack. In V. Cyrus, Editor, *Experiencing race, class, and gender in the United States,* 209–213. Mountain View, CA: Mayfield.

McLoyd, V. C. (1990). The impact of economic hardship on black families and children: Psychological distress, parenting, and socioemotional development. *Child Development, 61,* 311–346.

Medoff, P., and Sklar, H. (1994). *Streets of hope: The fall and rise of an urban neighborhood.* Boston: South End Press.

Melaville, A., and Blank, M. (1993). *Together we can: A guide for crafting a profamily system of education and human services.* Washington, DC: Government Printing Office.

Mermelstein, J., and Sundet, P. (1995). Rural social work is an anachronism: The perspective of twenty years of experience and debate. Paper presented at the Twentieth Annual Symposium on Social Work and Human Services in Rural Areas, July.

Merritt, J. (1994). Entering the story. *Winds of Change, 9*(4), 49–61.

Meyer, C. H. (1976). *Social work practice.* New York: Free Press.

————. (1983). *Clinical social work in the ecosystems perspective.* New York: Columbia University Press.

————. (1993). *Assessment in social work practice.* New York: Columbia University Press.

Miley, K. K., O'Melia, M., and DuBois, B. L. (1995). *Generalist social work practice: An empowering approach.* Boston: Allyn & Bacon.

Mill, J. S. (1963). *On liberty.* London: Oxford University Press.

Miller, D. W., and Starr, J. K. (1967). *The structure of human decision.* Englewood Cliffs, NJ: Prentice Hall.

Miller, G. P. (1974). *Decision making—a look at the process.* New York: Presidents Association of the American Management Associations.

Mintzberg, H. (1978). Crafting strategy. *Harvard Business Review,* July–August, 66–75.

Monroe, L. (1994). Student paper: Spirituality and religion. Unpublished document.

Montgomery, H., and Swenson, O., Editors. (1989). *Process and structure in human decision making.* New York: John Wiley and Sons.

Morris, E., Editor. (1982). *American heritage dictionary,* second edition. Boston: Houghton Mifflin.

Munch, S. (1995). Class lecture: Systems theory. Unpublished notes. Michigan State University, East Lansing.

Murphy, M. J. (1977). Community resources: How to find and use them. In F. M. Cox, J. L. Erlich, J. Rothman, and J. E. Tropman, Editors, *Tactics and techniques of community practice,* 35–42. Itasca, IL: F. E. Peacock Publishers.

National Association of Social Workers. (1981). *Standards for the classification of social work practice: Policy Statement IV.* Silver Spring, MD: NASW Press.

————. (1996). *Code of Ethics.* Washington, DC: NASW Press.

Neale, N. K. (1982). A social worker for all seasons: Rural social work in the 1980's. In L. A. B. Jorgensen and J. Smith, Editors, *The 80's: A decade for new roles in social work,* 169–180. Salt Lake City: University of Utah.

Netting, F. E., Kettner, P. M., and McMurtry, S. L. (1993). *Social work macro practice.* New York: Longman Publishing Group.

Noddings, N. (1984). *Caring: A feminine approach to ethics and moral education.* Berkeley: University of California Press.

Northen, H. (1982). *Clinical social work.* New York: Columbia University Press.

Novak, M. (1993). Neither WASP nor Jew nor black. In V. Cyrus, Editor, *Experiencing race, class, and gender in the United States,* 30–34. Mountain View, CA: Mayfield.

Nozick, R. (1974). *Anarchy, state, and utopia.* New York: Basic Books.

Nurius, P. S., and Gibson, J. W. (1990). Clinical observation, inference, reasoning, and judgment in social work: An update. *Social Work Research and Abstracts, 26*(2), June, 18–25.

O'Hanlon, W., and Weiner-Davis, M. (1989). *In search of solutions: A new direction in psychotherapy.* New York: W. W. Norton and Company.

O'Neil, M. (1984). *The general method of social work practice.* Englewood Cliffs, NJ: Prentice Hall.

Ortega y Gasset, J. (1957). *Revolt of the masses.* New York: W. W. Norton and Company.

————. (1962). *Meditations on Quixote.* New York: W. W. Norton and Company.

Osborn, A. (1963). *Applied imaginations,* third edition. New York: Scribner.

Pantoja, A., and Perry, W. (1995). Community development and restoration: A perspective. In Felix G. Rivera and John L. Erlich, Editors, *Community organizing in a diverse society,* second edition, 217–242. Boston: Allyn & Bacon.

Parry, A., and Doan, R. E. (1994). *Story re-visions: Narrative theory in the postmodern world.* New York: Guilford Press.

Paul, J. (1996). Student paper: Spirituality and religion. Unpublished document.

Pear, R. (1996). Clinton considers move to soften cuts in welfare. *New York Times,* November 27, A1, A14.

Peck, M. S. (1995). *In search of stones: A pilgrimage of faith, reason, and discovery.* New York: Hyperion.

Perlman, H. H. (1957). *Social casework: A problem solving process.* Chicago: University of Chicago Press.

————. (1979). *Relationship: The heart of helping people.* Chicago: University of Chicago Press.

Peters, T. (1995). *Thriving on chaos: Handbook for a management revolution.* New York: Alfred A. Knopf.

Phillips, K. (1990). *The politics of rich and poor: Wealth and the American electorate in the Reagan aftermath.* New York: Random House.

Pincus, A., and Minahan, A. (1973). *Social work practice: Model and method.* Itasca, IL: F. E. Peacock Publishers.

Pinderhughes, E. (1983). Empowerment for our clients and for ourselves. *Social Casework: The Journal of Contemporary Social Work, 64,* 331–338.

Pipher, M. (1996). *The shelter of each other: Rebuilding our families.* New York: G. P. Putnam's Sons.

Polansky, N. (1975). Classroom lecture, March.

Popkin, M. H. (1990). *Parenting of active teens, parent's guide.* Atlanta, GA: Active Parenting.

Posavac, E., and Carey, K. (1985). *Program evaluation methods and case studies.* Englewood Cliffs, NJ: Prentice Hall.

Prochaska, J., DiClemente, C., and Norcross, J. (1992). In search of how people change: Applications to addictive behaviors. *American Psychologist, 47*(9), 1102–1114.

Proctor, E. K., and Davis, L. E. (1994). The challenge of racial difference: Skills for clinical practice. *Social Work, 39*(3), May, 314–323.

Proctor, E. K., and Rosen, A. (1983). Problem formulation and its relation to treatment planning. *Social Work Research and Abstracts, 19*(3), 22–28.

Pruger, R. (1973). The good bureaucrat. *Social Work, 18*(4), 26–32.

————. (1978). Bureaucratic functioning as a social work skill. In Betty Baer and Ronald Federico, Editors, *Educating the baccalaureate social worker: Report of the undergraduate social work curriculum development project,* 149–163. Cambridge, MA: Ballinger Publishing Company.

Putnam, R. (1993). *Making democracy work.* Princeton, NJ: Princeton University Press.

Rainie, H. (1995). The lessons of Banana Kelly. *U. S. News and World Report,* June 5, p. 72.

Rapaport, J., Reischl, T., and Zimmerman, M. (1992). Mutual help mechanism in the empowerment of former mental patients. In D. Saleeby, Editor, *The strengths perspective in social work practice,* 84–97. New York: Longman Publishing Group.

Rapp, C. A. (1992). The strengths perspective of case management with persons suffering from severe mental illness. In D. Saleeby, Editor, *The strengths perspective in social work practice,* 45–58. New York: Longman Publishing Group.

Rawls, J. (1971). *A theory of justice.* Cambridge: Harvard University Press.

Reamer, F. (1993a). From the editor. *Journal of Social Work Education, 29*(1), 4.

_____ . (1993b). *The philosophical foundations of social welfare.* New York: Columbia University Press.

Reynolds, B. C. (1963). *An uncharted journey.* New York: Citadel Press.

Rich, A. (1986). *Blood, bread, and poetry: Selected prose 1979–1985.* New York: W. W. Norton and Company.

Rivera, F. G., and Erlich, J. L. (1992). Introduction: Prospects and challenges. In F. G. Rivera and J. L. Erlich, Editors, *Community organizing in a diverse society,* 1–16. Boston: Allyn & Bacon.

_____ . (1995). Epilog: Reaching toward the 21st century—fraud in the inducement? In F. G. Rivera and J. L. Erlich, Editors, *Community organizing in a diverse society,* second edition, 243–257. Boston: Allyn & Bacon.

Rivlin, L. G. (1990). Home and homelessness in the lives of children. In N. Boxill, Editor, *Homeless children: The watchers and the waiters,* 21–31. Binghamton, NY: Haworth Press.

Robey, D., and Sales, C. (1994). *Designing organizations,* fourth edition. Burr Ridge, IL: Richard D. Irwin.

Rogalla, T. (1996). Student paper: Spirituality and religion. Unpublished document.

Rompereud, A., Editor. (1993). *The collected poems of Langston Hughes.* New York: Alfred A. Knopf.

Rooney, R. R. (1992). *Strategies that work with involuntary clients.* New York: Columbia University Press.

Rosen, A., and Livne, S. (1992). Personal versus environmental emphases in social workers' perceptions of client problems. *Social Service Review, 64*(1), 86–96.

Rothman, J. (1989). Client self-determination: Untangling the knot. *Social Service Review,* December, pp. 598–612.

Rothman, J., and Tropman, J. (1987). Models of community organization and macro practice: Their mixing and phasing. In F. M. Cox, J. L. Erlich, J. Rothman, and J. E. Tropman, Editors, *Strategies of community organization: Macro practice,* 3–25. Itasca, IL: F. E. Peacock Publishers.

Royce, D. (1992). *Program evaluation: An introduction.* Chicago: Nelson-Hall Publishers.

Ryan, W. (1972). *Blaming the victim.* New York: Vintage Books.

Saleeby, D., Editor. (1992). *The strengths perspective in social work practice.* New York: Longman Publishing Group.

Salois, P. G. (1995). Spiritual healing and PTSD. *Clinical Quarterly: National Center for Post Traumatic Stress Disorder, 10*(5), 12.

Schacter, O. (1984). Human dignity as a normative concept. *The American Journal of International Law, 77,* 848–854.

Schank, R. (1990). *Tell me a story: A new look at real and artificial memory.* New York: Scribner's.

Schindler-Rainman, E., and Lippitt, R. (1977). *The volunteer community.* La Jolla, CA: University Associates.

Schon, D. A. (1987). *Educating the reflective practitioner.* San Francisco: Jossey-Bass.

Schorr, A. L. (1986). *Common decency: Domestic policies after Reagan.* New Haven, CT: Yale University Press.

Seidl, F. (1995). Program evaluation. In R. Edwards, Editor-in-Chief, *Encyclopedia of social work,* nineteenth edition, 1927–1932. Washington, DC: NASW Press.

Seltser, B., and Miller, D. (1993). *Homeless families: The struggle for dignity.* Urbana: University of Illinois Press.

Senge, P. (1990). *The fifth discipline: The art and practice of leading organizations.* New York: Doubleday.

Sharwell, G. (1982). How to testify before a legislative committee. In M. Mahaffey and J. Hanks, Editors, *Practical politics: Social work and political responsibility,* 85–98. Silver Spring, MD: NASW Press.

Sheafor, B. W., Horejsi, C. R., and Horejsi, G. A. (1994). *Techniques and guidelines for social work practice,* third edition. Boston: Allyn & Bacon.

Shimkus, J., and Winship, J. (1977). *Human service development: Working together in the community.* Athens, GA: University of Georgia Institute of Community and Area Development.

Shook, N. (1996). Student paper: Spirituality and religion. Unpublished document.

Shreeve, J. (1994). Terms of estrangement. In J. Kromkowski, Editor, *Race and ethnic relations: Annual edition,* 250–254. Guilford, CT: Dushkin.

Shulman, L. (1982). *The skills of helping individuals and groups.* Itasca, IL: F. E. Peacock Publishers.

_____ . (1992). *The skills of helping individuals, families, and small groups.* Itasca, IL: F. E. Peacock Publishers.

Simon, B. L. (1994). *The empowerment tradition in*

social work: A history. New York: Columbia University Press.

Siporin, M. (1975). *Introduction to social work practice.* New York: Macmillan Publishing Company.

Sklar, J. (1986). Injustice, injury, and inequality: An introduction. In Frank S. Lucash, Editor, *Justice and equality: Here and now,* 13–35. Ithaca, NY: Cornell University Press.

Snyder, G. (1992). *No nature: New and selected poems and prose.* New York: Pantheon.

Solomon, B. (1976). *Black empowerment: Social work in oppressed communities.* New York: Columbia University Press.

Souflee, F. (1993). A metatheoretical framework for social work practice. *Social Work, 38*(3), May, 317–331.

Sours, L. (1883–1993). Poster. Kotzebue, AK: Maniilaq Association Health Education Program.

Spiegelberg, H. (1970). Human dignity: A challenge to contemporary philosophy. In R. Gotesky and E. Laszlo, Editors, *Human dignity: This century and the next.* New York: Gordon and Bresch.

Sullivan, P. (1992). Reconsidering the environment as a helping resource. In D. Saleeby, Editor, *The strengths perspective in social work practice,* 148–157. New York: Longman Publishing Group.

Sundstrand Corporation. (1993). *Diversity in Sunstrand Aerospace.* Rockford, IL: Sundstrand Corporation.

Takaki, R. (1993). *A different mirror: A history of multicultural America,* first edition. Boston: Little, Brown & Company.

Taylor, R., Neighbors, H., and Broman, C. (1989). Evaluation of black Americans of the social service encounter during a serious personal problem. *Social Work, 34*(3), 205–211.

Terkel, S. (1992). *Race: How blacks and whites think and feel about the American obsession.* New York: New Press.

Töennies, F. (1957). *Community and society* (translated and edited by C. Loomis). New York: Harper & Row Publishers.

Trattner, W. I. (1994). *From poor law to welfare state: A history of social welfare in America,* fifth edition. New York: Free Press.

Tripodi, T. (1983). *Evaluative research for social workers.* Englewood Cliffs, NJ: Prentice Hall.

Truax, J. (1995). Personal communication, November 18.

Tung, M. (1985). Psychiatric care for Southeast Asians: How different is different. In T. Owens, Editor, *Southeast Asian mental health: Treatment, prevention, services, training, and research,* 5–40. Washington, DC: U. S. Department of Health and Human Services.

Turecki, S. (1994). *The emotional problems of normal children.* New York: Bantam Books.

Turner, K. A. (1985). Local churches and community social work providers as collaborators in rural social service delivery. In W. H. Whitaker, Editor, *Social work in rural areas: A celebration of rural people, place, and struggle,* 111–127. Orono, ME: Department of Sociology and Social Work, University of Maine at Orono.

Uba, L. (1994). *Asian Americans: Personality patterns, identity, and mental health.* New York: Guilford Press.

United Nations. (1987). *The United Nations and the International Court of Justice.* New York: United Nations Office of Public Information.

U.S. Bureau of the Census. (1992). *Statistical abstract of the United States, 1992.* Washington, DC: Government Printing Office.

U.S. Commission on Civil Rights. (1982). *Minority elderly services: New programs, old problems.* Washington, DC: Government Printing Office.

Verghese, A. (1994). *My own country: A doctor's story of a town and its people in the age of AIDS.* New York: Simon & Schuster.

Vigilante, F., and Mialick, M. (1985). Human behavior and the social environment: A sequence providing the theoretical base for teaching assessment. *Journal of Teaching in Social Work, 1,* 33–47.

Walker, A. (1968). *Once.* New York: Harcourt Brace Jovanovich.

Wallis, J. (1994). *The soul of politics.* New York: New Press and Orbis Books.

Walzer, M. (1983). *Spheres of justice: A defense of pluralism and equality.* New York: Basic Books.
————— . (1986). Justice here and now. In Frank S. Lucash, Editor, *Justice and equality: Here and now,* 136–150. Ithaca, NY: Cornell University Press.

Waters, D. B., and Lawrence, E. C. (1993). *Competence, courage, and change: An approach to family therapy.* New York: W. W. Norton and Company.

Webster, S., and Campbell, P. (1978). Changing dimensions in rural life: Is a new practice model needed? In R. K. Green and S. Webster, Editors, *Social work in rural areas: Preparation and practice,* 75–94. Knoxville: University of Tennessee, School of Social Work.

Weick, A. (1992). Building a strengths perspective for social work. In D. Saleeby, Editor, *The strengths perspective in social work practice,* 18–26. New York: Longman Publishing Group.

Weil, M. O., and Gamble, D. N. (1995). Community practice models. In R. Edwards, Editor-in-Chief, *Encyclopedia of social work,* nineteenth edition, 577–594. Washington, DC: NASW Press.

Weissman, A. (1976). Industrial social services: Linking technology. *Social Casework, 57,* 50–54.

West, C. (1993). *Race matters.* Boston: Beacon Press.

Whitaker, J. (1983). Mutual helping in human service practice. In J. Whitaker and J. Garbarino, Editors, *Social support networks: Informal helping in human services,* 33–67. New York: Aldine.

White, B. (1975). *The first three years of life.* Englewood Cliffs, NJ: Prentice Hall.

White, M., and Epston, D. (1990). *Narrative means to therapeutic ends.* New York: W. W. Norton and Company.

Whittington, B. (1985). The challenge of family work in a rural community. *The Social Worker, 53*(3), 104–107.

Wilson, W. J. (1996). *When work disappears: The world of the new urban poor.* New York: Alfred A. Knopf.

Winship, J. (1984). *An examination of the factors influencing voluntary county allocations to public welfare in Georgia.* Unpublished dissertation.

Wolf, G. (1994). Personal communication, spring semester.

Wood, D. (1995). U.S. Hispanics: To be and not to be. In J. Kromkowski, Editor, *Race and ethnic relations: Annual edition,* 106–107. Guilford, CT: Dushkin.

Wrobleski, C. J. (1993). *The seven Rs of volunteer development: A YMCA resource kit.* New York: Human Kinetics.

Wuthnow, J. (1994). *Sharing the journey: Support groups and America's new quest for community.* New York: Free Press.

Wyant, S., and Brooks, P., Editors. (1993). *The changing role of volunteerism.* Boston: United Hospital Fund.

Yin, R. K. (1984). *Case study research: Design and method.* Thousand Oaks, CA: Sage Publications.

Youth Service Bureau, Department of Health and Human Services. (1994). *Culturally competent services for runaway youth.* Washington, DC: Government Printing Office.

Zastrow, C. (1989). *The practice of social work,* third edition. Chicago: Dorsey Press.

Author Index

Subject Index

Credits

This page constitutes an extension of the copyright page. We have made every effort to trace the ownership of all copyrighted material and to secure permission from copyright holders. In the event of any question arising as to the use of any material, we will be pleased to make the necessary corrections in future printings. Thanks are due to the following authors, publishers, and agents for permission to use the material indicated.

Photo Credits

Page 1: © M. Bridwell / PhotoEdit. **Page 22:** © Allen Zak Photography / Mccsc Photo Research. **Page 67:** West Rim Enterprises. **Page 99:** © David Young-Wolff / PhotoEdit. **Page 120:** Jim Magdanz, Nome, Alaska. **Page 155:** Jim Magdanz, Nome, Alaska. **Page 186:** © John Boykin / PhotoEdit. **Page 232:** © 1996, Tasha Williams. **Page 250:** West Rim Enterprises. **Page 281:** © 1996, Fabrienne Jackson.

Text Credits

Page 4: Excerpt from Curriculum Policy Statement, Commission on Accreditation, Council on Social Work Education, Inc., 1992. Reprinted by permission. **Page 7:** Excerpt reproduced by permission of the publisher, F. E. Peacock Publishers Inc., Itasca, Illinois. From Allan Pincus and Anne Minihan, *Social Work Practice: Model and Method,* 1973 copyright, pp. 53-68, 102. **Page 10:** Excerpt from *The Strengths Perspective in Social Work Practice,* by P. Sullivan, pp. 153-154. Copyright © 1992 by Longman. Reprinted by permission. **Pages 11, 94:** Excerpts reprinted by permission of Penguin Putnam Inc. from THE SHELTER OF EACH OTHER by Mary Pipher. Copyright © 1996 by Mary Pipher. **Page 29:** Excerpt from *A Different Mirror: A History of Multicultural America* by Ronald Takaki, p. 4. Copyright © 1993 Little Brown and Company. Reprinted by permission. **Page 31:** Excerpt from *Story Revisions: Narrative Theory in the Postmodern World* by A. Parry and R. E. Doan, p. 25. Copyright © 1994 by The Guilford Press. Reprinted by permission. **Page 33:** Excerpt reproduced with permission from 77 A.J.I.L. 852 (1983), © The American Society of International Law. **Pages 39, 146-148:** Excerpts from *Narrative Means to Therapeutic Ends* by Michael White and David Epston. Copyright © 1990 by Dulwich Centre, Adelaide, South Australia. Reprinted by permission of W. W. Norton & Company, Inc. **Page 46:** Excerpt from *Women in Context: Toward a Feminist Reconstruction of Psychotherapy* by M. McGoldrick, p. xiii. Copyright © 1994 by The Guilford Press. Reprinted by permission. **Page 53:** Excerpt from *Makes Me Wanna Holler* by Nathan McCall. Copyright © 1994 by permission of Random House, Inc. **Pages 62, 63:** Excerpts from *Competence, Courage, and Change: An Approach to Family Therapy* by D. B. Waters and E. C. Lawrence. Copyright © 1993 by W. W. Norton & Company, Inc. Reprinted by permission. **Pages 64, 107:** Excerpts from "Building a Strengths Perspective for Social Work" by Ann Weick. In D. Saleeby (Ed.) *The Strengths Perspective in Social Work,* 1992, Longman Publishing Group. Reprinted by permission of Addison-Wesley Educational Publishers Inc. **Pages 71, 123:** Excerpts from *Social Work Macro Practice* by Netting, Kettner & McMurtry, copyright © 1993 Longman Publishing Group. Reprinted by permission of Addison-Wesley Educational Publishers Inc. **Page 92:** Excerpt from *The Good Society,* by R. N. Bellah, A. S. Sullivan, A. Swidler, and S. M. Tipton,

351

TO THE OWNER OF THIS BOOK:

We hope that you have found *Generalist Social Work Practice: Context, Story, and Partnerships* useful. So that this book can be improved in a future edition, would you take the time to complete this sheet and return it? Thank you.

School and address: _____

Department: _____

Instructor's name: _____

1. What I like most about this book is: _____

_____

_____

2. What I like least about this book is: _____

_____

_____

3. My general reaction to this book is: _____

_____

4. The name of the course in which I used this book is: _____

_____

5. Were all of the chapters of the book assigned for you to read? _____

   If not, which ones weren't? _____

6. In the space below, or on a separate sheet of paper, please write specific suggestions for improving this book and anything else you'd care to share about your experience in using the book.

_____

_____

_____

_____

_____

Optional:

Your name: _____ Date: _____

May Brooks/Cole quote you, either in promotion for *Generalist Social Work Practice: Context, Story, and Partnerships* or in future publishing ventures?

Yes: _____ No: _____

Sincerely,

Barry Locke
Rebecca Garrison
James Winship

FOLD HERE

- -

BUSINESS REPLY MAIL
FIRST CLASS   PERMIT NO. 358   PACIFIC GROVE, CA

POSTAGE WILL BE PAID BY ADDRESSEE

ATT: *Barry Locke, Rebecca Garrison, & James Winship*

Brooks/Cole Publishing Company
511 Forest Lodge Road
Pacific Grove, California 93950-9968

FOLD HERE

Brooks/Cole is dedicated to publishing quality publications for education in the human services fields. If you are interested in learning more about our publications, please fill in your name and address and request our latest catalogue.

Name: ————————————————————————

Street Address: ————————————————————

City, State, and Zip: ——————————————————

IN-BOOK SURVEY

At Brooks/Cole, we are excited about creating new types of learning materials that are interactive, three-dimensional, and fun to use. To guide us in our publishing/development process, we hope that you'll take just a few moments to fill out the survey below. Your answers can help us make decisions that will allow us to produce a wide variety of videos, CD-ROMs, and Internet-based learning systems to complement standard textbooks. If you're interested in working with us as a student Beta-tester, be sure to fill in your name, telephone number, and address. We look forward to hearing from you!

In addition to books, which of the following learning tools do you currently use in your counseling/human services/social work courses?

_____ **Video** _____ in class _____ school library _____ own VCR

_____ **CD-ROM** _____ in class _____ in lab _____ own computer

_____ **Macintosh disks** _____ in class _____ in lab _____ own computer

_____ **Windows disks** _____ in class _____ in lab _____ own computer

_____ **Internet** _____ in class _____ in lab _____ own computer

How often do you access the Internet? _____

My own home computer is:

_____ Macintosh _____ DOS _____ Windows _____ Windows 95

The computer I use in class for counseling/human services/social work courses is:

_____ Macintosh _____ DOS _____ Windows _____ Windows 95

If you are NOT currently using multimedia materials in your counseling/human services/social work courses, but can see ways that video, CD-ROM, Internet, or other technologies could enhance your learning, please comment below:

_____

_____

_____

Other comments (optional): _____

_____

Name _____ Telephone _____

Address _____

School _____

Professor/Course_____

You can fax this form to us at (408) 375-6414; e:mail to: info@brookscole.com; or detach, fold, secure, and mail.